Mapping the

Invisible Landscape

THE AMERICAN LAND AND LIFE SERIES

Edited by Wayne Franklin

Mapping the

Invisible Landscape

Folklore, Writing,

and the Sense of Place

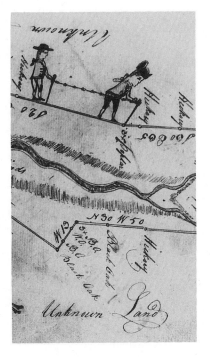

By Kent C. Ryden

Foreword by Wayne Franklin

Ψ

UNIVERSITY OF IOWA PRESS

IOWA CITY

University of Iowa Press, Iowa City 52242
Copyright © 1993 by the University of Iowa Press
All rights reserved
Printed in the United States of America

Design by Karen Copp

Printed on acid-free paper

Library of Congress Cataloging-in-Publication
Data
Ryden, Kent C., 1959–
    Mapping the invisible landscape: folklore,
writing, and the sense of place / by Kent C.
Ryden; foreword by Wayne Franklin.
        p.   cm.—(The American land and life
series)
    Includes bibliographical references and
index.
    ISBN 0-87745-406-X (cloth),
    ISBN 0-87745-414-0 (paper)
    1. Landscape assessment—United
States.   2. Geographical perception—
United States.   3. Folklore—United
States.   4. American essays—History and
criticism.   5. Folklore—Idaho—Coeur
d'Alene Region.   I. Title.   II. Series.
GF91.U6R93   1993
304.2'3—dc20   92-46529
                                  CIP

97 96 95 94 93 c 5 4 3 2 1
97   p 5 4 3 2

TO MY MOTHER

AND

TO THE MEMORY OF MY FATHER

Contents

≈≈≈≈≈≈≈≈≈≈≈≈≈≈≈≈≈≈≈≈≈≈≈≈≈≈≈≈≈≈≈≈≈≈≈≈≈≈

Foreword

BY WAYNE FRANKLIN

There's an art to finding out where you are, an art you may not recognize—or know you lack—until you need it. Over three hundred years ago, in the spring of 1676, a young English boy made his way out of his shelter and started moving off through the forest. He had been taken prisoner by the Indians during the bloody war then being fought under the leadership of "King Philip" to determine who was to control the land, and though he probably had been treated well and might have come to find the Indian manner of living more appealing than that of his own grim Puritan community, as many other English captives did, he had been brought up to hold the natives in dread, and hence he longed to run away and find his old home. Even in his dread, however, he must have known that finding his way in the dim woods would be extremely hard. As long as he remained with his captors, he didn't have to worry about where he was or where he was going. Once off on his own, however, he would have to orient himself and by intuition or sheer luck find his way back.

In his case, the answer was simple but ingenious. As he moved on in the gathering light, his eye caught small round stars of greenery dotting the floor of the forest, first one and then a few more, and then large numbers of them. The stars consisted of a ring of egg-shaped leaves, strongly lined and with a thick but hollow center stalk, spread out against the ground. From their centers rose thin spikes capped with tight green seedheads.

Anyone who tends a North American lawn today is probably familiar with the plant in question, which is called plantain. It dots the yard much as the young English boy found it dotting the forest, but it does not come from the forest, at least not originally. It is a common Eurasian plant which, like many of the weeds that vex the North American lawn or the garden or the farm field, came into this country with the Old World colonizers, hidden in bags of good seed or in animal bedding or in the nooks and crannies of the thousand items dragged ashore in Quebec or Boston or New Amsterdam or Philadelphia or Jamestown. Green invaders, such seeds stowed away on the emigrant ships and then, turned loose on shore, soon overran the countryside.

By 1676, a mere half-century after the English began arriving in earnest, the plantain was well known not only among the settlers but also among the Indians. In scorn, the natives called it "Englishman's foot," for its sole-like leaves had walked into their land with these foreigners— indeed, the plants themselves, spotting the landscape with their round marks, looked for all the world like a scattering of footprints. And the plantain's meaning was not lost, either, on that young English boy, the son of Thomas Eames of Sudbury, Massachusetts, who had been taken captive when his family's home was burned and his mother was killed on February 1. How young Eames found his way back illuminates, I think, a whole realm of significances. I quote the account of his escape published later in 1676 in London:

> though the Boy knew not a Step of the Way to any *English* town, and was in continual Danger of the skulking *Indians* in the Woods, and far from the *English*, yet God directed him aright and brought him to the Sight of *Plantane* (the Herb which the Indians call English-foot, because it grows only amongst us, and is not found in the Indian Plantations) whereupon he concluded he was not far from some *English* Town, and accordingly following of the *Plantane* he arrived safe amongst us.

This story is of interest, I think, because it offers a wonderfully concrete distillation of the history of the American landscape. As the environmental historian Richard White reminds us in speaking of the history of Island County, Washington (and by extension the past of any landscape), "The real history of the area is not political history, nor in a strict sense social history, although it contains elements of each. Instead it is the history of changes wrought in the natural environment by both Indian and white occupation and use of the land, and the consequences of these changes for the people who made them." Those Eurasian plantains in the woods of eastern Massachusetts in 1676 were, as American botanists would call them, the "escaped" consequence of that massive environmental change which was the founding of colonial America. In making his own escape back along this trail of plants, young Eames was a shrewd observer of his environment, a reader of landscape for whom this herb provided more than its usual remedies.

But the Indians who may have been in pursuit of him on that May afternoon also had their eyes trained on the changing text of the Northeast. Seeing the English plant, Eames knew its sudden appearance in the woods marked the nearness of his people's agricultural enclaves; for their part, the Indians knew that it was a sign of possession, a sign of the always-nearing trend of the Englishman's booted foot—and perhaps in quite literal ways. If it was birds that most likely carried the plantain seed out from Sudbury and Concord and Lancaster, surely some of the seed clung to the muddied soles of English footwear as settlers opened new fields to English crops, hunted for game in the forests, cut and brought in firewood from woodlots, or indeed pursued Indian warriors in 1636 or 1676. It was not by guns alone that the soldiers who had killed Conanchet a month before, and who were soon to kill King Philip himself, were wresting control of New England from their soon-to-be-conquered foes. Plants, too, were the implements of empire.

How do we know where we are? This is the deceptively simple question that forms the theme of Kent Ryden's wonderful book. In the case of his own central story, told through the words of the residents of a northern Idaho mining district, the feet we trace through the landscape need not be literal. We mark the landscape by a multitude of means. The mines of Silver Valley do so massively, as at one time did the now shriveled towns that the valley's silver built, such as Kellogg or Burke. There are the maps on paper, too, and in our heads—the lines of which manage to trace out the rudiments of structure that set one place off from another. But in Silver Valley (and, as we'll see in a moment, in much of North America and beyond) it is in our stories that we locate places most powerfully, and in so locating them gauge and assess their meaning. It is our lore, our written tales, our essays of place that succeed most of all in giving sense to place and thus in nurturing our inner sense of place.

Perhaps Euro-American and African-American settlers in the New World have felt special need for such reassuring orientation. They, like the plantain, "escaped" into the New World, bringing cultures with them that were not always suited to their new homes. Over the millennia of their solitary possession, Native Americans had evolved extraordinarily subtle place-maps, linguistic and visual and cognitive, for which the invading Europeans and the slaves they brought had no precise counterpart. Indian place-names might themselves function as maps, pinpointing a location by recalling the features surrounding it or the human uses it had. European place-names can serve a similar purpose ("Silver Valley" itself does), but more often they have reference to some inner, remembered place elsewhere or to some accidental association of the location in question. Because much of American culture so-called is in some final sense "lost"—a creolized, dislocated melange of forms and peoples whose cultural hearths lie far beyond the sea—place-names exhibit a curious vacillation between the immediate grasp of local features (as with Red Root Creek, New Jersey) and a play of reminiscence within a closed system, completely without reference to the setting (as with Paris, Texas).

It is the stories people tell, in any case, that are the real place-namings. Kent Ryden's collections from Idaho exhibit the depth and range of affection that the inhabitants of that landscape feel for and about their place. Appendages of an exploitative economy that is so characteristic of the Euro-American presence in the land, they yet display a profound sense of where they are, a sense they themselves have constructed. Their cognitive maps are grounded in their passage through space—experience, not a name or legal title, claims the land—and their language, in turn, copies and shapes that passage. Whereas we may think of folklore as a preeminently portable commodity which goes with a people wherever they go and in fact may keep its shape best when it is far-carried, Ryden shows how lore also springs from the places where people pause, generated by their movement and action and their need for attachment and a contemplative pause.

He does so in a wider, reflective context of his own. From his opening tale about his unearthings along the Rhode Island–Connecticut border to his final tale about the microchanges in his familiar world, he shows himself well-versed in the subtle marks by which one place fades off into another. More to the point, he shows how the oral tales of Idaho fit into a widely dispersed pattern of verbal place-making that reaches out to embrace the essays of E. B. White and the fiction of William Faulkner. With a clear grasp of both geography and language, he invites us to see how strands of significance run through many apparently diverse human activities in North America. It is in their relation to the invisible landscape of our minds and hearts that these activities come together. And for that invisible landscape there are few better guides than Kent Ryden. He is a topographer of North America as a cultural entity; he is a topographer as well of the human spirit. His book offers new understandings of the very old human activity of place-making, and new understandings, too, of how we feel about the places we make, how we internalize them and remember them after they or we are gone. It's a book, at last, about how we find our way back home by following the words that tie us to the land.

~~~~~~

Preface

There is a poem by James McGowan that I like very much. Its title is "On Writing an Illinois Poem," and its speaker is a would-be Midwestern bard who wants to write honestly and well about his adopted state. He finds himself unable to put pen to paper, though, sensing that he is not equipped for the task; he is stymied by a fundamental inability to grasp the meaning of Illinois.

> I shouldn't do it yet;
>> don't know this place.
>>> I've been here now three years and don't relate.
>
> One notes things, though:
>> the squares—of land that is;
>>> the prairie's laid in blocks
>>> and towns are just a smaller grid;
>>> roads meet in perpendicular
>>> and go in only four directions
>>>> (though a thousand miles in each).

He is put off by the very nature of the landscape that faces him, an alienating tableau of straight lines, compass points, and rectilinear fields, boring in its regularity, appalling in its monotony, intimidating in its spaciousness; it is a blank surface which resists his imagination and thwarts his understanding. He views it accordingly with a combination of fear and contempt, speaking with scorn of this smooth cold plane where "there is nothing for the mind to climb on" and which is farmed by

> men whose fields grow tall,
> while houses crack in years of wind
> and children split and wrinkle, die in their rows.

In the end, though, the speaker is sufficiently self-aware to realize that what he sees is somehow not the real Illinois, that his newcomer's perception bears none but the most superficial physical resemblance to the view of the state held by people who have spent their lives there. He senses that there is a deep world of human meaning laid atop that opaque surface which he eyes with such disdain, an invisible landscape which the natives see but which has not yet been revealed to him, and knows that he is not the person to write a poem about this place—at least not a poem that comes anywhere near capturing the voice of local truth.

> But yet I understand so few things of this land and people—
>> flats and facts and squares—
>>> I should not write.
>> I think, though, that there is
>>> there must be mystery, dimension, depth—
>>>> each citizen his soul, each grid its ghosts—
>>> I've heard of towering substance, strength, imagination,
>>> prairie art, and love—
>>>> (and rumors of the circles and the symbols out of sight,
>>>> behind thick blinds,
>>>>> in dark, in woody parlors).

This book is about that mystery, dimension, and depth—not only in Illinois, but in any place where people live and listen and remember and talk and write. It is about the words that we superimpose on land-scapes—the "Illinois poems" that sound in each of our lives. In it, I attempt to come to an understanding of the sense of place—that complex of meaning that gives a landscape significance in the eyes of the people who inhabit it, marking it off from the surrounding terra incognita—and demonstrate the ways in which that sense gains expression in words, words that map out the contours of that invisible landscape of meaning which McGowan's narrator would give voice to if he could. The sense of place achieves its clearest articulation through narrative, providing the thematic drive and focus for the stories that people tell about the places in their lives. These stories need not be limited to any one medium, for both folk and literary narratives about place bear a striking thematic and stylistic family resemblance; they are simply manifestations in two different media of the same narrative impulse, and I accordingly examine both kinds of narrative in this study. For my oral materials, I discuss stories which I collected in the Coeur d'Alene mining district in the Idaho panhandle; for my consideration of written works, I focus on what I call the "essay of place," the personal essay which takes as its subject a particular place and the writer's relationship to that place.

One of my hopes for this book is that it will lead readers to a renewed and enhanced appreciation of the places in their own lives and the invisible landscapes which surround them. It has done so in my case; indeed, since (like everyone else) I have been deeply engaged in landscapes and places every day by virtue of the simple fact of living, it is perhaps inevitable that I should contemplate my own relationships with place in conjunction with those being described in the texts that I study. I thus include some observations and words of my own in the prologue and epilogue of this book, answering in my way a challenge which Thoreau laid down in the opening pages of *Walden*. "I, on my side, require of every writer, first or last, a simple and sincere account of his own life," wrote Thoreau, "and not merely what he has heard of other men's lives; some such account as he would send to his kindred from a distant land; for if he has lived sincerely, it must have been in a distant land to me." Thoreau's excuse for writing in the first person was that "I should not talk so much about myself if there were any body else whom I knew as well"—nor might *I* be so inclined to include my own observations on place in addition to those of my informants and chosen writers if there were anyone else's that I knew with comparable intimacy. Accordingly, this book incorporates an account or two from "distant lands" in which I have lived—and, with Thoreau, "I will . . . ask those of my readers who feel no particular interest in me to pardon me."

There are many words in this book other than mine, though; I received a great deal of help from a great many guides in exploring and mapping the intellectual terrain that I staked out for myself. Perhaps my greatest thanks go to the people of the Coeur d'Alene mining district, whose stories and comments I share and write about in my third chapter and whose kindness and hospitality made gathering those stories and comments the most enjoyable academic work I've ever done. (Two of my informants, Maidell Clemets and Shirley Horning, have died in the time since I interviewed them. *Requiescat in pace.*) Special thanks to Bob Launhardt for his logistical help.

I suspect that the seeds for this book were somehow planted way back in high school, when David Bell's teaching first made me realize that studying American literature and culture was important and exciting and what I wanted to do. The book began its life as my doctoral dissertation in the Department of American Civilization at Brown University, and I remain grateful to the members of my dissertation committee—Bruce Rosenberg, George Monteiro, and Barton St. Armand—for their good advice and their unfailing support and encouragement. Thanks are also due to many other friends, colleagues, and kind strangers for words of wisdom, helpful comments, and other acts of practical and intangible assistance in getting the book (in both its incarnations) finished and on its way—particularly to Dave Moore, Mary Johnson, Laurent Ditmann, Sheila Blumstein, and especially Pat Flaherty; to Robert Emlen, Richard Candee, and the staff of the Brown University Art Slide Library, for assistance with procuring or reproducing illustrations; and to Carolyn Brown for her fine editorial work. Finally, Wayne Franklin's comments, suggestions, and general enthusiasm were invaluable when it came time to revise my dissertation into book form; I am pleased that my book has found a home in the American Land and Life series, and I hope that it proves to be a worthy addition.

Mapping the

Invisible Landscape

≈≈≈≈≈≈≈≈≈≈≈≈≈≈≈≈≈≈≈≈≈≈≈≈≈≈≈≈≈≈≈≈≈≈

Prologue: Reading the Border

It is a brilliant May morning, the first truly summer-like day of the year. I am walking back and forth on Route 101 at the Connecticut–Rhode Island border—an ordinary enough stretch of road, yet one rendered significant by my knowledge that a geographical boundary runs through here and by the insistent presence of road signs.

Borders and boundaries carry a certain mystery and fascination. They imply a transition between realms of experience, states of being; they draw an ineffable line between life as lived in one place and life as lived in another. The Romans had a god—Janus—who guarded gates and doors, testifying to the metaphorical power that his worshippers found in physical boundaries. The ground on either side of a border seems to mean different things—each such demarcated piece of land is under a different jurisdiction, has seen a different history. In a subtle and totally subjective way, each side of the border feels different; in the space of a few feet we pass from one geographical entity to another which looks exactly the same but is unique, has a different name, is in many ways a completely separate world from the one we just left. Look: it is even a different color on the map. This sense of passing from one world to another, of encompassing within a few steps two realms of experience, enchants and fascinates. This is why people have themselves photographed sprawled across the marker which outlines the Four Corners of Arizona, New Mexico, Utah, and Colorado; this is why visitors at the Royal Observatory in Greenwich have their pictures taken as they straddle the brass rod embedded in the forecourt which locates the Prime Meridian—only this way can they be in two (or four) places at once. Even in an essay which ultimately points out the frequently absurd and harmful aspects of international borders, Barry Lopez confesses to a sense of excitement as he hikes along the Alaskan Arctic coast and approaches the boundary with the Yukon Territory: "the romance of it—this foot in Canada, that one in Alaska—is fetching."[1] Now, on a brilliant blue May morning, I stand Janus-like on the border between Connecticut and Rhode Island, looking one way and then the other, letting each place tell me what it means.

The signs on each side do their best to let me know that their state is

1

distinctive and significant, that I would be glad should I decide to cross the line in that direction. They invite me in with strenuous bonhomie. I look into Connecticut, stroll down the road: an enormous blue sign stands on the right-hand side of the highway, big and vivid enough to catch the eye of any motorist who comes speeding by. It reads, in big white letters: "Connecticut Welcomes You. William A. O'Neill, Governor." The sign also incorporates a smaller, more colorful, bumper-sticker-like label, evidently the state's tourism slogan: "ClassiConnecticut / The Pride of New England." Finally, notification that I have just wandered across not only a state but also a municipal frontier: "Town of Killingly."

I turn and walk about 150 yards east, into Rhode Island. Here, another big blue sign sticks out its hand and tries to make me feel at home. A picture of the Rhode Island state house in Providence takes up one side of the sign. "Welcome to Rhode Island," reads the other side, followed by the logo of the state's latest tourist campaign—the words "RI 350 / The Spirit Burns Brighter" superimposed on a drawing of an anchor. Finally, the personal touch: along the bottom of the sign runs the name "Governor Edward D. DiPrete."

On the surface, these signs serve a basic geographical and political function, simply letting us know when we have passed from one U.S. state into another. As geographical markers, however, they are wildly inaccurate. Standing 150 yards apart, they cannot both mark the border, which in fact lies between them about 50 yards east of the Connecticut sign. Given these geographical limitations, the primary purpose of public, official welcoming signs such as these is to shape and manipulate the feelings of difference and distinction that we experience when we cross any geographical border. They are advertisements, hucksters of geographical impressions. As Wilbur Zelinsky points out, the highway welcoming sign is distinctive for "the commodity it purveys: the image of a particular locality. The ostensible purpose is to interest strangers in sampling the wonders of this extraordinary place or, at the least, to wander onward with lingering curiosity."[2] When we travel this stretch of Route 101, we sense that we have passed from one world to another, that Rhode Island and Connecticut are distinctive places with distinctive qualities, and in erecting these signs the governments of each state want to make absolutely sure that we are aware that that distinction exists and, moreover, want to suggest to us (as efficiently as they can in the few seconds it takes a car to breeze past a sign) just wherein that distinction lies—just what their states' special qualities are. We will be left with a certain image in the back of our minds after we read the signs, the sort of positive image which governments and chambers of commerce want us to have there.

Each state tries to impress us with its friendliness. The governor himself extends us a cheery welcome. Moreover, Rhode Island tries to give a sense of its historical depth and the barest hint, given the constraints of the highway sign as a communications medium, of what else can be found in the state. The tourism logo lists the state's age as an impressive 350 years old. The imposing figure of the state house implies a similar sense of historical depth and implicitly invites the motorist to Providence to view this impressive architectural landmark. The anchor in the tourism logo hints at both the state's recreational riches and its nautical heritage. In symbolic, telegraphic form, then, the sign reveals Rhode Island to be a land of history, heritage, friendliness, and fun, populated by people who are bursting with pride in this panoply of virtues—in Rhode Island, after all, "The Spirit Burns Brighter." Connecticut doesn't pack quite as much into its sign, contenting itself with the rather vague slogan, "ClassiConnecticut / The Pride of New England." Still, this slogan carries a certain resonance: most people carry an image of New England as a region of a certain historical heritage and distinctive, attractive landscapes, and if New England as a whole is most proud of Connecticut, then Connecticut must epitomize these New Englandly qualities. Instead of relying on overt pictorial imagery, then, the Connecticut sign draws upon geographical images and impressions which the passing motorist probably already carries in his head, sharpening them, heightening them, and concentrating them within the borders of a single state. In this way, the Connecticut sign tries to win the war of geographical impressions which it wages with the rival it faces down the road. If you liked Rhode Island, it says, you haven't seen anything yet. Over here, we're Rhode Island and then some—Rhode Island only more so.

Other elements in this border landscape serve to modify and deepen the geographical messages conveyed by the welcoming signs. Just inside the Rhode Island side of the boundary, a roadside picnic grove beckons travelers off the road to rest and refresh themselves. It is an attractive spot of land, quiet, cool and restful on a May morning, with birds singing, towering evergreens providing a soft carpet of brown needles, a handful of picnic tables and grills scattered about. It is also the first thing the motorist sees in Rhode Island, as it occupies the entire roadside between the border and the official welcoming sign. Rest, it suggests to the traveler. Get out and stretch. Enjoy the shade. Eat something. Here in Rhode Island, we care about your comfort and welfare.

The message of caring and concern that the picnic grove conveys is reinforced by another small sign that stands at its edge, about 50 yards before the welcoming sign. "Enjoy Rhode Island," the sign says. "Please Buckle Up." Along with the welcoming sign's greeting, history lesson, and preview of coming attractions, then, comes an impression of caring and nurturing—Rhode Island as mother. You'll like it here, this carefully planned border landscape says. We care about you.

In both directions, though, the border message is undercut by unintentional comedy. Just after the Rhode Island seatbelt sign stands another, grimmer placard erected by local residents. "WARNING," it growls. "This is a CRIME WATCH COMMUNITY. We immediately report all SUSPICIOUS PERSONS and activities to our Police Dept." The welcoming message is bathetically modified: We care about you, but watch yourself. We have a lot to offer, want you to see it, and don't want you to die, but that doesn't mean we trust you. The Connecticut welcoming sign is followed within 30 yards by another sign, equally big and blue, which snaps the motorist out of his newly induced New England reveries: "Connecticut Posted Speed Limits *Strictly Enforced.*" Once again the message is mitigated: welcome, but watch it, you potential scofflaw. We're glad to see you, but you're welcome here on *our* terms. I am tempted to waggishly suggest that, well, Connecticut is advertising itself as the pride of New England and this is just an example of that famous New England reserve. The comedy is surely unintended, however, and the delicious irony behind these mixed signs probably only apparent to a scholar afoot on the border with the time to sit in the picnic grove and puzzle out the implications of what he sees. Borders have traditionally been places where guards are posted, passports checked, police business carried out; here we see a vestige of that function. And the main message that the 50-mile-per-hour motorist carries away is the one posted most obviously and insistently—the positive one. Borders are also places of indoctrination, and the traveler continues on into the state with his first geographical impressions suggested to him. If he's never been in Rhode Island or Connecticut before, then at least for now, as geographical entities, those states mean what the government and tourism board want them to mean.

These signs are not all a matter of manipulation and salesmanship, however. To say so implies a cynicism behind the signs' construction which, while it may exist to a certain degree, undoubtedly overstates the case. While they probably don't experience and think of their states in the terms that the welcoming signs suggest they should, residents of

Rhode Island and Connecticut for the most part do think of their states as distinctive (for better or worse), as interesting, as possessing a personality and identity different from that state on the other side of the line. While it wears a simple public face and speaks the overstated language of boosterism and advertising, then, the welcoming sign also hints obliquely at the local residents' understanding of their place; behind its bluster are layers of lived meaning and unique geographical experience. The sign's "real audience," Zelinsky suggests, "is not the transient motorist or potential guest but the local population itself. It is a form of reassurance, a hopeful declaration that we are truly precious, somehow unique, and that the world will ignore us at its peril."[3] This declaration of geographical distinctiveness, this proud proclamation that here is a place like no other undertaken through the overblown imagery of public relations, is also loudly trumpeted by "roadside colossi," Karal Ann Marling's term for those grotesque, attention-grabbing, oversized fiberglass statues of people, animals, and objects which dot the Midwest. These colossi are "assertions of local identity. They mark off a stretch of time and a node of place from the continuum of the summertime highway." Drive, for example, to the small town of Olivia, Minnesota, where "that declaration of importance is rendered permanent, tactile, and somewhat alarming by the colossal ear of golden corn that stands atop a picnic shelter on the outskirts of Olivia. . . . Olivia's vegetal beacon in the sky jolts the passerby with the message that here— right here—begins an exceptional, nay extraordinary town, altogether different from the rest of the little burgs strung out like so many beads along Highway 212 from Glencoe to Granite Falls."[4] Few passing motorists will be able to forget such a sight (as much as they might like to), and so Olivia remains indelibly etched in their brains (and if they forget the exact name of the town, they will at least be able to remember and refer to "the place with the ear of corn"). At the same time, the act of erecting such an outrageous artifact on the roadside is a symbolic declaration of the local geographic distinctiveness that the denizens of the place feel, if not of the exact shape that that distinctiveness takes. They know their place is special, and so (if in a different way) they want to impress it as a unique locality on other people as well, whether they want to be so impressed or not.

Such concentrated nodes of geographical meaning are common in the American landscape, especially, it seems, in its small towns and villages. Elsewhere along the Rhode Island border, the tiny village of Adamsville nestles along the line between the towns of Little Compton,

Figure 1. The Adamsville "history park." 1989 photograph by the author.

Rhode Island, and Westport, Massachusetts. At an intersection in the center of the village, prominently located so that all passers-by can see it, the villagers have built what I think of as a "history park" (fig. 1). On a bit of roadside lawn, backed by an arc of stone wall, are a sign and a monument which together proclaim Adamsville to be a distinctive place like no other. The sign—simple, grey, and weathered—reads "Adams-ville / Rhode Island / 1675." Its possible use as a geographical marker is limited—it is located nowhere near the borders of the village. Its primary purpose is to proclaim, with grey and dignified understatement, the village's historicity. The sign says "age," resonates with history, and triggers imagination. We find ourselves standing in 300-year-old sur-roundings, impressive anywhere in a youthful country and a valid reason for Adamsville to assume a place in our geographical consciousness. At the same time, historically related questions fire off in our minds: how old, then, are these buildings around me? What was life like around here in 1675? What did the village look like? Who was Adams, anyway? The sign simultaneously slaps a date on a piece of geography, making it notable and giving it meaning, and calls our imaginations to further lay-ers of significance: we don't know *what* sort of history Adamsville has had, but we feel certain *that* it had a history, and so as a place it intrigues us. The date suggests a world of local experience which glimmers and resonates elusively in our sympathetic minds.

Our attempts to fill in historical blanks with whatever secondhand lore we may have available—images of colonial life, of Revolutionary exploits—may fade into quiet amusement when we contemplate the monument. A four-foot-high bronze plaque set into an upright slab of granite with an ornamental row of flowers planted in front, it is designed to catch the eye and educate the passer-by about the one important event in Adamsville's history, an occurrence whose effects have long reverberated in the wider world: on a nearby farm, the Rhode Island Red breed of poultry was developed (fig. 2). It is a monument to a chicken; in the historical landscape of Adamsville, a barnyard bird stands out as the highest peak. This may not sound like much, but someone was proud of it, proud enough to put up a monument. The plaque encapsulates a bit of the meaning of the place for the people who have lived there, a meaning which inevitably rubs off on the people who read it: I, for one, will never be able to think of Adamsville, Rhode Island, without thinking of chickens. In the process, my experience of Adamsville has been enriched—I have had an amusing and memorable experience which will always vivify that spot on the map for me. The history park as a whole, then—deliberately set off from the rest of the village, calling attention to itself as a history park and a source and repository of geographical meaning—colors the view of Adamsville carried away by the people who accept its invitation to pause and read. Its privileged setting, carefully tended appearance, and dual historical message testify to the villagers' sense of Adamsville as an unusual and special place, a distinctiveness they wish to communicate and share as best they can. At the same time, as it invites people to linger in the village for a moment it is a catalyst of geographical experience in its own right, as well as a stimulant to the geographical imagination: as we leave Adamsville, we look around and rebuild the countryside with landscapes of centuries gone by.

As the sun climbs in the May sky and I scrutinize the Route 101 border more closely, I find that it too supports a layer of historical nuance and implication for those who take the time and effort to seek it out. On the south side of the highway, about seven feet in from the road and six feet west of the line where the Connecticut road crew stopped when they recently repaved the road (at least we know where *they* think the border is), a rusty, weathered old boundary sign stands (fig. 3). In several border crossings by automobile I have never consciously noticed this sign (in fact, expecting only to write about the newer signs and their

Figure 2. The Rhode Island Red monument. 1989 photograph by the author.

effect on the experience of crossing the border, I am delighted to find it now); I may have subliminally registered a rusty smudge at the periphery of my field of vision, but that is all. It is rather small, too small to notice when you drive by it fast, especially since it has faded to subtle tones of orange and grey that blend into the background as you whoosh past. Although the sign still stands clearly by the side of the road, the eye is caught and pulled ahead by the larger, newer, brighter signs farther

Figure 3. The old boundary sign. 1989 photograph by the author.

along the road on either side of it which partially (if less accurately) duplicate its function as a geographical and political marker. Thus the motorist has no real reason or opportunity to seek the old sign out. Scaled to a different, older pace of travel, it rusts and fades in obscurity.

The square wooden post which supports the sign was painted white once, but I have to lean close to determine this; it has since weathered into grey. The sign was obviously erected by the Rhode Island highway department: the rusty sign attached to the east side of the post reads "State Highway Ends Here," whereas the placard on the Connecticut side reads "State Highway Begins Here." The sheer Rhode-Island-centricity of this sign delights me, with its implication that all known civilized roads end at this point despite the obvious fact that the road continues unimpeded into the next state. (Here is a brutal if unintended comparative statement of the merits of Rhode Island and Connecticut which far outstrips anything that the subtle Connecticut tourism agency has been able to come up with!) A set of faded metal finger signs, black letters on irregular grey background, sits atop the post about seven or eight feet off the ground. The sign pointing east reads "Foster, R.I.," while the one pointing west says "Killingly, Conn."; a third finger pointing perpendicular to the road, worn into near-illegibility, reads "State Line" as one leaves Rhode Island, "Town Line" as one enters (that delightful localism again: Killingly, apparently, is not a town). A vine climbs the sign, winding around the bottom of the post, clinging to the Rhode Island end-of-the-road warning, poking its tip into the sky above the finger signs, adding to the general air of neglected ruin and charming antiquity.

Leaving aside the ways in which it reveals the Rhode Island highway department's evidently Ptolemaic worldview, this sign carries no information as to how passing travelers should interpret and experience the lands which they are about to enter. It is a geographical and political marker pure and simple, a tangible sign that the traveler has just crossed over a particular line on the map. People crossing this border when the sign was new were left free to think of Connecticut or Rhode Island according to their own experience of them, or to seek out their own experience if they hadn't had one yet, free from geographical suggestions planted in the backs of their minds by glad-handing big blue signs. For the contemporary observer, though, the sign is historically suggestive, whispering of older landscapes, older ways of getting around, older modes of experiencing the world. As I study the sign, sketch it, photograph it, I have no idea when it was erected. Its aged state is plain to see, but I don't know how fast signs deteriorate with exposure to the elements. Its evident scaling to a different rate of travel, however, is suggestive: it must have been put here when people drove more slowly, when they were more concerned with local gradations and nuances of travel, perhaps when the road was narrower. Route 101 is also known as the Hartford Pike, a link in the most direct route between Providence and Hartford; although it is a rural two-lane highway, then, it carries a fairly large amount of traffic at 40 to 50 miles per hour. People in vehicles moving this fast, sometimes following or followed closely by others, certainly could not read a small finger sign telling them they are entering Foster or Killingly; driving by at speed later in the day, I barely feel comfortable pulling my eyes from the road to pick out the sign at all. Enormous blue placards, like big highway billboards, are much more appropriate to these conditions. Knowing of the older sign, however, encourages the imagination to wonder what this border crossing looked like when the sign was new: to picture older cars, a narrower road occupied by fewer people in less of a hurry to get between Hartford and Providence, a rate of speed and style of travel which encouraged, or at least allowed, closer attention to details in the roadside landscape. (A Burma-Shave-sign style of travel, if you will, rather than a billboard style.) An entire historical landscape of travel suggests itself, at least in vague and shadowy terms, to the person who notices and thinks about the old sign. It is simple, functional, and obviously obsolete, and for all of those reasons a spark to the engine of the geographical imagination.

Intrigued and delighted by the old sign, I wonder if there are any other border markers along the side of the road, markers which this sign rendered obsolete in its day, markers even more ancient and historically resonant. I search the ground around me and quickly spot a stubby stone post, about a foot and a half high, planted in the earth about seven feet west of the old sign (fig. 4). It looks man-made, seems roughly hewn: seen from the top, it is approximately flatiron-shaped, about a foot across each unsmoothed side and ten inches across its curved back. It must have been brought here from elsewhere, as I see no other rocks around which match its pinkish granite. If this roughly carved, deliberately planted artifact isn't in fact some sort of border marker, I muse, I'd like to think it is.

I sit on another nearby rock, lean close to measure, sketch, and photograph the post. It has lichen growing on it and is closely surrounded by small vines and other weedy roadside plants. (To my immediate chagrin, some of the plants have thorns on them; to my later, and much greater, chagrin, it becomes clear the next day that I wasn't careful

Figure 4. The stone post, with the letter *C* showing. 1989 photograph by the author.

enough around those plants that I thought looked like poison ivy. Bemused thoughts of ancient curses laid against those who would disturb the post race through my brain.) Suddenly, as I scrutinize and poke, it becomes clear to me that what I at first thought was a random curved gouge in the surface of the rough prism facing me is really a shallowly carved (or badly eroded) C, about six inches high. This is the west side of the post, so I decide that my hunch must be correct, that the C must stand for Connecticut, and that this must in fact be an old border marker. And if there is a C on this side, there must be an R and an I on the other. Excited, I step around to the Rhode Island side of the post and start probing its surface. After a close search, I finally make out the loop of an R, its stem and tail partially buried in the ground because the post leans into the side of a slight incline which slopes downhill from Rhode Island. The I is similarly partially buried, very faint, but nonetheless there. Without ever having expected to, I have taken yet another step back in the history of this border. This post looks old enough to have been put here when Roger Williams sent the first surveyors out.

It probably wasn't, of course, but much about it nonetheless suggests great age: at the very least, the lichen and the weathering and erosion of the rock and letters; the (to my uneducated eye) very old-fashioned quality of the carving; the vast difference in scale and seeming purpose between this humble and insignificant post and the gaudy blue placards facing it from either side. The post suggests history, emanates mystery, and draws questions out of the person contemplating it, questions which imply a history both of the artifact and of the landscape in which it is set. Whose hands carved the post? When? Who ordered it carved? When was it put here? The questions radiate out from the post to encompass its border surroundings and more: what was this road like back then (whenever then was)? What did it look like around here? What did people travel past this post in or on? Are there other, similar posts on other border-crossing roads—did one state or the other put this post here as part of a wider border-marking program?

The post sits mute. It demands that words and stories be woven around it, that questions be answered, that imagination be loosed in speculation, that research be done in the field and the library and written into history. Now the questions that it elicits become more mysterious and puzzling: *why* was the post carved? What purpose was it put here to serve? It doesn't seem adequate to serve the conventional purposes of a sign. It does mark the border and so locates an important geographical and political division, but since it is carved someone must have expected people to read it. But who? Not travelers: the post is too small and low, the letters too obscure to be read except by foot travelers squatting down and peering at it. In fact, it is so humble that it is difficult to notice from any distance at all. From across the road, it blends into the background and becomes indistinguishable from the other stones lying around unless you are deliberately looking for it, and it is next to impossible to pick out from a moving vehicle. Clearly it was not meant to announce a boundary crossing to passers-by, a feeling reinforced by the fact that the rock and carving seem rather crude—the rock is not squared off or polished, the carving is not deep. It seems not to be the work (or at least not the *careful* work) of a stonemason or headstone cutter; it is not "graveyard quality," seems not to have been meant to be easily legible and admired. Why not? Why not the best to mark the border along the important Hartford Pike? Who, finally, was supposed to read the letters—for whose satisfaction was the post put here? The expected answers seem not to be adequate upon reflection.

The post answers its questions with further questions, amusingly complex behavior in an unassuming artifact originally designed to perform one simple task: sit on a border and tell which side is which. In that designed function it predates and duplicates the purpose of its neighbor, the weathered old sign. It echoes that sign as well in the historical suggestions it makes, and in fact far outstrips it: the old post suggests historical landscapes even further removed from us in time, modes and rates of travel even more foreign to our experience. It resembles the Adamsville sign in its reference to antiquity and subsequent call to the geographical imagination, but to my mind it is much more deeply allusive and historically resonant because it was a witness. It participated in all the landscapes which it has seen pass. It is not a piece of new material with a date written on it; as a carved artifact, it is itself as old as any date we could accurately inscribe on its surface. It continues to participate in the Route 101 border landscape today, obscure and unremarked except by border-hopping scholars who find it because they expect, on a hunch, that it will be there. It encapsulates a depth of geographical meaning and suggestion that nothing else in this landscape does. With the rest of the signs and markers along this stretch of road, it forms a palimpset: a layered accumulation, with each new layer erasing and obscuring the last, of man-made frontier-announcing artifacts, of implied landscapes, of attitudes toward travel, of the unremarkable everyday history of this spot on the border. The new blue signs point toward the future (as boosters always do), toward the geographical impressions they hope travelers will form and take away with them. The old sign and the stone post point in a different direction, back and further back into the geographical past, forming imaginative impressions of their own and bidding us travel, not bodily but in our minds, through vanished landscapes and earlier worlds. I realize finally, as I straddle the border, that I am Janus-like not only in looking two ways from a physical boundary. In thinking about signs, in walking this road slowly and imaginatively rather than speeding through in a car from city to city, I stare simultaneously forward and backward from the border between the future and the past.

I retreat to a picnic table to write down some notes. Below me, an official-looking orange truck approaches from somewhere in Connecticut, pulls into a side road which leaves the highway just inside the Rhode Island side of the line, and parks. Three men get out and cross to the north side of the highway. After looking around for a while, they drive into the ground near the border a tall stake with a fluorescent orange banner tied to its top; they also tie an orange band around a nearby tree and spray-paint a white mark on the edge of the pavement, then return to their truck. Intrigued, excited, and amused by the serendipitous way that this day is turning out, I scramble down the hill to talk to them. Perhaps they are marking or resurveying the border and can tell me exactly where it is. Certainly nothing in the landscape can help me locate it precisely: old sign, new signs, stone post, the line where the road surface changes—all are in different locations, all are probably more or less inaccurate. The side road on the Rhode Island side of the boundary is marked by a yellow sign of the sort used by the Town of Foster; another road, which leaves the highway no more than 20 feet to the west of the one in Rhode Island, is marked by a green Town of Killingly sign. The road surface line, the old sign, and the stone post all stand between these two roads. I have begun to think of these few yards of highway as a border zone in which one state gradually fades into another rather than as a passage over a definite sharp line which cuts with hard geometric precision across the right-of-way. Perhaps these men can point out to me exactly where one place ends and another begins. Perhaps they can also give me some information and background on the mysterious stone post, can supply it with the voice which it lacks but which I wish it had.

As it turns out, they can do none of this, but that doesn't make my conversation with them any less interesting. They work for the Connecticut Department of Transportation and, when I meet them, are in the process of traveling around the state and locating geodetic survey markers—those small bronze disks which serve as known and measured spots of longitude, latitude, and elevation for the benefit of surveyors—so that they can be checked and measured even more accurately by the National Geodetic Survey. They aren't actually concerned with the state line at all—they tell me that they don't get out to the edges of the state very often, and in fact, given the multiplicity of confusing and vague boundary indications in the area, they are wondering themselves where the boundary runs. The survey monument whose general position they mark with their stake isn't actually on the border, doesn't offer a quick and easy way of finding it, but instead provides a known and fixed reference point if someone wants to precisely locate and measure the boundary with surveyors' equipment. Nor can they tell me anything about the history of the way in which the border has been located, measured, and marked. We each are interested in what the other is doing, though, have a friendly and question-filled chat, and go our separate ways having been reminded of a new and different way of looking at and thinking about this particular chunk of geography that we were examining in our specialized fashions.

As the surveyors drive off, I think about how radically different their professional view of the earth is from the one I am pursuing. I have been thinking about basic questions of human, cultural, and historical geography, about past landscapes and landscape change, about the human experience of crossing borders and the ways that border markers may affect our view of what's on the other side, about the meaning of a few yards of road and what lies on either side of it. Theirs is a view that replaces geography with geometry, meaning with measurement. The geodetic viewpoint sees the earth not as a collection of places to be experienced but as a surface to be measured, a featureless surface with nothing on it but mathematical coordinates of longitude and latitude. Theirs is the cartographic perspective carried to an extreme. Cartographers rely on the work of surveyors and the existence of geodetic survey markers in order to be able to draw accurate lines on their maps, but they also try to give an indication of the physical things that are on the land their map takes in, to translate into graphic symbols as best they can a portion of the earth's surface. The geodetic view doesn't take into account the multiplicity of stuff that is on the earth's surface, the things that can be thought about it, the words that can be said about it; it just looks from survey marker to survey marker, thinks about where one mathematical point is in relation to another mathematical point.

Just as I and the surveyors come to the border with radically different purposes and perspectives, then, so do the stone post and the geodetic survey marker imply different things, make us think in different ways. The post is silent, but it makes the observer think, wonder, ask a variety of questions. It is complex; it vivifies its surroundings with human meanings. The survey marker, on the other hand, says one simple thing but says it loudly, loudly enough to drown out other thoughts and conversations. Here I am, it shouts, right here on this exact spot of longitude and latitude. In its terms, I suddenly realize, no point on the earth's surface is unknown or unaccounted for, even if no one has ever been there; every spot on the land surface of the country is potentially locatable in relation to this or any other survey marker and from there can be tied in to a network of geodetic survey lines covering the entire globe.

When I came across the stone post that morning, I had felt a surge of discovery, a feeling (true or not) that I had stumbled across something that no one else knew about or that everyone else had forgotten about. I was reminded of geographer John K. Wright's comments about the earth still being largely a collection of unknown and undiscovered places: "If . . . *terra incognita* be conceived as an area within which no observed facts are on record in scientific literature or on maps, the interior of my place in Maine, no less than the interior of Antarctica, is a *terra incognita*, even though a tiny one. Indeed, if we look closely enough—if, in other words, the cartographical scale of our examination be sufficiently large—the entire earth appears as an immense patchwork of miniature *terrae incognitae*."[5] Here, I felt, was such a place—unmarked on any map, and unknown, I felt sure, to all but a few minds. I now realized that a bead could be drawn from it to a nearby survey marker and from there to any place in the world I pleased. In the process its meanings and mysteries would be temporarily disregarded, and it would simply become a known point in a network of other known points. As historian of cartography John Noble Wilford explains, "when a local surveyor checks the corners of your property and ties his work into the nearest Geodetic Survey marker, he is positioning your lot in relation to Meades Ranch,"[6] in Kansas, the "zero point" to which all survey markers in North America are tied indirectly. The idea of relating this humble post, so intimately tied to the Connecticut–Rhode Island border, to a spot in faraway Kansas is for me simultaneously fascinating, amusing, and completely foreign and irrelevant to my experience with it this morning. In geodetic terms, though, neither the post nor any other terra incognita you could think of is mysterious, secretive, silent, or obscure—as a featureless point, at least, if not as a meaningful location.

It has meaning for me now, though, as does this whole border zone—this vague and fuzzy region, bristling with signs and markers, where the Ocean State stops and the Nutmeg State begins. I can imagine myself translating it into words and stories—an anecdote about the role of serendipity in doing research, a wryly humorous warning to the effect that sometimes it's a good idea to wear long sleeves and gloves when doing fieldwork in rural areas in the spring. As I wander across the border one last time, no longer emulating Janus but anticipating the drive back across Rhode Island, all of the varied geographical approaches and perspectives to which I have been exposed and in which I have participated this day—the human experience of geographical transitions, the hints of historical geography which I read into the post, the newer cultural geography of roadside signs and picnic groves and the interpretations they invite, the far-reaching, detail-effacing perspective of surveyors and geodesists—fade before thoughts of the day's work and the experience of settling one last time on a mossy hillside, amidst piney shade and cool breezes, to write in my notebook.

1 Of Maps and Minds: The Invisible Landscape

Now when I was a little chap I had a passion for maps. I would look for hours at South America, or Africa, or Australia, and lose myself in all the glories of exploration. At that time there were many blank spaces on the earth, and when I saw one that looked particularly inviting on a map (but they all look that) I would put my finger on it and say, When I grow up I will go there.
—JOSEPH CONRAD, Heart of Darkness

I'd like to go to the real Correctionville someday. I have been living and working as a writer in the other Correctionville, the one in my mind. There, I am constantly tinkering with the maps of the Midwest, trying to damp the distortions as much as possible while realizing that each selected vision of the place is a map more detailed than the thing it represents.
—MICHAEL MARTONE, "Correctionville, Iowa"

Cartography and Imagination

To experience a geographical place, it seems, is to want to communicate about it. Innumerable works in a variety of media have been produced over the years as people have attempted to tell others what certain places look like and feel like, what they mean and how they got that way—efforts ranging from travel itineraries and guidebooks to landscape paintings and photographs to the formal academic descriptions of geographers and landscape historians. Of all the media of communication about geography, the map is probably the first that comes to most people's minds, and it has certainly been one of the most basic and long-lived. Maps of some sort have been produced by nearly all known cultures in all known times. Archaeologists have discovered maps of ancient Sumerian cities, preserved on clay tablets. Pacific Islanders make maps out of sticks in order to teach young men how to navigate among the far-flung islands which make up their community. Cartography was one of the most important and respected arts in medieval and Renaissance Europe, serving both to summarize the current state of geographical knowledge and belief and to spur explorers on to ever-wider-ranging voyages of discovery.[1]

Not only has the map been a perennially central form of geographical communication, it is probably one of the most densely packed communications media of any sort. Modern cartography in particular is capable of including an immense quantity of information about a place on a small rectangle of paper, with the efforts of the United States Geological Survey providing perhaps the most detailed and precise examples for Americans. Look, for example, at any of the USGS's topographic maps—say, the 7.5-minute quadrangle centering on New Milford, Connecticut. This map gives as complete a summary of the physical and cultural features of the New Milford area as is possible given its limitations of technology and scale. Through its system of contour lines, it clearly and graphically indicates the hilly nature of the local terrain. The map also indicates the kind of vegetation which covers that terrain, and pinpoints the location and course of lakes, rivers, and ponds. It also shows what has been done with this particular piece of geography. A thick blanket of cultural artifacts has been laid over the New Milford hills: buildings, roads, power lines, cemeteries, golf courses, parks, railroads—all are precisely located on the map, as are other, less physically obvious but no less present evidences of human occupation such as place-names and political boundaries. Through the precise graphic shorthand of modern cartography, the makers of this map have been able to summarize in a very small space a wealth of topographical and cultural information that would otherwise have taken pages and pages of verbal description and mathematical figures to contain.

While the modern map is a marvel of efficient geographical communication, though, in other important ways it does not tell us very much at all. The New Milford map provides an excellent example in this case, for I spent nine years of my childhood among those hills, houses, rivers, and names. The map tells me where certain hills are, but I retain in my legs the physical memory of what it feels like for a child to climb them. It tells me where certain buildings are, but I know what they look like inside and out—and not just as a photograph freezes an image, but what they look like at different times of the day and year. I look at the map and pick out my house, my childhood best friend's house, the buildings which were my church and school, and remember what I did in those buildings. The map reminds me of how dirt roads run off into the hills north of where we lived, but what it doesn't tell me—what I have to superimpose on it from my own experience, my own memory—is how one sunny fall day my father and I went exploring those roads in his beat-up old convertible, how I wasn't quite sure if he knew where he was going and didn't really care, how I wanted that afternoon and that car and those roads to go on forever. I see the river where I went swimming, the woods where I went exploring, the names which once seemed as much a part of my nature as my own. To me—to anyone intimately familiar with the area who views it—the New Milford map is even more densely packed with information than it is to the cartographer who drew it or the average outsider who reads it. Each square centimeter recalls to mind an image, a memory, a bit of history or half-forgotten experience.

The poet Elizabeth Bishop has written perceptively on the limitations inherent in cartography—the way in which maps provide only the most partial reflection of geographical experience. The speaker of her poem "The Map"[2] examines a map of the North Atlantic region and is struck by its arbitrariness, its static lifelessness, the way that it converts a complex geographical reality into a purified object of aesthetic contemplation. The map pays no heed to the ambiguities of that shifting, amorphous zone where land meets sea; it states firm conclusions in sharply etched lines and bright cartographic blues and greens, leaving the speaker to wonder for herself about the indeterminate interaction of beach and ocean and to summon from experience and memory an image of tawny sand of which the map's cool hues give no hint:

> . . . does the land lean down to lift the sea from under,
> drawing it unperturbed around itself?
> Along the fine tan sandy shelf
> is the land tugging at the sea from under?

The map does not answer these perhaps unanswerable questions, for they are irrelevant to its purpose. Instead it compresses the landscape's ambiguities into an arbitrary and simplified flatness—it is all surface, lacking depth. This lack of depth takes in the human dimension as well; just as the map freezes the landscape in stasis so that waves no longer lap at beach and land no longer pulls at water—"Mapped waters are more quiet than the land is," says Bishop later in the poem—so too does it depopulate the land, removing from it any vestige of life and movement and history. The map has nothing to do with the quality and character of human existence as it is lived and felt on the surfaces that it describes; all depends on the disinterested craft of the cartographer:

> Are they assigned, or can the countries pick their colors?
> —What suits the character of the native waters best.
> Topography displays no favorites; North's as near as West.
> More delicate than the historians' are the map-makers'
>   colors.

This is the cartographer's world, not the historian's: here, all is flat, dimensionless, washed-out, and lifeless. There is no layer of history here, no room for the historian's bold hues of red blood and green life. The mapmaker's colors instead seem effete and fragile, arbitrarily chosen from the cartographic palette, a pale imitation of the world they purport to depict. Instead of a faithful enactment of a vibrant and complex natural and human world, the map of the poem is an aesthetic object, little more than an artful arrangement of color and shape. It lies under glass like a painting on a wall: "We can stroke these lovely bays, / under a glass as if they were expected to blossom, / or as if to provide a clean cage for invisible fish." Like a plant in a terrarium, like a fish in an aquarium, the map is deliberately set off from life, abstracted from reality and put on display. Looking at a captured fish behind glass gives us little sense of a complex ocean environment; looking at a captured landscape behind glass gives us little sense of a complex human environment—although, like the fish, it may be pretty to look at.

Where the map fails, however, the imagination takes over. Shapes and colors on the map awaken echoes in the speaker's mind of things that she has seen and done in her life. She fills in physical details which do not fit on the map because they have nothing to do with its function, recalling images of "long sea-weeded ledges" and "the fine tan sandy shelf" in the shifting tidal zone where the land slips beneath the water. Her mind plays with the images suggested by the silhouettes of the map's landforms, so that the flat and static chart suddenly springs to bustling life: under the speaker's whimsical scrutiny, "These peninsulas take the water between thumb and finger / like women feeling for the smoothness of yard-goods," while "Norway's hare runs south in agitation, / profiles investigate the sea, where land is." Maps may be inadequate in themselves to express human life, they may resist poetry, but nevertheless they can inspire imagination, emotion, and words; Bishop superimposes her poetic creativity on the map, and her poem enacts the perennial urge to connect with landscape in an imaginative, human way, even if that landscape is only present in the attenuated form of a map.

As Bishop ultimately recognizes—and as I realize in contemplating New Milford's cartographic image—maps, while they have their limitations, nevertheless possess the power to summon up a deeply human response, appealing irresistibly to memory and creativity and dreams, connecting intimately with people's minds and lives. Much of the fascination of maps lies in the fact that they are simultaneously distillations of experience and invitations to experience. Modern maps look so precise and scientific that it is difficult to remember that (unless they are generated completely from aerial photographs and satellite data) they are summaries of the direct field observations and experiences of surveyors and geologists, not the anonymous productions of computers and machines. In this sense maps stand as segments of the professional autobiographies of their makers, and thus, inevitably, of their personal autobiographies as well. John McPhee has written about David Love, the supervisor of the United States Geological Survey's office in Laramie, Wyoming, who was born on a ranch in central Wyoming in 1913 and who has spent almost his entire professional career within the boundaries of his home state. Love is a prime illustration of McPhee's observation that "geologists tend to have been strongly influenced by the rocks among which they grew up." Having spent his youth among the mountains of Wyoming, gazing from horseback at the landscape surrounding him as he tended his family's livestock, idly trying to figure out how it got that way, Love "was drawn to be a geologist in much the way that someone growing up in Gloucester, Massachusetts, would be drawn to be a fisherman"—indeed, admits Love, "there was nothing else to be interested in." Love has spent countless days of his professional life studying this dramatic landscape which was so intimately intermingled with his childhood and his family history; he observes that he has probably spent a quarter of the nights of his life sleeping under the Wyoming stars, and reflects, while looking about him from a piece of high ground near the Tetons, that "I guess I've been on every summit I can see from here." In a sort of symbolic recapitulation of his personal and professional history, Love has twice been the senior author of the geologic map of Wyoming—a fitting piece of work for someone who, McPhee claims, "had the geologic map of Wyoming in his head."[3] To the ordinary map user, this map is a convenient summary of the way that the state of Wyoming is put together. To Love, it summarizes as well a past, a career, and a way of life.

At the same time, as the narrator Marlow in Joseph Conrad's *Heart of Darkness* demonstrates, maps are spurs to the imagination, beguiling catalysts for travel and exploration. After a childhood spent daydreaming over maps, Marlow as an adult remains fascinated by "one river especially, a mighty big river, that you could see on the map" of Africa, "resembling an immense snake uncoiled, with its head in the sea, its body at rest curving afar over a vast country, and its tail lost in the depths of the land." Drawn inexorably by his fascination, Marlow becomes a steamboat pilot on this river: "The snake had charmed me."[4] Maps have perennially inspired people to journey to the lands that they represent, to translate their signs and symbols into lived experience—fortunately, rarely with the nightmarish consequences that Marlow found. The history of world exploration is studded with journeys inspired by the tantalizing information proffered by maps and globes. In early times, this information was often fanciful and erroneous; as John Noble Wilford points out, until the Renaissance, "the only maps that could be trusted were confined to immediate surroundings. Those that essayed to describe distant lands and seas were, until the modern era, exercises in conjecture based on inadequate surveying, wishful thinking, theological dogma, or sheer imagination."[5] Nevertheless, these exercises in creative cartography took powerful hold on the minds of adventurous Europeans; says geographer John L. Allen,

> The imagination evokes certain responses and elicits certain activities from those who would explore. Thus, goals imaginatively set forth influence explorers in many different areas and periods as they search for imaginary objectives, despite the failure of others to find them. . . . Generations of explorers have devoted their careers to imaginary objectives—to the search for a Prester John, for a Passage to India, for the Lake of the Golden Man or a Golconda or an Ophir. These objectives, the lands of myth and waters of wonder, have themselves conditioned exploratory behavior and modified exploration's consequences.[6]

The map thus emerges as a powerful expression of dream and desire—a product of imagination in early times, a magnet for imagination at all times. Maps were once drawn, and even today are interpreted, according not only to what is objectively out there but also to what we wish were out there, or hope to find out there.

Christopher Columbus is perhaps the most famous of those whose actions have been influenced by the cartographic expression of geographical fancy. He was encouraged in his explorations and confirmed in his purpose by maps of the day which included, among other things, the mythical mid-Atlantic island of Antilia, which "was such a standard feature of fifteenth-century maps that Columbus seemed to have every expectation of finding it—and possibly using it as a way station—en route to the Indies."[7] He was also encouraged by a chart which he owned—a map from the Florentine scholar Paolo dal Pozzo Toscanelli, whose learning would have stamped his charts with incontrovertible authority—which demonstrated that a sea voyage from Europe to Asia was relatively short and entirely feasible (especially with that midocean stopover)—another geographical commonplace of the time. Map-motivated journeys were not, however, limited to the Age of Exploration. William Least Heat Moon wrote a 1982 best-seller, *Blue Highways*, about his journeys on some of America's more obscure thoroughfares. He explains his title: "On the old highway maps of America, the main roads were red and the back roads blue." Troubled by a painfully tumultuous personal life, Least Heat Moon sought solace in these little-traveled routes, setting off "in search of places where change did not mean ruin and where time and men and deeds connected."[8] Those narrow squiggles on the road map represent for Least Heat Moon the healing rhythms of a stable small-town American way of life, a frozen chunk of a fondly imagined past; they lead to a promised land which is just as hazy and fleeting as are the fabled realms sought by Columbus and his contemporaries.

It seems, then, that this intermingling of abstract geographical representation with imagination and memory characterizes cartography (and its contributing science, surveying), and conditions the way in which we read maps, to at least some extent in all times and places. As I was reminded when I met the surveying party on the Connecticut–Rhode Island border, however, and as is brought forcefully to my notice when I look at the USGS's map of New Milford, mapmaking and surveying today are abstract scientific exercises. The farther back we go in time from modern cartographic science, though, the more personal and communal experiences, perceptions, and understandings control the mapmaker's pen. The early history of political boundaries in Europe, for instance, was marked by a comfortable familiarity with the facts of local geography, as those who drew lines on the land and reproduced them on paper habitually sought out borders and markers already available and recognized in the landscape; the geography with which they dealt was emphatically a geography of human experience. "Traditionally," geographer David Lowenthal points out, "natural features and artifacts—trees and rocks, mountains and rivers, meadows and pastures, buildings and roads—demarcated both private and civil boundaries. . . . Landowners and local officials committed these landmarks to memory by regularly perambulating the bounds, and preserved such landmarks as irreplaceable evidence of possession."[9] From the earliest days of Christianity until the first village maps were drawn in the late sixteenth century, parish priests in England led annual processions around the boundaries of their villages in order to fulfill two functions, says Maurice Beresford: a religious one, "to ask a blessing on the coming agricultural year," and a social one, "to examine the boundaries of the fields," ascertain the village's property rights, and ensure "the education of the young in this important set of facts." Boundaries in medieval England were thus much more than abstract lines. They had ritual and religious meaning; they had the sanction of God's blessing and were constantly watched over and protected by a divine presence. Moreover, they were firmly grounded in the facts of experience. Their constancy could not be taken for granted; every year men had to struggle through field and forest to ascertain their location through the evidence of their senses. When surveyors and cartographers eventually came to fix village boundaries on paper, they too relied on knowledge derived from years of life in the local landscape: they drew their lines according to the testimony of courts of survey "made up of local inhabitants of substance and experience. Since the usages of the past were an important issue, the old men of the village were essential witnesses." These old men described the limits of their villages to the surveyors in terms of "landmarks that had become fixed in the memories of the townspeople: a hole by the riverside where there had once been a mill; a cross erected to record the bounds of Rushden; a suicide's grave in open country, unhallowed no-man's-land."[10] In this world, boundaries arose as natural outgrowths of custom and usage and were only important insofar as they impinged on local life and belief. They were recalled only in relation to the marks and monuments, both natural and artificial, which the land provided and which the people came up against every day.

Villagers and landowners in early America similarly conceived of boundaries in experiential terms. Life in the nucleated New England village, for instance, was directed inward, not outward. Social, civic, and economic life centered on the church and on the carefully cleared and ploughed fields which closely surrounded the area of settlement, and travel to other places was rare; few roads led from village to village, and people traveled on them only when compelled by necessity. Early New Englanders distrusted the wilderness which lay beyond the fields; it was the home of wild beasts and wild men, it was traditionally understood to be Satan's realm, and its tangled disorder stood in fearful and unsettling contrast to the topographical and social order of the village. Moreover, as landscape historian John Stilgoe points out, the forest was simply terra incognita. The New Englander's dislike and distrust of the woods in large part "derived from his own limited experience. . . . The typical husbandman named his fields, bounded them, measured them, and wrote down his private perception of them when he sold them, but he rarely left them or the town of which they were a part." The boundaries of his fields were familiar and exact because they formed the basis of his life and livelihood; the town boundaries, since he feared the wilderness in which they lay and had no compelling reason to approach or revere them, remained for the New England farmer vague and shadowy, known in theory but not in experience. Town officials still walked the boundaries annually, in the traditional way, but even as new fields expanded outward from the village center "the narrow zones abutting [the borders] went unvisited by townspeople still guided by old centripetal roads. . . . The narrow zones of vestigial wilderness reinforced the vision of a town as a discrete, special place focused inward upon itself."[11] The "real" village boundaries—the ones developed through local patterns of life and belief—thus stood well within the official political frontier.

As in medieval England, then, the only boundaries that ultimately mattered in early New England were those established from the inside, pushed out by the daily round of life and work—and, as the narrow compass of the New England farmer's day-to-day existence made clear, the most important and familiar of these boundaries were property lines. In early New England, as in the rest of the country, property was not surveyed in relation to abstract geometrical points and established geodetic baselines as it is today. Instead, landholdings were outlined through the "metes-and-bounds" system, a means of measurement which depended on the surveyor's immediate personal contact with the landscape. The surveyor delineated a piece of property by measuring a series of straight lines from one landmark to another; when these landmarks were connected on paper, the resulting irregular polygon defined the "metes and bounds," or limits, of the property. Frequently these landmarks took the form of "witness trees," durable hardwoods whose relative permanence in the landscape seemed certain and which could be easily marked by an ax with distinctive identifying blazes: a plat from around 1790 of the property belonging to the Georgian landowner William Few, to take one typical example, indicated hickory, black

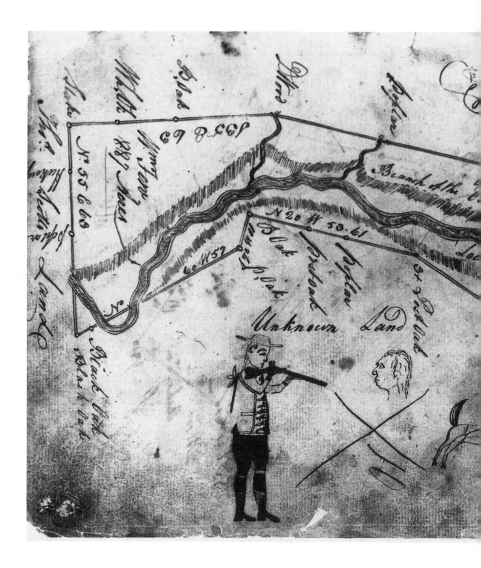

oak, poplar, white oak, dogwood, and post oak among its witness trees (fig. 5). The measurement process thus brought surveying teams into intimate contact with the land; they had to come face to face with the terrain they were mapping before they could draw lines on it. Helen Hooven Santmyer provides something of the flavor, of the intense geographical immediacy, of surveying in the days when the land around her home town of Xenia, Ohio, was platted: "And as one walked through the weeds that grow today in all fence corners, the imagination could be exercised by picturing how the first surveyor, after struggling through the crowded forest, crashing among saplings with his instruments, hacking down the wild grapevines that twisted about his shoulders—how he

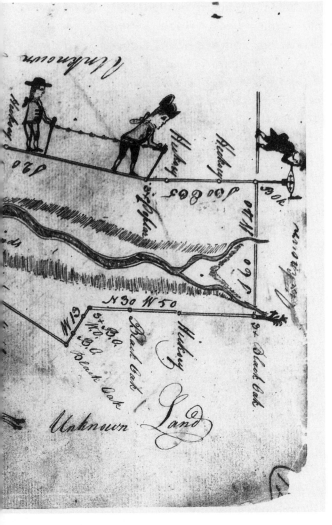

Figure 5. Survey plat
for William Few,
c. 1790. Courtesy
Georgia Department of
Archives and History.

found these particular trees at the end of the line he had traced with so
much difficulty, and marked them, triumphantly, with his axe."[12] As
when English villagers walked the boundaries of their villages in order
to ascertain their limits, the metes-and-bounds system of surveying approached pieces of land, and the lines which delineated them, in the
terms in which local residents understood them: as lived, experiential
realities.

When early American surveyors, and the cartographers who relied
upon their work, came to draw maps of the lands which they had measured and bounded, they occasionally strayed from the strict and abstract delineation of lines on the ground, opting instead to flesh out their

diagrams with colorful, detailed drawings of the things that were done and found on those lands. William Few's surveyor, for instance, decorated his plat of Few's landholding with sketches of the survey party at work, providing a view not only of a piece of land but of the process by which that particular property was bounded and measured. Cut off from the mainstream of cartographic convention through geographical or cultural isolation, these cartographers reverted to an earlier, premodern style of mapmaking, one which concentrated on geographical meanings far more than on geographical locations and which attempted to give as full an impression as possible of the lived texture of the local landscape. Only in the modern world, says E. V. Walter, do we "take it for granted that a map will not inform us how it feels to be in a certain place, or about the kind of experience to expect there, or . . . indicate perils of the soul on the way from one place to another. Yet, objectivity is the rule for a certain kind of map. It is not inherent in the nature of maps. Ancient maps differ from ours not only because they are graphically and mathematically naive, but also because they follow different rules." Such maps, concludes Walter, "show the spirits of places, and they preserve the memory of how people *felt* about places."[13] They are closely akin to those medieval world maps to which Allen alluded: maps which found room on the earth's surface for such legendary and mythological places as Paradise, St. Brendan's Island, the land of Gog and Magog, and the kingdom of Prester John, and which filled the blank spaces of Asia and Africa with drawings of strange monsters which were believed to dwell there—maps which "were more ecclesiastical than cartographic," in John Noble Wilford's words, "more symbolic than realistic," and which existed as "a representation of the mind more than of the Earth."[14] While not relying on an experiential understanding of the earth's surface, these medieval world maps reflect a belief that all geography is charged with religious and supernatural significance, a belief further indicated by their tendency to place Jerusalem at their centers. This understanding of the meaning of geography applied just as much to the ground under one's feet as to the mythical lands on the earth's fringes. All maps in this earlier cartographic style, then, elevate subjective interpretation over objective geographical reality; they warp and supplement cartographic space so that it reflects an understanding of an experienced world.[15]

While not "ancient" by any means, Shaker cartographers in the nineteenth century adhered closely to this early mapmaking style; they "conceived of their maps experientially rather than diagrammatically," says

Robert Emlen, "and thought it only reasonable to represent both the structures and the landscape they knew." These mapmakers drew illustrated maps of their villages, superimposing three-dimensional pictures of buildings upon two-dimensional diagrams of roads, fields, orchards, and woodlots (fig. 6). It was not uncommon for certain rather unexpected elements to stand out in these maps—a system of granite walkways, a botanical garden—indicating that these features of the landscape had special meaning for the mapmakers; the maps thus hinted at autobiography as well as providing a documentary record of the built environment, a personal touch of the sort which the knowing may read into David Love's Wyoming map but which is rarely found so overtly in cartography. Many Shaker maps were animated with drawings of farm animals and of people going about their daily business, giving the map-reader a sense of the patterns of daily life in the village—such maps, suggests Emlen, "had begun to function as narrative scenes."[16] The local landscape was not simply presented to the viewer in Shaker maps, then—it was assigned meaning and actively interpreted, explained in the terms by which local residents understood it. Shaker mapmakers drew little distinction between the depiction of geography in cartography and the experience of geography in their lives. In their maps they tried to suggest as fully as they could not only what made up the local landscape but also what it looked like and what it was like to live in it.

William and John Godsoe, a grandfather and grandson who worked as surveyors and cartographers in Kittery, Maine, in the late seventeenth and early eighteenth centuries, took similar pains to deepen the meaning of their maps with pictorial representations of the local landscape, both natural and man-made. As they went about their work in the town, measuring new parcels of land and settling boundary disputes between quarrelsome neighbors, the Godsoes produced maps enlivened by "illustrations of houses, barns, a meetinghouse, sawmills, fences, cornfields, orchards, and roads as well as such topographic features as marshes, creeks, and rivers replete with boats and waterfowl." Taken together, the Godsoes' maps paint a picture not only of Kittery's property divisions but also of its ecology, economic base, settlement history, architectural tastes—a brief yet wide-ranging summary of the local landscape and ways of life (fig. 7). The conditions which encouraged this personal and descriptive style of cartography, however, began to vanish in the eighteenth century. In Maine, as in the rest of the country, more and more wilderness land was being opened up for new occupation, and for the first time that land was subdivided into even, geometrical units before it

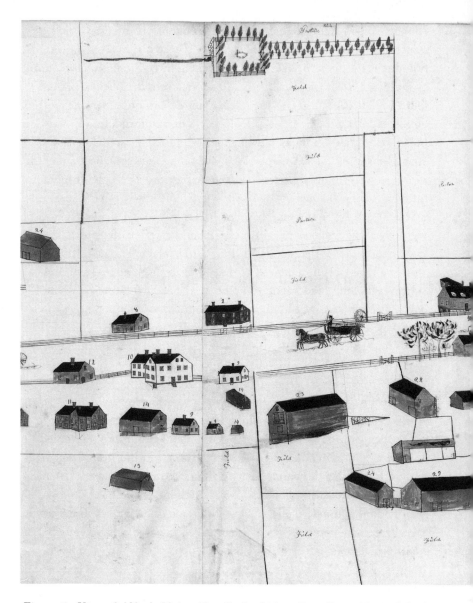

Figure 6. View of Alfred, Maine (detail), by Joshua Bussell, c. 1848. Gift of
Dr. J. J. C. McCue. Courtesy Museum of Fine Arts, Boston.

was actually occupied. No longer could Americans simply strike out for
no man's land and carve out a ragged piece of property for themselves;
from now on, regular surveying preceded settlement. Thus John Godsoe
found himself spending most of his professional time inscribing straight
lines on land where no one even lived yet, not drawing pictorial maps
of the familiar precincts of Kittery. These changes in the way people

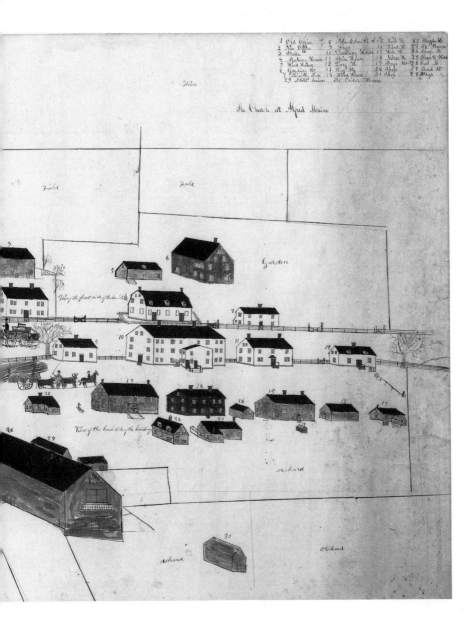

The Church at Alfred Maine

thought about the distribution, division, and settlement of land caused the practices of land measurement and mapmaking to drift away from their earlier grounding in the subtleties of geographical experience. What resulted was a style of surveying and cartography which took little heed of nuance and detail in landscape, which viewed land as an abstract entity to be measured and divided impartially and impersonally;

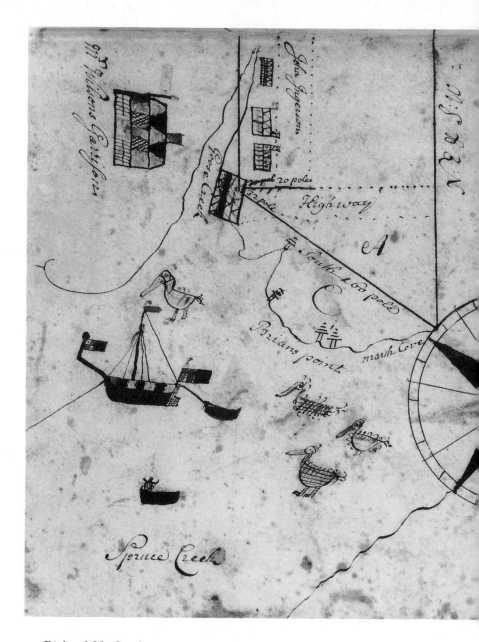

as Richard M. Candee comments, "Large tracts of land, often held for speculative purposes, do not call for the attention to small detail—the houses, ships, or ducks—that enlivened the seventeenth-century maps of Kittery."[17]

Today, with modern surveying and cartographic techniques, land measurement and mapmaking continue in the direction which John Godsoe and others pioneered. Modern maps are largely a matter of transits

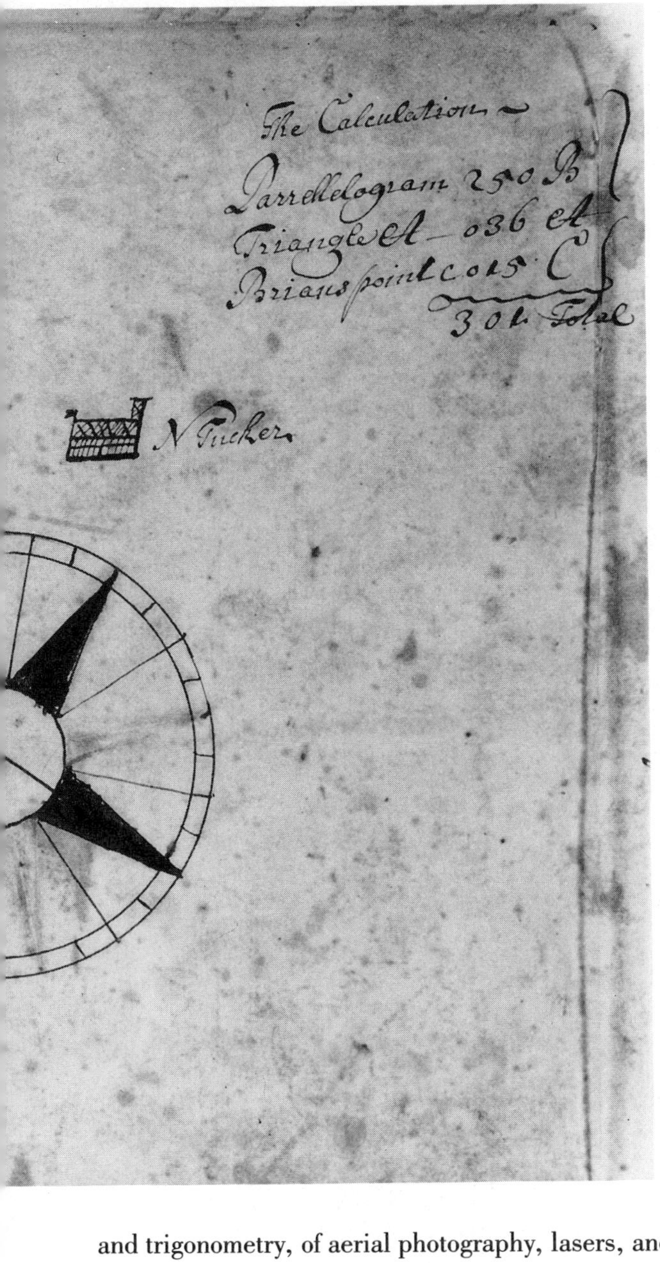

The Calculation ~
Parrellogram 250 B
Triangle A 036 A
Brians point C 015 C
301 Total

N Tucker

Figure 7. William Godsoe's survey of Elihu Gunnison's land at Brian's Point, Kittery, Maine (detail), March 1696/7. Courtesy Richard M. Candee.

and trigonometry, of aerial photography, lasers, and satellite technology; we can map the surface of the moon as easily as we can that of our own planet. No longer does the cartographer need to take to the field in order to inscribe the lines that divide up the land; instead, as Lowenthal says, "we now trace boundaries on an abstract grid and reproduce them mechanically, obviating the need either to recall or to retain old physical features."[18] The Land Ordinance of 1785 established that two-thirds of the United States—everything north of the Ohio River and west of the Pennsylvania-Ohio border—would be surveyed into six-square-mile townships, each divided into thirty-six square sections. This system of land division inscribed a network of potential boundaries on the landscape long before people lived on it; the result was the now-familiar grid of straight and square borders, roads, and fields which covers much of the nation. These geometrical survey lines march laser-straight across the country, taking no heed of the conditions and subtleties of the topography over which they pass. Their artificiality is frequently striking: the perfect rectangles of Colorado and Wyoming, for instance, seem incongruous in the jagged and mountainous West. These mathematically precise boundaries, imposed from miles away by legislative fiat, are a far cry from the meandering line between mill site and suicide's grave walked annually by the medieval priest; no one (except possibly David Love) has ever walked the Wyoming line, committing landmarks to memory, nor would anyone have reason to or, probably, even want to. No border could be farther from the lives of people on the land; it is little wonder that, as Stilgoe points out, "many colonists distrusted surveying . . . , thinking of it as a sort of evil magic that trapped their land in a web of invisible lines drawn by a mysterious figure knowing things beyond common knowledge" [19]—a bizarre departure, that is, from the ways of normal geographical experience, of approaching borders and their markers on foot and grasping them with hands, eyes, and mind.

Space, Place, and Narrative: The Invisible Landscape

Modern cartographic information, then, while extremely rich and retaining a degree of suggestive power over the imagination, is also extremely narrow and limited. Modern maps are concerned only with the spatial distributions of things—physical or cultural phenomena—and with helping their users accomplish certain specific tasks, depending on the type of map: wayfinding, education, delineating property, and so on. The cartographic imagination of our era is concerned with, and responds to, the things that are in a particular location but must necessarily stop short of dealing with the *meanings* of that location and the objects that it contains. Spurred by a growing realization that a strictly scientific approach to geographical understanding reveals only part of the nature of a location or a landscape—and in fact "falls embarrassingly short of being able to capture important intangibles of place: meaning, essence, and character," in geographer James R. Shortridge's words—humanistically oriented geographers have come to oppose "the somewhat sterile, theoretical term *space*" to "the equally important but emotion-laden and particularistic term *place*."[20] Space is abstract, geometrical, undifferentiated. Considered as space, the world is a blank surface on which areal relationships, physical landforms, and social patterns are dispassionately outlined; it is a matrix of objective geographical facts distilled from the messiness of real life—"an object for reflection,"[21] in the words of geographer Edward Relph, and not a subject to be experienced. Space "has no trodden paths and signposts," says geographer Yi-Fu Tuan. "It has no fixed pattern of established human meaning; it is like a blank sheet on which meaning may be imposed,"[22] meaning which is frequently foreign to the ways of life of the people who occupy the space in question. Looked at in spatial terms, the Connecticut–Rhode Island border is an exercise in mathematics, not a congeries of allusive artifacts and sensations. Space is primarily two-dimensional, a pattern of locations, a system in which the places of human experience have significance primarily as geometrical coordinates or identical dots on a map. The grid established by the 1785 Land Ordinance epitomizes the view of geography as space; ignoring the texture of the terrain over which it passes and the exigencies of the lives that people live on the land, it covers the country with a uniform blanket of identical squares and evenly spaced intersections. Space is geography viewed from a distance, coolly pondered and figured out, calmly waiting to have meaning assigned to it.

It is difficult, however, to think about space without soon thinking as well about the related concept of place. Sooner or later, we pull our eyes away from the horizon and turn them to the dirt under our feet and the neighborhood which surrounds us; we look at the dot on the map and find ourselves wondering what the place looks like and what kind of people live there. Space contains place, but it also misrepresents place; space is an object of thought, whereas place, according to Tuan, is "a center of meaning constructed by experience."[23] As E. V. Walter points out, the two terms represent completely different ways of understanding geography:

Modern "space" is universal and abstract, whereas a "place" is concrete and particular. People do not experience abstract space; they experience places. A place is seen, heard, smelled, imagined, loved, hated, feared, revered, enjoyed, or avoided. Abstract space is infinite; in modern thinking it means a framework of possibilities. A place is immediate, concrete, particular, bounded, finite, unique. Abstract space is repetitive and uniform. Abstraction moves away from the fullness of experience. Abstract space against concrete place contrasts abstract representation with the pulse of life feeling. The rationalization of space breaks the unity of located experience.[24]

A place, in this sense, is much more than a point in space. To be sure, a place is necessarily anchored to a specific location which can be identified by a particular set of cartographic coordinates, but it takes in as well the landscape found at that location and the meanings which people assign to that landscape through the process of living in it. A sense of place results gradually and unconsciously from inhabiting a landscape over time, becoming familiar with its physical properties, accruing a history within its confines. "What begins as undifferentiated space becomes place as we get to know it better and endow it with value," says Tuan. We may move to a new town, a city which we have known only as a name and a dot on a map: "In time we know a few landmarks and the routes connecting them. Eventually what was strange town and unknown space becomes familiar place. Abstract space, lacking significance other than strangeness, becomes concrete place, filled with meaning."[25] When space takes on three dimensions, when it acquires depth, it becomes place.

Part of this depth is physical. A knowledge of place is grounded in those aspects of the environment which we appreciate through the senses and through movement: color, texture, slope, quality of light, the feel of wind, the sounds and scents carried by that wind. This is literally a *sense* of place; this sense, says Tuan, "is made up of experiences, mostly fleeting and undramatic, repeated day after day and over the span of years. It is a unique blend of sights, sounds, and smells, a unique harmony of natural and artificial rhythms such as times of sunrise and sunset, of work and play. The feel of a place is registered in one's muscles and bones."[26] While "the importance of particular associations of physical features, both natural or man-made, in defining place cannot be denied," Edward Relph warns nonetheless that "it is hardly possible to understand all place experiences as landscape experiences."[27] The depth that characterizes a place is human as well as physical and sensory, a thick layer of history, memory, association, and attachment that builds up in a location as a result of our experiences in it. What vivifies an arbitrarily labeled chunk of space, says Walter, is the personal and communal history that we can attach to it, the things that happened to us there: "Every event happens some *where*, but we don't often locate an experience by its latitude and longitude. We say this experience happened to me in Manchester, or I felt this way in New York, or I did such and such in Boston. A place has a name and a history, which is an account of the experience located in that position."[28] This is not to say that all places must be as big (or as small) as a city, or even that they must necessarily have names, for, as Tuan points out, "experience constructs place at different scales. The fireplace and the home are both places. Neighborhood, town, and city are places; a distinctive region is a place, and so is a nation." What binds these various places together is that "they are all centers of meaning to individuals and to groups."[29] What makes them stand out is that they fuse history to location and give that location significance.

Since places are fusions of experience, landscape, and location, they are necessarily bound up with time and memory as well. The experiences which create and establish places recede inevitably into the past, so that one important quality of places is that they are "the present expressions of past experiences and events"[30]—contemplation of place quickly brings to mind earlier stages in one's life, episodes in the history of a community, formative and notable events and experiences. The landscape of a place is an objectification of the past, a catalyst for memory. Few of us remember our pasts with complete objectivity; the memory of an event calls forth the emotions with which we experienced that event, so that insofar as a place is a locus of experience it is a locus of feeling as well. "Place can acquire deep meaning," says Tuan, "through the steady accretion of sentiment over the years," although on the other hand one brief powerful emotion can illuminate a place for life—"the quality and intensity of experience matters more than simple duration."[31] For most people, though, the landscapes in which they invest the most emotion are those in which they have spent the most time: homes, favorite haunts, the landscapes of childhood. "A person in the process of time invests bits of his emotional life in his home, and beyond the home in his neighborhood";[32] such places, weaving themselves inextricably into the fabric of daily existence, gather to themselves some of the same emotions that we feel toward any other partner in life.

Part of the sentiment which people feel for places derives from the feelings of identification that they form with those places. We commonly and casually identify ourselves in terms of geographical labels, as being Midwesterners or New Yorkers; more important, if we feel that our present selves are inextricably bound to our pasts—that our lives have historical continuity, that we are the products of our past experiences—and if we tie memory to the landscape, then in contemplating place we contemplate ourselves. Says Relph, "There is for virtually everyone a deep association with and consciousness of the places where we were born and grew up, where we live now, or where we have had particularly moving experiences. This association seems to constitute a vital source of both individual and cultural identity and security, a point of departure from which we orient ourselves in the world."[33] This sense of identity may be one of the strongest of the feelings with which we regard places: when our meaningful places are threatened, we feel threatened as well. Along with the other elements of the sense of place, this feeling of identity helps give order, structure, and value to the geographical world. Experience, memory, and feeling combine with the physical environment to push peaks of human meaning above the abstract plain of space. We approach space through the mind, trying to figure out what it means with the help of books and measurements. As E. V. Walter reminds us, though, such a view requires that we willfully ignore much of what the mind *really* knows about the geographical world, for "the mind includes more than intellect. It contains a history of what we learn through our feet. It grasps the world that meets the eye, the city we know through our legs, the places we know in our hearts, in our guts, in our memories, in our imaginations. It includes the world we feel in our bones."[34]

For those who have developed a sense of place, then, it is as though there is an unseen layer of usage, memory, and significance—an invisible landscape, if you will, of imaginative landmarks—superimposed upon the geographical surface and the two-dimensional map. To passing observers, however, that landscape will remain invisible unless it is somehow called to their attention, as it was once brought to the notice of the philosopher William James. While taking a journey through the Blue Ridge Mountains of North Carolina, James contemplated the landscape around him, which had recently been settled by farmers. What he saw appalled him:

The impression on my mind was one of unmitigated squalor. The settler had in every case cut down the more manageable trees, and left their charred stumps standing. The larger trees he had girdled and killed, in order that their foliage should not cast a shade. He had then built a log cabin, plastering its chinks with clay, and had set up a tall zigzag rail fence around the scene of his havoc, to keep the pigs and cattle out. Finally, he had irregularly planted the intervals between the stumps and trees with Indian corn, which grew among the chips; and there he dwelt with his wife and babes—an ax, a gun, a few utensils, and some pigs and chickens feeding in the woods, being the sum total of his possessions.

So far, James's description is for the most part realistic and straightforward. His emotional reaction, however, is one of near-melodramatic distress: "The forest had been destroyed," he decides, "and what had 'improved' it out of existence was hideous, a sort of ulcer, without a single element of artificial grace to make up for the loss of Nature's beauty."

Finding himself "oppressed by the dreariness" of the scene, James asks his driver, a local mountaineer, what sort of people would possibly want to construct and live in such an eyesore. "All of us," the man replies. "Why, we ain't happy here, unless we are getting one of these coves under cultivation." James immediately feels abashed:

> I instantly felt that I had been losing the whole inward significance of the situation. Because to me the clearings spoke of naught but denudation, I thought that to those whose sturdy arms and obedient axes had made them they could tell no other story. But, when *they* looked on the hideous stumps, what they thought of was personal victory. The chips, the girdled trees, and the vile split rails spoke of honest sweat, persistent toil and final reward. The cabin was a warrant of safety for self and wife and babes. In short, the clearing, which to me was a mere ugly picture on the retina, was to them a symbol redolent with moral memories and sang a very paean of duty, struggle, and success.

In sum, James realizes that "the spectator's judgment is sure to miss the root of the matter, and to possess no truth. The subject judged knows a part of the world of reality which the judging spectator fails to see."[35] There is clearly more to this landscape than the bald physical facts which James sees—there is in addition an invisible landscape of meanings, memories, and associations, factors which constitute a "part of the world of reality" to which the mountaineer, an insider, is privy but to which James, the traveler, the outsider, is not. Both see the same physical scene, but James sees *only* that scene and judges it solely by imported aesthetic standards, while the local farmers see much more. James did not dream of the existence of the invisible landscape until the mountaineer spoke; his words opened up an entire new world before James's astonished eyes.

James reveals the key to seeing, understanding, and sharing with others the invisible landscape, the means through which to restore to maps that layer of meaning which they incorporated as a matter of course in earlier times. Mapreaders bring to maps their own associations, memories, and dreams. When they want to communicate to others what to them are the true meanings of the places that the maps describe, however, they must turn to words. As Barbara Johnstone argues, place is in fact as much a verbal as a physical or geographical phenomenon: "our sense of place . . . is rooted in narration. A person is at home in a place when the place evokes stories and, conversely, stories can serve to create places."[36] Art and photography may reveal the physical appearance of a place in a way that maps cannot and may capture something of the mood and meaning of that place, but their range is limited; they capture a moment, a facet, but lack the discursive, exploratory depth of words. Maps are strictly denotative; words are connotative. While words may be ill-suited to describe spatial arrangements precisely, then, they are eminently well-suited to reveal the depth and range of meaning that a place holds for those who are familiar with it, who have had enough experience of and in a place to enable them to transcend the cartographic imagination. As cartographers Arthur H. Robinson and Barbara Bartz Petchenik put it, "The two systems, map and language, are essentially incompatible. To be sure, we use the term 'language' loosely to denote any method of communication; but to believe that the language systems of maps and words are somehow equivalent and therefore convertible is as wrong as asserting that the 'language' of algebra could be used to communicate the meaning of a Rembrandt."[37]

Anthropologist Hugh Brody provides an example of this difference between mapped reality and experiential, narrative reality. As part of an effort to preserve traditional Indian ways of life in the face of an oil pipeline project proposed for northeastern British Columbia, Brody had members of the region's Indian tribes take standard topographic maps of the area and construct what he called "map biographies," graphic outlines of traditional Indian land-use practices. "Hunters, trappers, fishermen, and berry pickers mapped out all the land they had ever used in their lifetimes, encircling hunting areas species by species, marking gathering locations and camping sites—everything their life on the land had entailed that could be marked on a map." In other words, the Indians took a standard cartographic view of their place and personalized it, reinterpreted it so that it reflected their experience on the land and therefore *meant* something. They literally superimposed an additional layer of meaning upon the "official" maps they had been given, thereby incidentally revealing the communicative shortcomings of modern maps.

Brody describes one Indian in the process of drawing his map biography: "Joseph had his own agenda and his own explanations to give. He stood by the table, looked at the map, and located himself by identifying the streams and trails that he used. Periodically he returned to the map as a subject in its own right, intrigued by the pattern of contours, symbols, and colours and perhaps also by his recognition of the work that had brought us to his home. But if the map had any real importance for him, it seemed to be through its evocation of other times and other places." As for Bishop, as for me, the map here serves for Joseph primarily as a catalyst for imaginative wanderings, associations, memories, a sense of geographically anchored personal identity—and, importantly, for words, as he transcends the marks of his map biography and explains the meanings of the marks in story; the layer of significance that he superimposes on the map is a layer not only of land use but of narrative. Brody describes how Joseph provides a sort of running commentary as he makes his map, telling stories of how and why his family first came to the place he now calls home, of how a dream prophecy influenced them to stay; pointing out all of his hunting and trapping spots and explaining what one can find there; in the process explaining not only where his home place is but what it means to him and why. "The reminiscence thus spoken, and accompanied by an occasional search on the map . . . , slowly established his way of life."[38] Joseph has reinscribed on the map that narrative, expository element that modern cartography refuses to acknowledge.

The modern, detached cartographic imagination has much in common with the touristic imagination, the viewpoint of outsiders who come into a place with little prior knowledge of, or thought about, what they are going to see. Such viewers will frequently be limited to largely aesthetic impressions—they will comment to themselves on how the local landscape fits in with their notions of what makes for pretty or ugly scenery and leave it at that. They share with the cartographer (and the cartographically minded) a concern with surfaces, with the things that a place contains. The people who live in that place, however, could tell that viewer of a wide variety of mythic, legendary, historical, and personal meanings overlying what may have seemed to be a largely neutral chunk of geography. Nowhere is this difference in views clearer than in central Australia. The middle of the Australian continent is, to most visitors, a singularly forbidding place: a harsh, hot desert, usually flat, sometimes craggy. It carries little meaning for outsiders other than discomfort and the feelings of foreboding and fear that usually accompany the contem-

plation of disorganized and hostile wilderness. Bruce Chatwin, coming
across a preserved Aboriginal sacred site in the town of Alice Springs,
finds that it means nothing more to him than its appearance suggests:
"There wasn't much to see, for a white man anyway: a broken barbed-
wire fence, some crumbly stones lying this way and that, and a lot
of broken bottles in the bristly grass."[39] This aesthetic dismissal, this
impenetrable opacity of the geographical surface, is typical of the traveler's—of the white person's—experience with the central Australian
landscape.

To the Australian Aborigine, however, that same landscape is alive
with mythic and sacred meaning. In traditional Aboriginal thought,
all landscape features were formed by the Ancestral Beings during the
Dreamtime, that mythic time before historical time when the world and
everything in it were made. The Ancestors walked across the length and
breadth of Australia, creating the known world as they went. Landscape
features are to Aborigines, then, nothing less than evidences—physical
records—of the experiences and activities of their totemic ancestors
during the Dreamtime. Members of a totemic "family" can walk the path
of their ancestors and trace their story; while they are unable to read
geographical features elsewhere, they realize that they have similar significances to other totemic groups. All Australian landscape, then, has
significance to Aborigines, if not to whites—religious significance, political significance in that the routes of the Ancestors provide a basis for
determining tribal territories, and personal significance in that the same
life force that created the landscape also created the tribal members who
live in it; land and humankind are, in a fundamental spiritual sense,
one. Aborigines see themselves in seeing the landscape; it is a basic
source of personal identity. As Peter Sutton summarizes this Aboriginal
world view, "The Ancestral Beings, or Dreamings, who carved forms
out of the formless world and molded the shapes of the creeks and desert sandhills and rainforests also brought human sociality and culture.
Thus, there is no geography without meaning or without history. . . .
The land is already a narrative—an artifact of intelligence—before
people represent it. There is no wilderness."[40]

The Aborigines traditionally express their interpretation of the landscape in extremely stylized paintings of the Ancestors and their travels
and experiences—and, again, in words, speaking that narrative which
is the land. As Bruce Chatwin discovers in *The Songlines*, the activities of each Ancestor in the Dreamtime are summarized in song. As the
Ancestors wandered Australia, they literally sang the world into exis-

tence: geographical features sprang into being as they sang out their names. These long and wandering songs remain alive in Aboriginal tradition, with each phrase and line corresponding to a segment of the Ancestors' path, their "songline"; those who know the path and the song can follow the one and sing the other in the same way the Ancestors did, recreating the mythic creative process, reasserting their identities. Aboriginal myth thus provides a particularly potent example of the connection between the meanings overlying the bald facts of physical geography and the expressive power of words.

Joseph annotates the map with personal experience narratives, stories of the ways in which he and his people have traditionally used and interpreted the land. The Aborigines draw a map all their own through mythic tales, labeling the land with the words and stories of their songs, sketching imaginative contours and dramatic peaks through repeating their traditional narratives. Together, they demonstrate that folk narrative is a vital and powerful means by which knowledge of the invisible landscape is communicated, expressed, and maintained. In fact, the sense of place—the sense of dwelling in the invisible landscape—is in large part a creation of folklore and is expressed most eloquently through folklore. It is through traditional narratives, both personal and communal, that the human meanings with which the landscape is imbued are given form, perpetuated, and shared; the meaning of a place for the people who live there is best captured by the stories that they tell about it, about the elements that comprise it, and about the events that took place within its bounds. Barry Lopez expresses this truth in a recent essay in which he ruminates on the nature of geographical knowledge. In this essay, Lopez considers how he can best come to understand the meaning of a place for the people who live there—how he can sift through obscuring layers of image and learning and formally presented history to reach the underlying bedrock of local and lived significance. How can a visitor, an outsider, hope to approximate a wisdom born of deep-rooted experience? "If I were to now visit another country," suggests Lopez,

> I would ask my local companion, before I saw any museum or library, any factory or fabled town, to walk me in the country of his or her youth, to tell me the names of things and how, traditionally, they have been fitted together in a community. I would ask for the stories, the voice of memory over the land. . . . I would ask about the history of storms there, the age of the trees, the winter color of the hills. Only then would I ask to see the

museums. I would want first the sense of a real place, to know that I was not inhabiting an idea. I would want to know the lay of the land first, the real geography, and take some measure of the love of it in my companion before I stood before the paintings or read works of scholarship. I would want to have something real and remembered against which I might hope to measure their truth.[41]

He would want a companion, in other words, like William James's driver, for whom every bit of local landscape tells a story. He would want to listen carefully and at length to John McPhee's David Love, whose encyclopedic knowledge of Wyoming's geology gains authority from a lifetime spent roaming the state, for whom the pursuit of that knowledge is finally an outgrowth of a childhood spent riding and camping among the rugged Rockies. It is stories—narratives formal or informal, elaborate and detailed or offhand and telegraphic—of what happened to people in a place, of what they have done with the things that they found there, that best reveal the "real geography": geography, that is, experienced and understood as place.

Folklore, however, is not the only means by which the insider's invisible landscape can be communicated; certain categories of literature, too, play their part, using words to transcend the strictly mappable aspects of the landscape. This implicit connection between landscape and narrative, this inchoate awareness that maps can be brought to life and given meaning through words, bursts forth from time to time in American literary history as a motive force behind powerful works of literature—and of all American writers, William Faulkner is probably the most sensitive to the ways in which landscapes and stories are intertwined. Much of Faulkner's work is set in Mississippi's fictional Yoknapatawpha County, a vividly realized world which in its geographical and cartographical structure closely resembles the actual Lafayette County in which he lived. Geographer Charles S. Aiken has demonstrated that Faulkner's descriptions of his fictional landscapes accurately mirror the geographical reality on which they are based—that the topography, ground cover, economic geography, and cultural geography of Yoknapatawpha and Lafayette are essentially the same, and that the fictional county seat of Jefferson and the real county seat of Oxford resemble each other down to the details of their respective courthouse squares. While many of Yoknapatawpha's features are of Faulkner's invention—to take only one example, there never was a plantation in southeastern Oxford where Compson's Mile is located in Jefferson—the general correspondences between the actual and the fictional map are striking, and Aiken concludes that Yoknapatawpha County is "a fictional mutation with certain of its geographical components drawn from a reality that was deliberately altered" and that "Faulkner transmuted Lafayette into Yoknapatawpha by combining the real, the modified, and the imaginary."[42] Faulkner's work, then, is more particular than is sometimes assumed: rather than create and write about a microcosmic South, broadly representative of the larger region in its geography, history, and culture, Faulkner created "a place within the South,"[43] crafting his fiction primarily from materials mined from the visible and invisible landscapes of the particular place in which he lived.

Yoknapatawpha County was a complete, detailed, realistic geographical whole in Faulkner's mind: his descriptions of its landscape are remarkably consistent from story to story and novel to novel, and in 1936 he drew a map of the county to include as an endpaper in *Absalom, Absalom!* (fig. 8). This map closely resembles Lafayette County in its details, providing further evidence of the extent to which Faulkner's fictional county was based on fact. And not only does this map sketch out Yoknapatawpha's visible landscape, but it hints at the shape of its invisible landscape as well. Faulkner includes brief allusions to episodes from his novels next to certain of the map's features: thus, for example, we see the "church which Thomas Sutpen rode fast to" from *Absalom, Absalom!*, the "saw mill where Byron Bunch first saw Lena Grove" from *Light in August*, "Compson's, where they sold the pasture to the golf club" from *The Sound and the Fury*, the "bridge which washed away so Anse Bundren and his sons could not cross it with Addie's body" from *As I Lay Dying*, and "Varner's store, where Flem Snopes got his start" from *The Hamlet*. Faulkner has annotated the map of Yoknapatawpha to give some hint of the thick layer of narrative which overlies it, narrative which can be found in its complete form in his fiction; in an important sense, his entire career consists of annotating that map. Faulkner has created in his map and work a fictional imitation of any town or county where people have accumulated histories; he has done in fictional form what many people could do orally for their own towns after having spent many years living and listening there. His map, says critic Jules Zanger, is "essentially a record of human actions rather than of political boundaries or of topographical details";[44] critic Elizabeth Duvert agrees, arguing that "the map becomes an icon of Faulkner's vision of landscape as spatialized time. Place becomes synonymous with event; <u>landscape becomes history</u>; and the map of Yoknapatawpha, Faulkner's image of re-

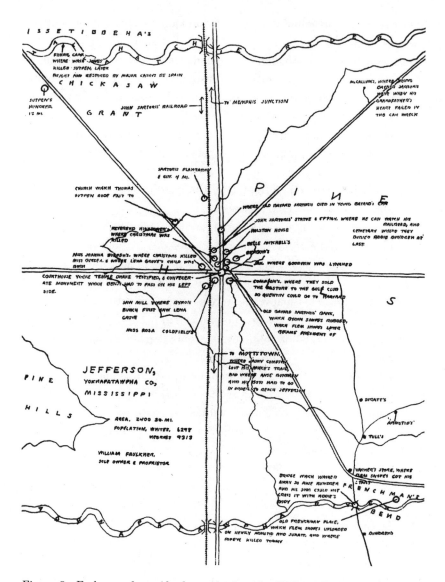

Figure 8. Endpaper from *Absalom, Absalom!* by William Faulkner. Copyright 1936 by William Faulkner and renewed 1964 by Jill Faulkner Summers. Reprinted by permission of Random House, Inc.

ality as shaped by the history of place."[45] In his map as in his work, Faulkner demonstrates a keen awareness of the way in which history piles up on the land, of the way terrain absorbs and recalls history, of the way narrative is an unstated component of any map and thus of any landscape. More than any other writer of fiction, perhaps, Faulkner un-

derstands and recreates—cumulatively, through the body of his work—
the sense of place.

His work *is* fiction, however, and fiction, like a map, is an approxi-
mation and distillation of real life—a selection of details to be translated
into symbolic form, a pointing of theme, a translation of life's messiness
into a version that is portable and comprehensible. Moreover, fiction
reaches beyond the particular into the universal; as many critics have
pointed out, Flem Snopes is not only a recognizable Southern type but
also represents the soullessness of encroaching mercantile capitalism,
and the tragedy of Thomas Sutpen is that of Captain Ahab, of Jay Gatsby,
or of any self-absorbed innocent who desperately wants to put a mark on
a world or universe which refuses to acknowledge his importance. Faulkner himself pointed out that he used the particular to get at the universal,
saying that "I was trying to talk about people, using the only tool I knew,
which was the country that I knew"; significantly, as Aiken points out,
Faulkner's Yoknapatawpha map has no external boundaries, and so
"symbolically, Yoknapatawpha is a place with a core, but the county has
no isolating walls"[46] and instead reaches out to form connections with
people and places everywhere. Fiction, in the end, usually comments
on geographical meaning tangentially on its way to some other destination or focuses on a particular place in order to get at larger truths. As
D. W. Meinig has commented while contemplating the relationship between geography and literature, "the skillful novelist often seems to
come closest of all in capturing the full flavor of the environment. His
sensitivity to a scene, to the seasons, to the special qualities of life in a
particular locality are often vividly evocative. And yet his main emphasis will almost certainly be upon the interactions of personalities, and it
is likely that his real purpose is to transcend the local to display something of the universals in human life."[47] The complex intersection of
geography, experience, imagination, emotion, and meaning is in and of
itself a rare and somewhat limited subject for the conventional genres
of fiction and poetry. Literary critic Leonard Lutwack, speaking of these
genres as they deal with geography, finds that "the literal and geographic
aspect of place is always under the strain that all literature feels to attain
the condition of poetry, of symbol," and thus that "all places in literature
are used for symbolic purposes even though in their descriptiveness they
may be rooted in fact."[48]

Given these literary limitations of fiction, I would like to propose an
unconventional and loosely organized genre of *non*fiction writing that
takes as its subject matter precisely that complex intersection of life and

landscape that I have been discussing and which we may conceptualize with the help of the idea of what E. V. Walter has called "chorography." Walter derives this idea from the ancient geographer Claudius Ptolemy, who drew a distinction between the fields of geography and chorography. "According to Ptolemy," explains Walter, "geography pictorially represented the earth as a whole, describing its nature, position, and general features. It showed the world through the perspective of unity and continuity, and this special task required mathematics. Chorography, by contrast, set off a part of the world, exhibiting it separately, representing exactly and in minute detail nearly everything contained within it. . . . [N]o one could practice chorography, in Ptolemy's words, unless he were an artist." If geographers make maps and formulate interpretations of the physical landscape, chorographers are mappers and interpreters of the invisible landscape. In Walter's view, the chorographer must be an artist because a place contains much more than a simple array of physical objects that can be mathematically arranged. "We get to know a place when we participate in the local imagination. The whole synthesis of located experience—including what we imagine as well as the sights, stories, feelings, and concepts—gives us the sense of a place."[49] To capture and express that sense, that complex intersection and interaction of geography and mind, we need art—specifically, the art of words. In grasping the difference between geography and chorography we are back at the basic conflict between the cartographer and the storyteller, between map and memory, between the outsider and the insider, between the tourist and the native. Writers who practice chorography, who "set off a part of the world" and attempt to tell its stories, to capture its emotions, to display its imagination—mappers of the invisible landscape, if you will—stand with their feet firmly planted in Lopez's "real geography"; they are the imaginative allies of oral narrators, restoring to the map that layer of words and experience that was so integral a part of earlier styles of cartography.

Mark Twain provides a fine example of the American chorographer in action. As he began scribbling notes for the book that would be published as *Life on the Mississippi*, Twain suggested to himself that he "cut the map of the Mississippi into 20 pieces (full page size) & interleave it along through the book"[50] for the guidance of his readers; he eventually obtained a large map from the office of the Secretary of War, although he decided in the end not to incorporate it into the final work. The fact that Twain had a map in mind even in the earliest stages of planning his book, though, is important for understanding his conception of the book's nature and structure: he meant it to follow the map and to be keyed to the map's features; the book was to be, essentially, a map in words. The "map" which he intended to write, however, was not to be the static slice of geography, the frozen image of a particular moment of topographical time, that most cartographers produce; it was to incorporate into its structure a complex stratum of history, a chorus of voices weaving a thick layer of stories—it was to be a statement and revelation of place. Critic Horst H. Kruse has convincingly demonstrated that Mark Twain meant *Life on the Mississippi* to be a "standard work" about the river—that is, a book which is not fiction and is not simply autobiographical, but one which "does not rest on invention and memory so much as on observation and, in modern terms, the 'field trip,'" one which follows the "purpose of conveying information and instruction" and is rooted in "documentary and historiographic intentions."[51] Twain's intention to write a standard work about the river accounts for the book's diverse and bewildering variety of sources, ranging from Twain's personal observations as noted on a journey which he took down the river in 1882, to his early autobiographical experiences as recounted in the chapters which had originally been published in 1875 as "Old Times on the Mississippi," to commentary gleaned from the travel books of English visitors published earlier in the century, to academic histories and promotional pamphlets, to a gallery of fanciful yarns which often seem only tangentially related to the points along the river which inspired Twain to recall and include them. Twain realized that in order to write his standard work he would have to explore the river's past as well as its present, and, importantly, that he would have to take account of many voices other than his own in order to be able to tell the river's story accurately and completely. In other words, Twain seems to have begun his work from the premise, and with the knowledge, that an invisible landscape of some sort overlay the river and that his job as the writer of a standard work was to seek that landscape out and get it down on paper. In this sense, his work on *Life on the Mississippi* was essentially a mapping expedition; writing the book with a real map in mind, he charts on its pages as thickly detailed a "map" as possible of the river's invisible topography, inscribing as many people's words on the paper map as he can find in addition to his own, orchestrating a chorus of voices to reveal the layers of time and experience which the river bears.

In America, literary explorations of the sense of place have taken a variety of nonfictional forms; after all, maps are drawn to many different scales according to a variety of projections in order to serve a wide range of purposes, and so are maps of the invisible landscape. While some such writings, like *Life on the Mississippi*, take the form of comprehensive book-length atlases, however, more frequently they take the form of brief, essay-length, freehand sketches—what in later chapters I will call the "essay of place." Some writers, like E. B. White in his personal essays on the state of Maine or Wendell Berry in his writings from the Kentucky hills, reveal the layers of meaning which they have deposited atop the landscapes in which they have spent their lives, emphasizing the close relationship between the writer and the writer's chosen place. Others, like the itinerant Barry Lopez, roam North America in order to explore and report on the invisible landscapes of people in places other than their own. While they may differ in matters of scale and point of view, however, all these writers—all such literary cartographers— concentrate on trying to portray both the exterior, visible landscape— the world that can be mapped with mathematics and surveying equipment, the one that the casual visitor sees—and, more important, the interior, invisible landscape that lies atop it—a world of deep and subtle meaning for the people who live there, one that can be mapped only with words. Their writings, their stories, thus echo the purposes and functions of place-based folklore.

Maps certainly have their uses. Few people have not had occasion to consult one, or even to sketch one out, at some point in their lives. Still, most people are at heart chorographers, not geographers; storytellers and story listeners, not cartographers. Maps do not tell us nearly all there is to know about the environment and probably do not tell us all that we *want* to know. To learn all there is to know about a place, we must emulate Conrad's narrator Marlow in the epigraph to this chapter and let our imaginations take over when we contemplate a map; or better yet, we must turn away from the map at some point and hearken to words.

2 *Folklore and the Sense of Place*

I placed a jar in Tennessee,
And round it was, upon a hill.
It made the slovenly wilderness
Surround that hill.
—WALLACE STEVENS, "Anecdote of the Jar"

She was the single artificer of the world
In which she sang. And when she sang, the sea,
Whatever self it had, became the self
That was her song, for she was the maker. Then we,
As we beheld her striding there alone,
Knew that there never was a world for her
Except the one she sang and, singing, made.
—WALLACE STEVENS, "The Idea of Order at Key West"

Folklore and Geography

Wallace Stevens's "Anecdote of the Jar" reminds us of the necessary role that artifacts of human intelligence play in organizing our surroundings and making them meaningful. His jar imposes a pattern on the wilderness chaos; things can be located in relation to the fixed center which it provides; its symmetrical, geometrical shape seems to diffuse a sense of calm and structure as the woods surround the jar in a ring echoing the container's circular form. The wilderness takes on the character of the ordering human intelligence of which the jar is the emissary: it "sprawled around," says Stevens later in the poem, "no longer wild." Other human constructs serve similar ordering functions in our contemplation of geography—with maps, as we have seen, providing the best-known example. Maps take a random lump of geography and flatten it out, reduce it to graphic symbols, draw grids and coordinates on it, clearly mark the important parts, and generally translate it into a form that we can easily get our minds around. We're lost, we pass a prominent

53

landmark, we find it on the map: oh, so *that's* where I am. Among their other functions, maps translate geography into clearly understood locations, routes, and spatial relationships. With map in hand, we find that the world is no longer wild; we find where we are, establish ourselves as a center, and thus make the slovenly wilderness surround us.

We needn't, and in fact don't, entrust professional cartographers with all of the important business of mapmaking. As geographers and psychologists have established, we are all perforce cartographers of a sort. In his influential book *The Image of the City*, Kevin Lynch broached the idea of the "environmental image"—"the generalized mental picture of the exterior physical world that is held by an individual. This image is the product both of immediate sensation and of the memory of past experience, and it is used to interpret information and to guide action."[1] The environmental image that we hold of our surroundings is vital to our sense of orientation and to wayfinding—our ability to simply get around in our physical milieu. Building on Lynch's approach, Roger M. Downs and David Stea have suggested that people actually organize the components of their environmental images into cartographic form—that they construct "cognitive maps" of the worlds in which they live from day to day, on which they have pinpointed the important locations, landmarks, and routes of those worlds, and which they "follow" as they go about their quotidian travels. "A cognitive map is . . . a person's organized representation of some part of the spatial environment. . . . We use schools, stores, parks, and so on, in everyday life and so we need to know their locations, how far away they are, what's there, how good they are, and how to get to them. Cognitive mapping is our way of acquiring and storing this essential information, of being able to use it to decide where to go and how to get there."[2] Like explorers drafting charts of newly discovered lands, we draw these cognitive maps as a result of our needs and experiences in a particular environment. Depending as they do largely on experience, they tend to be highly subjective—our sense of distance may be wildly inaccurate, for instance, and we will only remember and "mark down" places that are for some reason important to us. Nevertheless, people inevitably act as mental cartographers of their immediate milieux, producing representations of the local geography that they could transcribe onto paper if they were asked to.

As they would with conventional maps, though, they would want to talk about the symbols that they drew, to explain the nature and meaning of their experiences in geographical space, not merely to indicate the bald fact that they *had* experiences in geographical space. Just as when we look at maps on paper, we apply layers of meaning to our cognitive maps, be that meaning secondhand and derivative or personal and experiential. Downs and Stea recognize as much when they compare cognitive maps to skeletons, bare-bones structures for organizing the environment: "The skeleton must be fleshed out with *personal* meaning: John lives there; here is a convenient 24-hour drug store; that corner is dangerous because of the pedestrian traffic; don't walk there because of a teenage gang; and so on. In this way, our cognitive representations recognize that the spatial environment is *full of personal meaning* and, in themselves, become meaningful."[3] Such meanings can of course be secondhand as much as experiential: we can know about the street gang's turf because we've heard about it, not necessarily because we were once attacked or intimidated there.

Peter Gould and Rodney White further discuss this secondhand aspect of cognitive cartography in their book *Mental Maps.* In asking British and American students where in their countries they would most like to live or visit, they found that in each country certain areas were consistently ranked as highly desirable (for instance, California and Colorado in America, and Devon, Cornwall, and the Lake District in England), while others could just as well be wiped off the face of the earth for all the students cared (like the Dakotas and the Deep South in the one instance, and the industrial Midlands in the other, although understandably natives of these regions demurred from the national patterns).[4] Only rarely were these opinions formed as a result of travel; in the absence of hard experiential information about the landscapes and culture of a place, people rely on positive and negative stereotypes of the kind found in movies, television, newspapers, advertisements, popular music, and books.[5] People thus can and do attach meaning to places they've never been to. The students that Gould and White talked to clearly see things in their minds when they look at their national maps; the fact that what they see is frequently distorted or simply wrong is secondary to the evidence they offer that, to most people, no geography is wholly meaningless, no wilderness completely slovenly. We tend to view the physical world in simultaneously cartographic and humanly meaningful terms, even on the most dubious evidence. Even if we've never been to Tennessee, most of us can place some sort of mental jar there.

Still, the experiential meanings we ascribe to places are much fuller, more complex, and more vivid than the ones we pick up secondhand. Each element of a cognitive map has a memory attached; each is an allusive shorthand notation for part of a life story. As Downs and Stea point out, "In some very fundamental but inexpressible way, our own self-identity is inextricably bound up with knowledge of the spatial environment. We can organize personal experience along the twin dimensions of space and time. But the dimensions are inseparable—there can be no personal biography of 'what' things happened 'when' *without* a sense of the place in which they happened. Cognitive maps serve as coathangers for assorted memories. They provide a vehicle for recall—an image of 'where' brings back a recollection of 'who' and 'what.' "[6] Cognitive maps, that is, just as much as paper maps, serve as catalysts for words: let me tell you what happened to me here; let me tell you what I heard happened to someone else there. Stories—and folklore in general—are inextricably linked with landscapes, overlying them snugly, bound to them and coloring them like paint on a barn wall. They are a central means by which people organize their physical surroundings.

This symbiosis between lore and landscape gets at a vital and often unappreciated relationship between geography and folklore. Traditionally, scholars who contemplate the relationships between folklore and geography do so in one of three ways. Some concentrate on how folklore spreads across geography over time: this is the root of the historical-geographical study of folklore, or Finnish method, which posits the existence of an original version of an item of lore and traces that version's changes as it diffuses through temporal and geographical space. The Finnish-method scholar seeks three things, says Richard Dorson: "the hypothetical Ur-type from which all variants of the tale or ballad as originally composed have sprung; its geographical starting point; and its historical routes of travel."[7] Others concentrate on the ways in which folklore is used to categorize or classify geography, in that areal distribution patterns of selected items or complexes of lore can be used to divide up the land into geographical regions. Geographer E. Estyn Evans, for instance, points out that geographers' and folklorists' "concern with areal differentiation leads to the detailed study of small regions; and this is one of the first points of contact between the geographer and the student of folklife."[8] The folklorist using this approach differs little from the standard cultural geographer in approaching a region as (to borrow an early definition from Henry Glassie) "a section of a geographical whole established by an analysis of comparable material found throughout the whole."[9] Finally, some folklorists concentrate on how folklore sometimes derives or is constructed directly from the materials available in the local landscape. This approach is usually limited to the study of material folk culture: W. F. H. Nicolaisen, for instance, argues that while "there are numerous traits in any regional folk culture which quite clearly have their origins in man's response to his natural environment, . . . these traits are mostly to be found in the more materially oriented aspects of a folk culture."[10]

These approaches to the relationships between folklore and geography, while valid and important, can sometimes seem dry and lifeless, more quantitative than qualitative. The folklorist engaged in these pursuits figuratively hovers high above the landscape, counting things and drawing lines around them. ("For the systematist and the user of systematic data," notes Fred B. Kniffen tellingly in an aside in his classic study of folk regions as determined by house types, "here is important raw material that can be divided into well-defined types and counted."[11]) Such approaches can divorce the folk from the lore if they concentrate on questions like "Where did we find this?" and "Where do we stop finding it?" and "What is it made of?" at the expense of questions like "What does this *mean*?" The things that folklorists count would not exist, after all, if real people had not created them. Items of folklore are artifacts of human intelligence first and foremost; they are created and repeated for a reason, because they encode and carry important personal and cultural messages; they are deciphered the same way. The messages behind the patterns finally matter more than the patterns themselves.

To return to the metaphor with which Stevens supplies us, what is ultimately important is not that there is a jar in Tennessee and that it is made of glass made from sand from a particular stretch of the Tennessee River Valley and that it is of a type that seems to derive from the Pennsylvania Culture Region and was probably brought to Tennessee by the Scotch-Irish settlers who moved south and west down the back side of the Appalachians, interesting and important though such matters are. What matters is that the jar gains meaning from and gives meaning to its geographical surroundings. It turns the wilderness into an active, living thing: the wilderness is made to surround, it sprawls like a big tame cat. What can be lost sight of is that folklore *vivifies* geography, brings it alive with meaning and significance, reveals it to be a deeply known and active partner in life. Geographer Edmunds V. Bunkśe recognizes this when he indicates that "folklore can be . . . an indicator of the culture of a people, their collective sense of place in the world, and of the meanings with which they imbue the landscape."[12] There is more to the study of folklore and geography than drawing lines around distribution patterns or comparing houses in place A with houses in place B. The job is not finished until we determine what those delimited and circumscribed items of lore signify to their creators and users—until we find out how they contribute to the ways in which people reconstruct their worlds in their heads and superimpose on those worlds layers of meaning.

We all, then, resemble Stevens's singer, ordering and structuring the random and chaotic ocean through the words of her song as she strides beside the sea at Key West. As long as there are people to perceive it, experience it, live in it, and communicate about it, it is misleading to ever think of the world as a meaningless blank. We assign it meaning through the things we do in it and hear about it and translate those lived and vicarious experiences into song—into folklore. Folklore becomes our means of understanding the world and the medium through which we make our understandings available and legible to others. We re-create and vivify geography through our traditional comments upon it. There never is a world for us except the one we sing and, singing, make.

The Folkloric Sense of Place

In America, regional folklore provides perhaps the best indication of the sense of place held by the people who live in a certain area. By "regional folklore," however, I do not mean the totality of all folklore which is current and can be collected within a certain set of geographical boundaries, as some types of folklore are clearly more regional than others. Some items of lore found in a place can also be found almost anywhere else in the country or can more accurately be thought of as the folklore of religious, ethnic, or occupational groups a few members of which just happen to live in a certain locality. Other items of lore, however, are so region-specific, so dependent on local cultural, historical, and geographical factors for their meanings, that they will not appear or necessarily be understood anywhere outside of the region; as folklorist William E. Lightfoot puts it, "Clearly, folklore that owes its existence and perpetuation to a particular geographic area is more indicative of regional consciousness and is more subject to regional interpretation and analysis than is nonenchorial folklore such as 'Barbara Allen,' 'knock-knock' jokes, or the proverb 'Haste makes waste.' A distinction should be made, in other words, between regional folklore and the folklore of regions."[13]

By making this distinction, folklorists show themselves to be sensitive to the insider's sense of place of a region, as the "regional consciousness" which regional lore displays is in large part identical to the invisible landscape of the region's inhabitants. Lightfoot indicates as much when he describes the ideal field of study of the regional folklorist: "Regional folklorists . . . are interested in groupings of people who have acquired self-perceived notions of location, identity, differentiation, and homogeneity, and who share common sets of experiences, attitudes, and values that give them a distinct regional character."[14] Folklorist Suzi Jones agrees, while putting more explicit emphasis on the specifically geographical, place-bound element of this type of regional folklore study: the regional folklorist, she says, should seek out "instances where people share a body of folklore because they live in a certain geographical area; their geographical location is the primary basis for a shared identity that is expressed in their lore, and they themselves are conscious of their regional identity."[15] Geography, in this view, is clearly much more than buildings and dirt—it supports a complex structure of personal and cultural significance. Such descriptions of regional folklore coincide closely with the notion of sense of place as formulated by humanistic geographers: the strong sense of rootedness in a location, of identification with (and self-identification in terms of) that location, of membership in a unified place-based community, and of a common world view as a result of a common geographical experience are all key elements in the formation of the local understanding of geographical meaning.

This sensitivity to the invisible landscape on the part of regional folklorists is a relatively recent phenomenon. While published collections of regional folklore have been abundantly produced for years, only since the late 1970s and early 1980s have folklorists sought to analyze their collections explicitly in terms of regional geographic consciousness, as a means of understanding what a particular chunk of geography means to the people who live in it. The career of one of the major figures in American folkloristics, Richard M. Dorson, provides an example of this evolution in the emphasis of regional folklore studies. Dorson's first book of regional folklore, *Bloodstoppers and Bearwalkers: Folk Traditions of the Upper Peninsula*, was published in 1952. It contains a wealth of northern Michigan folklore, but it is lore that is largely "the folklore of a region," to use Lightfoot's phrase. Dorson's strategy seems primarily to have been to collect as much folklore as he could within the political-geographical entity known as the Upper Peninsula of Michigan and then to organize it according to who told it. As he admits in his introduction, he was attracted to the Upper Peninsula because of the wide variety of stories and storytellers he knew he could find there, since "the Peninsula contains in minuscule the nation's varied folk culture. A dramatic century of land and water conquest, of mining and lumber booms, has generated a rich historical and local lore. On the European side, a dozen nationalities jostle each other in every town and provide a dazzling conglomeration of imported folkstuff, in contrast with the predominantly Yankee Lower Peninsula. The Indian element there, living now on scattered reservation villages, are the very Ojibwa from whom the great Schoolcraft had first gathered American Indian tales."[16] In 1952, Dorson was not particularly concerned with how folklore can grow out of a place, did not care about collecting region-specific lore; he cheerfully collected well-traveled occupational lore, imported European folktales—whatever he could get his hands on, just so long as he found it between Lake Superior and the Wisconsin border. This geographical constraint emerges in the book as little more than a collecting convenience; Dorson defines his region from the outside folklorist's point of view, not the native's, and evinces little concern for the invisible landscape, the meaning of the Upper Peninsula for the people who live there.

By 1981, on the other hand, Dorson had decided to approach regional folklore from the insider's perspective. In that year he published *Land of the Millrats*, a study of the folklore of the Calumet Region of Indiana, the heavily industrialized northwest corner of the state consisting primarily of the cities of Gary, Whiting, Hammond, and East Chicago. While this book also studies the lore of specific groups within a region—here, the lore of steelworkers, blacks, and ethnics—Dorson realizes that this lore can be studied most profitably within an understanding of what the region—the physical entity itself—means to the people who inhabit it. For his purposes, Dorson now defines "region" as "the section or provincial locality to which loyalties, patriotism, and folkways adhere":

> This . . . defines very well the folklorist's concept of the region, which may involve historical, economic, geographical, and political factors, insofar as they contribute to a sense of one's home ground. Common points of reference, common attitudes and expressions and behavior patterns, define this folk region. . . . In each folk region a set of traditional themes and values links the inhabitants, and the folklorist in his field inquiries should set his sights on those cementing ideas. The folk region . . . lies in the mind and spirit as much as in physical boundaries; consequently, those boundaries may shift as the social networks that maintain the region's folkways and symbols stretch or contract in spatial areas.[17]

This understanding of what a folk region is differs greatly from Dorson's earlier definition. He approached the Upper Peninsula as mainly a distinctively shaped, physiographically and politically defined area which was interesting primarily because of the diversity of people who lived there, and who, for all one could tell from looking at their folklore, could have lived almost anywhere; the Calumet Region, by contrast, is seen primarily as an insider's mental construct, a state of mind instead of a corner of a state, an area defined according to the natives' sense of place—their intimacy with their physical surroundings and with the distinctive political and economic circumstances and history of the region. Folklore that arises from and contributes to this sense of place—folklore that does not travel well, in a sense—is the true focus of the regional folklorist's concerns.

An additional difference between the "new" regional folklore and what came before it is that earlier studies tended to concentrate only on the traditional genres of lore—and then usually only on one, such as songs or legends—that could be found in a particular region. Dorson's early book, for instance, consists exclusively of tales, as do most of the pioneering collections of regional lore. Newer studies, however, have as a goal the elucidation of the meaning of a place for its inhabitants, not just the collection and publication of all the folklore of a region; thus, they tend to be much more multigeneric or willing to delve into unconventional genres in order to reach that goal. They teach us that the sense of place is learned, expressed, and transmitted through a variety of genres and forms of expression simultaneously, not just through storytelling (although stories tend to express that sense most vividly and accessibly). Sense of place is the result of *living* in a place in all the complex ways that that word implies; no narrowly focused study will do full justice to the meaning that a place holds for its people.

Philosopher Gary Comstock has commented pertinently on the distinction between what he calls "places of little sense" and "places of big sense," a distinction which we should keep in mind before embarking on a dissection and analysis of the folkloric sense of place. Places of little sense, says Comstock, "have very much sense; it is just of a modest, local, sort: farmers in orange feed caps discussing whether the girls' basketball team hadn't oughta switched to five-player rules, doughnut makers showing sixteen-year-olds how to boil potatoes to make broth for Page's Bakery cinnamon rolls, children encouraged by their parents on Saturday night to lay out their Sunday clothes. Such people have a good deal of practical wisdom, knowledge located in bones and bellies." The sense of such little, unpretentious places derives from the everyday round of localized experience. It emerges, piecemeal and humble, in custom and conversation. Places of big sense, on the other hand, are characterized by the University of Chicago, where Comstock went to graduate school, where daily conversation is devoted to big ideas and grand abstract theories, a place populated by "philosophers spending their lives searching for the key to all moralities, dinner guests telling intimate details about the lives of G. E. Moore and Paul Tillich. There is plenty of knowledge here, of a cerebral sort. Often, the bones are brittle."[18]

There is a clear contrast here, and an implied warning. The contrast is between the perspectives on life fostered by places of big and little sense, the contrast we saw William James stumble across in the first chapter: the philosophers (if they are scrupulously true to their craft) wandering with heads in the clouds through a place without ever realizing they've been there, the farmers never having heard of G. E. Moore and Paul Tillich and not giving a damn. The warning grows directly out of this incompatibility (and applies, I fear, to me). As Comstock puts it, "We should not try to explain places of little sense. There is no General Theory of Little Places into which each particular Iowa county, farm community, or religious sect can be fit. How do we talk about such places? By telling stories about them, one by one."[19] This caveat is, in an important sense, absolutely true and is a point well taken. Each place of little sense is distinctive and unique, as distinctive as the dot which marks its location on the map, as unique as the history it has seen, the topography on which it sits, and the ways of life it encloses. To borrow Comstock's metaphor, the skeleton of each is put together in a different way and clothed in and given life by a flesh of stories such as is found no place else. Nevertheless, bones have names, muscles can be categorized. While theory must never overwhelm stories, a consideration of the folklore (and not only the stories, but the material folklife as well) of different places of little sense suggests a common pattern to people's experience of places, a common set of ways in which they organize what they know about where they live. Each set of bones, while providing a sturdy structure of meaning for one place only, recognizably belongs to the same species.

So, into the breach: a reading and consolidation of regional folklore suggests that this lore reveals four categories or layers of meaning which overlie the facts of the physical world, four general ways in which local residents augment the surface impressions garnered by visitors to their region or the graphic symbols drawn on a map of their place by a cartographer. First, local lore, especially material folklore, reveals the depth and intricacy of local knowledge of the nature and physical properties and limitations of the geographical milieu. The traditional ways in which people use the materials which surround them, and the tools which they have developed to manipulate those materials most effectively, demonstrate a deeply lived familiarity with the nature and properties of the hard physical stuff of geography. The sensually descriptive folk names which people attach to the flora, fauna, and topographical features of a place provide a similar view of the local knowledge and interpretation of the physical components of that place, as do a few types of place-based narrative—like local legends and tall tales—which rely for much of their meaning on the nature of their physical setting. Such lore goes beyond cartographic symbols to get its hands dirty among the things that the symbols represent; it gets out of the tourist's car and walks around, picking things up, smelling and tasting them.

Second, regional folklore encapsulates and transmits the intimate and otherwise unrecorded history of a place; it reveals the meaning of a place to be in large part a deeply known and felt awareness of the things that happened there. Such history can be either directly experienced or learned through tradition (and thus in some cases may be apocryphal); it can be personal, it can pertain to the folk group as a whole, or it can refer to people outside the group—to things that happened to visitors or that happened in a long-dead time—just as long as the events it records happened within the bounds of the region. This local history need not—and in fact usually does not—concern itself with the important and prominent events of "official" history, of the sort which get commemorated by statues, plaques, and history books. For most people, this sense of local history consists of personal and intimate events: landmarks are remembered and found significant because of something striking that once happened there to the person doing the remembering, because they provided the physical context for significant social connections and relationships, or simply because of their perpetual presence in the course of the daily routine.

Often, though, we are aware of important local events which happened outside of our personal experience. In some places this sort of awareness is all but unavoidable; I imagine it is difficult for residents of Massachusetts towns such as Salem, Lexington, Plymouth, and Concord not to have at least a vague sense of what happened in their communities during colonial times. Residents of north County Louth, Ireland, reach back into mythic time and derive a strong sense of place from their region's association with the ancient Irish saga *Táin Bó Cuailnge*, commemorating the tale's characters and events in signs and signposts, tourism campaigns, public murals, community drama, and sporting events; while the saga is legendary, local residents see it as the starting point of their place's history, understanding myth and history to be parts of a single continuum.[20] Even in less storied places, though, the process of living through time, looking around, and listening to others makes local residents aware of the things that happened there before they came along, even if those things are not prominently commemorated in the landscape. "History is the essence of the idea of place," argues Henry Glassie, with that history consisting of both the unexceptional evolutionary history of local social and economic development, which is inscribed on the everyday landscape, and the exceptional tales of great people and events, which are preserved in words—legends and songs—and are attached in the local mind to the physical places where they transpired. Thus:

> the person who is in place, located, understands two histories. One is a matter of continuity, of endless growth and decay. The other is a matter of centers, of immortal and moral issues. Everyone is a part of the first and obliged to adapt to its power as to a climate, the sun and storm of every day. The other preserves great personages in deathless life. . . . Both histories surround people, echoing, screaming from the land they walk daily, demanding that they choose their path and find their way consciously. Inescapably inscribed in the land, history is intrinsic to the idea of place that forces people to be human.[21]

To live in a place is to see and know what the people who lived there before you did with it; to hear talk about a place is to understand what else happened there that has been deemed worth remembering. To live in a place is also to inscribe deeply on its face the paths, patterns, and events of one's own life, phenomena which enter one's own talk. To do all of these things—to see, listen, and talk about a place—is to understand and perpetuate the history of a place, history which lives simultaneously on a number of levels and colors the meaning of that place in a number of ways.

Third, local lore provides a strong sense of personal and group identity. Sense of self becomes inextricably linked to the physical components of a place, or to participation in place-bound ways of life, or to an awareness of the folk history of a region; folklore reveals the ways in which these links are made. In arguing that "one of the ways individuals define their own identity is through folklore," Alan Dundes points out particularly that "place can be, and often is, an extremely meaningful component of individual identity."[22] For Dundes, place-based identity is a relative matter; people simultaneously feel they belong to many concentric places, ranging from a continent or country down to a particular house in a particular neighborhood of a particular city. This sense of identity becomes stronger the closer we get to the center of this ring of concentric places. As anthropologist Anthony Cohen explains, "I might choose to identify myself as British, Scots, Shetlander, Whalsayman, or as belonging to some particular kinship-neighborhood nexus in Whalsay. The significant point is that with each 'ascending' level I increasingly simplify (and thereby misrepresent) the message about myself. At each descending level I present myself through increasingly informed and complex pictures. It should therefore be recognised that 'belonging to locality,' far from being a parochial triviality, is very much more of a cultural reality than is association with gross region or nation."[23] We have much more direct experience of neighborhood or town than of state or country, have much more of our lives invested in the little places than in the big places. We also therefore tend to know and repeat more folklore of the local, experiential region than of the larger, externally defined region—folklore grounded in place just as we are.

In expressing sense of place through folklore, then, we simultaneously express sense of self. For Henry Glassie, place-based identity depends on one's connection with the history, both factual and mythic, that is so central a component of the sense of place. Among his informants in rural Northern Ireland, Glassie found that sense of self was inextricably linked with the folkloric story of place, that locals understood themselves as historically and genealogically linked with the past as it transpired in that place—as the living end results of a historical process—and that they thus could not be fully understood or known without a knowledge of local history: "When Hugh Patrick Owens begins the story of the Ford [a historical legend of a 400-year-old event] with his own genealogy, he merges with the [River] Arney and the battle as part of this locale. . . . Simultaneously changing and unchangeable, history is place. Place joins those who make and mark the land with those who remake it, accepting its tasks. It joins saint to rebel, warrior to farmer, God to man. In place, the person is part of history."[24] In recounting stories of local history, people recount and reaffirm who they are. This also holds true for the more personal, intimate kind of history: I define myself through my own history, I am the product of what I do, and in contemplating and discussing where I did it I contemplate and discuss myself. People can also be defined and labeled, identified to themselves and others, in terms of the simple physical components of a place; geography in a sense can, by providing a particular arena for action and set of materials to work with, strongly influence local and individual identity. The folk name "Pineys" for denizens of the New Jersey Pine Barrens hints at such an influence, and within the complex ecosystem of the Pinelands identity is further particularized: "An informal nomenclature for groups in the region, addressing a wide variety of relationships to the land, suggests that people occur as ecotypes: woodsmen, baymen, stumpjumpers, snakehunters, farmers, gatherers, collectors, and mud-wallopers. . . . To be a woodsman, bayman, or farmer is to grasp the unseen connections and mutual influences exerted among components of the environment"[25]—that is, it is to grasp the nature of the Pinelands deeply and experientially and to assert one's own identity as one interacts with those surroundings through the processes of folklore. Whether it be a feeling that one somehow belongs to a particular piece of named ground through long association with it, that one's nature is bound up with one's relationship with the physical environment, or that one feels genetically related to and descended from the history that overlies those physical facts, one's identity as it is dependent on place provides another layer of meaning to superimpose on the map.

Finally, and most difficult to describe, regional folklore indicates the emotions which local residents attach to their place and the components of their place, feelings which arise from a knowledge of place-based history and identity and which inevitably tinge their contemplation of their physical surroundings. Here we enter the realm of what geographer Yi-Fu Tuan has called "topophilia"—"the affective bond between people and place or setting,"[26] a bond which is forged by a variety of factors. Extended residence in a place tends to make us feel toward it almost as toward a living thing, for better or worse: through propinquity we have come to learn all about it and to love it or hate it for its nurturing comforts or alienating discomforts. The place has become a shaping partner in our lives, we partially define ourselves in its terms, and it carries the emotional charge of a family member or any other influential human agent. Moreover, people tend to project their own feelings onto their physical surroundings: if something pleasant happens to us somewhere, we feel fondly toward that place, whereas if we have a traumatic experience we see the place in which it happened as malevolent and dangerous. Likewise, we can emotionally color sites which witnessed events we have only heard about: the dangerous parts of town strike us as nasty and intimidating even if we have never come to harm there. In other words, the emotions which we apply to the history of a place—the feelings we had when we experienced or heard about something which happened there—inevitably become applied to the place itself, providing the final layer of our complex sense of what a particular piece of geography means and tinging the way we talk about it.

The editors of a recent book on the traditions of the New Jersey Pine Barrens, *Pinelands Folklife*, provide a useful summary through their definition of the folkloric sense of place: "Sense of place is the totality of perceptions and knowledge of a place gained by residents through their long experience in it, and intensified by their feelings for it."[27] Folklore uniquely reveals this complex of knowledge and emotion. Material folklore builds on a lifetime of sensory perception to demonstrate an intimate knowledge of the physical facts of a place. A variety of forms of oral lore echo this awareness and add to it a detailed understanding of local history and of one's self as it is inextricably bound to place. Overlying these layers of meaning, and anchored firmly to the facts of geography, history, and identity, is a final stratum of emotion, a level of feeling which is inseparable from place, which intensifies local knowledge of that place, and which probably contributes most to separating the perspective of the insider from that of the outsider. For those who know the local folk traditions, a map or a tourist snapshot is only the most cursory of starting points, the briefest of allusions to a rich and multivalent world of meaning.

In a review of the exhibition for which *Pinelands Folklife* was the catalogue, Robert Blair St. George commented archly that "the 'sense of place' that binds the natural, social, economic, and aesthetic resources of a region into a seamless unity" was "more often evoked than analytically explored."[28] The Pinelands study and other recent regional explorations, however, have paid increasing attention to the subjective experience of place, throwing off outmoded concepts of region and regional folklore and instead examining a wide variety of folkloric genres from new perspectives in an attempt to get at local geographic meanings from the inside. The director of the Pinelands project, Mary Hufford, has in fact proposed the concept of "what we might call 'genres of place'— songs, stories, poems, paintings, recipes, rituals, tools, technologies, names, and ways of doing things in which knowledge of the place, its past, and its people is formalized and presented. They are genres of place because they are bound to the locale."[29] Suzi Jones also argues that "some genres are more readily regionalized than others"[30]—that is, are more susceptible to becoming attached to (and giving meaning to) a specific geographical location—with legends and tall tales topping her list.

I would go Hufford and Jones one better, though, and nominate the sense of place itself as a genre of folklore, or at least as a traditional attitude or stance vis-à-vis the physical world which underlies much folklore and for which Hufford's and Jones's genres of place provide the overt expression. The four elements of the sense of place derive from our experience with the hard physical facts of geography and become encapsulated, summarized, reenacted, and symbolized in folklore. That folklore in turn reiterates and teaches two things to its performers and audiences—in general, the elements of the sense of place, that traditional four-part way of experiencing and thinking about our physical environs; in particular, the individual form that one or more of those elements has taken on for *this* performer in *this* place. The sense of place logically precedes place-based folklore, provides the thematic drive behind that lore, and determines the kinds of stories people tell about places and the kinds of subjects and meanings those stories tend to have. The folklore which it generates condenses and summarizes our geographical experience, validating it and giving it the sanction of tradition. It is of course necessary and vital to discuss place-based folklore in generic terms—some genres are better than others at illuminating particular layers of the sense of place, and without that illumination it would be difficult to understand the sense of place at all—but to concentrate solely on genres of place is finally misleading. What is important is the kernel of meaning, the traditional structure of geographical experience and understanding that those genres individually and collectively reveal. This structure finally underlies all place-based lore; this sense of place, common in its outline to everyone who talks about or hears about places, provides the layers of meaning which comprise our invisible landscapes.

Genres of Place

A wide variety of folklore genres help reveal the multiple strata of the sense of place. One unconventional genre of lore (if it can even be called that) that residents of a folk region share is an unspoken sense of the physical boundaries of the area, a feeling of familiar and meaningful geographical space which emerges as a by-product of other, more conventional forms of place-based lore: we sense we are reaching the edge of our world when we run out of stories to tell about the places we see. Borders and boundaries usually tend to be thought of more as abstract geographical, legal, and political constructs than as lived realities, as arbitrary lines inked onto the map but not reflected on the land. Nevertheless, boundaries—not those drawn by surveyors and cartographers and marked by fences and signs but those superimposed on the land and inscribed in the mind through the daily experience of inhabiting a locality; not those erected fiercely from without but those pushed out gently from within—are frequently an important component of people's lived sense of place. Such borders, more than political demarcations, give geography order and meaning and help carve a place out of undifferentiated space; in landscape historian J. B. Jackson's words, "They give a permanent human quality to what would otherwise be an amorphous stretch of land."[31] Lightfoot addresses the issue of folk boundaries when, in his overview of regional folkloristics, he points out the difference between "ad hoc" and "ontic" regions. Ad hoc regions are artificial and contrived, imposed or invented by outside observers according to whatever single-factor variables they choose, however irrelevant those criteria are to the residents of the region. "Ontic regions, on the other hand, owe their existence to geographical, social, or cultural 'facts,' such as mountains, rivers, settlement history, or whatever else, and may or may not have within them corresponding cultural groupings. It is, of course, ontic cultural patterns or areas that are of interest to folklorists."[32] Such regions, self-consciously known and defined by the people within them, may or may not correspond with prominent and visible features on the landscape or with conventional political divisions; what is important is that the people themselves know and can point out the boundaries of their regions—the regions are accurately defined only from within, not without, and outside the figurative walls lies unfamiliar and somewhat intimidating terra incognita.

This folk sense of territory and boundaries is common to folk regions in a variety of geographical contexts. Often, these boundaries grow out of patterns of local and communal history: the sense of place ends at that point on the ground where the long story of the past is no longer known, where the land and the stories on the other side belong to someone else. Barbara Allen has written, for instance, of the "genealogical landscape" enfolding the community of Rock Bridge, Kentucky—a landscape delineated and given meaning in local minds through knowing the families "who live or have lived within the boundaries of the community and the land they live or lived on," so that "when the people of Rock Bridge look around them, they see the landscape as a complex web of human lives lived on it." People in Rock Bridge identify community members according to the houses (and surrounding acreage) that they own and reside in, or that their families used to own and occupy, and conversely identify houses and properties according to the individuals or families that have owned and lived in them—the old So-and-so place—even if the houses on those properties have collapsed or stood vacant for years. Land, people, and genealogical history are inextricably intertwined; when neighborhood residents can no longer attach names and family stories to the land, they know they have left Rock Bridge: "the landscape is strange and empty in Rock Bridgers' eyes if they don't know who lives on it."[33]

While folk boundaries often arise from a strong sense of the local past, just as often they accrete from the patterns of the present, from the daily round of living. As Richard Reuss points out in commenting on the folklore of suburbs, for instance,

> Any person living in a suburb will soon internalize a largely unspoken folk concept of his or her neighborhood. Almost always smaller than the suburb as a whole, the "folk" neighborhood may comprise just a few streets and adjacent areas such as school yards, ball fields, the nearby Dairy Queen, and so on. The folk boundaries may be busy street crossings, undeveloped lots, brooks, fences, railroad tracks or whatever; they may overlap school district lines, less often town political boundaries, and will tend to shift somewhat in the minds of residents living in different parts of the same neighborhood. All the same, the general outlines of the "folk map" will be clear to anyone who bothers to check. Inherent in the folk concept of neighborhood are all the associated notions of home, security, territoriality, and license. One who ventures outside this inner sanctum will find different ground rules.[34]

This sense of folk regionality, of ineffable but definite and powerful folk boundaries, is not limited to rural communities and suburban neighborhoods. Urban neighborhoods share them as well; Gerald Warshaver points out that in cities, neighborhoods as defined in folk terms are much smaller than they are conceived of by politicians and planners, and that "residents feel the 'true' or folk neighborhood to be the behavioral environment where 'everyone knows who belongs and who doesn't.' "[35] In his study of the Little Dixie region of Missouri, Howard Wight Marshall takes a more universal approach, claiming that "Little Dixie is the world with your county in the middle";[36] each folk region is Ptolemaic in a sense, consisting of a well-bounded sphere of known territory around which the rest of the world wends its mysterious way.

This is not to suggest, however, that all residents of a place necessarily sense a sharp break between their region and its surrounding foreign territories—that they can take a map and draw clear and definite boundaries between where they belong and where they don't, that their home place is surrounded by a conceptual wall of some sort. As Henry Glassie suggests in his study of the Northern Irish folk community of Ballymenone, the sense of place, and feeling for place, may focus on certain centers of intense meaning and then dissipate with distance from those centers. Finding oneself outside of one's place is thus not a matter of crossing the border and going through a conceptual checkpoint; it is instead a matter of passing through a hazy area in which feeling for place and knowledge of place gradually lessen, as though one were driving away from a radio station and gradually losing the signal, and suddenly realizing that one has left one's place without really realizing that (or when) it happened. As Glassie says in writing of the Irish home, "the world . . . expands away from the red fleck of the hearth, drifting from light to dark, heat to cold, dry to damp, familiar to unknown, controlled to uncontrolled. The hearth is the center of the dwelling, the dwelling of the house, the house of the home place; then fields roll, broken by hedged ditches, to merge with other farms. Edges are lost space as fields join, gathering the warm homes of the upland into the center of each townland, before fading toward cold, wet, unoccupied peripheries. The community is comparably a thing of centers, not margins."[37] Perhaps we should pay closer attention to Marshall's Ptolemaic imagery: in the Ptolemaic universe, after all, the earth stood at the center and its circumambient universe faded off into darkness. Attention was trained inward, not outward; the focus of meaning was at the center, and the edges could take care of themselves.

Sometimes, however, residents may choose a prominent physical symbol as a sort of gateway to their region, a marker to show where the land of the barbarians begins and to give concrete form to their folk sense of boundaries. One group of people in the Adirondack Mountains of New York have adopted such a monolith as a symbol of the distinctive quality of their place: "Ask them about [that quality] in the environs of South Colton and one is very apt to hear about Sunday Rock, which rests alongside Route 56 just north of town. As Charlie Berry put it, the huge glacial boulder is nothing less than the equivalent of the 'local Plymouth Rock,' for 'in the old days, life took on a different character beyond that rock: there were no ministers, no schools.'" The old boulder has survived several road reconstruction projects over the years because of the strength of local sentiment, and today "Sunday Rock rests in permanent symbolic testimony to a lifestyle as it has developed beyond the valley."[38] And it also serves as a catalyst for words and stories: a reference to the rock easily calls forth descriptions of the distinctive history and character of the region.

Related to this sense of folk boundaries is an inchoate knowledge of the physical things that properly belong within those boundaries—an unspoken awareness of the organic and man-made forms, unconsciously memorized through prolonged sensory experience, which fill the landscape and give it its characteristic "look," and an equally unspoken, unscientific folk taxonomy which organizes those forms into meaningful categories and thus imposes order on the landscape. Over time, a resident of a place becomes "a geographer of the micro-region," in David Sopher's phrase, "putting together, perhaps not wittingly, a mental composite of features that tell of home: a profile of hillside, the hue and texture of houses, the pitch of church steeples, the color of cattle."[39] Mary T. Hufford, in her discussion of the folkloric sense of place of the New Jersey Pinelands, has referred to this sense of what belongs and how it is rightly arranged as "environmental literacy," a phenomenon by which, interestingly, geography and words metaphorically become one. Environmental literacy is a folk knowledge which figuratively enables one to read one's surroundings: "Sense of place literally begins with the senses, with an ability to make sense of the environment, not only to tell what is there, but to understand the relationships between environmental elements. Outdoorsmen working in what we might call the endemic folklife habitats of the Pinelands may or may not express ecological relationships in scientific terms, but they know what the place looks, sounds, tastes, smells, and feels like at different times of the day and in different seasons." If environmental literacy enables one to read one's surroundings as if they were a text, that text must be made up of intelligible words, sentences, and paragraphs. The folk sense of place provides these units of meaning. As with any language, this sort of literacy is best gained through incessant practice and exposure; also as with any language, those who cannot read it will see the text as a meaningless jumble. "What appear to be monotonous woodlands to outsiders are teeming with categorical forms in the eyes of woodsmen. . . . 'Islands,' 'sloughs,' and 'bottom' are landscape motifs, grammatical units in the language of those who read the environment. These units may be natural entities that are mentally discerned and endowed with meaning, or they may be human constructions with historic legacies, such as channels, ditches, dams, bogs, sand roads, corduroy roads, and charcoal pits."[40] Each folk region encodes a language all its own. Residents of adjacent or antipodal regions may not be able to communicate with each other on this level—these languages are nothing if not private and difficult to learn—but within their own boundaries they can read rich and complex tales in their physical surroundings.

The material folklife of a region also provides an indication of the deep understanding and intimate knowledge that people have of their physical environs. The kinds of artifacts that can be produced in a region are, of course, in part determined by the available materials. Log houses, for instance, were an easy and natural choice in the wooded East, as were sod houses on the grassy plains and adobe houses in the barren Southwest. In addition to being partially determined by the environment, however, artifacts also embody a sort of interpretation of that environment on the part of the people who make them. Residents of a place combine with their knowledge of what items belong within their boundaries an awareness of the properties and potentialities of those items. They become familiar with the physical components of their place through prolonged sensory experience; in turn, "sensory familiarity is a basis for concepts of place that are expressed in folklife forms. Through these forms, residents both organize and tell about their knowledge of the place."[41] Material folklife, then, is on the one hand an inventory of the materials found within the boundaries of a place, a display of what is out there and what can be done with it. Also, the specific forms that artifacts take on demonstrate their makers' detailed knowledge of the qualities and demands of their environment; they tailor their artifacts carefully to conform and adapt to the physical conditions imposed by their surroundings, thus demonstrating the depth of their experiential knowledge of place.

This process is elegantly embodied, for example, in the configuration of the type of boat favored by the hunters of the New Jersey Pinelands—the Barnegat Bay sneakbox, which according to Hufford "comprises a distinctive response to distinctively regional conditions, a tool whereby local men distinguish themselves as inhabitants of a singular region."[42] Hufford elaborates:

The Barnegat Bay sneakbox, one of the most elegant forms to emerge from the region, effectively synthesizes the observations of generations of baymen of water, land, air, man, and mud. It was custom made for the marshes and estuaries of South Jersey. In its form we see every contingency neatly anticipated. Its spoon-shaped hull enables it to glide through areas marked as land on coastal maps. . . . [It] is light enough for one man to haul over land between channels. It is equipped with a mast-hole, centerboard well, and detachable rudder for sailing; winter and summer sails; folding oarlocks and a removable decoy rack to suppress its profile; runners for traveling on ice; and two kinds of accessory ice hooks for breaking up slushy ("porridge") and hard ("pane") ice. Its sloping transom allows a hunter to row backward in channels that are too narrow to turn around in. . . . In the sneakbox the shapes of men and meadows are fused.[43]

The form of this boat, and of the other indigenous material folklife expressions of the Pinelands, reveals a deep understanding of place and provides a glimpse of the local landscape as its inhabitants experience it. The people who build and use these boats know the requirements that the local meadows and marshes impose on their hunting activities, and they know just how to shape their materials (Atlantic white cedar) to meet those conditions. These boats reveal a perfect adaptation of people to place and demonstrate the successful encounter of imagination with environment. The meadows and marshes, rather than being simply amorphous swamps, are revealed as deeply known and understood hunting environments, their qualities and vicissitudes already grasped and planned for. An artifact such as the Barnegat sneakbox provides eloquent testimony to the local interpretation of the physical components of place.

Sometimes certain artifacts, rather than interpreting the environments from which they are built and in which they are used every day, are seen by their makers as synecdochic expressions of landscapes and places far distant in time and space. Such material expressions tend to refer more to the personal and emotional than to the physical component of place, like the deeply allusive wooden chains whose elderly Indiana carvers Simon Bronner has studied. Bronner found that his subjects generally had turned to chain carving—a craft remembered from their rural boyhoods—as a means of connecting themselves imaginatively to a fondly remembered past in the face of the encroaching infirmities of age, and as a way of resisting a modern industrial world in which they felt out of place. Carving a chain out of a single piece of wood depends on knowing the properties of particular kinds of wood; thus (as with the makers of sneakboxes), in the carvers' minds, "carving was connected to recognizing and using the natural landscape," particularly the farm landscapes of their youths. As they carve, these men travel in their minds to valued scenes of their past, scenes which they connect in an important way with their identities, scenes which they contrast favorably with their present surroundings: as they carve, "they think about tradition and their sense of self. They recall landscapes—country and city, old and new, natural and man-made. They admire the chain emerging from nature's wooden grip."[44] Artifacts, then, do not necessarily have to derive physically from a certain region or be historically connected with a locality to be repositories of place-based meaning. The notion of sense of place would be impossible without memory, the recollection of personal history grounded in a particular landscape or set of landscapes. Anything that awakens such memories or keeps them alive—even a stick of wood whittled and manipulated until meanings as well as chain links are released from their confinement within its grains and fibers—can be understood as an expression of the sense of place.

Folk architecture is another means by which the sense of place inscribes itself on the landscape, visible as well as invisible, as can be seen in the Little Dixie region of Missouri. Howard Wight Marshall feels that "patterns in traditional building, discovered directly by field documentation, furnish an index to regional personality"; Little Dixie was settled by emigrants from the upland South, and is now marked by a predominance of "Southern" building types—in particular, the transverse-crib barn and the central-hall I house—the extent and frequency of which determine the extent of the region. "These patterns of building mirror the region's identification as an island of upland southern folk culture in the lower Midwest with ties of history and mood to Virginia, the Carolinas, and Bluegrass Kentucky that are enormously important to many of the settlers' descendents today."[45] In other words, Southern folk houses provide the same sort of reminder of the area's cherished Southern heritage that the region's folk name does, a heritage which contributes in large part to the self-perceived identity of the region and the people who live in it. The extent to which identification with a place is tied to traditional architecture is further suggested by the fate of the Head of Hollybush settlement in the Kentucky Appalachians: Hollybush was a close-knit agricultural community, marked by a distinctive style of regional architecture, until the area moved closer to the mainstream of American life with the advent of coal mining, nonagricultural work outside of the narrow Hollybush valley and the community's resultant exposure to a national consumer culture. Hollybush's traditional architecture and building practices soon began to decay, to be supplanted by more standardized and less meticulous forms; as the local sense of place and ties to that place were diluted, in other words, so was the physical fabric which helped to define and sustain the place. Eventually the settlement was abandoned.[46]

In addition, house types and other man-made alterations to the landscape contribute to the folk sense of boundaries by providing visual reminders of the extent of a folk region, serving to outline an area beyond the limits of which the landscape doesn't "look right." The built forms of the region inscribe themselves in the minds and memories of residents and create a comfortable sense of familiarity and belonging; outside of the region, the world may prove to be disconcerting through its sheer physical foreignness. Little Dixie's "Southern" houses fulfill this function; as Marshall points out, "Traditional builders adapt old ways to new landscapes in the course of settlement, and as each new land is tampered with by carpenters and masons and farmers a sense of place gradually appears. Regions when effectively settled take on the appearance of possession, and they take on a special character that local citizens come to know and identify with home and community. Architectural patterns are a basic factor in the process of regionalization . . . wherein local landscapes are made."[47] The sense of place which the built environment creates and invokes can be found in any environment, not just in rural areas where folk-created houses and barns loom large in the landscape. Even suburban householders have a well-developed sense of what looks (and therefore feels) right: "Within each suburb, the houses, lawns, gardens, garages, sidewalks, and other landscape features are arranged in patterns dictated by custom as much as by zoning laws or town regulations."[48] The ways in which people alter their environments effectively demonstrate and externalize the physical component of their internal sense of place and at the same time provide physical forms around which feelings of community solidarity and personal identity can coalesce.

Such feelings are not limited solely to man-made elements of the landscape. Any setting can become a symbol of and element of personal and group identity through sufficient familiarity and propinquity. Through extensive interaction with a place, people may begin to define themselves in terms of their relationship with and residence in that place, to the extent that they cannot really express who they are without inevitably taking into account the setting which surrounds them as well. The geographic component of personal identity is strong in the minds of Adirondack woodsmen, for instance:

In general, working-class men who grow up in the foothills are expected to be at home in the woods. Such familiarity is a major component of male identity. . . . [This] explains . . . why local men, much more so than women, spend a good deal of time talking about the woods and male recreational activities within it. To woodsmen the environment offers something more than a forest retreat. To be in the woods means something special, . . . [f]or in woodsmen's eyes the woods is a particularly male domain. In the woods individual men and groups of peers confront natural phenomena, self, and other men on male terms. Their casual talk and yarns emphasize the male pursuit of life as defined and elaborated in outdoor contexts.[49]

These woodsmen define themselves in terms of their life and activities within the woods, an environment they know intimately through years of work and play. Their sense of self—as people and particularly as men—is determined almost exclusively by what they do, and what they do is determined almost exclusively by where they are. Their oral lore—their talk and yarns about the woods and woods life—in turn reveals both their sense of place—their understanding of what the woods means—and their personal identity as attached to and determined by that place. In this instance, then, geography transcends its immediate role as a physical delimiter of place, providing much more than a familiar and comforting ambience that "looks right."

The simultaneous use of such things as houses and rocks to evoke, encode, and communicate the sense of place emphasizes the multigeneric fashion in which invisible landscapes are constructed and maintained by regional communities. As the case of the Adirondack woodsmen and their "casual talk and yarns" indicates, however, the physical environment, while it may indicate a lot about a place in its own right, also inevitably and necessarily provides a bridge back to oral forms of place-based lore. Folklorists could not convincingly and completely explain the meaning and local significance of the physical environment, after all, if local residents did not tell them; every place has words attached. In considering material genres of place-based folklore, we need to remember that insofar as houses and artifacts connect to memory, they allude to narratives. As Barbara Johnstone argues, while a place necessarily has a physical geographical existence, our sense of place is primarily a narrative construction: "The texture of a familiar neighborhood is a narrative texture, too; when a neighborhood feels like home, the houses and people one passes on its streets evoke stories."[50] We remember and respond to that narrative texture as much as to the physical texture, if not more so—stories bring the physical place to life, giving it vivid human meaning. While artifacts serve importantly to delineate the folk region and interpret the local landscape, they connect most compellingly to place and provide the most immediate glimpse into local residents' sense of the region, insofar as they lead to verbal expression: people in the New Jersey Pinelands turn cranberry scoops into magazine racks, sneakboxes into coffee tables, and fishing and clamming tools into restaurant decorations because they like to "surround themselves with evidence that they are at home, in a place with a usable past. The tools and resources are thus recycled into touchstones for stories about the region."[51]

The names which people give their regions and the things within their regions are one verbal form that provides a good indication of regional consciousness and a sense of living in a distinctive place, especially when they are names such as are not found on maps or in standard reference books. As Hufford points out, "Information about the landscape, its places and people, its economic and seasonal cycles, its past, and its multiple realities, is encapsulated in the names for things within it." Vernacular names for local flora and fauna, as opposed to formal biological taxonomies and more widely known common names, provide an especially good indication of regional environmental literacy: "Local names . . . encapsulate human experience with the species on this landscape, conveying that 'knowledge of' the place that is born of repeated experience with it. . . . Local names for plants and animals . . . spring from experience with a place. Taken as a whole, they graphically catalog its sights, sounds, smells, and impressions";[52] they thus tend to be blunt, practical, and sense-oriented. People in the Pinelands tend to name plants according to such attributes as what they look like, where they grow, what they do—names like brown burr, rabbit's foot, cat's paws, cottontail grass, pearly everlasting, Old Field balsam, hog huckleberries, killcalf, staggerbush.[53] Such names tend to be known only by locals and thus provide insight into the ways in which they see, experience, and interpret their place. They also help consolidate a feeling of local identity, providing a private language which outsiders will probably find impenetrable.

As with folk names of things, so with folk names of places. The informal, unofficial names which people apply to their regions imply a strong insider's sense of local history and regional identity and provide locals with a feeling of belonging in the form of a "code name" for their region whose full range of meaning and nuance will be lost on the uninitiated. As Hufford puts it, "Place names, linked with landscape features, encode the shared past, distinguishing members of one group from another. . . . Places and their names are sources of identity and security."[54] Dorson, in his study of the Calumet Region, found that its residents "invidiously referred to the general area as 'de Region.' As a folklorist interested in regional theory and the common traditions shaping a region, I was intrigued by the notion of an urbanized region, seemingly a contradiction in terms, and one so self-aware that it pinned the label on itself."[55] Accustomed to thinking of regions strictly in rural terms and unable to see any obvious physical markers or boundaries, Dorson was not tipped off to the existence of this urban region until he became aware of the folk name.

The provenance of such names is a mysterious process, but regional residents cling to them fiercely. "Little Dixie" is a folk term for a region of central Missouri which was thickly settled by upland Southerners in the years before the Civil War. As these settlers unhappily found themselves surrounded by Yankees after the war, they found solace and security in the idea of being a fiercely proud enclave of Southernness in a hostile Northern land. The name "Little Dixie" soon sprang into being as a symbol of historically based regional identity, a symbol which maintains its power even today:

> For farmers and townspeople alike, Little Dixie is a name that can convey a meaningful sense of place, a sense of belonging, of inheritance, and a connection (dimly or sharply perceived) based on a selective community memory of a common past kept alive for current and future uses. . . . Little Dixie has no commonly repeated or standard "place-name story," but the belief and the attitude are more important than some set repertoire of narratives. The name operates as a label for regional awareness based both on actual history and on impressionistic history, and as a device for public and commercial interests.

The name "Little Dixie" is as much a source of personal and communal identity today as it was in the postwar days in which it was first coined, serving to remind people of the shared Southern past of the region and to bind them to their geographical surroundings. Even local businesses share in (or take advantage of) this proud regional awareness and identification; Little Dixie Eggs and Little Dixie Ham are sold in the area, and people borrow books from the Little Dixie Regional Library System, uses of the name which, Marshall feels, "refer us to a living, vital place that grew from within, not one invented by historians, civic clubs, or journalists."[56] This pattern of folk naming also holds true in the Upper Cumberland region along the Kentucky-Tennessee border. The name "Upper Cumberland" was first applied to the area in the 1830s with the arrival of the steamboat trade on the Cumberland River above Carthage, Tennessee. Residents along that stretch of the river soon adopted the name as their own, and today dozens of businesses and governmental agencies in the region include the words "Upper Cumberland" somewhere in their names—an onomastic pattern which, according to folklorist William Lynwood Montell, "makes clear the inhabitants' preference that their territory be referred to by this name,"[57] a name which grew directly out of the local riverine way of life. The folk name emerges as one of the most succinct yet most powerful embodiments of the meanings of a place for the people who use it.

In addition to the way that they accumulate folk names, physical places seem to have a particularly close relationship to personal experience stories and community oral history. In fact, Montell found in his study of the Upper Cumberland region that "the one genre that is present above all others in the region is the oral historical narrative, in the form of both traditional stories and accounts of personal experiences."[58] I would generalize from Montell's observation and suggest that the oral historical narrative may well be the most common genre found in *any* place. Events happen in places; when we remember or are told about the events, we remember or are told about the places; historical narratives, whether firsthand or secondhand, thus adhere firmly to and cluster thickly upon the landscape. Any component of the local geography, be it natural or man-made, can serve as the setting, focus, or catalyst for a tale. Charles Martin, in his Hollybush fieldwork, found that old buildings and building sites served to spur the memories of former Hollybush residents with whom he toured the area, bringing back reminiscences of "other families, Hollybush history, and personal experiences," as well as "personal experiences between inhabitants, customs, farming techniques, and agricultural history." One old house, which Martin "saw only as an inanimate ruin," turned out to be highly significant to his informant as the place where his mother died. Such an occurrence, while indicating the extent to which memories of personal and communal experiences adhere to the physical settings in which they take place so that a reminder of one is a reminder of the other, also reminds us of the inevitable and yawning gap between the insider's and the outsider's knowledge of a place. As Martin realized while contemplating an anonymous Hollybush grave, "I knew then, as I stood over the unnamed, that I would never really understand the subtle pattern of life in Hollybush, but only fragmented perceptions. A lifetime of study could not duplicate the knowledge inherent in hoeing corn on the hillside for one day when the Head was a living community."[59]

As Martin's informants indicate, the folkloric sense of place is closely related to local community history, particularly as it circulates in oral tradition. The local landscape summarizes and objectifies local history in concrete form; objects in the landscape become prominent in the local mind because of important or striking events which took place there. Conversely, historical narratives vivify the local landscape, transforming it from a neutral chunk of geography into a combination of stage set for historical events and important actor in significant local dramas of the past. A large part of the local meaning of Little Dixie, for instance, lies in its settlement history. "The people's own vision of Little Dixie" is based primarily on "a 'southern' past (which some call 'the old slave days') of tobacco farms, log houses, country ham, fox hunts, rail fences, 'old southern mansions' (only remotely like the famous manor houses on big Deep South plantations), and what they imagine to have been a more genteel life-style."[60] When Little Dixieites look around them, they see their surroundings through the historical haze of a romanticized, Southern-flavored past, the memory of which is kept alive through the stories they tell about it. The oral tradition of the Upper Cumberland is anchored firmly in the river which runs through the region: "because the river dominated commerce and transportation in the region from the late 1780s until 1930, the Cumberland River remained the central element in regional consciousness. Many people associated with the river have become legendary in the minds of the present residents of the Upper Cumberland area. Oral stories about them reflect a close affinity with the river and the human dramas enacted upon its waters."[61] Folksingers in the Adirondacks have a similar historical bent: "the thrust of their creativity in song reflected an overriding desire to chronicle woods-work events and personalities."[62] They attempt to tell the history of the woods in two primary ways: as personal history, through singing about their own careers as loggers and hunters, and as impressionistic communal history, through relating real and legendary tales of dramatic events such as logging catastrophes. Their body of folksong (now found mainly in the memories of old-timers) tells the historical tale of both a place (the Adirondack woods) and the community it encloses (the people who worked there).

At the same time, many of the Adirondack woodsmen's songs transcend their immediate historical function to hint at the emotional valuation which the singers and their local audiences put on their place, a valuation which rises out of the often turbulent and violent events of local history. "'Good' songs, like good poems, fuse memorable form with memorable content," says Bethke. "They are expressive links to persons, places, and emotions." This fusion of person and place with the emotions associated with that place because of the actions of that person is illustrated by a song which one of Bethke's informants, Ham Ferry, composed about the death of Jim Hickey. According to Ferry's later summary of the events of the song, there was once a massive logjam on the nearby Raquette River: "Well, Jim Hickey went out to break the jam. They were warpin'. They had ropes they'd hook in and find the key log that was holdin' it. And they'd take the rope back to the rest of the men on the bank and they'd pull on it. He was out to hook the log and started back. He hollered to the boys to pull. And they pulled on it. And the first thing you know, he fell. That was the last they ever saw of him till they found him down the river. The jam broke and he went right on down through with the logs."[63] Not only does this song commemorate a tragic event in local history and anchor that event firmly in a local river, it also provides a sobering interpretation of the nature of that river and of the whole woods environment. The woodsmen's occupations in the lumbering industry brought them into intimate proximity with the physical components of their place, and the dangerous nature of their work seems to have given a dark tinge to their evaluation of that place: the woods are revealed, disturbingly, as an unpredictably antagonistic force, a place of physical challenge, threat, and danger.

The local view of the meaning of the woods thus contains little romance, little sense of the Thoreauvian closeness to nature or frontier-style adventure that outsiders might expect. Instead, local loggers explain their place with calm yet sombre realism through the medium of historical songs and stories about events which have, in a certain sense, been *caused* by that place—Hickey would never have died, after all, if there had not been big trees in the area and if the river had not been full of big rocks behind which jammed logs could pile up. Other, less specifically place-anchored songs similar in plot and theme to the Hickey tale were also popular in the Adirondack woods, the most widely known being "The Jam on Gerry's Rock," a traditional song in the American logger's repertoire which resembles Ham Ferry's homemade folksong almost point for point (with the addition of six more deaths and a grieving sweetheart).[64] Such songs found a home in the Adirondacks, though, only because they agreed with and confirmed the indigenous sense of place as derived from local history and captured in indigenous stories and songs. "The special appeal of such songs is understandable," comments Bethke. "More than a tribute to occupational heroism and sacrifice, they were a constant reminder of the dangers on foothills rivers. The association was immediate and lasting, a kind of loggers' *memento mori*."[65] Several others of Bethke's informants could tell of similar deaths in the woods—deaths of friends, family members, coworkers. Songs—be they historical like Ham Ferry's or apocryphal like "The Jam on Gerry's Rock"—serve to crystallize and make visible and vivid the sense of place to which those deaths contributed.

"The Jam on Gerry's Rock" is a migratory piece of folklore, one that tends to wander in and settle down wherever people chop down trees and float them down rivers. In its footloose ways it resembles the subgenre of the migratory legend—the traditional narrative, found in many different areas at many different times (and often at the same time), which floats into a place and becomes temporarily localized, anchored on known and named features in the local landscape. Migratory legends join with historical narratives and songs to recount the events associated (or thought to be associated) with a place and also to reveal the local community's emotional evaluation of those events and therefore of that place; together they tell of history, then move beyond memory to feeling. And since migratory legends, while usually believed to be true by those who hear and tell them, are rarely strictly factual or historical (how could the exact same thing happen in the exact same way in so many places?), they are in fact primarily concerned with feeling rather than memory. They serve mainly to give narrative shape to emotions lingering in the local air, not to create quasi-history—as "The Jam on Gerry's Rock" indicates, such legends migrate into a region most readily when the emotional as well as the physical and historical geography of the place supports them: there must be wariness as well as woods, potential tragedy as well as trees.

Migratory legends, then, often become attached to real features in the local landscape because they confirm lurking feelings that local residents already have about those places. Occasionally, though, they may settle on places perfectly innocently, because they demand a certain setting and one just happens to be on hand in the local scene; once they become so anchored, however, they may change forever the way that people feel about those places. Urban legends provide a good example of both of these processes. These brief tales of ordinary people who unexpectedly find themselves involved in embarrassing, violent, traumatic, and sometimes humorous events are almost exclusively floating legends, circulating widely through many parts of the country simultaneously and evading all attempts to track them down to a point and time of origin. Nevertheless, as they float into a place they tend to settle gently but firmly on the ground; as Richard Reuss points out, a large percentage of urban legends "are set, either explicitly or implicitly, in a suburban locale. . . . All these stories . . . circulate nationally, yet they are invariably placed in a neighborhood setting; if they did not originate in the suburbs, they have followed the suburbanites to their current domiciles from either the city or the country."[66] Usually the settings of these tales attain great geographical specificity. Noted urban legend scholar Jan Harold Brunvand observes that "in the world of modern urban legends there is usually no geographical or generational gap between teller and event. . . . The legends' physical settings are often close by, real, and sometimes even locally renowned for such happenings." While the events in the tales almost certainly never actually happened in the places to which they are attached, what is important is that tellers and listeners *believe* that they did. Such legends thus provide the "folk history, or rather quasi-history," of a place. As Brunvand points out, though, they quickly move beyond history (of whatever sort) to "reflect many of the hopes, fears, and anxieties of our time."[67] And in the process, they reveal the folk interpretation of some of the places, and some of the common categories of places, in our urban and suburban landscapes.

Many urban legends, for instance, cluster around suburban shopping areas. These tales tend to focus on such unlovely subjects as contaminated food, suspect merchandise, and occasional random violence. Whenever they are told, they are almost always said to have occurred at a specific store or mall in the region—or, at least, in an unnamed outlet of a major retail or fast-food chain, all of whose stores are so similar that a story told about any of them will immediately cast suspicion on the local branch. Stories about deep-fried rats being sold by Kentucky Fried Chicken outlets, for instance, have circulated widely in recent years.[68] In the late 1960s, there was a small spate of stories about customers being bitten by poisonous snakes lying hidden in blankets which had been imported from Asia; specific stores in New York, Maryland, Indiana, South Dakota, Minnesota, Wisconsin, Texas, and Idaho—many of them K-Marts—were simultaneously identified as being the site of the fatal bite.[69] One gruesome group of legends centers on shopping-mall or department-store restrooms: they involve the attempted kidnapping of girls and the bloody castration of boys who wander into the restroom unaccompanied by their parents. All such legends inevitably become tied to local shopping centers.[70] Tales like these touch on a variety of themes: distrust of impersonal big business and modern commercial forces, the perceived importance of fulfilling traditional domestic functions like making home-cooked meals and looking after the kids, xenophobia (in the case of the imported blankets), and so on. Looked at in terms of the way they reflect and contribute to the local sense of place, though, they also indicate how tale tellers and audiences interpret some of the important commercial sites in their area and in fact can contribute largely to the nature of those interpretations. As places, the shopping mall and commercial strip are distrusted, even feared. They awaken unpleasant associations in local residents, associations which may derive in part from experience: tellers and listeners have had distressing or annoying things happen to them at the mall or on the strip and so are all too eager to lend credence to urban legends which portray those places as sites of death and mayhem. These tales distill, sharpen, and exaggerate experientially derived place impressions which are already alive in the community.

Conversely, tales like these may *create* place impressions. Chain stores attract urban legends like magnets; put up a K-Mart or a McDonald's and you can immediately expect lurid tales to come flocking around. Not knowing any better, people listen to these compelling and entertaining stories and use them as the *a priori* basis for their emotional evaluation of the strip and the mall. Instead of beginning with a place experience and gradually adding a layer of emotional evaluation which gains expression in legend form, such people begin with the legend, with the emotional impression, and work their way down to the concrete place experience: when they next visit the site named in the story (or another one identical to it), their view of that place will be colored by the emotions inspired by the legend which the place calls to mind. The subgenre of the urban legend, and the migratory legend in general, demonstrates in miniature the ways in which narratives can both reveal and influence place-based emotion; if tragic events had not darkened the Adirondacks and inspired Ham Ferry to write his song and express the local impression of the woods and rivers, it is entirely possible that the popular logger's song "The Jam on Gerry's Rock" would have drifted in and created that impression anyway.

Personal experience stories, while taking as their overt subject episodes of an individual's history as played out in a particular landscape or set of landscapes, also provide a vivid glimpse of the emotional interpretations which people put on the places around them. These tales might at first seem to reveal only the idiosyncratic emotion of the teller; the content of the story, after all, is the unique experience of an individual narrator, and so the emotions carried by the narrative might seem to be unique to the situation and to the particular person involved as he or she reacted to that situation. Looked at more closely, however, personal experience stories reveal place-anchored emotions which are common to the group of local residents, and therefore to the place, as a whole. For one thing, these tales are rarely told in isolation. They are most frequently told in the context of other similar tales, with one teller prompting another to tell a related story, and so the stories which the teller is likely to keep at hand in his or her repertoire will be those which fit in most smoothly with the tales, and the themes and emotions couched in those tales, that are told in the community at large. Indeed, insofar as personal experience stories center on places, the local sense of place will inevitably form the thematic core of the tale. As folklorist Sandra Stahl points out, "personal narratives contain traditional attitudes, cultural 'evaluations' if you will, that are not necessarily consciously employed but do in their covert stance make the stories significant, give them meaning." She continues, arguing for the universality within the folk group of these attitudes and evaluations: "no attitude itself will exist independently, idiosyncratically: it will always be shared by group members, varying only in the degree of relative importance each individual personality affords it. This degree of importance attached to the attitude will easily display itself in personal narratives, since the attitude is what gives the narrative its meaning; it is the point of the story and therefore is an attitude regarded as important by the teller and presumably by his audience."[71] I have already argued that the sense of place is such a traditional attitude or stance—here, a stance regarding the significance of the geographical world. As a cultural "evaluation" of the meaning of a location, then, the local sense of place, even if it is not fully and consciously articulated by the teller, provides the bulk of the significance of the place-based personal experience story. That the teller feels comfortable telling it in story-trading sessions, sure that he or she will receive a sympathetic response, and that the audience responds favorably and reacts by telling similar stories of their own suggests not only how widely held the local sense of place is but also that the personal experience narrative may in fact be one of the most common and accessible folkloric manifestations of that sense of place.

As folklorist Eleanor Wachs tells us in her study of the crime-victim story tradition of New York City, the shared sense of place is an integral aspect of this subgenre of the personal experience narrative. Most New Yorkers, it seems, tell such stories: "One of the most popular traditions among New Yorkers is telling stories about significant events in their daily lives. The specific content of these urban tales may vary, but they often share common characteristics and themes [that is, a common sense of place]. . . . As storytellers, they select their accounts from an extensive repertoire of narratives that includes other stories, perhaps more personal or intimate. Yet, whether intimate or commonplace, many of these tales deal with some aspect of crime victimization or some feature of urban life." New Yorkers would not feel compelled to tell these tales if the events which they recount were not an integral and compelling part of their everyday lives, and the traumatic character of these events inevitably colors the teller's perception of the milieu in which they take place: after describing an all-female tale-swapping session, Wachs asserts that the stories "present a world view shared by the women. They all expected New York City to be a dangerous place to live. Throughout the swapping of tales, several of the women made comments such as, 'This is New York,' or 'Where else *but* New York?' " The tales reveal New York as seen through the eyes of native storytellers, and that city is "a world of chaos and unexplainable violence,"[72] one that cannot be contemplated with equanimity but only with the most raw-edged and painful emotions: Wachs repeatedly describes her informants as angry, shouting, obviously still moved by the fear and distress which the crime caused them. Even people who recount stories that they have heard secondhand are outraged that such things could happen. Crime-victim stories reveal personal history within a locality, then, and suggest through their ubiquity that in New York crime is part of everyone's history. More centrally, they also provide a particularly potent example of the way in which personal experience narratives can demonstrate the emotional component of the local sense of place. Few people can contemplate those experiences which they deem important enough to enter their personal-narrative repertoire without feeling some sort of emotion, and this emotion surfaces in the telling.

As with other folkloric manifestations of the sense of place, though, the emotional evaluation of New York is built upon a firm grasp of local geographical facts. As Wachs tells us, crime-victim narratives are always definitely and precisely located:

> [T]he narrator focuses immediately on the location of the incident, grounding it in time and space and establishing its veracity. In effect, the world of the story becomes real, having recognizable and familiar places and scenes. . . . Such stories are set in common urban places—apartment lobbies, elevators, vestibules, subways, buses, the open street. The locales provide another way to highlight the story action. But because the settings are so ordinary, victims and nonvictims, narrators and listeners, are apt to re-evaluate their environments after an incident occurs. . . . The elevator becomes the danger room, the city street the murder place, the subway car the den of thieves.

In other words, not only can the personal experience narrative reveal the significances that the teller has attached to the components of her physical surroundings because of her history in those surroundings, it can also serve to teach others about the local sense of place—to expand and sharpen the knowledge of residents, to initiate newcomers. It can attach layers of meaning to places not yet seen. In the case of Wachs's study, "as a result of hearing about a crime incident, or being victimized themselves, many people indicated that they had significantly altered their cognitive maps and took additional precautions to afford themselves an added sense of security." The storyteller imparts to others the (in this case negative) emotional charges she has attached to certain real, specifically identified and located parts of the geographical environment. In most cases, though, the act of imparting such information serves merely to reinforce perceptions and emotions that the audience already shares; personal experience stories often serve to confirm a group in a shared traditional attitude—here, a shared sense of place. In New York, in fact, the crime-victim narrative is largely an insider's genre: such stories are frequently used as "conversational icebreakers. This is because tellers and audience share a common frame of reference [that is, a sense of the meaning of New York]. They assume that there is no escape from crime in the city world. Thus, lengthy preliminaries are not necessary, except for outsiders, newcomers to New York City."[73] Tellers and listeners already know what New York is like; by exchanging stories, they confirm themselves in this knowledge, in their identity as experienced New Yorkers. All elements of the folkloric sense of place, then—location, history, identity, and emotion—fuse in the telling of place-anchored personal experience narratives, whether in New York or elsewhere.

The tall tale, that traditionally American genre, similarly expresses sense of place on many levels simultaneously. The successful tall tale is grounded firmly in, and provides a complex commentary upon, the geographical facts of a particular place. To be sure, these facts would be likely to take root in local consciousness and provide the basis for local stories at any rate. Noting the ever-present threat of tornadoes on the Great Plains and the devastating effect that that region's mercurial weather can have on local economies and ways of life, for instance, folklorist Larry Danielson finds that "tornado stories are commonplace in contemporary oral tradition of the central United States" and that these stories express "something significant about living on the prairie and about regional identity: the obvious importance of weather in agricultural life, providential intervention in human affairs, and the strength of Plains character in the face of natural disaster." While often amazing, typically describing striking images of delicate objects which remained untouched while walls and roofs were blown to splinters around them, these stories nevertheless remain realistic: they are, says Danielson, "informal credible accounts that describe the incredible." [74] Tall tales, on the other hand, leap gleefully over the line into full-blown incredibility. In the tall tale, the teller takes local geographical facts, plays with them, enhances them, fuzzes the boundary between reality and hyperbole, and produces outrageous deadpan comedy from the ground that he or she walks on every day. "Knowledge of the familiar, of the local environment," is thus the basis of the "whopper" according to folklorist Suzi Jones. "The whopper is usually a humorous exaggeration of some aspect of the local environment" which "must provide a ludicrous image which rests on truth" in order to succeed. A region's powerful winds cannot simply be described as violent and strong, that is, but must instead become an outrageously comic force. Jones elaborates: "For instance, in southeastern Oregon they tell about suspending a section of log chain from a pole to reckon the wind. When the section of chain is blowing straight out, they say it's a gentle breeze, but when the links of that chain start snapping off, they know a good wind is blowing. And the cows in that part of the country must stand on their hay to keep it from blowing away." [75] Tall tales such as these are legion in America's better-ventilated regions: "one hears," notes Barre Toelken, "that the sand is blown out from around prairie dog holes (the animals fall and break their necks), that car lights are blown off the road, wells are blown over into the neighbor's yard, and that a hen was seen laying the same egg five times."[76] Much of the humor and meaning of whoppers like these is lost on people who have never been to the place being joked about—says Jones, "the wind is a persistent reality in southeastern Oregon and so are cows, and this then is a humorous and regionally informed way of expressing the fact of the wind's persistence."[77] Only those who have been hit in the face a few times by a good Oregon wind, it seems, will fully understand the wry truth behind the impossible image of a heavy chain whipping and breaking in the wind like a motheaten pennant. While the wind may never actually be that strong, some days it certainly may feel like it.

At the same time, tall tales often concentrate not so much on the geographical configuration of a place as on the local emotional evaluation of that place. Insofar as they have commented on particular geographic locations, tall tales have tended to emerge and become popular in places marked by extremes of topography, of climate, and of fertility—places like southeastern Oregon, or like the trans-Appalachian frontier and the trans-Mississippi West in the nineteenth century, where stories of incredible prodigies of nature—massive game animals, outlandish geological features—arose and filtered back East into the channels of national popular humor. In its comic exaggeration, the tall tale expresses the excitement and exuberance, or masks with bravado the fear and apprehension, that life in such a challenging place inspires. Bethke comments on the continued popularity of the "big story" in the Adirondack foothills in this century: "The woods has an importance exaggerated beyond its mere presence as landscape. The Big Woods is a testing ground—big in its geographical expanse, the challenges it presents, and its role in shaping male experience. It is little wonder that woodsmen love to tell 'big stories' ('lies,' 'tall tales') about events in those Big Woods. Through hyperbole, the yarns transform recognizable situations and encounters into larger-than-life confrontations, ones commensurate with the Big Woods as a heroic plane of action." The emotions raised through facing the challenges of the woods environment are effectively vented through the ebullient fancy of the tall tale. At the same time, of course, the Adirondack tall tale drily alludes to the scale and scope of nature in the woods; as Bethke points out, "Big Woods events sometimes do take on implausible and fabulous qualities. The 'big story' genre merely capitalized on inherent potential."[78] Bethke includes a long string of tall tales told by his informant, Ham Ferry: tales about swarms of black flies so thick that he left a path through them when he walked around; about deer with antlers so big they had to walk through the woods backwards; about a massive pet angleworm that chased fish out of the water; and so on. The spirit and exaggerated content of these tales correspond to, and grow out of, the meaning of the woods as experienced by the men who live there.

Sometimes a prominent local character is elevated to folk-hero status at least in part because, in his mastery of the harsh conditions imposed by the local terrain, he crystallizes local geographical experience. On the surface, such lore concentrates on a human hero, but the local landscape nonetheless looms large over his shoulder, conditioning not only what he does but who he is. Outsiders may enjoy hearing and reading these tales, but they will not appreciate them in the same way as does the audience which shares the land in which the hero and his acts are rooted. This geographical commentary is certainly the impetus behind much of the hero-centered tall folk humor which grew up on the nineteenth-century frontier and was captured by and adapted to the popular almanacs of the day. When Davy Crockett, for instance, finds that the earth has become frozen on its axis one bitterly cold morning and gets it moving again through the judicious application of bear grease (freshly squeezed from a live bear captured expressly for the purpose) and a good swift kick,[79] he is doing more than engaging in stock tall-tale-hero hijinks for the entertainment of Eastern almanac-readers. Tales like these were popular on the frontier (leaving aside the reasons for their popularity in the nation as a whole) because they expressed in distilled and heightened form an appreciation of the harsh nature and brutal demands of the local, bitterly cold, bear-infested winters. Crockett, or the humbler local heroes about whom the stories were first told before they drifted into the powerful gravitational field of the better-known Crockett, was popular because his tall-tale experiences epitomized local geographical knowledge and experience and because he was able to surmount, in flamboyant and triumphant fashion, the conditions which geography imposed.

The master of geography as legendary hero is not merely a phenomenon of the previous century, found now only in old almanacs, archives, and folklore collections; in some places he remains a celebrated figure today. George Magoon, for example, the folk hero of Washington County, Maine, is popular in part for geographical reasons. Washington County has always been the home of hunters, hunters who don't much like the law telling them what and when they can and cannot hunt; and Magoon, a noted poacher, has become renowned for his exploits in confronting, outrunning, and outwitting game wardens and other meddling representatives of the state government who insist on quashing the local way of life. In addition to his central and heroic role in this tense cultural conflict, though, Magoon is also admired and celebrated for the deep knowledge and mastery of the woods of Washington County that he displays as he goes about his exploits. In a region where considerable geographical expertise has historically been a prerequisite for personal and economic survival, George Magoon is an example and an inspiration. Edward Ives discusses Magoon's starring role in the local battle of man versus nature: "He is incredibly tough, to begin with, being absolutely impervious to cold and snow—reveling in them, in fact—and certain it is that eastern Maine is a cold and snowy country. In addition he can lug a sackful of heavy bear traps for miles through the woods, outrun the best athletes they can put on his trail, take to the water like an otter, thrash his way through the worst thickets, leap blowdowns like a deer, and—perhaps most wonderful of all—always know where he is and where he will come out." Geographically speaking, in the stories told about him George Magoon emerges as a modern (if slightly more subdued and less omnipotent) Crockett. "To tell about George is—for that fleeting moment it takes the breath to pass—to assume his strength along with his spirit of denial," says Ives. "There is sustenance in that for ordinary men."[80]

As a genre, the tall tale is particularly well-suited to creating and reinforcing a sense of group identity, a sense which grows out of that shared intimate knowledge of the physical nature and experiential meaning of the local environs which fuels the popularity of a George Magoon. The tall tale is emphatically an in-group form of folklore: in telling a tale to a group of insiders, the teller knows that they will understand its exaggerations and respond to the emotional overtones of its wild humor because they share with him or her a lifetime of exciting or frustrating experience within the challenging local physical environment. That shared experience of place provides the kernel of meaning which the words and events of the tale uproariously illuminate; only locals will fully understand the story as anything more than an extended joke. The tale thus binds the group together through their shared knowledge of place and in the process excludes outsiders who do not understand the nature and meaning of the region; as Carolyn S. Brown points out, "As the narrator uses the group's peculiarities of experience, knowledge, and values to draw his listeners into the tale, he also reinforces group identity—sometimes by proudly flaunting the group's self-image. Tall tales about poor soil or rough weather inflate the hardiness of those who can cope with such troubles, and thereby imply the inferiority of those who need not."[81] The performance of the tall tale "usually occurs in the presence of naïve outsiders whose ignorance of the region renders them unable to distinguish the boundary between truth and exaggeration,"[82] and these outsiders, who do not fully understand the meaning of the tall tale, who do not quite see when the description of local conditions tips over into hyperbole or who realize too late that the line has been crossed, prove through their incomprehension that they do not belong to that place. Through reaffirming local place knowledge and through aggressively excluding outsiders, the tall tale is an effective and popular genre for asserting and celebrating a sense of place-based identity.

From an initial discussion of folk boundaries, we have wandered a long and circuitous route to end at the tall tale. I doubt that we have approached any boundaries of our own here: the sense of place clothes itself in too many guises to admit of any final circumscription. Our tour was by no means exhaustive, although it covered a lot of ground. It might at first seem difficult to hold together in our minds a carved chain and a tale of urban crime, to mention rationally in the same breath a woods ballad and a wooden boat, to reconcile the rambunctious image of George Magoon crashing through the forest with the calm quiet of a leisurely stroll through a comfortably known and bounded neighborhood. Some of the items of lore we have surveyed are primarily urban, some are rural; some are constructed of words, others sit quietly and wait to be talked about before their meanings can be released. All are linked, however, through being rooted in a common ground. They are genres of place. Together and apart, subtly or obstreperously, they offer thoughtful and heartfelt commentary on the geographical surfaces which the casual eye sweeps across. That eye takes in the visible landscape; the *mind's* eye, in concert with the hands and especially with the ears and tongue, lingers on the scene a while longer to take in the invisible landscape as well.

The Value of Place and the Motive for Stories

On Sunday, May 21, 1989, a ten-story, thirty-five-year-old public-housing apartment building in Providence was scheduled to be dynamited to the ground. That demolition ultimately failed—the building turned out to be stronger than expected, and demolition crews finally had to go after it with a wrecking ball—but several former residents turned out to watch, saddened that their old home was going to be destroyed. On the surface, the old tower didn't look like much—a drab, unprepossessing concrete pile, standing shabby and stark among a handful of other buildings just like it—but these former residents saw more than that surface. They viewed the doomed structure through a refracting haze of memory and association.

"I just see all the memories there," said Perina Brunetti, who had lived in the building from 1958 to 1965. "I met a lot of people there I still know. It was beautiful then. . . . It's going to seem funny coming down the street and not seeing it anymore. It's funny, huh?"[83] Brunetti's emotional attachment to the building is clear: in a newspaper photograph she is looking down tearfully, with a hand in front of her face, as the demolition attempt is made. To her, and to others like her, this familiar and expected landmark is inextricably associated with friends and family. Place enfolds relationships; relationships shape memory; memory sparks stories; stories cling to place, with such tenacity that the destruction of place threatens the entire structure—the fear is that stories will fly away unanchored, memory will dim, emotion will fade, identity will become tenuous if the geographical root is cut. The day before the building was slated to fall, Perina Brunetti had a friend take her picture in front of it. In a photograph, at least, place is permanent. Brunetti and the building are forever inextricably linked on film; the complex bond between person and place is noted down in shorthand on a glossy piece of paper, ready to awaken memory and words when called upon.

Other groups of displaced people have felt similar emotional distress and personal threat when their places have been destroyed, and they have responded energetically to keep place alive in memory and tradition so that its nature and meanings, so important to their lives, will not follow its physical presence into oblivion. Much of the Upper Cumberland region, for instance, has been flooded by reservoirs rising behind modern dams. William Lynwood Montell writes:

Although the dams have been beneficial to the region, there is no way to measure the intense grief and mental anguish of the unfortunate families who were forced from their homes. . . . [O]ne out of four persons in [Pickett] county was moved from land that had been handed down from one generation to the next since before Tennessee was a state. Willow Grove, a thriving Clay County town of three hundred residents which possessed its own grade and high schools through the 1930s, perished completely. Former residents gather annually in Celina for the Willow Grove Homecoming and talk about the old days. They vow orally and in local newspaper columns that their children and grandchildren will know about the Willow Grove of their memories.[84]

By now it should be clear that a place—any place—is much more than a chunk of geography. That geography is thickly layered with significance—the sense of place as revealed by folklore. While Perina Brunetti and the former residents of Willow Grove may mourn the loss in the world of a physical location, that loss is mitigated both by the sense of place which remains in their memories and their words and by their evident determination to keep those memories and words alive in whatever way they can. Stories remain even when places change radically or vanish; the sense of place can outlast place itself. The actual physical place may drown or be blown up, but the layers of the sense of place remain, like stacks of valuable china on a table after the magician has whisked the tablecloth away.

Sense of place endures all vicissitudes, then, sustaining identity, providing connections to a personal and collective past, offering an emotional center. It is a rooted and anchored locus of meaning and value. This may finally be why we develop a strong sense of place, why it is worth thinking and writing about place, why so much folklore adopts it as a theme either directly or obliquely: places, or our understanding of and attachment to vanished places, sometimes feel like all that is solid in a world of change, all that has undiminished value in a world of maddening flux. Philosopher of religion Gary Comstock writes of the difficulty today of living a life that does not contradict his religious beliefs, of being one of those who

drive alone in cars that waste unrenewable fuels, spray Pam on their pans releasing ozone-destroying chlorofluorocarbons, eat meals that waste calories by turning grains into meats, defecate in woefully inefficient toilets, neglect their children to secure their careers. Is it possible any more to be Christian without engaging in practical contradictions? I do not know. The only apparent answer for me is to try to separate myself—to one degree or another—from the institutions and arrangements that contradict our convictions. One way to figure out how to do this is to identify the real places—the little places—in which we actually live and move and have our being. Then, we can start clinging obstinately to the memories that hang on, and the hopes that spring up, in these specific crannies.[85]

Most of us, I think, have already identified these places in our own lives, already cling to the memories they shelter, already formulate their value in folklore. As Comstock suggests, when we feel morally buffeted, emotionally strained, cut loose from any source or center of value, sometimes the best thing we can do is dig down into place, think, start talking, and listen carefully to what we say. As Wallace Stevens began this chapter, so let him finish: we need place, ultimately, to make the slovenly wilderness surround us, to make a bewildering world no longer wild.

3 The Folklore of Place: The Coeur d'Alene Mining District, North Idaho

> *To do this well, to really come to an understanding
> of a specific American geography, requires not only time
> but a kind of local expertise, an intimacy with place few
> of us ever develop. There is no way around the former
> requirement: if you want to know you must take the
> time. It is not in books. A specific geographical under-
> standing, however, can be sought out and borrowed. It
> resides with men and women more or less sworn to a
> place, who abide there, who have a feel for the soil and
> history, for the turn of leaves and night sounds. Often
> they are glad to take the outlander in tow.*
>
> *These local geniuses of American landscape, in my
> experience, are people in whom geography thrives.
> They are the antithesis of geographical ignorance.
> Rarely known outside their own communities, they
> often seem, at the first encounter, unremarkable and
> anonymous . . . ; but they are nearly flawless in the
> respect they bear these places they love. Their knowl-
> edge is intimate rather than encyclopedic, human but
> not necessarily scholarly. It rings with the concrete de-
> tails of experience.*
>
> —BARRY LOPEZ, "The American Geographies"

> *You know, there's a lot of these personal experiences I've
> had and so forth, and I suppose they're entwined with
> the history of the area; I mean, you can't live in an
> area without being involved in it.*
>
> —LEONARD HEIKKILA

Region and Narrative

In late September of 1989, I traveled to the South Fork
of the Coeur d'Alene River in northern Idaho in search of Lopez's "local

geniuses of American landscape." The valley through which the river runs is a deep gash which winds sinuously through the Coeur d'Alene Mountains of the Idaho panhandle. Motorists traverse it on Interstate 90: descending from Lookout Pass on the Montana border, they drive west through a string of small cities and towns—Mullan, Wallace, Osburn, Kellogg, Smelterville, Pinehurst, Kingston, Cataldo—before climbing to Fourth of July Pass on the canyon's western end and continuing on to the city of Coeur d'Alene (fig. 9). The valley's sides are steep, its course serpentine; in places, its floor lies in deep shadow even in midafternoon, while its twistings and turnings rarely allow one to see very far to the east or west: inevitably, a mountain thrusts a shaggy shoulder in the way. Its narrowness is striking: in places it is only wide enough to accommodate the river, the highway, and a railroad track (fig. 10). It is bounded by mountains on the north and south; these mountains are penetrated at intervals by narrow gulches and canyons—Burke Canyon, Ninemile Canyon, Big Creek, Milo Gulch, Pine Creek—which are lined with working or defunct mines. Mining has always been the life blood of this valley: its mines are among the richest producers of silver, lead, and zinc in the country and have been the area's largest employers by far for over one hundred years. The landscape here is striking and dramatic, a tableau of hard-working settlements set against a rugged and roughhewn backdrop.

The people who live in the valley call it by several names. Having visited this area in the past, I had come to know it as the Silver Valley, and given the importance of silver mining in the region, I assumed that this was an old and traditional name. I found, however, that the name was actually coined only a few years ago. "The term Silver Valley here is fairly recent," explained retired Kellogg newspaper editor Wendell Brainard. "They call this the Silver Valley, and before it was always called the Coeur d'Alene mining district."[1] The Silver Valley name arose in response to economic depression in the mining industry in the early 1980s, as a means of polishing the area's image in hopes of attracting more visitors: "Since the hard times," noted Cataldo resident Alida Sverdsten, "when they've been promoting it as a tourist place, why, they've started calling it the Silver Valley and advertising it as that." The name has been self-consciously adopted in the area; it is not a natural outgrowth of local life. Some residents theorize that the name did not even originate with local people: geologist Don Long suggests that "the Chamber of Commerce, people out of Spokane and Coeur d'Alene or other people started it; and then, of course, the local chambers got to using the Silver Valley name." By now, though, many people in the area use the name as a matter of course, particularly those not involved in mining. Miners, however, still tend to refer to their place as "the mining district" or simply "the district." Many people also casually refer to the area as "the valley." Despite the fact that there is no uniform local name for the place, though, each of the terms which people use clearly implies an awareness of and belief in the region's distinctiveness, whether that distinctiveness lies in its topographical or economic features. Each local name implies a geographical area which is clearly set off from the surrounding world, which stands as a discrete unit in the minds of the people who live within it.

I chose to study this area in part because of its geographical distinctiveness. To my outlander's eye, the South Fork area stands clearly as a natural physiographical region, bounded on the north and south by mountain ridges and on the east and west by high mountain passes. It is a natural trench isolated in a thinly populated part of the country, a trench which it takes a good deal of travel and effort to climb out of. This was more true in past years than it is today—some of my informants told me that many area roads were not paved until the 1920s, that punctured tires and mired automobiles were commonplace, that a trip to nearby Coeur d'Alene was a major undertaking, and that a journey to Spokane required an overnight stay—but it still takes a lot of driving to reach the outside world, and it is not at all unusual for the passes to be closed by winter snows. I wanted to see how the valley's natural borders, self-contained geography, and distinctive physical appearance affected the sense of place of the people who live there.

I also wanted to show that landscapes and places do not have to be national centers of cultural attention or to have accreted a thick sediment of well-publicized history in order to be richly significant—that a complex, deeply felt sense of place can emerge whenever and wherever people settle on the land long enough to develop shared experiences and tell stories about those experiences. Tucked away in remote mountain valleys and hollows, toiling in obscurity in the thinly populated reaches of out-of-the-way regions like central Montana and northern Minnesota, America's mining districts exist on the outermost fringes of the national mind—and when they are thought about at all, they are usually contemplated with disdain. In his examination of the landscape of America's historic mining districts, Richard Francaviglia notes that "in comparison to greener or less industrialized places, . . . mining landscapes are viewed as industrial and exploitative," bleak panoramas of ravaged land,

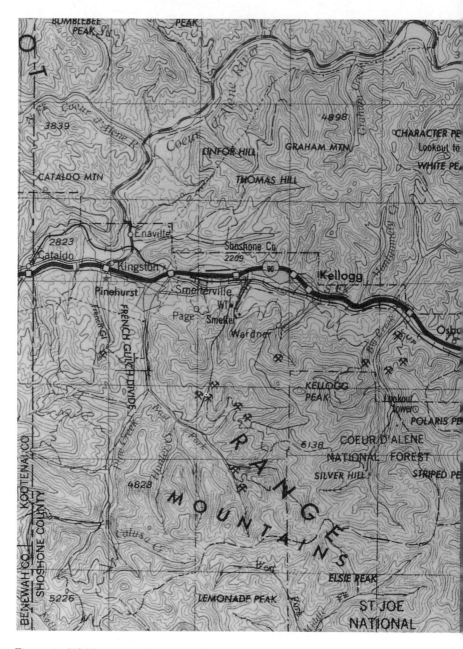

Figure 9. USGS topographic map of the area comprising the Coeur d'Alene mining district.

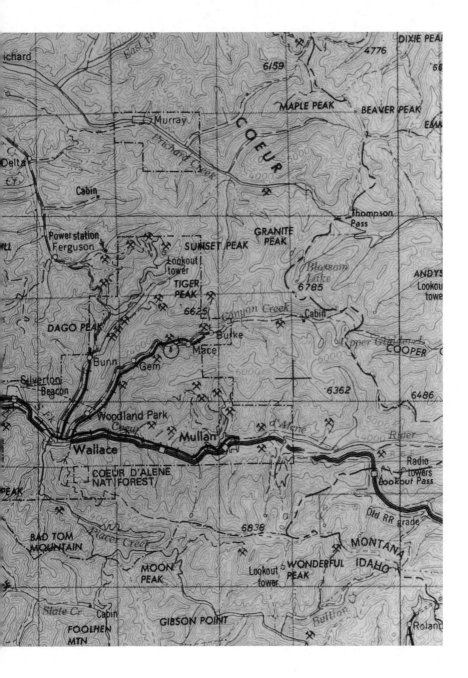

Figure 10. The valley floor between Mullan and Wallace. 1989 photograph by the author.

foul air, and murky water; thus, "many observers are likely to characterize mining country as a ruined, hellish wasteland." That is, if they observe mining country at all: in America, as Francaviglia observes, "mining seems to occupy marginal, often hidden locations."[2] In traveling to the Coeur d'Alene mining district, I hoped to explore and reveal

Figure 11. Murray as it appears today. 1989 photograph by the author.

the vibrant invisible landscape that overlies this little-known and unprepossessing part of the world and thus demonstrate that the marginal can (and should) be seen as meaningful—that the obscure backwater that the outside observer may view in a negative light can be a positive, nurturing place for the people who live there.

Moreover, the area's economy, and thus its history, has always depended overwhelmingly on mining and to a lesser extent on logging—on industries which extract the natural resources which the distinctive landscape of the valley provides. The human history of the South Fork region grows out of the physical exigencies of local geography to an extent rarely found elsewhere.[3] Mining in the area began in 1883 with the discovery of gold along Prichard Creek, a tributary of the adjacent North Fork of the Coeur d'Alene. A full-fledged gold rush ensued the following year: by the autumn of 1884, over ten thousand people lived in the Prichard Creek boom towns of Eagle and Murray. Eager miners quickly exhausted the placer gold fields along the North Fork, though, and after 1886 the population quickly drained from the North Fork mining camps: although some of the original buildings are still standing in Murray, only about sixty people now live there (fig. 11), and Eagle has vanished completely. By the time the gold fields were played out, however, many prospectors had already wandered over the ridge to the South Fork,

Figure 12. Cornwall, Idaho—one of the old mining settlements along Burke Canyon. 1989 photograph by the author.

staked claims, and begun working the valley's veins of rich galena ore. By the end of 1884, most of the claims that would become the region's most important mines—among them, the Sunshine, Tiger, Poorman, Hecla, Morning, Black Bear, Gem, and Frisco mines—had been located, and when prospector Noah Kellogg wandered up Milo Gulch in September of 1885 and discovered the vein that would be developed into the wealthy and successful Bunker Hill mine, he set off another "rush"— this time to the South Fork and its deposits of silver and lead. The valley's mines immediately began producing huge quantities of high-grade ore, and bustling towns soon sprang up around them. Large-scale logging began at about the same time, once the area had been opened by mining. By 1890, the Coeur d'Alene mining district, as it became known, was a vigorous center of social and economic activity. Mining has continued to dominate the area in the ensuing century. Some mines have bottomed out or fallen victim to economic circumstances—Burke Canyon, once a string of rich mines and lively towns, is now largely abandoned (fig. 12)—and the area as a whole has endured boom-and-bust cycles driven by the vicissitudes of metal prices, but the unremarkable everyday history of life in the valley has continued to be directed by the mines.

That history has not been entirely unremarkable, though; the area has seen dramatic and tragic events over the years, many of them centering on the mines. In the 1890s, unionized miners repeatedly clashed with management over wages and working conditions, sometimes with literally explosive results. In 1892, after shutting the mines down for several months in an effort to drive metal prices up, the district's mine owners reopened with a plan to cut the wages of shovelers and carmen, arguing that their jobs were not as skilled as those of drillers and blasters. Feeling that all underground jobs were equally hazardous and demanding, the miners refused to report back to work unless they were guaranteed that all underground wages would be equal. The owners responded by bringing in nonunion workers and armed guards, a move which quickly led to violent conflict with the local unions. On July 11, shooting broke out at the Frisco mine in Burke Canyon between nonunion miners and guards, who had barricaded themselves in mine buildings, and union men who occupied the surrounding hills. At the height of the shooting, the union miners dropped dynamite down the sluice of the Frisco's concentrating mill, blowing the building to pieces. Similar fighting erupted at the nearby Gem mine, and the nonunion miners surrendered at both places. With the whole area now under armed union control, over five hundred miners advanced to the Bunker Hill mine, a notorious anti-union stronghold, and threatened to blow up its mill unless all nonunion workers were let go; the owners felt they had little choice but to give in, and all nonunion miners left the district by the first available trains. The next day, however, Governor Norman Willey declared martial law, and fifteen hundred federal troops swept through the area, arresting six hundred union miners. Of these men, only seventeen were convicted of any crime—four of conspiracy, thirteen of violating a court injunction against interfering with nonunion miners—and they only served short terms in prison. Still, the power of the unions was temporarily broken, and mine owners were once again able to operate as they liked. The miners' setback was short-lived, however: the unions quickly regained strength and numbers, and their members had long memories.

Local miners had always resented the Bunker Hill because it was the only mine in the district that had never been unionized and because its owners consistently refused to pay the union wage to shovelers and carmen. It stood as a constant threat to organized labor in the district. In April of 1899, with the aid and support of the district's other union locals, miners at the Bunker Hill decided to move openly to form a union. The mine's owners agreed to pay the uniform underground wage but balked at recognizing the union and demanded that all members of the nascent organization quit their jobs. The new union men did so, but the owners' recalcitrance ultimately provoked the area's unions to violence once again. On April 29, all the unions in the district met and organized a mass movement of miners to the Bunker Hill mill. Members of the Burke union commandeered a train, loaded one of its cars with dynamite which they stole from the Frisco mine's powder house, and forced the engineer to take the train to the Bunker Hill, picking up other miners along the way. By the time the train reached the Bunker Hill, it carried nearly a thousand angry riders, many of them wearing masks and carrying guns. Once they arrived, the miners set fire to the company's offices and boarding house. They then unloaded the dynamite, placed it carefully in the mill, blew the building to kindling, got back on the train, and went home. This time, though, retribution was swift and thorough and ultimately destroyed the unions completely. Governor Frank Steunenberg immediately declared martial law, and federal troops arrested every miner who could not prove where he was on the day the mill was blown up, which amounted to most of the men in the district: of 1,148 area miners, only 199 had reported to work that day. The union miners were incarcerated in "bullpens"—makeshift stockades—in the embryonic city of Kellogg for up to four months. Only fourteen men were ultimately tried, and most of those on charges of interfering with a train that was carrying mail, but the long imprisonment seemed to sap the strength and spirit of the unions. Moreover, the district's mine owners instituted a blacklist which ensured that union men involved in the conflict would never be rehired, and set up a central hiring bureau (which operated until 1948) to assure them of a steady supply of workers sworn never to join a union. Labor relations in the district have thus remained calm for the bulk of the twentieth century. Still, because of their explosive violence and the depths of the passions which drove them, the "mining wars" of the 1890s stand out as high peaks in the history of the valley.

Such historical peaks are not limited to the activities of mines and miners. In 1890, for example, a fire destroyed almost the entire city of Wallace. Then, in the summer of 1910, a huge fire swept the Northwest, destroying millions of acres of forest in parts of three states and sending up smoke that was visible for hundreds of miles. The conflagration swept into Wallace on August 20, ultimately destroying the eastern third of the town. As the flames crested the ridge south of the city, women and children frantically boarded trains to be taken to the safety of Missoula and Spokane; all able-bodied men stayed behind to save as much of the city

as they could. Evidence of this fire remains in the landscape for those
who know how to interpret it. The hills surrounding Kellogg, denuded
by the flames, remain bare because fumes from the Bunker Hill smelter
prevented vegetation from growing back, while Pinehurst resident Marylinn Heikkila knows of places where charred survivors of the inferno still
stand: "Take the road over to Avery and you can still see some of the big
cedar trees which were burned out and part of it is still standing, from
the 1910 fire." For the most part, though, the mines have continued to
provide the high points in the texture of local history. On May 2, 1972,
ninety-one men died in an underground fire in the Sunshine mine. In
1981, in response to a precipitous decline in metal prices, the Bunker
Hill mine and smelter in Kellogg shut down. Bunker Hill was the biggest
employer in the district, and its closing threw over two thousand men
out of work—this in a valley whose population was not much more than
sixteen thousand. In its exceptional events as well as its mundane details, then, the history of the South Fork valley has been overwhelmingly
dominated by the mines. I predicted that this distinctive history would
have produced a large body of stories, narratives that would reveal the
meaning of the place for the people who live in it.

I did find stories in colorful profusion, but not necessarily the sorts
that I thought I would find. I thought certainly that I would find traditions
about the mining wars: such dramatic events, such elemental confrontations between worker and manager in an area still dominated by mining—confrontations which occurred in mines and towns which are still
standing—must, I thought, have left behind a thick residue of oral tradition. In fact, only one of my informants was able to pass on to me a
version of the events of the mining wars which had come down to him
orally; while other people knew of these battles and could even supply
me with details, they pointed out to me that they drew their knowledge
from books. Bob Anderson, a retired mining engineer for the Sunshine
Mining Company and a native of Wallace, told me that only old-timers
discussed the mining wars in his youth, and that he paid little attention:

No. No, those were history then, you know, in my time; I wasn't born
until '14, well, that was long gone. Oh, grownups, sure; grownups talked
about it amongst themselves, and there was a great deal of animosity all
their lives because of that. Because not only were the places blown up,
but then the troops were brought in, federal troops; state troops, and then
federal troops. And the union men were rounded up and put in what they
called bullpens, big stockades. Kept in there for some time, then some

of the men were tried and imprisoned; a few were imprisoned, not many. [. . .] But, you know, for people like me, growing up, not being born until '14, so not really paying any attention to history probably for another fifteen years; and then, history was a thing that then had to be drilled into most of us [chuckles]. Often you're not interested in history until you get out of school.

Mr. Anderson knew the events of those turbulent days, but he learned them by reading, not by listening. After our interview, he lent me a book so that I might read of that period in the district's history for myself.

When I asked one of his colleagues for any stories he might have heard about the early days in the region, however, I got a different response. Sunshine geologist Don Long had moved to Burke with his family in 1937, long after the days of labor violence; among the miners in the community, though, memory of the mining wars remained bitter and strong. Mr. Long recalls

stories that come from the Bunker Hill; that was before that time, you know, way back in the 1890s and early 1900s, that they had the union trouble in the district. . . . Yeah, they were always talking about the—that was a period of time in the district when there was a lot of strife, really, because the union was trying to get in; the people were trying to get unionized, and I'm sure there were abuses because of the companies' attitude towards the miners. The pay was low, and so they were trying to get the unions in. The companies didn't pay any attention to them until they started, really, a lot of trouble; that is, they actually went in and—it was around 1900, or the early 1900s, they went down and blew up the Bunker Hill mill, for instance. That's the big mill complex that's down at Kellogg. They put powder on some flatcars and pushed it into the mill and just blew the whole complex. And then, of course, the other miners up above, then, in the Frisco and some of the other mines up towards Burke, also all joined into that same effort, and they had a lot of problems with the miners, then, because they were very angry, and they blew the other mills and other buildings, and did a lot of damage to the mines and the mine complexes. Anyway, the federal troops were sent in at that time, [. . .] and that didn't set well with the miners at all. And they put all these guys in a big bullpen; they rounded up all the dissident [chuckles] miners that were causing this trouble, and put them in a bullpen in Kellogg, and that really made those guys mad. Well, finally that strife was taken care of and the unions did get into these mines.

Historically speaking, the story that Mr. Long tells is not entirely accurate. It conflates the events of 1892 and 1899, implying that "other mills and other buildings" were destroyed at the same time as the Bunker Hill mill, and ignores the fact that the unions were already powerful antagonists of management at the time of the violence, having unionized all mines but the Bunker Hill and carried out several successful and non-violent strikes before tensions erupted in war. Moreover, instead of getting the unions into the mines, the blowing up of the Bunker Hill mill ultimately destroyed them. What Mr. Long's narrative lacks in objective historical accuracy, however, it makes up in its concentration on meaning. By conflating the two battles into one, it suggests that they are but two episodes in the same ongoing confrontation and that their significance is essentially identical. By downplaying the unions' earlier strength and opting for a "happy ending," the narrative plays up the unions' heroism: their backs against the proverbial wall, the miners lashed out with righteous violence at the callous mine owners and achieved their goals. As Mr. Long tells it, this story summarizes (or did for the miners from whom he heard it) what must have been important elements of the self-image and group identity of miners in the Coeur d'Alenes, emphasizing as it does their pride, their independence, their feelings of solidarity and cohesion, and their tough, no-nonsense way of dealing with life. It reveals an image of a group whose identity was forged in the traumatic events of their place's history.

This tradition seems not to have been widely shared, however: it was limited at the time to a single occupational group and is now lost largely in the past. When other people in the region tell stories about the mining wars, they emphasize their personal perspective on those battles' dramatic events, sharing brief tales, passed down from older relatives, of how their family members were involved. Those days are alive with meaning today only insofar as they touched one's parents or uncles; otherwise, as Mr. Anderson says, they are just "history"—events which, according to books, happened in the valley but live today only on those books' pages and have no real relevance to the present or to the people who talk about them. Bill Noyen, a Smelterville grocer and onetime Shoshone County commissioner who has lived and worked in the valley since 1946, repeats one such narrative told to him by his father-in-law:

Hazel's dad, who farmed in the Palouse country, came into the—his folks came into the Palouse country around Potlatch in 18 . . . I think it was 1880, 1888, somewhere around in there. When he was a young man, when they had that blowup at the Bunker Hill, when they blew up the mill at the Bunker Hill, and they came down from Burke, I guess it was, and blew it up—I think it was about 1898, or somewhere around in there. So they had a bunch of strikebreakers come down, and Hazel's dad was offered a—he was short of work, and things were tough on the farm, and he heard that there was work up here in the Coeur d'Alenes, so he come up and he was one of the strikebreakers. He didn't last long! He didn't know what it was all about, and when he found out what it was about he got the heck out of here. But yeah, I can remember; he told about those days, you betcha. Darn right.

Bill Dunphy, who moved with his family to Burke at age five in 1915 and who worked in the Star mine for his entire career, similarly shares family traditions when asked for stories about the mining wars, fleshing out the historical events of that time with their effects on his male relatives:

[W]hen they had the big strikes and the troubles up there, they brought in the National Guard to keep the peace after the union miners had blown up the Frisco mill. And the story that I got from my cousin about my dad's brother, my uncle John—they brought all these National Guardsmen in by train, in boxcars, and nobody knew they were coming, and they just took them up the Burke Canyon and unloaded them, and they just swept the whole canyon and arrested everybody who had a union card. But of course somebody got onto it real quick and started putting the word out, and then of course the guys just headed for the hills and headed up the road and so on. Well, my aunt says that my uncle, he was not too well, but when he came along, why—when these guys were getting pretty close, why, he just ran home, and my aunt got a pillowcase and stuffed—she was baking bread, and she threw all the bread she was baking into that thing and whatever food they had, and up the hill they went! And the National Guardsmen, she says, were down plinking at them as they were going up the hill.

Mr. Dunphy's father was in Burke at the time and took to the hills in the same fashion as his uncle: "My dad was in town, but he was a six-foot-three-inch, athletic type of a Irishman, and he just took off [chuckles] walking, and they couldn't have caught him with a pack horse. He walked clear over to Thompson Falls, twenty-five or thirty miles over the hill, and grabbed a train and got in to Spokane and went back to Canada, where we'd come from [chuckles]." These family stories are thematically similar to Mr. Long's narrative, emphasizing in Mr. Dunphy's case the miner's independence and instinctive resistance to authority and in Mr. Noyen's story a sympathy with the cause of the unions, but instead of sketching the labor battles as a whole they concern themselves with those battles only as they impinge on individual lives. They reveal and share important themes that miners have extracted from their experience in their place, but the history of the place as constructed through such stories is more a matter of individual and not communal experience: the hills of Burke Canyon matter more because of the concrete image of Uncle John scrambling over them with a pillowcase full of bread than because of the larger picture of which that image is a part. The sense of place that these stories reveal, while its broad outlines may be held in common throughout the region, is accordingly much more experiential than it is learned and absorbed through tradition. The people of the valley have each evolved a variation on the regional sense of place through their individual experiences in the valley, through the personal perspective each has gained on the shared materials of life in the district; they have then shared that sense through the stories they have made out of the things they have done.

This emphasis on the experiential over the materials of received tradition, on encoding the sense of place in stories of one's own manufacture, holds true today as vigorously as ever. When Mr. Dunphy brings up the 1910 fire, he discusses it strictly as a historical fact, strictly in terms of numbers and magnitude—the sort of information that could be gotten out of a book: "Nineteen ten was the year of the big fire, too, you know, the one that burned the biggest burn in the history of the United States, except for one back someplace in Minnesota or somewhere where they have big logging; they had a big fire back there, too. It killed more people; it killed ninety people in the forest fire, or more; I really don't know for sure. But it went all the way from below Wallace clear over to . . . oh, it went over to Taft, Montana, and clear back into the St. Joe, and back on both sides, oh, it was a tremendous thing." He seems not to have heard any stories about this fire, no anecdotes with which to enliven his summary of events. There was another fire in the valley in 1923, however, one which looms much larger in his mind because he was there:

I was burned out. We had [several words drowned out by background noise] that was running the Dunphy Hotel, the boarding house, and we were doing well. God, I had everything a kid at that time would want—

sleds and baseball bats and all that. But another kid and I took off and went to Wallace to swim. Wallace had an open swimming pool at that time; there was none in Burke. They did build a big one later. But we rode horses down to Wallace seven miles, and swam for a couple, three hours, and came back. And when we got about a mile and a half below, they said, "Burke's on fire." And so we goosed the horses and rode them to Burke, but when we got there you couldn't go through at all. And so I was burned out. I had a pair of jeans, a denim shirt, and a pair of tennis shoes, and that's all in the world that I had. A kid that had Sunday-go-to-meeting suits and the whole thing; all burned. They didn't save them. Boy, when that went, it was—it was all clapboard houses, you know; dry cedar wouldn't burn any faster, big piles of it. And it just went right up that canyon like a storm, and just burned the whole thing, and then got to the mine and burned the mine. Men were down in the mine, too. And so they had to climb; some of them had to climb out three thousand feet up ladders to get out on the hillside up above Burke. Took a whole day to get everybody out of there; some of them were not in too good a shape to climb that far.

Unlike the 1910 fire, which happened before his time and is emphatically part of the lost past, this fire is intensely meaningful: Mr. Dunphy's narrative is enlivened by the sense of remembered excitement with which he tells it and by his personal sense of loss—this is not just a story of destruction but of how the fire affected the life of an individual boy. As he tells it, then, the story of the fire alludes to and awakens echoes of other memories of Mr. Dunphy's childhood in Burke, becoming not only a narrative of an important episode in a particular place but also a window onto the way one resident experienced that place, a look at how that event wove itself firmly into the fabric of his life in Burke. He does not stint the communal story of the fire—the threat to mines and miners, the destruction of Burke's distinctive ramshackle architecture—but he relegates that story to a secondary position, almost as an afterthought, behind his own understanding of the fire's meaning and the narrative form that that understanding takes.

Compare this with Bob Anderson's discussion of the 1910 fire. When asked if his parents, who lived in Wallace at the time of the fire, ever talked about it, he replied, "Yeah, my mother was put on the train, because my brother was born in 1910, so women and children first. The way it turned out, they didn't need to." They could have been spared the trouble because the fire "didn't burn out the whole town, let's put it that way; it only burned out half the town. It didn't burn out my granddad's house or my folks' house. Well, my folks weren't up on the hill at that time; it didn't burn out my granddad's house. His was not burned out in the fire of 1890, either. That was because he had his own waterworks, and other people put their furniture in his yard at that time, the 1890 fire. And it was about the only thing that was not burned in that fire, the fire of 1890." Mr. Anderson's parents and grandparents were there in 1890 and 1910, witnessing the destruction, avoiding the flames, relieved when their property was spared. His knowledge of the 1910 fire has more life, more depth, than does Mr. Dunphy's, because the fire had worked its way into Anderson family tradition while managing to avoid entering the tradition of the region as a whole. The fires which swept through Wallace have thus influenced and enlivened Mr. Anderson's understanding of the area's history and have shaped his appreciation of the physical face of Wallace as well: as he points out, "Most everything was replaced after that fire of 1890; in fact, they started two or three days later, making everything of brick. So Wallace was a very well-built city because of that; all the buildings downtown are brick." His grandparents' house, standing unscathed on the hill in 1890, remains in his mind as a sort of monument, the lone survivor of a local catastrophe; it stands out, along with his grandfather's wetting down his property with water from his waterworks, as an emblem of resilience and survival in the face of one of the place's periodic natural disasters. When Mr. Anderson contemplates Wallace today, then, family tradition enables him to see and understand the Wallace of 83 and 103 years ago as well and to incorporate them as living elements into his knowledge of the place.

In seeking out traditional narratives in the Coeur d'Alene mining district, then, I found very few stories which were held in common by large numbers of people—freefloating stories with no identifiable "author." Instead, while each illuminates in its own fashion a sense of place shared widely throughout the region, the stories I found tend to belong to more limited narrative traditions, within which narratives can usually be traced to some specific point of origin—to belong, that is, to the repertoires of individuals, of families, of specific occupational or recreational folk groups, of workers in a single mine or residents in a single town. My findings confirm those of William Lynwood Montell in the Upper Cumberland region of Kentucky and Tennessee, who found that "the one genre that is present above all others in the region is the oral historical narrative, in the form of both traditional stories and accounts of personal experiences. . . . The people there like a good story, and conditions and events within the region provided grist for narrators." The bulk of the oral traditional narratives that Montell found were second-hand reminiscences of past events, which he characterizes as the sort of stories you repeat from your grandmother when she tells you about something that she once did or witnessed—the stories that Bill Noyen and Bill Dunphy tell about the days of the mining wars, for example. Even more than these traditional narratives, though, Montell found that "people like to relate personal experience narratives about people and events within their own lifetimes. John I. Cummings of Clinton County, for example, admitted having knowledge of guerillas such as Champ Ferguson and Dave Beaty and of divided loyalties during the Civil War, but he brushed aside questions about them in order to talk about his personal logging and rafting experiences on the Wolf River."[4] So, too, do residents of the Coeur d'Alene mining district tend to dismiss the events of the distant and communal past—"history," as Mr. Anderson put it—in favor of telling stories of life in a mining town or narratives of hunting adventures in the surrounding woods, revealing the region's sense of place primarily as they themselves have experienced it, claiming and delineating their niche in the larger structure of local history and experience—a niche that is private in its particulars but shared in its broad outlines by the other people in the region who participate in the region's distinctive ways of life. Here, as in the Upper Cumberland, the personal narrative is the preferred storytelling genre.

Folklorist Sandra Dolby Stahl disagrees with Montell's implication that personal narratives are strictly idiosyncratic and not traditional, that "accounts of personal experiences" should be kept in a separate category from "traditional stories." True, she defines the personal narrative as "a prose narrative relating a personal experience; it is usually told in the first person, and its content is nontraditional." Still, the meanings which such narratives reveal are highly traditional: "Strictly speaking, personal narratives are not folklore, but they are a primary means by which a special kind of folklore is expressed." Stahl notes that in memorates, first-person narratives concerning supernatural beliefs, these beliefs "play a significant generative role"—

that is, the belief usually precedes the experience and thus influences the storyteller's perception of the incident that forms the core of the memorate. If the personal narrative is the secular equivalent of the memorate, then the secular beliefs represented by such academic terms as *values*, *attitudes*, or Alan Dundes's term *folk ideas* would form the core of these secular narratives. I would identify such "nonverbalized folklore" as the folkloric content of personal narratives. The folklore, in this case, is neither verbal nor material, nor even customary in the sense of *recognized* behavior patterns. Instead it is the nonverbalized, tacit knowledge that collectively makes up an individual's world view.[5]

The sense of place is part of this body of nonverbalized folklore, shaping the way people understand their experiences in the world and the way they talk about those experiences, generating personal narratives out of the stuff of daily living. People pull events out of the seamless flow of memory and experience and shape them into discrete units and coherent narratives because they understand those events, however hazily, to illustrate certain important aspects of their sense of place—the emotions they feel about their environs, their sense of identity as it is shaped by their interactions with the landscape, the important themes and conflicts they sense in the ongoing history of their place, and so on. In telling stories about their lives in the valley, then, the people who live along the South Fork of the Coeur d'Alene approach and illuminate from a variety of perspectives the local sense of place; without that sense, those stories would not have taken the shape they have in the first place.

To the full-blown narrative genres described by Montell and Stahl, I would add a third genre of sorts: what I think of as the "compressed narrative" or "narrative allusion." By this I mean a brief reference to a remembered event, to a narrative heard in the past, or to a typical or habitual pattern of past behavior, which evidently has a skeletal narrative structure in the speaker's memory but which has not yet grown into a full narrative performance or about which the narrative details have been forgotten. Bob Anderson's accounts of his family's difficulties in the 1890 and 1910 fires are such compressed narratives: while he has obviously at some time been told the story of his family's experiences in the fires, those stories are now compressed in his mind so that just the essence of activity and meaning remains. For another example, consider Bill Dunphy's account of his favorite way of spending childhood afternoons: "I had a buddy, and we'd sit and maybe at noon we'd decide, well, nothing to do, let's hike to the top of that mountain. We'd take off and go up there and pick huckleberries, of course, during huckleberry season. We'd sell them for a dollar a gallon; you get fifteen dollars for a gallon now. But if you got a dollar, it was a big piece of change." This account is a distillation of countless afternoons spent roaming the hills above Burke Canyon, any one of which could probably at one time have provided the matter for an unremarkable but richly and lovingly detailed narrative. Because time brings a loss of detail, though, and because those afternoons were individually undramatic but collectively memorable, they have melded together into a brief summary of a fondly recalled pattern of behavior in the landscape. Compressed narratives such as these are the essence of stories, the kernels or raw materials out of which fuller narratives could be (or once were) constructed—"proto-folklore," if you will, and a primary component of one's personal sense of place. (We cannot be expected, after all, to have turned every memorable experience in a place into a story.) They join the fully developed personal narrative and secondhand traditional story as the primary oral genres which I found along the South Fork; together they grow out of and reveal the local sense of place.

Landscape and Life—The Woods

It is difficult to travel far in the South Fork valley without encountering the physical presence of mining in the region. As you drive east on Interstate 90 and crest the small rise between Kingston and Pinehurst, the scarred brown hills which surround Smelterville and Kellogg begin to rise before you, their rutted and eroded surfaces providing mute evidence of their years of exposure to corrosive smelter smoke (fig. 13). In the years since the Bunker Hill smelter shut down, scrubby plants have begun to reclaim these hills, and for several years the mine sponsored a tree-planting program; on the occasion of a recent high-school reunion, Marylinn Heikkila was amused by "the people who came back who hadn't been in Kellogg for twenty, thirty years: 'It's so *green!*' Just astounded." Despite this veneer of new growth, however, the underlying ravages are still apparent. In Kellogg itself, the massive smokestacks of the Bunker Hill smelter dominate the sky, and heaps of black tailings sit piled beside the highway. If you turn up one of the side canyons, you soon find either working mines still hauling ore out of the earth or else abandoned mining camps, once teeming with activity but now sitting silent, their mine buildings slowly collapsing or else vanished altogether (fig. 14). Over the entire human landscape loom mountains and thick evergreen forests; kept at a distance in the more industrialized parts of the valley, these forests are rapidly reclaiming the abandoned mine sites. Despite over one hundred years of mining in the district, the wilderness is never far away. Even today, people occasionally see elk on the hillsides above the streets of Wallace, and bears wander down into people's yards in years when huckleberries are scarce.

Figure 13. The view from the hill between Kingston and Pinehurst, with the bare hills around Kellogg in the background. 1989 photograph by the author.

Figure 14. Disused mine workings in Burke. 1989 photograph by the author.

The towns in the valley are humble and unpretentious, standing physically close to the wilderness which surrounds them and spiritually close to the mines which are their raison d'être. They grew as the mines grew, providing places for miners, managers, merchants, and professional people to live and socialize. Not all the towns in the area grew the same way, though: while Wallace, the district's commercial center and the seat of Shoshone County, filled with prosperous-looking brick buildings and impressive homes on tree-lined streets, a mining town like Kellogg sprang up in a more haphazard and roughhewn way, befitting the style and way of life of the miners who lived there. Maidell Clemets captures something of the feel and physical character of Kellogg in his discussion of "twilight houses":

> All the houses in Kellogg were built in the twilight hours. Just like an old fellow told me, and I know what he's talking about: he worked in the Osburn area, he said, in '37; the Depression was on, and him and his wife lived in a little tent. And the fellows told him, they said, if you go up on Big Creek and cut some trees up there, you can get enough to make a log house. He went up there, he said, and he cut the logs, and then the forestry department said he couldn't have them, because they had to be used only on the mining property. If he was going to build a cabin with them in Osburn, it wasn't going to be used on the mining property. So he went back and told his friend; his friend says, tell the forestry department to go to hell; take them. So he said he took them and he built the cabin. Said he got a job, and wasn't making very much; he was working four days a week. So, he said, about that time a baby would show up, and they had to have more room in the cabin, so he built a room onto the cabin, but he didn't get any raise in wages or anything like that. The only place that money could come from, he said, was out of the sugar bowl. And he'd buy a few boards each payday and nail them on. That's the way most of the houses were built in Kellogg; that's twilight houses.

Bill Dunphy recalls growing up among rickety houses like these, which had been jammed into the narrow canyon at Burke—houses that "were built so close together, I don't even know how they got the—they had to nail the walls up, then raise them"; houses that burned like tinder in the 1923 fire. Such houses, while shabby and ramshackle in construction, also illustrate the miner's resilience, his resourcefulness, and, in the case of the cabin in Osburn built from poached logs, his instinctive, independent-minded willingness to stubbornly defend his own welfare in the face of a disapproving authority—the same qualities which motivated and sustained him in his strikes in the 1890s. They stand for both the character and the socioeconomic condition of the men who built them. The district's towns have filled with more modern homes since 1937—Mr. Clemets himself lived in a modern ranch-style house on an attractively landscaped street in Osburn—but they still closely mirror the welfare and conditions of the mines: they have suffered through recent hard times in the mining industry, and many homes and businesses in the area now stand empty. And, like the mines whose character they reflect, they nestle close to the circumambient wilderness: dead-end streets in Smelterville run straight into the side of a mountain; Wallace is jammed so tightly into its canyon that a new stretch of freeway had to be built high up on a hillside. One of the joys of growing up in Wallace, Bob Anderson recalls, was the ability it offered to "just go out the back door and go up Placer Creek and, in fifteen minutes, be fishing."

This juxtaposition of people and nature—the physical presence of mines and mining in the area, the towns which depend on and reflect them, the whole human landscape closely surrounded by wilderness— shapes the way that people think about the region. It is difficult for them to contemplate one of these environments separate from the other, and most area residents are comfortable in both milieux: many local men and women go hunting every year, and even the most town-bound people enjoy heading into the surrounding mountains for an afternoon to pick huckleberries. In this regard they resemble the fishermen whom folklorist Timothy Cochrane studied on Isle Royale in Lake Superior: "Outside the borders of gardens and houses, fishermen lived in two disparate landscapes: one littered with rusty and moldy equipment—half a machinaw boat turned up to make an outhouse—and the other unmistakably wild. Fishermen felt comfortable in both the 'functional landscape' of gutted equipment, net reels, and narrow foot paths and the wild-lands inhabited by moose, beaver, and wolves." In its character both as wilderness and as a working landscape, Cochrane found that "the island was a dynamic and experiential part of fishermen's lives" and that "place as experienced and reformulated in expressive culture is a critical contextual factor in fishermen's folklore forms."[6] Such is also the case along the South Fork of the Coeur d'Alene: residents' simultaneous understanding of their place as wilderness and as industrial settlement, an understanding pieced together from their daily experience with the landscape, deeply influences the sorts of stories they tell about it.

This understanding gains immediate expression in the mental image that local people have formed of their physical environs. When asked

Figure 15. The Sunshine mine complex. 1989 photograph by the author.

what image or picture would best summarize the region for her, for instance, Hazel Noyen supplies a shorthand description both of the landscape and of the ways of life it supports: "Miners and mines and trees
and loggers—that's about it." Don Long sketches a tableau of mine and
mountains as his emblematic picture of the area; it is just this juxtaposition, in fact, which makes the district visually distinctive for him compared to other regions he has visited: "Well, you know, this is a very
beautiful area, actually; most mining areas aren't like this. The aerial
pictures, say, of the Sunshine complex up here; that's a nice picture.
And people do come up and take pictures just of the Sunshine; oh, it's
a very old plant, and I think plants like Sunshine's present one sort
of—it's what people really picture as a mining site" (fig. 15). He points
out that other mining areas in the West are scarred by open pits, like
the famous copper mine at Butte, Montana. "But my idea is more like
the Coeur d'Alene district mines, where you got the head frames, and the
mills right by the head frames. [. . .] Plus the nice mountains. It is a
beautiful area, really, as compared with other areas that mining has been
done in."

Not everyone, however, thinks first of mining when contemplating the
region. Like Mr. Long, Bob Anderson has worked in mining all his adult
life. When asked to describe an emblematic image which summarizes

the area for him, though, his mind's eye wanders away from head frames and mills toward Striped Peak near Wallace.

> And it's not a peaked peak; it's a flat peak [chuckles], called Striped Peak because of the formation on it: the various formations outcropping gave it the appearance of stripes. I picked that one because that's where we used to hike; we'd hike up to Striped Peak and talk with the Forest Service lookout up there, and either come back or come down a different direction: going past there and come down to Lost Lake, and down past the Galena mine and down to the highway and walk back to Wallace, a mile and a half. So all in all it was probably a fifteen-mile hike. But that's also where we used to always go huckleberrying when I was young. So to me, that's a picture of the whole district, even though it's not typical; the peak itself is not typical.

The compressed narrative which Striped Peak evokes in Mr. Anderson's mind reveals that, to him, the district's character lies primarily in its distinctive topography and in the recreational opportunities which that topography supports—it is a rugged, visually compelling landscape which invites hiking and huckleberrying. Insofar as Striped Peak is a picture of the district, it is a picture which calls forth in Mr. Anderson a host of associated memories of times spent simply enjoying himself in the wilderness. The mines, while inevitably present in the landscape (he has to mentally walk by the Galena on his way back to town), are evidently not the most important or deeply felt part of his lifelong experience of the place.

When people think, and then talk, about the valley, their understanding of it tends to follow one of the two paths suggested by this dual mental image—an image born both of the nature of the physical landscape, which they see every day and whose components they have quietly internalized, and of the qualities of the working landscape in which they earn their livings and pursue their recreations. When they talk about the region, that is, their narratives tend to cluster around one of two themes, two modes of conceptualizing place: the woods and the mining camp. Both the woods and the camp are understood as places to work—specifically to work at extracting the resources which occur naturally as part of the local geography through felling trees and mining ore—and as places that support certain kinds of recreation: hunting and huckleberrying on the one hand, the close-knit and sometimes rambunctious socializing of a mining community on the other. While the woods and the mining camp may seem on the surface to be quite different places, the stories that people tell about what has happened in them reveal common themes, common understandings of and feelings toward the area, common ways in which the local geography has worked its way into the identities of the storytellers—common elements, that is, of a shared local sense of place.

Of all the people whom I met and interviewed in Idaho, Alida Sverdsten was the best storyteller. Born in Plains, Montana, she came to the valley in 1926 when she met and married her husband, Ed, a logger. The family has owned and operated a logging company since that time; Mrs. Sverdsten's sons all went into the business, and in earlier years Mrs. Sverdsten herself occasionally helped out in the woods when she was needed. She was also an enthusiastic hunter and huckleberry picker when she was younger and has gone as far afield as India in search of game: a museum in Coeur d'Alene houses the stuffed and mounted skin of a man-eating tiger that she bagged on that trip, along with mounted bears and elk that she and her husband brought down closer to home. Ed Sverdsten died in 1977, and Mrs. Sverdsten now lives alone in Cataldo, in a house whose front picture-window commands a striking view of mountains and forests—"And sometimes [we'll] have an afternoon or evening thunderstorm, and the evening sun'll come out and there'll be a rainbow across to over there; it's awful pretty. That window's hard to beat."

As an avid hunter and sometime logger, Mrs. Sverdsten has spent much of her life in the woods. She has seen many changes in her time: when her husband started his logging business, for instance, loggers relied on horses to skid logs out of the woods and load them onto trucks, and they lived for months at a time in roughhewn camps in the woods, whereas now they use powerful, sophisticated mechanical equipment and drive to work every day from modern homes. The early days of logging in America produced an extensive and well-documented body of folklore, much of it having to do, in folklorist Roger Mitchell's words, with "the outstanding bosses, the strong men, the pranksters, the cautionary tales of accidents that could have been avoided, the ability to withstand adversity,"[7] and Mrs. Sverdsten shows at least a passing awareness of these traditions, gleaned at second hand from her husband and his employees. Ed Sverdsten sometimes got well back into the wilderness in the days of horse-logging.

And so they had camps along there, a long ways from habitation. And the men that worked in those camps were mostly single men, the type of men that they told stories about, like, when they died they'd find the buttons from six suits of underwear in their shoes or something like that! [Laughs.] Because they didn't have the facilities to keep themselves clean even if they'd wanted to. And they were the kind of men that went out in the fall when everything closed down and maybe blew their whole summer's earnings in one big drunk or something like that.

Compressed narratives like these reveal the logger's understanding of the woods as a realm set apart from the world most people live in, a place defined in part by its distinctively crude and boisterous style of life, and provide humorous commentary on the harsh conditions of life in the camps. Mrs. Sverdsten similarly sees the woods as a special, distinctive place, but the particulars of her understanding differ from those of the male loggers of earlier years—after alluding to those loggers' narrative traditions, she admits that "I don't have stories like that to tell." She sees the wilderness not as a traditionally severe, demanding, masculine arena of brute strength and physical deprivation, but according to the themes and lessons suggested by the life she has lived among its trees and mountains; like miners discussing the mining wars of the 1890s, her understanding is experiential, not received.

Mrs. Sverdsten has spent so much time in the woods and knows the north Idaho wilderness so extensively that is it difficult for her to choose any one local landmark or scene as a favorite regional emblem. I asked her if she could pick out and describe such an image; her answer reveals much about her impressions and memories of the area, and her feelings toward it.

I'd have to say no, I guess, because it's all pretty and it's all dear to me, and all that, and I don't know, I don't have any real favorite places that I'd want to go, you know, if I could get around any more like I used to. Because all of it was—I used to hunt a lot when I was younger, and I used to go out hunting by myself and hunted all these mountains over here in various directions. But I had to give that up when my husband died, because—well, I was getting pretty old, but I even had to give up going out scouting for huckleberries by myself, because after he was gone nobody knew where I was, you see. Now, when he was here, even though he was going to work, I'd always tell him what I was going to do that day and where I was going to go. And I used to do a lot of driving around by myself looking for huckleberry patches; then on Saturday and Sunday, why, we'd get some of the family together and go to where we knew the berries were. But after he died I thought I'd continue doing that, and it wasn't the same, because I'd go up and be driving around looking for huckleberries and I'd think to myself, now, if I get to gawking at huckleberry patches and roll the car over the bank and not be able to get out of it again, nobody would know where I was. So that kind of ended my trips.

The reason she cannot pick out any one prominent mental image or landmark is that the entire area blends together in her mind as a field for hunting and huckleberrying—it is *all* her favorite place. Like Bob Anderson talking about boyhood days spent roaming around Striped Peak, she alludes fondly to her habitual patterns of behavior in the landscape. This recreational behavior is central to her definition of the place: a question about the local geography makes her think, evidently as a matter of course, about the particular uses she has made of that geography. This definition, though, is now confined largely to the past and to memory: in the course of her reminiscence, Mrs. Sverdsten admits that age no longer allows her to hunt elk and "scout" for huckleberries, and her discussion takes on a nostalgic, regretful tone. Contact with the woods was important to her, and she has evidently based part of her sense of identity on her wilderness activities: when she pictures the landscape she pictures herself in it, with gun in hand or with eyes peeled for berries, as though that is where she naturally belongs. Through her stories she keeps this integration of self and landscape alive in words. Her extensive repertoire of personal narratives centers largely on work and recreation in the woods, keeping her in close imaginative contact with a beloved landscape, one which is "dear" to her but which she can no longer visit in person.

Mrs. Sverdsten is well known in the Cataldo area for her colorful hunting and working exploits. Marylinn Heikkila was glad to hear that I had talked to her, asking, "Now did Mrs. Sverdsten tell you that she used to drive logging trucks? [. . .] That was one of the first things I heard about her." She had indeed told me about that part of her life: she sometimes drove "cross-haul teams," teams of horses which lifted logs onto trucks, and later occasionally operated the mechanical "jammers" that replaced horses in that function.

And I even hauled a few loads of logs myself, and I remember one time, my husband had to take off and go to Spokane or Portland on business, and a job was being finished up that next day, and the roads were icy, and one of the truck drivers broke his arm cranking his car. Now you're too young to remember that, but in the old days we had to crank cars by hand, and if they kicked and broke your arm, that happened quite frequently; and I got word—I guess his wife come over or something and told me about it, so I took his truck out that day and hauled two or three loads, and the roads were icy, and chains had to be put on and taken off, and I—oh, I'm kind of a legend in a way about that sort of thing because that was—I didn't do *much* of that sort of thing, just when somebody was hurt or couldn't come on the job or something.

Despite her self-deprecation, Mrs. Sverdsten's feat is noteworthy for several reasons and provides ample reason for her becoming "a legend . . . about that sort of thing," a worthy and meaningful topic of discussion in the community. The north Idaho wilderness is rugged, its logging roads are rough, and its winters are harsh, making the removal of its resources a difficult and dangerous task. Wrestling a logging truck through this demanding landscape was hazardous and challenging under the best of conditions, and a layer of ice only made things worse; as Mrs. Sverdsten continues, "those roads were icy, and my brother was on the crew, on the loading crew up in the woods, and after I took off with the last load, he, my brother and this other man come down of a ways behind me. And that other man, he said, 'We'll find that truck piled up on just any curve now.'" The fact that she successfully met the challenge posed by the local geography, that she arrived safely at the other end of the road having completed a task that others did not expect her to finish, accordingly lends her a subtle aura of strength and accomplishment which she accepts with amused humility.

In addition to proving her great skill with a logging truck—a valued and admired talent in this part of the country—this little narrative provides insight into the way that Mrs. Sverdsten interprets the local geography. On the one hand, the land is generous and bounteous, amply providing riches for people to take. The life of the entire area is based on such interaction with the earth: loggers and miners are "very much the same," she told me at another point in our interview, because "they both do real hard work with natural resources" and have abundantly harvested those resources for years. On the other hand, the landscape does not always give up its riches lightly, but resists and frustrates man's economic pursuits through its rugged severity. Defeating these geographical obstacles is a necessary condition of success in the region. By successfully overcoming this resistance, then, Mrs. Sverdsten becomes a small-scale local hero, her mastery of geographical conditions proving her fitness as a resident of the place. This interpretation of place will recur repeatedly in Mrs. Sverdsten's stories of her life in the valley.

Not everyone successfully overcomes the resistance thrown up by the landscape. "All logging is dangerous," Mrs. Sverdsten observes. "There's lots of accidents in logging. No matter how careful the men are, there's things that happen out in the woods that are sort of unpredictable." One of her sons died in a helicopter crash while inspecting a future logging job from the air, and she knows of other men who have died when limbs and dead branches have been knocked from neighboring trees by falling timber.

> And sometimes big limbs get knocked out of other trees that are brushed by a falling tree and they'll fly through the air quite a ways and get the sawyer where he thinks he's in a safe place. I had a brother killed like that in the woods; he was a sawyer, and a very experienced one too, a good sawyer. And he and his partner—they were out on the coast in big timber, that wasn't here—and all week long, they looked at that tree; they knew it was dangerous. I can't remember now why they knew it was dangerous, but they thought about it all week. It killed him [voice choking up a little]. They waited 'til the last thing on Friday night to fall that tree.

Like loggers elsewhere who sing "The Jam on Gerry's Rock," Mrs. Sverdsten sees the woods as a dangerous place—and not only dangerous but capricious and malevolent, acting with almost conscious intent. She speaks as though the tree were a murderer: "It killed him." The tree seems to have known exactly what it was doing; despite her brother's caution, despite his decision to avoid it until the last minute, the tree waited patiently and struck down its victim with seeming inevitability. Once this "dangerous" tree made up its mind, the story suggests, her brother was fated to die. Mrs. Sverdsten's implicit characterization of the tree, and her emotional pause at the moment of death, reveal that to her the woods—on the coast where her brother died, in Idaho where, as she notes, "we've had men killed on our job like that, under similar circumstances"—are not just an inert resource to be exploited or a particularly troubling component of a generally difficult landscape but a living force, an active participant in a local drama of economic survival. The events of her life have shown her that the woods are both a generous partner and a treacherous antagonist in local life, and as such her emotional response to them is both appropriate and inevitable.

Working in the woods has also provided Mrs. Sverdsten with an arena for working out her sense of identity—not only as a resident of a region in which mastery of geographical conditions is valued but also as a woman. One of the reasons that the man who followed her logging truck down the icy road expected her to crash, in addition to the slick surface, was that she was female: "He says, 'No woman can drive a truck on roads like this.'" She reports that she encountered resistance to her logging work, that "a lot of the men didn't like it. They thought that anything a woman did was taking a job away from a man—you know, that women should stay home." Only men, it seems, were expected to work extensively in the landscape, a way of life which was evidently central to their sense of self; the woods belonged to the men, they felt, and the home belonged to the women. Rather than accept and adapt to conventional notions of female identity, and the geographical limits implied by that identity, Mrs. Sverdsten openly challenged those notions, forging a new identity which even today she reveals and proudly proclaims through her mastery of the physical conditions of her place as recounted in her stories. Her logging-truck narrative shows her challenging, confronting, and reworking assumptions about who she is through her activities in the landscape, through the confident way she crosses the boundaries of gender posted invisibly yet emphatically on that landscape: just as much as the men, she is a logger, someone at home in whatever conditions the woods confront her with. She is "kind of a legend," then, not only because of her mastery of local geographical conditions but because her very presence among those conditions was unusual for a woman and was widely recognized as such. This sense of self as worked out through her experiences in the woods remains a source of pride for her and is a strong and recurring motif in her stories.

Lumber is not the only source of bounty in the north Idaho woods. The mountain forests are home to deer, elk, bear, and wild huckleberries, resources which figure largely in local patterns of recreation: as has been mentioned, many people enjoy driving deep into the mountains to pick huckleberries and use the berries extensively in foods, preserves, and homemade wine. Many people hunt as well, setting off annually to track down the wild animals which inhabit the region's forests. In addition to providing sport and food, these animals and fruits carry important symbolic meanings in the local mind. Often residents of an area will informally nominate one of the indigenous flora or fauna as a sort of regional emblem, feeling that it encapsulates something of the nature and character of the region and discussing that character in their stories about it. The Isle Royale fishermen whom Timothy Cochrane studied, for instance, adopted the moose as their island's emblem, feeling that moose "were more common on Isle Royale than on the mainland, and so represented a unique island resource. . . . Fishermen saw moose as symbols of their conception of Isle Royale as unusual, wild, and separate from mainland life."[8] In the same way, many residents of the valley think of elk, bear, and huckleberries as standing for the distinctive qualities of their place. By far the largest part of Mrs. Sverdsten's repertoire of personal narratives, for instance, is devoted to tales of her recreational experiences in search of game and huckleberries, tales which incorporate many of the motifs seen in her logging narratives: the temptations and frustrations offered by the local environment, her competence as a master of local geographical conditions and the important role this mastery plays in her sense of identity, the way she has imbued the landscape with the emotions incident to the life she has lived within it, her intimate knowledge of the physical details of her place. These stories grow directly out of those physical details, recounting Mrs. Sverdsten's confrontations with the forms of life supported by the local landscape, seeking the meaning that inheres there, reflecting a style of living which has responded and adapted to the distinctive congeries of recreational opportunities that this bit of earth offers. Mrs. Sverdsten's recreational narratives are rooted deeply in her experience of the local geography—and, as they concern activities in which many other local residents engage as well, they help reveal an understanding of the woods that is widely shared in the valley as a whole.

Hunting and huckleberrying are closely related to mining and logging, the other ways of life that the region supports, in that all are attempts to harvest the resources that the land offers. As the sad story of Mrs. Sverdsten's brother indicates, however, the land does not give up its riches easily but instead holds off its exploiters with one hand after proffering its wealth with the other: the trees are abundant and easy to find, but the work is highly dangerous. Hunting and huckleberrying offer additional frustrations in that every such expedition is a gamble: it is often difficult to find animals or fruit-bearing bushes, and even then success is not guaranteed once you get them in your sights. Unlike logging, unsuccessful forays into the woods rarely end in tragedy. Mrs. Sverdsten tells one humorous narrative of a recent huckleberrying expedition, one in which the humble huckleberry emerges as a symbol of the simultaneous attractiveness and treachery that characterizes the local landscape for the people who work and play in it. She prefaces her story by explaining that "huckleberries are not easy to find around here. You find a good patch one year and you go back there the next and there isn't anything there. Huckleberries are kind of notional." By describing them as "notional," Mrs. Sverdsten endows the berries with personality and devious mental abilities: they are crafty and unpredictable, taking it into their heads to appear only when and where they want to. Like the tree that killed her brother, albeit in a much less threatening way, they are capricious antagonists in a local way of life. In their "notionality," in their fleeting, will-o'-the-wisp manner, huckleberries encapsulate the nature of the local relationship with and understanding of the land, as Mrs. Sverdsten's ensuing narrative drama of people against nature makes clear.

The expedition began just like any other huckleberrying trip, except with a rare guarantee of success: despite their notorious notionality, this time the berries had been tracked to their lair. Although she can no longer get around in the woods as well as she used to, Mrs. Sverdsten decided to make the effort:

Well, then, I'm really too old to be going out in a huckleberry patch, and I've got a sister-in-law who is about as helpless as I am out in the woods, and my son Terry took us huckleberrying a year ago. He had been over on a business trip into western Montana, and he had a four-wheel-drive pickup, and he come over an abandoned road that he knew about, up over the Idaho-Montana divide, to see if he could see any huckleberries along the way. And he run into a very fine patch—not a big patch, but the ground wasn't too steep, he thought Dorothy and I could manage it. And so he stopped, and he showed us the berries—he had a gallon bucket with him, and he picked a gallon bucket full in a little over an hour, and he showed them to us on the way home, and then the following day he took us up there. And it was about seventy miles from here, but we had to go back about twenty miles on that abandoned road that he'd come over. And we just got within about a mile of the huckleberry patch, he ran over an unknown sharp object and ruined two tires on the same side—front and the back tire. We only had one spare, so he had to walk out for help, it was twenty miles back on an abandoned road. But we didn't know whether anybody'd come over it that way, you know. So he had to leave Dorothy and me stranded, we were stranded for about six and a half hours, right on top of the Idaho-Montana divide. And we weren't able to walk down to that patch and pick, and he didn't want to walk twenty miles back over that abandoned road, so he cut right down off of the high mountain, down to the Shoshone Creek road, which is a mighty long ways; there are pretty high mountains there. It took him three and a half hours to make the trip from the top of the mountain down to the road down at the bottom. And then he had to walk a ways before a car come along, because that road wasn't too much traveled. But he was lucky: that car was a deputy sheriff, he was cruising around on his beat, and he took Terry to the nearest phone, which was several miles away, and waited until he was sure that he had got help at home. You see, we weren't sure that any of his sons would be home on Sunday afternoon. But he was lucky. The deputy sheriff stayed with him, and he appreciated that [chuckles]. So the son got a spare tire and wheel—he had an extra one for his own pickup, and it was the same make of pickup, but it wasn't the same year; it was an older pickup than what my son had up in the woods. And they made that trip up there, and the wheel wouldn't fit. Now that was the same kind of pickup—a Dodge and all that—and the same weight classification and all, but they have to make them a little different every year, so you can't interchange parts, you know [laughs]. So the four of us had to ride back, and they had to go back the next day with the proper wheel—cost a hundred and twelve dollars apiece for each of those ruined tires. We didn't get to the huckleberry patch.

Like the Sirens of mythology, the huckleberries lure Mrs. Sverdsten and company to destruction on the rocks. Lush and easily accessible, they tempt their pursuers deep into the wilderness, only to strand them there: what must have been a sharp rock in the abandoned dirt road punctures two tires, leaving the would-be berry pickers stranded in the woods with the berries tantalizingly out of reach. Both aspects of Mrs. Sverdsten's perception of the environment are present here: the rich resources which wait to be collected and used by humans, the lurking danger which frustrates the pursuers of those riches before they reach their goal. The elaborate and maddening process of trying to fix the truck—the vehicle which brought the party into the woods, the means by which the berries' antagonist approaches them—suggests in its extremity a sort of punishment, a cruel penance they must perform for their temerity and presumption. It is as if the berry pickers were, through their stranding, being shown just how out of place they were in that environment that they came so casually to exploit—that the land, through the agency of berries and the "unknown sharp object," wanted to teach someone a lesson. Happily, no one was hurt, and the story is essentially comic—Mrs. Sverdsten reports that her sister-in-law excitedly told the story to everyone she knew and that "she thought that was great. She didn't complain." Still, the story serves as a vivid dramatization of the local tension between people and their place, as well as a reminder that it is not always people that get the upper hand.

Other local residents tell similar comic stories of the frustrations they have encountered in their pursuit of the resources which the land makes available. It is evidently a common experience for people to be offered tantalizing glimpses of the region's recreational wealth, only to have those riches mysteriously withdrawn at the last minute—an experience which, given the strong urge that they feel to re-create it in narrative, seems to capture something central in the way that the valley's people think and feel about their local environment. Helen Bondurant recalls a memorable fishing experience that she and her retired miner husband, Bill, had one day just over Lookout Pass on the St. Regis River in Montana:

> Yeah, we used to go fishing. He'd be on day shift, and he'd get off about 3:30, four o'clock, and I'd have the hamper fixed and put it in the car, and I'd meet him up there in the parking lot. We'd take off right for Montana, and spend an evening fishing. [. . .] I'll never forget this one time we went over there. And I never fished; I never cared to fish. I'm a very impatient person; if I put a line out there, I want something on the end of it. And I hadn't even got the fire started; I was just kind of messing around there, trying to get the camp going. And he went down the stream, and it didn't seem like he was gone fifteen, twenty minutes, and he came back, and he was plodding along, looking all down, and I says, "What happened?" He says, [in a downcast voice] "I got my limit" [laughs]. And he just [caught fish] just as fast as he put that thing down. So we *really* hurried up, and cooked them up, and he went back, and he never got another bite! [Laughs.]

Fish, it seems, are just as notional as huckleberries. In part, this narrative emphasizes the huge quantities of trout that are waiting to be caught in local streams: they eagerly and cooperatively impale themselves on hooks as soon as they see them. This bounty vanishes, however, as soon as Mr. Bondurant turns his back; when he returns to the river there is not a fish to be found. Fishing streams, then, are of a piece with the woods through which they run in the capricious face that they present to the people who come to them for recreation. At the same time, a central point of the story is that the Bondurants were deservedly thwarted in an attempt to cheat: having caught their limit of trout, they promptly ate all the evidence and tried to catch more but found to their surprise that they could not. In her laughter Mrs. Bondurant recognizes the justice of this frustration: legally they were not allowed to catch more fish, so it was only right that the fish should avoid the hook. The story underscores the tenuous, balanced relationship that the region's people have with their place—the sense comes through in their narratives that the land calmly yet firmly ensures that its visitors remain circumspect and slightly off-balance, humbling them periodically lest they become too proud, too greedy, too casual in carrying away the land's resources. The wilderness guards its treasures carefully, doling them out only as it sees fit.

By far the largest group of Mrs. Sverdsten's personal narratives consists of what she herself recognizes as a favorite subgenre, her "hunting stories"—as she told me, "I got lots of good hunting stories." These stories center on striking, dramatic, or humorous experiences she has had while hunting in the woods, events which stand out and are crafted into stories because they reveal important themes in her interpretation of her environment and in her sense of identity. Taken together, the stories chronicle the development of a hunter: starting out as a tentative beginner who is not quite comfortable in the woods, Mrs. Sverdsten becomes a skilled woods veteran whose mastery of her environment is complete and who confidently overcomes any obstacle the wilderness throws at her, no matter how threatening. In the course of her development, she confounds the expectations of the men who hunt with her, creating her own identity through triumphant confrontations with the natural environment at play just as she did at work. Although often delivered with humorous self-deprecation, Mrs. Sverdsten's hunting stories collectively sketch a portrait of someone who knows her place intimately, who respects it as a worthy adversary, who accepts its challenges, and who, in a part of the country where geography dominates life and where knowledge and control of that geography are valued, consistently demonstrates her resourcefulness and competence. In a valley where personal and communal identity are shaped through interaction with the physical conditions imposed by geographical circumstance—with veins of ore running deep into the mountains, with stands of timber on remote hillsides, with the flora and fauna native to the region—the Mrs. Sverdsten of the hunting stories stands as an exemplar.

In stories of her early hunting experiences, Mrs. Sverdsten portrays herself as an apprentice of sorts, setting challenges for herself, learning the ways of the wilderness, proving her worthiness in the woods. Her story about learning to hunt bears recounts a deliberate effort to overcome wilderness fears, to vanquish self-doubts and the doubts of others, and to establish herself as a competent and confident hunter.

> My family just laughed their heads off when I said I was going to go bear hunting, because they knew I was scared of bears [laughs]. When we'd go to a park or something like that and see bears pretty close, you know, why, I always showed my fear of bears. But when I'd be getting ready for elk season, I always hiked a lot out in the woods, but I didn't carry a weapon, and never worried about bears. I know they usually run if they hear you coming. The only thing to be afraid about is if you get around a mother with her cubs. And one year—the bear season was open, you see, when elk season and deer season were closed, and I said, "I'm going to carry my gun with me when I go on my hikes and hunt for bear." Oh, the family, they laughed, but they didn't laugh so much when I got a bear! [Laughs.] It was a funny psychological effect that that had on me—when I started carrying my gun, immediately every squirrel that threw a pine cone out of a tree made my hair stand up on end; I just knew it was a bear. Kind of scared me! [Laughs.] But I got several bears.

Before she sets out hunting, Mrs. Sverdsten's knowledge of the woods is balanced with a lurking fear of the things that the woods contain: she is aware, as part of her body of wilderness knowledge, that bears pose little danger to hikers, but there is still a small but insistent part of her that is afraid of them. By deciding to carry a gun with her and fire at any bears that she sees, she makes a deliberate effort to reconcile these disparate feelings toward bears and the wilderness, to dispel her fears and, as a result, face the woods with unalloyed confidence. The effort is traumatic at first—knowing that she is expecting herself to shoot at any bears she sees intensifies her fears to the point that she jumps nervously at the smallest noises—but she suppresses her dread, shoots a bear, and, a true hunter now, goes on to shoot several more in her lifetime; her tenderfoot fears are banished, her confidence and competence in the woods are now complete. And by impressing her skeptical family and silencing their doubts, she establishes her identity as a hunter, a woods expert, in their eyes as well; hers is a public and not just a private identity, one that she comes to share with other hunters in the region.

It was not easy for her to establish this identity, however—both because she was a neophyte and because she was a woman trying to prove her competence in what had always been seen as primarily a male activity. Her story of her first elk demonstrates these difficulties: despite her having brought the elk down herself, and despite its being a museum-quality mount, the circumstances under which she shot it conspired to cast her abilities into doubt. This kill was not yet the "masterpiece" that would end her apprenticeship.

> But my first elk was something, and that's in the museum, too. I shot an elk, and I fired signal shots and my husband started coming back, and he was some distance off, and heard me and come down where I was butchering the elk. And I had cut its throat, and I had it opened up and was doing a pretty good job butchering it when he got there, and before he got to it he said, "Well, look at that!" Forest service telephone wire wrapped back and forth [around its antlers]. That animal had been caught in Forest Service telephone wire and had broken loose. Now, they sometimes find skeletons where they didn't break loose. But this one broke loose, and it was remarkable how it went back and forth and back and forth in figure eights, before he wore it out, I guess; metal fatigue set in and the metal crystallized. That was my first elk and it was worthy of the museum, too. It wasn't a big set of horns, but . . . Well, all my men friends and all my family, which were all menfolks—my husband and three sons—they said, "Well, of course you could kill an elk when it was tied up!" [Laughs.] But I killed a few more. Fortunately for me I didn't kill as many as the men in the family did, so they could feel a little superior toward me [laughs].

This episode was clearly important in her development as a hunter: as she modestly puts it, she moved on and in later seasons "killed a few more." Moreover, anyone who can calmly begin to field-dress an elk moments after killing it and before help arrives must have a fairly high level of woods competence to begin with. But two facts combine to cheapen her achievement in the eyes of the men who hear about it: the elk had its antlers entangled in wire, and she is a woman. That the elk was mobile despite its encumbrance—it had not starved to death like so many of its unfortunate fellows—seems not to matter to her critics, or at least not to get in the way of their fun: they resist the idea of a successful woman hunter, and the fact of the telephone wire enables them conveniently to explain her achievement away. Mrs. Sverdsten has demonstrated that she is an equal in their field, that she is a skilled and able hunter, but she will have to prove herself under more difficult and challenging circumstances before men will accept this valuation of her.

Eventually she does so, amply proving her woods competence and talent as a hunter—although, as she notes with amusement at the end of the story, male resistance to the very idea was so ingrained, and male egos so large and easily bruised, that it did not do to flaunt her abilities. At the same time, though, her laughter implies that she may well have been able to had she wanted to, but the strain on family harmony would have been too great: while men may recognize her self-proclaimed identity and geographical mastery only grudgingly, she, at least, is secure in her sense of who she is, and observes and accommodates the discomfort and insecurity of those around her with amused tolerance. Her husband had been among those who doubted her woods competence, but just as the circumstances surrounding her first elk called her abilities into question, the circumstances surrounding a later hunt completely silenced all criticism:

And when you shot an animal, then the work began—a lot of work, getting it butchered and the meat taken care of and everything. My husband kept saying to me, "One of these days when you're hunting by yourself"—because I always hunted by myself; I couldn't keep up with the men. They might have been off a distance, but I didn't hunt with them, right with them. And lots of times I went out by myself. He says, "One of these days you're going to kill a big elk that you can't butcher, and then what are you going to do?" Well, it happened. I shot an elk and it fell on a steep hillside with one leg under the, or was it three legs? I can't remember how many legs it had under the windfall, and one or two legs over the windfall. It wasn't a big windfall, maybe a foot through. And that made it awful hard to get to the entrails, laying like that. And its belly was downhill, too. If it had been uphill, then I could have done different, but of course it had to be the other way because it fell down the hill, you see. I fired signal shots; this time, I was hunting with three men, my husband and two other men. We were making a long drive, we had left camp and we made a long drive, the younger men went toward the top of the mountain, and my husband medium, and I was the one that took the lower part of the mountain. Well, they were there—quite a distance apart, but they were there. And I fired two shots quick; that was our signal. And my husband heard it, but he was deaf and wore a hearing aid and he couldn't locate sound good. And so he didn't hear me the first time, and I shot several times. And I didn't want to shoot all my shells away, and finally I decided I had to do something with that elk. And the windfall was about a foot off of the ground. And I was able to reach under and split down the flank, and then I went around to the upper side of the rib cage and opened the diaphragm between the ribs and reached in and cut the diaphragm in there. And the entrails rolled out underneath the windfall and rolled down the hill, and that was the easiest [rest of sentence lost in laughter]. Well, of course I still didn't have it skinned or anything, but getting the entrails out, that's the important thing. Then, of course, I had to get the skin off so it could cool. But before I started that I picked up my rifle and fired twice more, and my husband answered. I told him which way to come, but there was a little draw between us, and when he went down into that draw, suddenly he couldn't hear me any more, so he figured he was going in the wrong direction. He had to go back where he could hear me before. And I'd keep telling him. Finally, I had to take my hatchet and blaze a trail, because it was thick brush and I wanted to be able to find my elk again. And I had to blaze a trail over to where I could get him and bring him back to where that was. And after he saw what I had done there, he never said again, "What are you going to do if you kill an elk you can't butcher?" [Laughs.]

Despite being unable to "keep up with the men" all the time, Mrs. Sverdsten proves herself amply able to meet any exigency that the woods throw at her, conveniently answering the one question that her husband had always had about her abilities. If he is the "master" whose approval she needs to end her apprenticeship, she gains it here. Moreover, she demonstrates skilled woodcraft in other aspects of the story as well, marking a trail through the forest and finding her husband when he is unable to locate her signal shots. In this story, Mrs. Sverdsten confronts the local landscape in its characteristic two-faced form, as it tempts her with readily available game yet frustrates her by attempting to put her kill out of her reach. By outsmarting the wilderness at its favorite trick, then, she declares her mastery over the conditions of local geography in the way that matters most in the region: she is not just a successful hunter, she is a successful North Idaho hunter, meeting and solving the geographical paradox that characterizes the North Idaho environment in the minds of the people who live there. This story culminates her account, and her perception, of her development as a hunter: in response to my asking what the hunting in the area had been like for her, she told her three stories in an uninterrupted sequence, recounting her growing competence and confidence as well as the increasing respect and acceptance that she won among other hunters. By the time she finished this last story, she had successfully and entertainingly completed a portrait of herself as a full-fledged hunter whose knowledge and mastery of her place are complete.

Despite this demonstrated mastery, however, she remains aware that her woods competence and her identity as a hunter remain publicly in doubt, that many people are prepared and eager to discount her abilities simply because she is a woman; her sense of herself as a hunter, and not primarily as a *female* hunter, remains strong, and she continues to chafe under the criticisms of those who would put her in a separate category because of her gender. She tells a comic anecdote of an encounter with a game warden which not only encapsulates traditional attitudes toward female hunters but also reveals one way in which women's hunting abilities were reflexively dismissed out of hand and their supposed ineptitude taken advantage of by men:

> Women hunters, they got a better reputation now, but back when most of this happened, twenty to forty years ago, everybody took it for granted that if a woman had her tag on an elk or anything, well, the menfolks in the party got it for her, you know, and of course that did happen in a lot of cases. But I sure surprised one of the—we went through a check station, and the deputy game warden, when he was checking our tags, we were short one elk. I was the only woman in the party, and my tag was the one that was not used. "Well," he said, "that's really a switch." He says, "Usually [laughs] the women get their elk first."

Apparently it had been common practice at one time for the women in a hunting party to surrender their tags to the men so that the men could shoot more than one elk, with the women not in fact "getting their elk" at all; since they were unlikely to shoot anything anyway, the thinking went, why waste the tags? By holding on to her tag, by sticking to her determination to get her own elk, Mrs. Sverdsten confounded the expectations and contradicted the experience of the game warden. She followed this story immediately with a secondhand narrative about another woman in a similar situation, a woman who acts out the frustration that Mrs. Sverdsten felt when teased by skeptical and patronizing men:

> And of course, quite a while prior to that we heard a story—now it could be a lie, but I don't know, with the attitudes it might not be—a woman come out with her elk in her party and the deputy game warden kidded her a little bit, whether she really got it herself or not. And she dared him to hang his watch out on a post a hundred yards away, and he did, and she smashed it for him! [Laughs.] Turned out she was an inspector for the Winchester Repeating Arms company, firing guns to make sure they shot straight when they left the factory. Now I don't know whether

that was so or not, but after hearing that story I always hoped that some-body would ask me whether I got my own elk or not. I was going to dare him to put his watch up.

This unnamed woman emerges as a sort of hero for Mrs. Sverdsten, an admired and exemplary figure: confident and competent, she has great skill as a sharpshooter and as a hunter and is not afraid to emphatically prove it when faced by male doubts and pressures. Through her ac-tions, she embodies both Mrs. Sverdsten's sense of her own abilities and her anger at having those abilities doubted. Since she has repeatedly demonstrated her hunting talents, since she has confronted the land-scape and met its terms on the same footing that male hunters have, Mrs. Sverdsten still thinks it unfair that she should not always have been accepted at the same valuation that men were.

And the conditions that the landscape imposes are often harsh and threatening. Just as loggers stand in constant danger of being killed by falling limbs, hunters must take extreme care against getting disoriented or becoming separated from the hunting party; if they do get lost, a long cold night and the effects of exposure await them. Moreover, when hunt-ing and wounding wild animals, there is always a chance that the ani-mals may decide to hunt and wound the hunter instead. Mrs. Sverdsten has faced many such dangers during her time in the woods but has al-ways emerged triumphantly. Once a faulty rifle imperiled her life:

> I killed a bear one time a long ways from the car, and incidentally it was the only bear hunt that had an element of danger in it. I had just had my rifle to the gunsmith for something, and I shot this bear and wounded him, and he went a ways; I tried to reload my rifle, and I couldn't get a cartridge out of the magazine. So I had to fish in my pocket and get a shell and put it in the breech, and then I put a fatal shot in the bear. The gunsmith had put something in upside-down, and that's why the car-tridges in the magazine wouldn't come into the—but the bear didn't come toward me; it was wounded, but didn't come toward me.

By great good fortune the bear decided to run instead of attack. In part, it seems, the secret of success in the woods lies in being lucky: she is lucky that the wounded bear did not press its temporary advantage, and she admits that, in the case of the elk that collapsed on the fallen tree, "It was just luck that it fell on that windfall. It was bad luck that it fell on the windfall, but it was good luck that the windfall was a foot off the ground." Luck in the woods is a recurrent motif in Mrs. Sverdsten's hunting stories, to the extent that it sometimes seems as though her life is charmed in some way, that she receives a special exemption from misfortune in recognition of her talent and fitness as a hunter. With good-natured humility, she tells of a poorly placed shot that ends up killing its target after all:

> Well, in case I've been bragging myself up as a good marksman, I shot a deer one time that—it was a pretty good shot in a way: it was running, and it was across the draw from me quite a ways away, probably three or four hundred yards, and I knew I had to lead it, so I did lead it. And the deer fell, just like that, and never kicked or anything. And I thought, "I'm really a pretty good shot!" And when I got over there, I had hit that deer at the base of the tail, and evidently—my husband said, "Why, that was no fatal shot," but it did hit the spine at the base of the tail. And it didn't spoil an ounce of meat, and it killed the deer dead; it never went even a jump or two. But I wasn't as good a shot as I thought I was.

Anyone who can bring down a deer by nicking it at the base of the spine is clearly one of the woods elite, someone who is no longer held to the standards of accuracy expected from ordinary hunters. While Mrs. Sverdsten means this story to deflect attention away from her impressive skills, she in fact achieves the opposite effect: few people could come anywhere near hitting any part of a running deer at that distance, and so the story reveals, while it attempts to obscure, just how extraordinarily good and masterful a hunter she is—she really did get off "a pretty good shot in a way." While Mrs. Sverdsten may appear lucky in her stories, then, that luck is in part an outgrowth of her finely honed hunting abilities: only after performing impressive feats of marksmanship and woodcraft is she in a position for "luck" to work its effects at all.

Not all of her scrapes in the woods, however, have been resolved by the timely intervention of good fortune. In other situations in which her life has been threatened, Mrs. Sverdsten reveals, she has had to rely on her well-developed and finely tuned knowledge of the physical qualities and details of the local environment in order to escape unharmed. She recalls one occasion when she got lost and almost was forced to spend the night in the woods:

> [M]y two oldest sons and my husband went back to Cleveland to drive trucks out instead of buying them from the local dealer. And I wanted to go deer hunting locally, up on Copper Mountain, and I told my son, who was home and who was going to high school, that I was going hunting up

on Copper Mountain, and I would be back pretty late, along toward dark, because that's when game comes out and moves around lots of times, late. And that was the only time in my life I ever carried a compass. And I thought I'd learn how to use a compass. And when I got ready to come home I went down the wrong ridge, because there were parallel ridges and I got on the wrong one, but even though it didn't look quite right to me the compass said I was going exactly in the right direction, toward the car. So I kept on going, until I come to something that I *knew* was not—I was on the wrong ridge. Well, I wasn't lost, in that I could hear the big trucks on the freeway a couple of miles away, so I had my directions straight, but I knew that I had to go back and get on that other ridge. And I knew I couldn't make it to the car before dark, but I figured I'd have to make a campfire and wait all night or 'til somebody come after me. But I would walk as far back to the car as I could before dark, and as I was walking I felt in my pocket for my matches which I *always* carried, and my pocket was empty. And I think it got pulled out with a handkerchief as I pulled it out. Because I always carried that. And I was wearing women's clothes that didn't have deep pockets; not as deep as men's pockets in their clothes. So I figured I would have to walk around a tree all night to keep warm. Well, when it got dark I kept going, but I unloaded my rifle and I used it for a cane; I swung it forward so that I wouldn't—I had to keep moving to keep warm, you see. So I moved very slowly, and sometimes around a windfall it was kind of hard to get around, but at least it was keeping me active, and I could hear a truck now and then so . . . Well, my son come home from school and he was scared to death, and he got the neighbors out, a couple of them, and they come up there and they fired a couple of shots to see if I'd answer. And I didn't answer. I didn't think anybody was hunting for *me*. I thought that somebody else was lost on the mountain because earlier in the evening, before it got dark, I had seen the glow of a campfire off down the ridge quite a ways, and I had heard a signal shot or two from down there. So I figured that the party was separated down there. And I kept on going, and the search party come on down that direction, and they fired several times before I finally put a shell in my gun and shot [laughs]. Well, you have heard, I know, that some people, when they get lost, they panic or they do crazy things. And that, I can see—now that was certainly a crazy thing, because when they got down there, I told them—"Didn't you hear? Why didn't you fire a single shot sooner?" "Well, I thought you were hunting for somebody else!" [Laughs.] Well, one of my friends, a neighbor, said, "Well, don't you think a search party would be glad if they found somebody that they weren't looking for that was lost?" [Laughs.] I hadn't thought about that; I thought they'd be mad—I actually thought they'd be aggravated that somebody had answered who wasn't who they were looking for.

The story sets up an elemental confrontation between the local geography and a person who has consistently demonstrated her knowledge of and control over that geography; it is a test of everything that Mrs. Sverdsten knows about her place. The narrative demonstrates in sobering fashion that the woods always harbor the power to defeat and harm those who work and play in them, that they command respect and discourage complacency; echoes of the unknown sharp object that guards the huckleberry patch, of the tree limb that killed Mrs. Sverdsten's brother, of the windfall that threatens to rob her of her trophy, of the dangerously wounded bear, all lie behind this story. Significantly, Mrs. Sverdsten allows her attention to be drawn from her accumulated experiential knowledge of the landscape and focused instead on her compass, and it is this distraction that gets her in trouble in the first place: she obediently walks in the direction that the compass indicates, even though the ridge she was on "didn't look quite right to me." Only when she encounters incontrovertible proof that she is on the wrong ridge does she revert to the finely shaded sense of direction and location that she has developed through years of hunting, relying on her woods competence to return her to safety. She turns her full attention to her wilderness adversary: she orients herself by picking up the familiar sound of the highway, and, despite losing her matches, develops a strategy to survive the night. In fact, she does not even seem to consider herself truly lost or in grave danger: although she says that her decision not to respond to the search party's signal shots was a "crazy thing" done under the stress of the moment, anyone less comfortable in the woods than she was would undoubtedly have listened anxiously for, and responded gratefully to, any sign of aid. Alone in the woods at night without even a book of matches to push away the cold and darkness, she keeps her head and defeats the wilderness. This is a story of competence in the woods that, in its magnitude and seriousness, far outstrips any of her most impressive hunting stories.

In the nature and magnitude of her geographical exploits as recounted in her stories, Mrs. Sverdsten seems at least distantly related to folk heroes in other times and places, like Davy Crockett on the nineteenth-century frontier and George Magoon in the forests of Maine. These men gained renown because of their complete mastery of the local environment, and stories about them elevated that mastery to superhuman or near-superhuman levels. While her woods narratives are a personal tradition, and the actions they describe are well within the realm of the humanly possible, nonetheless Mrs. Sverdsten resembles these legendary figures in the complete and indomitable control that she exercises over her region's terrain, as well as in concentrating in one character the distinctive geographical experience of a region's people. It is not surprising, then, that stories of her experiences in the landscape sometimes amaze through the magnitude of the efforts they describe, or that she should be able to transfer her geographical mastery to landscapes that she has never seen before.

Well, I got lost another time. I crossed a mountain ridge; and this was in strange country. Up there where I just told about, I knew that country, how those ridges laid; I'd hunted up there many times. But over in an area where I wasn't familiar, I crossed a ridge, and when I thought I was heading back toward camp I was going down the mountain in the other direction. And it was not a sunny day, so I couldn't tell my directions by the sun, and it was quite timbered, so I couldn't see out to get my bearings; it was *very* timbered—I couldn't see the mountains, really. Well, I walked down until I thought I was about close to camp. And I come out to where I could see. Got out of the forest where I could see, and I knew then I was on the wrong side of the mountain. And I come out at a campsite; that was how I could see out: this campsite was in a clearing. And there was a ladder leaning against a tree; evidently they had hung game up high so that bears couldn't get it or something like that. And I thought that was the funniest-looking thing to see out in the woods, to see that homemade ladder. But I turned around, and when I got back to camp—I didn't think I'd make it home that night, but I thought if I got up to the top where I could at least fire signal shots or build a fire that they could see or something. And, you know, the adrenaline got to pumping and I made it to the top in record time, and when I got down that evening all the rest of the party were in camp: three men. But one of the packers had stopped by to see if they had any game and needed them to come in and pack it out with horses. And they were all sitting there visiting; they hadn't missed me yet because it wasn't time for me to get supper yet [chuckles]. And they asked me what I'd been doing, and I said I went down the wrong side of the mountain and had a long hike getting home. And nobody paid much attention until I said, "I come out at a campsite where there was a ladder leaning against a tree." And that woke the packer up. He said, "Why, that camp's eight miles from here." And quite a high mountain in between—quite a high ridge. So that could have turned out pretty bad.

Not being in her own place, away from the area where (compasses aside) she knows "how those ridges laid," she understandably becomes disoriented. Knowing how to orient herself in the outdoors, though, she immediately realizes her mistake and sets out in the right direction, arriving safely at camp before she is even missed; her geographical competence evidently extends to any wooded, mountainous terrain. The magnitude of her task becomes clear when she describes her journey: she has hiked sixteen miles over steep, rugged terrain and arrived back before nightfall. This feat earns the surprise and respect of the packer, who functions in the story to provide testimony to the impressive scale and range of her abilities in the woods; his quiet awe increases the listener's respect for the storyteller, imbuing Mrs. Sverdsten with a bit of the aura that surrounds her tall-tale congeners. That the feat was accomplished by a woman makes it even more impressive: waiting for Mrs. Sverdsten to return so she could make their dinner, the men in camp hardly expected to hear that she had spent the day hiking back and forth over entire mountains. Just as she does in her hunting stories, she stakes her claim to, and defines herself in terms of, that knowledge of and competence in the landscape which has traditionally been the province of men. And what is more, she again calmly defeats a landscape which seems to be doing its best to frustrate and harm her—the situation, she says, "could have turned out pretty bad," but its outcome seems to have been in little doubt. Here as elsewhere in her stories, Mrs. Sverdsten emerges as a quietly invincible figure, completely at home in the wilderness environment—and, as such, an exemplar of local identity.

That the geographical attitudes, experiences, and expertise which Mrs. Sverdsten outlines in her stories figure largely in the valley's shared sense of identity is made clear by one of her favorite local narratives, one which features a bumbling visitor from the plains whose appalling ignorance of wilderness ways makes him a laughingstock for the entire region.

Well, the best story I can think about about this area doesn't have anything to do with me hunting. But, years ago, there was a season that, for some reason, the bears were plentiful, and they were hungry, and they were around garbage dumps. And in those days, the road over Lookout Summit, east of Mullan, there was a nice spring there and it was set up as a rest stop. And a businessman and his wife from Kellogg happened to be there when a Missouri tourist came along. And a bear was raiding a garbage can right at that time, and it had tipped the garbage can over; it probably wasn't a very big bear, maybe a yearling or something, but it had tipped the garbage can over, and it was in the garbage can, just its tail end sticking out. And this Missouri tourist got out of his car and walked over and hit the bear a good spat across the backside, and the bear come tearing out of the garbage can and grabbed him by the knee, and he had to be taken to the hospital to get some repairs done to his knee. And the Missouri tourist was very angry; he said, "Why, those animals are wild; they shouldn't be allowed on the highway!" I don't really think that that story was stretched, because at that time my sister was a nurse in the hospital up there. And that man was taken to the emergency room to have his bear bites taken care of, and of course the word was all over the hospital and it got all over the country.

From T. B. Thorpe's 1841 story "The Big Bear of Arkansas" to William Faulkner's "The Bear," *Ursus americanus* has figured prominently in American culture as the embodiment of wilderness. In the nineteenth century, writes folklorist Daniel J. Gelo, "the bear took on a potent symbolic characterization, becoming all that was terrifying and ferocious on the frontier, all that must be overcome in the realization of Manifest Destiny"[9]—a characterization which it has never lost. It is significant that Mrs. Sverdsten felt that she had to confront and kill a bear to become fully comfortable in the woods—that, like Faulkner's Ike McCaslin, she needed to face down the essence of all that was wild in order to prove she fully belonged to her place. Out of their experience with the local wilderness and its creatures, the people of the valley have corroborated and renewed the bear's traditional symbolic quality, investing in its shaggy form a sense of all that is savage in the local woods and mountains.

In picking a fight with a foraging bear, then, the Missouri tourist confronts the living, breathing, angry embodiment of all that the valley's residents know and feel about their place. The reason that word of the poor man's predicament spreads so quickly through the valley, from Mullan clear down to Cataldo, is that his behavior so thoroughly, stupidly, and amazingly violates the local understanding of the wilderness—the understanding that is outlined so colorfully in Mrs. Sverdsten's hunting stories. Bears, while they are attractive in their wildness and make treasured hunting trophies, are potentially dangerous and should be approached with respect, like the rest of the woods in which they live; they stand for the simultaneous attraction and repulsion of the woods environment that forms so large a component of the local sense of place. As his label implies, the Missouri tourist, a visitor from the flatlands, has probably never passed through the Western wilderness before. He has evidently seen bears only in zoos and circuses or else is firmly under the influence of "the Bambi complex"—a recent, revisionist cultural conception of wild animals which sees them as cute and cuddly and which leads vacationing Americans in national parks "to approach real bears as if they were the storybook kind."[10] By walking blithely up to a bear and spanking it he reveals just how completely foreign his understanding of the valley is to that of the people who live there, and he deservedly earns contempt and ridicule in the process. He is a foil against which those who tell the story can measure and take pride in their ways of life, knowledge of the local environment, and attitude toward their place; he is emphatically an outsider whose presence sharpens their sense of belonging. By enabling local people to affirm collectively their sense of place by contrast with his ignorance and ineptitude, the hapless Missouri tourist is a catalyst for a communal assertion of regional identity, an identity distilled from lives spent surrounded by the beauty, bounty, strength, savagery, and mercurial personality of the North Idaho landscape.

Landscape and Life—The Mines

Having spent almost all of her adult life in Cataldo and its surrounding mountains, Mrs. Sverdsten has never had extensive contact with the mines and mining towns which lie upstream on the South Fork. The valley widens west of Pinehurst and the old Pine Creek mining district: to the east of this line lie the mineral deposits and the settlements which have grown up around them, while small farms occupy the valley floor between Pinehurst and Fourth of July Canyon (fig. 16). The ways of life of the two halves of the valley have traditionally overlapped to a certain extent: as Mrs. Sverdsten explains, in earlier years it was difficult for her husband's horse-logging crews to work in cold, snowy conditions, so "they had to close down in the wintertime, and most of his crew went to work in the mines, and worked in the mines through the winter, and went into the woods in the spring, when the woods opened up again." Similarly, as she points out, "the farms around here are so small that the people have to, the men have to either log or work in the mine part of

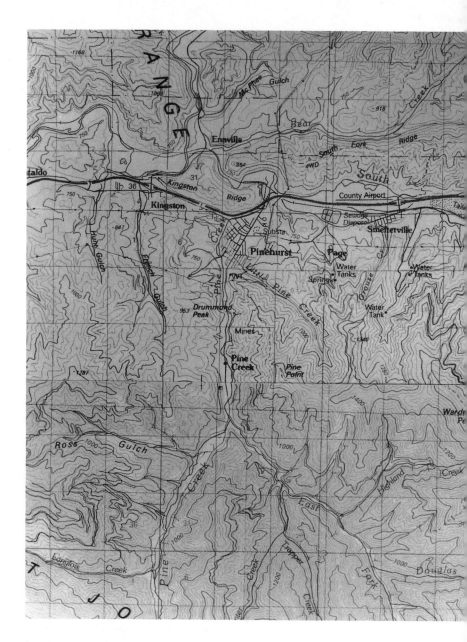

the time to support their families." Leonard Heikkila grew up on such a
farm near Cataldo; his father had been a miner as a young man, and he
and his brothers all worked briefly for the mining companies at one time
or another. Despite this degree of fluidity between the mining communities and the logging and farming communities, however, the two halves
·of the valley remain conceptually distinct in people's minds. Sunshine
geologist Don Long, for instance, thinks of his region as coterminous

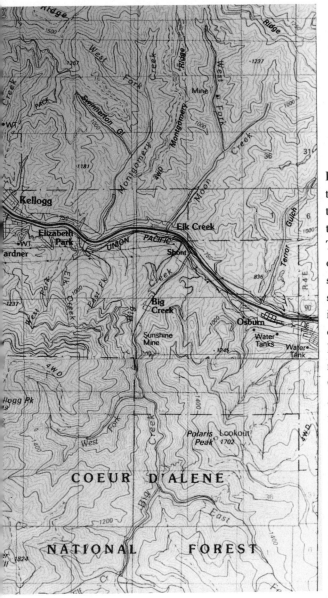

Figure 16. USGS topographic map of the western section of the mining district. This map is sufficiently detailed to show the locations of several sites discussed in this chapter, including the Bunker Hill and Sunshine mines, the old Pine Creek district, and the abandoned Highland mine site (located on Highland Creek, a tributary of the East Fork of Pine Creek). The Sunshine miners' memorial (see fig. 17) is located next to Interstate 90 where it intersects the road leading up Big Creek to the Sunshine mine.

with the Coeur d'Alene mining district, which "goes from about Pinehurst—there's Pine Creek on the west, and to Lookout Pass on the east." Wendell Brainard, retired editor of the Kellogg newspaper, also speaks of the region as the Coeur d'Alene mining district, which in his mind "doesn't go, it just—the Pine Creek area right out here at Pinehurst, it doesn't go any farther—well, they've had, even down in the Fourth of July Canyon there, where you go through there, when they were cutting the road through there they [chuckles] supposedly cut a gold vein in there, and they had a little rush down there for a while; that subsided, and the Indians supposedly had found some gold down there. But no, that's just about the end of it." To these men, the region is unified by mining. Because the two halves of the valley have two different economic bases and support two different ways of life, they are not understood to be part of a seamless, undifferentiated geographical unit.

Despite their physical and economic differences, however, the eastern and western sections of the valley are united by the sense of place that their inhabitants share, by a common understanding and interpretation of their differing geographies that local residents have developed through similar experiences in their disparate landscapes. After all, as we have seen Mrs. Sverdsten point out, loggers and miners are "very much the same" in that "they both do real hard work with natural resources." People in each half of the valley, that is, have traditionally seen the land as harboring resources to be harvested, resources that the land has made available with generous abundance: the mountainsides are shaggy with trees and teeming with game, and the mining district has been one of the richest in the country for the last hundred years. At the same time, those resources have often proven to be maddeningly elusive: prospecting for minerals is as hit-or-miss an enterprise as shooting at a distant elk or trying to find a good huckleberry patch. Moreover, there is as much danger in mining as there is in hunting and logging, if not more; the mountains exact a fearful toll in death and injury from those who tear them open to extract their riches. Finally, though, mining is a way of life which its practitioners proudly embrace. The miners of the district define and identify themselves in terms of their occupation, an occupation which, like logging and hunting, depends for its nature and its very existence on the physical conditions of the local landscape.

If there is any one story with which most residents of the district are familiar, it is the legend of how Noah Kellogg discovered the ore body that became the Bunker Hill mine. Kellogg had been among the thousands who had poured into Eagle and Murray during the gold rush. In the summer of 1885, he talked two Murray storekeepers into giving him a grubstake so he could go prospecting along the South Fork. One day, as Don Long summarizes the story, "he was up on the hill above Kellogg, in Milo Gulch, and his mule supposedly got lost up there, and so he went up to find the mule, or the donkey, whatever he called it; I guess it was a jackass, he called it [laughs]. And so he went up there to find the jackass, and supposedly he found the outcrop on the Bunker Hill." This is the central motif in the Kellogg legend: that, as Bob Anderson put it, "the Bunker Hill [was] supposedly found by a jackass." The event is endlessly commemorated in the public landscape of Kellogg's namesake city. Noah's moment of discovery is captured on murals in the post office and in the lobby of a local motel, as well as in a sculpture on one of Kellogg's main streets; Silverhorn, the ski area that sits atop Wardner Peak above Kellogg, was originally called Jackass Bowl; Jackass Creek runs out of the mountains north of town; and comic postcards proclaim that Kellogg was founded by a jackass and is now populated by his descendants. The legend, as well as its public reinforcement, clearly establish mines and mining as the raison d'être of the city of Kellogg—as well as of the district as a whole—in the minds of local residents.

The details of the legend, as various people tell it, reveal some important attitudes that the narrators hold toward their place. Bob Anderson, for instance, describes the particular circumstances under which Kellogg found his fateful outcrop:

Well, the prospector came over from the North Fork, from Prichard area, where the gold rush was. And he borrowed enough money, or borrowed the food and grub, as we call it; he got a grubstake from one of the store owners over there at Prichard or Murray; got a grubstake and borrowed the jackass, came over here looking. And it was quite a trip coming over, no trail, coming through the brush and following a deer trail, perhaps. But anyway, tough trip to get over here. And so, after tying the jackass, putting it out, staking it out to have something to eat, why, the next morning he couldn't find it. And here it was, somehow or other, had gone, climbed up over downfalled trees and so forth. He found the jackass just standing on the hill, just looking, staring across the canyon. And he got up and looked, and here it was the sun shining on this big outcrop of lead, of galena ore, shiny galena ore; looked like a mirror [chuckles]. So that's the story of him finding, of the jackass finding the ore.

The central motifs of the legend become clear: the lost jackass, Kellogg's scramble to find it, the outcrop of ore shining like a beacon or a grail, the air of incredible good luck hanging over it all. Wendell Brainard's version of the story also incorporates these motifs, and in the process he goes out of his way to correct the legend's factual inaccuracies:

Oh, they got different—there's no doubt that the guy, Noah Kellogg, used a jackass to carry supplies over there and everything, and the story spread that, you know, the jackass ran away and went up on the steep mountain right up there; that's called Wardner, the old town up there that joins to Kellogg right up there. There's not much left, but I was born up in Wardner, and crawled all over those hills up there. But anyhow, the story was that the jackass wandered away and he climbed up on the hillside, pawing at this outcropping of lead ore up there. Of course, there's some discrepancies in it, because lead—you know what lead looks like, don't you? [. . .] [L]ead is shiny; lead's real shiny. Silver—that's what gets people mixed up; silver is not shiny. They call it "grey copper." It's a dull, black, greasy—the greasier-looking, the richer it is; it's called tetrahedrite silver. People think silver is shiny, but it isn't. And lead's the opposite; lead is a show-off metal. But anyhow, when it's out on the surface like that and it's oxidized, it's black. So the story was the sun was shining down on that, making a big—which is wrong, because [chuckles] the stuff was—you go up there today, get up to, they call it the glory hole, where it was first discovered, and there are boulders in there half as big as this room in here that have come down off of there, and they're all black; they don't shine. But anyhow, he took the samples back to Murray with him, and the guys that had grubstaked him, that owned the burro, they found out that it was lead, and he got in cahoots with this fellow named Phil O'Rourke; he was an old miner from Leadville, Colorado, and he recognized that it was good lead ore. [. . .] And it became a big mine after that, and that was the story.

Having lived his entire life in the vicinity of the Bunker Hill mine, a mine whose physical presence has woven itself firmly into his life and memory to the point that he cannot discuss the legend without mentioning his own childhood forays over the same ground, Mr. Brainard has developed a refined sense of local environmental literacy. He knows from experience that exposed ore does not shine, and thus shows that the Kellogg legend could not literally have been true. The fact that narrators have retained the motif of the shiny ore despite the fact that it contradicts what they know about the physical facts of their place suggests its evident importance to the meaning of the legend—the ore must glitter and shine; for the story to retain its point, Kellogg cannot have found it in any sort of prosaic, realistic way. In its unnatural gleaming, the ore has a magical and numinous air, appearing to Kellogg as a revelation of sorts, as though he and his jackass were being chosen specially to find the valley's riches and set its human history in motion. The glittering outcrop also reminds the hearer of the shiny refined silver and gold that have come out of the district; it alludes to the great mineral wealth which lies beneath the region's surface. At the same time, though, there is a large element of luck in Kellogg's story. He has to claw his way over rough terrain to get anywhere near the outcrop in the first place and would never have found it if he had known how to tie better knots and keep his jackass in camp. The ore is elusive and demanding, leading Kellogg on a difficult dance before he can claim his reward. In its events and its striking imagery, then, the legend of Noah Kellogg hints at a two-edged understanding of the local land and its mineral wealth: the land is rich and generous but teases and frustrates as well. While it may seem unrelated to the world of the woods, then, the Kellogg legend suggests that in the way people think and feel about it the mining district is conceptually of a piece with the surrounding wilderness. A common sense of place arches over them both.

Other stories that have come out of the district reinforce the themes which underlie and shape the Kellogg legend: instances of the landscape's bounty, combined with its maddening propensity for concealing that bounty or suddenly snatching it away, dominate local mining narratives. Bob Anderson tells of another mine that was supposedly discovered under circumstances similar to those of the Bunker Hill: "The Tiger was located—pack trains coming over from Montana, the horses going along this trail, they uncovered, their horseshoes uncovered ore that this one fellow spotted; the galena ore up there at Burke, right in the valley. So he located that one day and his partners located the claim across the valley the next; that's a very narrow valley up there at Burke. So that was located also by horses [chuckles], by animals." The area was so cluttered with mineral wealth, it seems, that you could not help but stumble over it on the surface; while the streets of Burke Canyon may not have been paved with gold, its supply trails were at least paved with galena ore. This brief narrative blows a whiff of fantastic, tall-tale air across the local landscape; while the area was certainly rich in ore, the discovery of the Tiger was probably not this easy and fortuitous. Still, the story encapsulates and perpetuates the excited perceptions of early miners.[11] And in the relative ease with which it made its riches available, the Tiger closely resembles not only the Bunker Hill but other mines in the area, like the Mother Lode gold mine near Murray. While Murray is not on the South Fork, many people nevertheless connect it in thought with the local mining towns: people "really don't include the Murray district in the Silver Valley," says Wendell Brainard, although "it's in the mining district all right." Mr. Brainard describes the Mother Lode's origins:

That mine, the old Mother Lode, was started from the two prospectors who were looking for outcropping and stuff, and right along the creek there was a slab, big slab outcrop there, just lousy with gold. They called it the Golden Slab. And they said the gold was just sticking out there. In fact, they guarded it all the time; they even set up a shack there and slept there because they didn't want anybody to swipe that ore. And they finally got hard up, and they ground it up, and I think they took about two, three thousand dollars worth of gold out of it at the old price, just from that one slab of gold there.

The Mother Lode was so rich that it even enriched downstream claims: its owners used an inefficient stamp mill to crush the ore, and, Mr. Brainard continues, "the other miners down the creek below them that owned the claims down there, they were running their stamp mill and a lot of the stuff was going down the creek that they weren't recovering, and these guys down below were picking it up down below [chuckles], getting it for nothing, getting it free—free gold [chuckles]." It is no longer nearly so easy as it once was to recover the area's mineral wealth: the rich Sunshine silver mine did not tap into the "bonanza ore," as Don Long put it, until the shaft had reached the 1,700-foot level, and the people who developed the Hercules mine around the turn of the century hand-drilled their tunnel for twelve years before they reached the ore vein. Moreover, many of the district's mines bottomed out many years ago and are now abandoned. Still, the fact that these narratives of easily available ore still live suggests that, in the local imagination at least, the landscape remains rich, glittering, and generous.

If the ground was lousy with gold, however, it still took some luck to find that gold. The landscape did not reveal and surrender its wealth to just anyone. Wendell Brainard tells of another rich gold deposit whose discovery suggests the workings of the same mysterious agency that led Noah Kellogg to the Bunker Hill.

Between Prichard and Murray. There's a gulch there called Dream Gulch. And it got its name [chuckles] from a guy lived over in Washington somewhere; I think it was Kennewick or somewhere in that country. And this is back in the gold-rush days. He had a dream that he found this gulch that was just full of gold. And he came up to Murray and looked around, and this gulch was right what he figured in his dream. And it actually became one of the good gold-producing gulches, so they called it Dream Gulch after him. And they took quite a bit of gold out of there.

The gulch is a magic cavern of sorts, like Ali Baba's cave, standing undisturbed in the midst of the gold rush, waiting for the chosen person to come along and empty it of its riches. On the one hand, this place-name legend alludes to the magnitude of the area's mineral wealth, a bounty that seemed almost too good to be true; it is, literally, the stuff that dreams are made of. On the other hand, as in the Kellogg legend, there is a sense that this wealth is selective and capricious, that it is not necessarily available to everyone, that it does not wait as a reward for the meritorious and hard working but falls unpredictably to a lucky few—here, to a sleeping man in Washington. The land ultimately gives of itself of its own volition, it seems, rewarding and punishing whomever it chooses, and so man's control over it is partial at best. In the way it disposes of its riches, finally, the land is as notional as Mrs. Sverdsten's huckleberries.

Not all worthwhile deposits lay on the surface, waiting for passing horses to kick them over or transfixing jackasses with their gleam. Most early prospectors did not depend on luck, dreams, or the land's caprice to lead them to the ore but relied instead on hard work, careful observation, and a subtle, detailed knowledge of the landscape. They attempted to outwit the land, to discover its deep secrets, through developing and exercising a finely shaded environmental literacy. They were driven by glittering visions of the wealth they knew was there, but counted less on mysterious revelations than on their ability to decipher and interpret complex geographical clues. In conversation with me, Bob Anderson describes the days when "there were men all over the hills like deer and bear, or rabbits."

RYDEN: What would they look for? How did they locate these mines?

ANDERSON: Look for something that looks unusual. Instead of just the plain rock, which you see everywhere, you look for some that's stained with manganese, black manganese oxide, or with red iron oxide. And they'd look for quartz veins; you'd look for siderite veins, siderite being iron carbonate, which oxidizes into limonite, which is a red iron oxide; limonite and/or hematite. So you'd look for odd . . .

RYDEN: Different colors, it sounds like.

ANDERSON: Uh-huh. [. . .] And, for instance, if you came up a creek here, if you were fishing in the creek, wading the creek or along each side, and you saw a rock in the creek that was entirely different from all the others, and then as you kept going up the creek you maybe found more, and then pretty soon you found none, then if that particular type of vein material looked of interest to you, then you'd start up the hill to see where it came from.

RYDEN: Because it would have washed down, you mean?

ANDERSON: Mm-hm. Well, it would have rolled down first [chuckles], and washed to some extent. If it were gold, or any other vein; perhaps the vein cut right across the creek. But anyway, that's the way generally you'd start looking; you'd look along the creeks, because that's where you would find rock that was not covered with soil, so it was visible.

Although he has technical knowledge that the early prospectors would not have had, being able to identify different local minerals and explain why they turn different colors, Mr. Anderson gives a good sense of how those prospectors found worthwhile outcrops and were able to stake paying claims. Having developed a detailed sense of the district's physical texture—its structure and colors, its rocks and their distribution—both through deliberate exploration and through simply living and working in the region and keeping their eyes open, they then looked around for anomalies that stood out against the familiar background, for aberrations in the land's wonted surface. For these prospectors, such anomalies represented cracks in the land's smooth inscrutable mask, hints of where hidden riches lay. Having deciphered the landscape, they then located their claims, shouldered their tools, and went to work.

Miners and prospectors in the district always took great pride in their ability to read the landscape in this way, to locate paying properties and to identify ore-bearing rock at a glance. This sensitivity to the subtleties of local geography became an identifying feature of miners in the district, one which anchored them firmly in their place and distinguished them from outsiders and tenderfoot prospectors. Maidell Clemets tells a story about the dreams and explorations of an environmentally illiterate Civilian Conservation Corps worker from the eastern United States, a comic figure who in his innocence and naivete rivals Alida Sverdsten's Missouri tourist as a foil against which local identity and knowledge of place can be defined—yet one who, in this case, leaves behind him an unintended note of mystery and irony.

Well, I think one of the favorite experiences I had was—it was a hot summer's day, and I was up in Wallace, the Wallace Corner, having a beer. And the place was filled up, but I had a booth there, though; I saw a seat, and I sat down. And an old fellow come in, and he had sort of an old acquaintance look on his face, you know, and wanted to know if he could sit there, and I told him, "Sure." Well, then he told me that during the Depression he had been a bartender up there in Wallace at that very same place, and that he always liked Wallace. He told me that he had made a friend there when the CC's come into town, the CC boys, and the boy's name was Johnny Dever. And Johnny said he was going to get out of the CC's, and of course they'd remonetized the price of gold up to thirty-four dollars; there was quite a good deal of stir for gold at that time. And Johnny, he wanted to go prospecting. And so he wanted a grubstake. Well, [the bartender] said, he only had about twenty-five dollars, and he gave it to Johnny and told him, heck, he's young and he had enthusiasm. He backed him up. He said, well, he worried about the boy all the time after he left. He says, he come back; in about thirty days he was back, all right, and he said, well, he'd found it. He said he had quartz rock; said you could see the gold in it, and he's showing it around the bar to the fellows there. Why, they began to laugh, and they said, well, that's iron pyrite; that's fool's gold. Nobody but a damn fool would pick that up, you know. So [the bartender] said he felt sort of bad about it. He said [he'd been] made the laughingstock of the town. But he [kept] it, though; he said he set a big chunk of that quartz rock with the pyrite on the back bar. He said Johnny left; he went back east; thought he was from around New Jersey somewhere. Well, later on, he said, a mining engineer come in and wanted to know if he could look at that rock on the back of the bar, and he thought, well, some of the boys have told him about that, you know, and are going to have some more fun at my expense. He said [the engineer] got looking at this [rock]; boy, he said, get a few tons of that, you could pay up all your debts and have some money. Well, he was sort of dubious about it. But, he said, the more I thought about it, why, he just took the darn rock over to a metallurgist, Murphy, up there in Wallace, ran an assayer's shop, and told him to assay it. Well, it came back fourteen dollars a ton gold. Pyrite was carrying gold with it. And, God, he said, he didn't know what to do. He said he tried to look up Johnny Dever in the CC's; he couldn't find any trace of him. But then he sold out in Wallace and went down to San Francisco, and he had a bar down there, he said, and he made money down there. But, he said, all the time he got thinking about Wallace and that gold. So he come back, he said, to Wallace, he did, like a lodestone just pulled him there. Well, he said that he knows damn well that one of these days Johnny's going to come walking through that door! And he's going to have his mine then. And I told him, well, that's a pretty interesting story you told [laughs].

Johnny is laughed out of town because he cannot make the simple distinction between real gold and fool's gold. Thinking that he can walk blithely out into the mountains and assure his fortune by picking up the first shiny yellow thing he sees, he makes a fool of himself in front of the veteran miners who know that finding mineral wealth is a difficult process, one which requires endless hours of exploration and patient scrutiny of the landscape. In their laughter, the miners of the story share and reaffirm their sense of the difficulty and frequent obscurity of the local geographical surface and seal their communal identity as Coeur d'Alene miners, expert decoders of that surface. In the sequel, however, their local knowledge is confounded, their reading of the rocks not subtle enough. Johnny was fooled into thinking that iron pyrite was gold, but the miners were fooled into thinking that the rock necessarily contained no gold at all. Rather than give up its riches easily or as a reward for hard work and subtle experiential understanding, the land here is coy and sly, disguising its true nature behind a mask of scorned pyrite, never allowing those who seek its wealth to understand it completely no matter how exhaustive they think their knowledge is, always seeking to divert their attention or hide its bounty after a brief tantalizing glimpse. As the bartender realizes at the end of the story, there is a lost mine out there in the Idaho hills which may never be found again.[12] The land contains great wealth, but all too often that wealth is elusive, fugitive, and notional.

Many other miners found similar frustration; even after using all his wiles to find a promising spot, the prospector was rarely guaranteed success. Bob Anderson points out that "this whole district, for about eighteen miles long and several miles wide, is covered with mining claims now," many of them located in the 1880s. Few of these claims were ever actually developed; fewer still became producing mines, let alone wealthy ones. Miners frequently burrowed deep into mountainsides, following narrow veins that they expected would lead to great wealth, only to have their hopes dashed because of the faulting conditions in the area; as Wendell Brainard explains, "Now, a fault is a—you may be following an ore vein, and the fault will come in and just whack it off or displace it somewhere else. That's the way they lose their ore bodies." Once a vein was lost in this way, it took a great deal of time and money to find it again—if, indeed, it could ever be found at all. And when ore bodies were not vanishing entirely, they sometimes turned out to contain a completely different (and less valuable) type of ore from what was expected. Mr. Brainard tells the story of one such disappointment, an episode which he witnessed personally:

I knew a fellow, he worked down at—we had a mine right over the hill here in town called the old Stewart mine, and it was a good producer. And they worked it out; this fellow had worked in there, and he got a lease on—what happens if the mines work out, if there's still ore in there, it isn't worth the company's time, but a leaser, or get a partner or something, they can go in and they can make money by taking out what ore is left, you know. Besides, they're working for themselves, so they'll be working twice as hard as if they're working for the company anyhow. So anyhow, there was an outcropping off to the north that the company hadn't explored. So he got a lease, and he went out there at the end of the dump and he started to hand tunnel in; they had machinery there, but he wasn't using that. And he was driving this by hand. I've done some of that hand mining; you just take a piece of steel, you know, and you hit it with a hammer, turn it; you can make about two feet a day if you get enough holes poked in there. He drove that tunnel in there by hand by himself; he was a little guy, about five-foot two, so he didn't make the tunnel any bigger than he had to. In fact, he got my dad mixed up in the deal, and he was grubstaking him by giving him the powder, the dynamite, to do the work with. And I'd take it out to him, and I was working in a mine in Wardner, and he said, "Old Jim needs some more powder out there," so I had a Model A Ford roadster, and I put it in the rumble seat, two boxes of powder, fifty pounds apiece, and hauled them out there and packed them up the dump. And I'd go in the tunnel to see what the old fellow was doing, and I'd have to bend over to get in there. I could hear him singing; he'd be singing away back in there. And instead of hitting the steel this way [overhand], he would go like this [underhand]. Easier on the arm; he'd drive all these holes upward, so he'd just let his arm swing. And he'd be swinging away, and I would look what he was doing, you know. Anyhow, he drove that tunnel in there nine hundred feet by hand; took him two years. He finally hit the vein in there—and it was zinc! [Chuckles.] And this was when zinc wasn't worth anything. He got so mad, he drifted a little ways to see if it would—sometimes the zinc will turn to lead, or it'd be more one or the other. And what ore he did take out, he got so mad he just threw it over the dump, and then that was it. He gave it up. Zinc wasn't worth anything. That's just one of the stories of the old hand miners.

Having come upon what to all appearances was a rare and rich opportunity—an undeveloped outcrop on a paying mine property—and having spent months and months of hard physical labor to reach the ore body, poor Jim finally nets nothing but disappointment and frustration. For much of this century, the price of zinc was so low that it cost more to process the ore than the metal could be sold for; it was viewed as a contaminant in more valuable ores. As Mr. Brainard put it, "Zinc was a dirty word here in the old days. [. . .] If you had zinc in your ore and you shipped it to the smelter here in Kellogg, they not only wouldn't pay you for it, you got penalized for it, and they just threw the zinc away." Jim's disastrous mining adventure emphasizes, in a black-humorous way, the treacherous and elusive quality of mineral wealth in the valley. What seems easily within reach sometimes vanishes altogether; in a sort of reverse alchemy, valued and eagerly sought substances change before the miner's astonished eyes into duller, baser metals.

Not only are ore bodies baffling and coy, but pursuing them is difficult and dangerous work. The history of mining in the Coeur d'Alenes is punctuated with accidents and deaths, and the long hours spent underground wear men down in more gradual ways as well. As Maidell Clemets explains, "mining is a very hazardous occupation. And the life expectancy of a man ain't too great to that either. If he gyppos down there in a mine [that is, gets paid by how far he advances the tunnel each day and not by the hour], and he's working at a very high pace, and his air isn't very good; they don't have the ventilation, either, they should have. He physically exerts, and if he stays at that, about five years' time he's burned out. Can't do it." The drills that miners used in the early part of the twentieth century ultimately ruined the health of many of them. Years of breathing rock dust drove Leonard Heikkila's father out of the mines completely, for instance, leading him to take up farming instead. As Mr. Heikkila explains,

he had worked all of his life in the mine, and in the early years of mining they worked with what they call a dry buzzy, which was a drilling machine, but it didn't have any water. The present-day machines, when they're drilling, they have water there that they put on so it cuts the dust. But those early days, they didn't have those, and they were just called dry buzzies. And so, in the mine, drilling, they got a lot of dust, and he got a lot of dust in his lungs, and he had what today is known as emphysema, I guess. They had a different name in those days for it: miner's consumption, they had some other names.

Miner's consumption, or "miner's con"—or silicosis, as it is technically known—was a common crippler in the district. People who have been around mining all their lives remember the devastating effect that the disease had on men in the community, and some have even been touched by it themselves: as Mr. Clemets says, "I worked in mines for years, worked in mining for eighteen years. I've got enough rocks in my lungs to give everybody in town some. I worked with dry machines." One of the first things that Don Long told me he remembered about growing up in the district was the shattered health and the early deaths of many of the men in Burke Canyon: "And at that time, most of the miners that had been working in the mine, when they were forty years old, they had emphysema or miner's con, and they were dying at the age of forty. [. . .] And they would start in at eighteen years old, and when they were forty, then, most of them died, because of that silica dust in their lungs. It's, I guess, in a way kind of like the black lung that the coal miners get. But I can remember that quite readily, because a lot of those fellows were fairly young men, yet they were dying." Men working together often died together, brought down by the same foul air. Mr. Clemets tells of the fate of thirty-two men who drove a raise together in the Bunker Hill, "and at the end, a year after the raise was driven, there wasn't a single man alive that worked in that raise. All dead." Even today, many retired miners in the district serve as living reminders of mining's deadly early days. Bill Bondurant, for instance, notes that "I've got a few old friends here; they're all dusted up so bad that they can't go do anything. [. . .] We just talked to a fella in Mullan day before yesterday, and he can't even stand furniture polish in the house, he's got it so bad; and another one up here in Woodland Park, an old partner of mine, visited here, oh, about a month ago. He says, 'I gotta get down out of here, it's just'—he could hardly breathe." As long as men like these live in the district, and as long as memories like these live in the minds of the district's residents, the mines can never be seen simply as repositories of temporarily trapped wealth. They will always be touched by shadow, always be eyed with a degree of distrust. Like the woods, the mines harbor riches for the taking, but they exact a human cost.

Hazards to health and life in the mines go far beyond the debilitating effects of dust-laden air. The Sunshine mine fire of May 2, 1972, which killed ninety-one men, casts a long black shadow across the communal memory. No one seems quite sure what caused the fire: mining company officials and federal inspectors blamed it on spontaneous combustion in an abandoned stope (an excavation from which ore was once removed), while experienced mining men like Sunshine geologist Don Long and retired miner and one-time state mining inspector Bill Bondurant—who assisted in the official investigation—theorize that it must have been caused by welding slag "for the main reason," as Mr. Bondurant says, "that most mine fires nowadays are caused by welding slag." Whatever the cause, the carbon monoxide produced by the fire, as well as toxic fumes released when the fire burned the foam barriers that sealed off the abandoned stope, entered the mine's ventilation system, circulated quickly through the tunnels, and asphyxiated the trapped miners. The effect of a tragedy of this magnitude on the small and close-knit local mining community was devastating. Many families lost husbands, sons, brothers; if they were not related to victims of the fire, most valley residents at least knew some of them. Since it was common for miners to work in several of the area's mines over the course of their working lives, many men in the district had been coworkers of the dead miners at some point, laboring beside them to extract ore from the earth; besides felling their comrades, the fire served as a chilling reminder of how fragile and precarious their own lives were. As well as claiming ninety-one lives, then, the Sunshine fire tore a gaping, jagged hole in the communal fabric of the region. It scarred and ravaged the social and emotional landscape of the district as deeply as years of smelter smoke devastated the physical landscape around Kellogg.

Few people talk about the fire today; the memory is still too painful. It lies beneath the surface of local thought, unexpressed but always present; to express the events of that day publicly in words would be to bump too hard against emotional bruises, impeding their healing. Only to outsiders is the fire a fit subject for verbal examination and deliberate contemplation: as Bob Anderson explains, "I think the locals all like to try to forget it. The only ones that it comes up is somebody from Spokane comes up and wants to write something about it, or remind the people about it on an anniversary, and they want to write a column or story; or somebody from Boise or whatever. But locals, no; they try to forget it." The Sunshine fire, then, stands as a mute, colossal, awful fact astride the local landscape, not overtly acknowledged but impossible to ignore. It is made visible not in narrative but in the dramatic form of a memorial statue erected to the memory of the fallen miners at the spot where the road leading to the Sunshine intersects Interstate 90. The statue is a visually arresting, larger-than-life metal figure of a miner, one leg braced behind him, his drill thrust against the sky, his dimensions and stance suggesting strength, defiance, and heroism (fig. 17). A small grove of

Figure 17. The memorial statue to the miners who died in the Sunshine mine fire. 1989 photograph by the author.

evergreens, an informational sign, and a plaque inscribed with the names of the dead men complete the memorial. Created by a man named Ken Lonn, a former local miner who later became a sculptor, and drawn from his own experience and memory of work and fellowship in the district—as Don Long explains, "he would take, say, the profile off some miner that he worked with in Bunker Hill [. . .] or someplace else, and then that would be—see, the profile of this miner that's on the sculpture down here is actually somebody's face"—the statue is a fitting and moving tribute to the fire's victims and a striking memento mori for the region's inhabitants. For the families and friends of the dead miners, it provides a catalyst for quiet memories and silent, sober contemplation—"when I look at the statue," says Mr. Anderson, "I think about the men that I knew. [. . .] I think of the various men whose names are on the plaque. I don't have to go look, you know; I just think of certain individuals." Public recognition of the Sunshine fire is restricted to the monument and the annual memorial service held before it; otherwise, quiet inner voices, rather than the voice of shared narrative, keep alive the memory of the men who perished.

The fire was also made visible in a negative way, by the subtraction rather than the addition of things—that is, by the absence of the men whose lives it took, by the yawning gaps which local residents saw in the community. These violent disruptions in the flow and fellowship of local life were unsettling, unnerving; they spread a chilling gloom through the valley's towns. Bill Bondurant describes the effect of the fire: "Oh, just like a pall, just like a giant—well, ninety-one people died, and it was just like a giant funeral pall all over the area. You looked, well, so-and-so is missing; he died in the fire. So-and-so is missing; he died in the fire. Five of them were good friends of mine, and on the memorial, I checked out and I knew twenty of them. These are the guys you missed." Having so many familiar faces torn from the region's communal portrait, disfiguring it beyond repair, proved the most haunting and disturbing reminder of the fire's ravages and of the threats and dangers inhering in the mines. The pall that those ninety-one deaths produced hangs as a dark mist through which those who lived through the time of the fire inevitably contemplate their place.

In response to the tensions and anxieties engendered by laboring in hazardous work environments, workers in many industries frequently create and perpetuate folk beliefs—omens, signs, and behaviors which they believe to cause or predict either good or bad fortune. Patrick Mullen has written, for instance, about the uncertain world of the commercial fishing crews on the gulf coast of Texas: "When he sets out to sea on a long voyage, he does not know exactly what dangers he may confront: heavy seas, a leaky boat, mechanical troubles, or any of a number of things. As the fisherman leaves port he needs some sort of assurance that his voyage will be successful and that he will return safely." He

finds this assurance in an elaborate system of magic and empirical beliefs. Superstitions—proscriptions against mentioning certain words or
bringing certain objects on board, omens of bad luck in the offing—
"seek to alleviate the natural hazards of the sea such as hurricanes,
storms, waterspouts, drowning, and sinking,"[13] and provide the illusion
of human control over a powerful and potentially deadly environment:
the success of the fishing trip is seen as depending directly upon what
the crew does or omits to do. Empirical beliefs, primarily in the form of
signs for predicting the gulf's mercurial weather and finding elusive
schools of fish, similarly allow fishing crews to gain a degree of mental
control over their uncertain occupation and the dangerous milieu in
which they pursue it.

Like Mullen's gulf fishing crews, miners in the Coeur d'Alene district
have been known to rely on such folk beliefs in recognition of, and in an
attempt to remain unscathed by, the hazardous nature and economic
uncertainty of the mines. While professing not to believe them himself,
Bill Bondurant told of superstitions which spread from the Cornish miners who used to work in the region. Rockbursts are a constant hazard in
mining, yet miners were often able to avoid them with the aid, the belief
went, of supernatural guardians: "And you've no doubt read about these
rockbursts in this area. They had them in Cornwall, England, Wales.
And the rock would pop, pop, pop. And they called them tommyknockers. And that was a common expression in this country. When the rock
was working a little bit, you could hear ping, ping, ping; they said that
the tommyknockers—trolls—were warning you to get out of there." In
its way, this is an empirical belief just as much as is a knowledge that
certain sky colors and cloud conditions presage rain: from years of listening to the rock and surviving its attacks, miners have collectively
learned to discern the aural clues which tell that a rockburst is imminent. At the same time, talk of trolls invests the mine with a sense of
living power beyond the mere physical force of shifting strata of rock.
Explosive, dangerous strength lurks behind the tunnel walls, a strength
which the trolls sense and warn against and which miners can dodge by
listening carefully, behaving properly, and passing this knowledge on to
their fellows. In this way they can gain a tenuous mastery of an environment which seems to do its best to thwart and harm them; they can learn
to cheat its power.

Mr. Bondurant told of another belief about how not to jeopardize hard-
won success in the mines, one which has become outmoded through
changing social conditions: "Oh, there used to be a superstition that

you'd lose the vein if a woman looked on the vein, but that's—since women have worked in the mines, well, that superstition is pretty well forgotten." Still, this belief was fiercely held in earlier times, and many men would immediately walk out of a mine if a woman came underground. Ore veins are just as notional as huckleberries, it seems, and will moodily vanish if not properly propitiated. Finally, Helen Bondurant told of another superstition which miners used to cheat death: "Oh, and another thing is you never work the last shift. [. . .] You know: you'd get killed your last shift. See: 'It would have been his last shift, but he got killed.'" Miners knew that their job was deadly, that every shift could be their last, so in adopting the tradition of not working the last shift before they quit a job they respectfully and ritualistically acknowledged the mine's dangerous and violent strength and also helped assure themselves of continued survival by refusing to tempt fate one last time. Bill Bondurant indicates that beliefs like these have dwindled in the present, telling me that he'd "have to get next to an old Cornishman" to remember any more, but they survive in the memories of district veterans like him, and together they imply a collective vision of the mining landscape as an unpredictable and sometimes violent environment which was to be both respected and feared—yet one which, through the application of folk belief, could be at least temporarily and tenuously controlled.

Miners' feelings of wariness toward their place are not confined to the mines. They extend to the surrounding landscape as well, a landscape which has in many cases been altered and rendered dangerous by the demands and practices of nearby mines. Snow slides, for instance, were a common and deadly occurrence in Burke Canyon in the early days of mining; on March 29, 1894, there were seven slides in the canyon in a single day, one of which destroyed much of the mining village of Black Bear.[14] Many of these catastrophes still live in the repertoires of older residents. In describing one such avalanche which swept through the town of Mace in 1910, Bill Dunphy shows that snow slides could not have been as frequent and devastating as they were if it were not for the insatiable curiosity of prospectors and the voracious appetites of their mines:

Well, the reason for [the frequent snow slides] was all the prospecting that was done. And every one of these draws would have a creek running in it, you know, and it was worn down into a draw. And that was a sign, of course, that there was faulted ground; it wasn't hard rock. And so that's where the ore could be, in one of those faults; that's where they found all the ore veins. So they'd get up on these hills and they'd get right off the side of the creek and drive their tunnel in. And they'd cut all the timber that they needed out of the hills on both sides there. So they just made a great big chute down the side. Well, then up on the top of the hill was bare, and it was—well, we always called rock slides, but they didn't slide, they had weathered down from a thousand feet higher or so, who knows, into great big rocks, and it was all bare for maybe a quarter of a mile on each side of the ridge. And the snow would pile up there, and then it would cone over in the wind. Then if you got a Chinook, look out below, because you were liable to get a snow slide. And that's what happened in the snow slide of 1910, when they had all the snow slides that killed all the people; the snow must have been twelve foot deep up on those ridges, and then they got warm weather and a rainy Chinook. And you can hear a snow slide building hours before it comes: whoooo, you hear that Chinook wind blowing up on the hills, and boy, you better get the hell out of those snow slide draws. But it came down at night, of course, and caught all those people down in Mace, and there was a slug of them killed.

A contemporary postcard published by the Barnard Studio in Wallace shows the devastation wrought by the Mace snow slide: the massive pile of snow entombing the valley floor, the wreckage of houses scattered atop the pile, the dwarfed figures of rescuers searching for signs of life (fig. 18). The destructive power revealed by this photograph derived from more than simply the force and weight of onrushing snow: as Mr. Dunphy explains, "The mass of snow in the slide pushes the air in front of it at tremendous speed—a real hurricane. The buildings in its path are blown high into the air and come down on the spent slide. Makes it difficult to find the people buried." [15] It may seem odd, and slightly unsettling, that this disaster was deemed a suitable subject for a postcard. In the first two decades of this century, however, picture postcards were enormously popular both to send and to collect, and many small-town photographic studios—the Barnard Studio among them—produced hundreds of cards depicting both the typical scenes and the noteworthy happenings of their communities; their output comprised an informal pictorial record of the life and times of a town or region, suitable for keeping in one's memory book or sending to friends and family around the country. Just as they often are today, local picture postcards were both a form of promotion and advertising and a medium of self-identification, de-

Snow Slide at Mace, Idaho, February 27, 1910
16 Killed, 25 Injured

Figure 18. Picture postcard of the Mace snow slide. Courtesy Bill Dunphy.

picting as a rule the defining landmarks, scenes, and events of a place. The fact that the Barnard Studio chose to publish a postcard depicting the aftermath of a deadly snow slide—grim, offputting, and altogether unlikely an image as this may seem to send to a relative or paste into an album—indicates that Burke Canyon's tenuous relationship with slope and snow was an integral part of its self-image and, in turn, the image it chose to present to the rest of the world.

As Mr. Dunphy's description makes clear, snow slides like the one which tore through Mace were intensely place-specific, resulting from a unique combination of historical, economic, geographical, and meteorological circumstances which converged on this remote spot in the Idaho panhandle. The faulting patterns of the terrain around Burke Canyon brought ore close to the surface, luring eager prospectors who denuded the surrounding slopes as they cut timbers to shore up the tunnels of their mines, thus clearing and smoothing a downward path for snow piling up on the bare mountain summits. As northern Idaho receives heavy snows every winter and lies in the path of warm southerly Chinook winds, it was inevitable that massive snow slides would result. In a sense, then, snow slides were directly caused not simply by nature but by the especially enthusiastic brand of local mining as practiced under Burke Canyon's specific geographical conditions. Neither mining nor

Figure 19. The village of Black Bear as it appears today. 1989 photograph by the author.

mountains alone are sufficient to assure death by snow; the land has to be shaped just right, the miners have to be particularly in need of the easiest available timber. In the local mind, snow slides thus became a unique and distinguishing characteristic of this place, the product of a particular conjunction of life and landscape. The danger they once presented is now past—nowadays an entire glacier could scour most parts of Burke Canyon and not injure a soul, and trees have long since grown back in the narrow draws (fig. 19)—but avalanches still echo in the minds of people like Bill Dunphy as powerful reminders of the toll in human lives which mining in the area has historically demanded.

Along the way, Mr. Dunphy's discussion of snow slides also reveals a sensitive environmental literacy: his knowledge of man's role in shaping the canyon landscape, his awareness of the geological reasons behind the easy availability of ore in the district, his ability to decipher the aural signs which warned that danger was imminent (not unlike Mr. Bondurant's miners listening carefully for tommyknockers), his expertise in local patterns of wind and snow and the way that these elements typically interact with the local topography—all bespeak a long life spent quietly absorbing, through talk and experience, the components, textures, patterns, and meanings of the canyon landscape. In the course of skillfully explaining a specific phenomenon, Mr. Dunphy's discussion of snow slides reaches far afield to suggest a variety of ways of looking at and interpreting the local geographical surface, alluding by turns to his familiarity with the geological processes of faulting and erosion which shaped the district, with the traditional topographical clues which prospectors used to find new ore bodies, with the practical needs and material demands of mine developers, and with the evident and striking fact of the dramatic, jagged local terrain. In the space of a brief explanation, then, Mr. Dunphy reveals a deep and multivalent sense of place. He encapsulates in extremely condensed form much of the natural and human history of Burke Canyon, an awareness which simultaneously reflects the technical knowledge he has acquired from his professional life as a mining man, the historical knowledge he has drawn from his informal researches as a curious citizen of his place, and the unremarkable knowledge about slope and snow and sound that he has quietly accumulated through years of simply living in the landscape. His talk of snow slides may cast light on another facet of the dark and demanding quality which inheres in the place, yet at the same time it suggests how the full sense of that place, even for a single observer, gathers contributions from the full range of thought and experience which the locality supports and is finally deeper and more complex than any single, temporary interpretation which it may generate.

Many other people in the district match Mr. Dunphy in combining a detailed mental image of the local landscape with a wary and sobering sense of the ways in which the mines have shaped and stunted that landscape. Images of pollution, of fouled streams and barren ground, recur plentifully in perceptions and descriptions of the valley environment. During their many years of vigorous operation, the mining companies extracted and processed ore with little thought for the environmental consequences of their actions—"in those old days," comments Bill Dunphy, "you threw your waste in the creek, and that was your sewer, and the hillsides were ate up with smelter smoke. There wouldn't be a tree growing nowhere, or a lawn nowhere, within three or four miles, or five miles, of Kellogg." Economic concerns far outweighed worries about environmental damage or public health; as Leonard Heikkila explains the mining company ethic, "it was more important for the economy; that's all they were looking at: the mines were bringing in—there were all these jobs for the men, and it was providing work for them, and so they didn't think much of the environment; the environment was secondary, and the money and the jobs were first." As a result of this ethic, the town of

Kellogg, according to Maidell Clemets, "was called, at one time, the dirtiest town in the United States. So that's not really anything to boast about. And for years there was a creek out there that ran; there was a concentrator that was just pouring their mine wastes right in the creek, going down to the lake; they didn't have to impound any tailings or anything like that. And smelters were running wide open; they didn't care what pollutants they put out, you know." Kellogg has earned a reputation for filthiness in the rest of the state; an exoteric image which local residents commonly encounter as they travel outside the district. Marylinn Heikkila recounts an experience which happened to her daughter: "But I remember our daughter one day was talking to somebody down when she was going to school at ISU [Idaho State University, in Pocatello], and said she was from Kellogg: well, how could anything good—how could anything with any intelligence whatever come out of Kellogg? You know, that's just impossible [chuckles]." Lead poisoning and its concomitant brain damage, the thinking went, were endemic in Kellogg and its vicinity. In proud reaction to these attitudes, Mrs. Heikkila justly derives satisfaction from seeing outsiders' stereotyped images proved wrong, when "they come up here now and look: 'You have *trees!*' "

Still, Mrs. Heikkila vividly remembers how the South Fork of the Coeur d'Alene river ran grey with lead-laden mine wastes when she moved to the valley in 1961: "I can remember the grey river in '61. And you think of an icky grey sludge, and that is what the river looked like. And where the South Fork joined the North Fork up at Enaville, you had the clear one and the icky one becoming a murky one." She thinks also of the effects that corrosive smelter fumes had on the outside walls of houses in certain neighborhoods in Kellogg in the late 1970s, when the smelter was running at its heaviest and dirtiest: "In fact, there were some beautiful homes up at the far end of the Silver King draw, up past the smelter. Absolutely beautiful large brick homes up in there, well kept. Right in the midst of that. And then the houses that were directly east of the zinc plant, on the old highway—well, it's the road that goes up to the Bunker workings—there were some, oh, some lovely homes in there. Lovely homes. And then those particular years, no matter what kind of siding you'd have on your house, they took it off in that area. It's just—it was bad." Bill Noyen has similar memories of Smelterville at the time he moved there to run his grocery store, in 1946:

Well, the smelter was going, the zinc plant; everything like that was going. The air was foul with their smoke and the like of that; there was very little control on the smoke that was emitted from the stacks. [. . .] All the mines up and down the valley, up all the way from Burke and Mullan and Kellogg and Wallace, dumped whatever they had, all their waste was dumped in the rivers. And it wasn't until, oh, I think in the early 1970s, somewhere around in there, that they started cleaning them up. [. . .] It was a kind of a dirty place to come to.

Images of Kellogg as an industrial wasteland bulk large in local memory, their details etched deeply into the mental picture which people have formed of the district. Reinforced by the continued presence of the scarred brown hills which loom over the town, their ancient ravages showing through the ragged and patchy garment of new growth which has been thrown over them, this picture deeply influences not only the way that other Idahoans define the valley but the way that local residents define it as well.

Still, new growth *is* sprouting, and the rivers today are clear. Mines carefully impound their tailings, and the Bunker Hill smelter shut down when the mine closed in 1981; although the mine is working once again, the smelter remains closed. Valley residents contrast earlier images of sterile ground and sewer-like streams with the cleaner, greener landscape which surrounds them now, and they are heartened by the change. As it was with mining, when disappointment could be supplanted suddenly by unexpected wealth, so it is with the local environment—people sense the resilience of their landscape and are optimistic about its future. As far as Bill Noyen is concerned, one of the most noteworthy events he has witnessed in his years in the district is "the cleaning up of the river. Where it used to be, why, you wouldn't even dare to go down to the river and even put your foot in it; but now, now you can—there's fish coming up that creek now, so, yeah, it's changed an awfully lot since the time we came. That's forty-three years, and that's quite a change in forty-three years. And the greening of the hills and everything like that; and the sewage disposal, all of that has helped. There's a lot of things happened since we've been here." Marylinn Heikkila agrees: in her evaluation of local history, "one of the biggest things is a slow thing which—I hope I live another thirty years, so I can see what the trees are going to look like that they have planted on the hills." The thrilling fact of new trees is a recurring motif in people's discussion of their environmental image: Bill Etherton, a retired mining man and lifelong resident of the now-abandoned Pine Creek mining district, pointed out on a drive up Pine Creek that the surrounding hills had all been bare when he was a child. Those mountains have become reforested in his lifetime, a fact which gladdens him. He considers trees to be very valuable now—probably, he theorizes, because there were not very many around when he was a boy. People speak of the new growth with a gentle note of wonder, pleased and slightly amazed that new life is rising out of the abused earth: it is a form of once-buried and newly revealed wealth as dazzling and delightful as the gold and silver which miners have long sought to disinter from the mountains. Past images of barrenness and pollution stand juxtaposed with present scenes of greening hillsides and fish returning to waters that would have killed them not long ago. In their contemplation of the valley landscape, and in sifting that landscape through time and memory, local residents see in quick succession the threat and the promise which characterize their interpretation of their place, with new evidence of that promise present to their senses whenever they look out the window.

This same spirit of resilience and optimism also characterizes the way in which local residents think and talk about mining: despite the tales of disappointment which people tell, and despite the mine closings of recent years, the promise of success has always remained alive. In local minds, the land continues to harbor great wealth, wealth that awaits those who are lucky or skilled enough to find it; the glittering light of Noah Kellogg's outcrop continues to illuminate the district. Burke Canyon may be a string of ghost towns now, but elsewhere, up by Murray, people continue to work small claims. Wendell Brainard owns such claims and tells of the owner of a neighboring claim who sold his rights to a Canadian mining company, reserving a small section for himself: "He said, 'I call that my treasure vault.'" While many miners have found only disappointment in the district, many other seeming disappointments have turned suddenly into huge successes; as Bill Dunphy notes, "This is full of places where guys just quit and sold his interest, and somebody took it for a debt, and cursed it to high heavens, and wound up a millionaire." The district has seen enough stories of unexpected success to sustain its positive view of the land, to fuel its dreams of wealth—the story of the humble owners of the Hercules, for instance, who put their own money and work into the mine for twelve long years before they hit the ore and became millionaires, or the story of one of the owners of the Standard mine as Bill Dunphy heard it:

And the Standard mine was a real good one. [. . .] And when they hit the ore, these guys that were in the bond really had it made. And I know,

I got a story [that] Charlie Tilford in Spokane told me, and his folks had told him about it, that one of the guys who went in there and dug out, that found the ore in the Standard; his name was Leonard, that was his last name. He'd gone to work, and he came home, and they'd hit that beautiful galena ore down there, and he walked in the door and he threw his lunch pail behind the stove, and took off his diggers and threw them on the floor, and said, "Well, I'll never use them again!" Said his wife took off her apron or something, threw it down, and she said, "I'll never need this again!" [Laughs.] They didn't, either; they were worth a big bundle of money.

Traditions like these sustain people in their sense that, despite the way it has let so many of them down, the landscape's fundamental bounty and promise remain valid.

This sense ultimately grows out of and helps sustain the miner's traditional and fundamental attitude of optimism, his accustomed stance vis-à-vis the world—the "nonverbalized folklore," to revert to Sandra Dolby Stahl's term, that underlies and generates so many local narratives. As Bob Anderson puts it, "Yeah, hope springs eternal, especially in the mining. It's always one foot to a million dollars, the next foot [chuckles]." Maidell Clemets colorfully summarizes this traditional attitude:

But there's something about a mining town, though; there are a lot of optimistic people. In order to be a miner, you've got to be an optimist. You've got to be a great expecter. A miner is a greater expecter than a Christian, I believe. A Christian, he's expecting to go to heaven, but a miner, he's expecting to hit it big [chuckles]. [. . .] They say there's only two miners who ever went to hell, and one of them, he was working with a dull pick, and the other one, he had underestimated the size of the ore body. So that's one thing about it. It seems as though a miner, if he'd been a cat and had nine lives, why, he'd put seven of them in dreaming about his big strike he was going to make, and two of them trying to rustle up enough money to make it.

In a new expression of this old sense of optimism, the city of Kellogg is building a funicular railway from the center of town to the Silverhorn ski area on top of Wardner Peak: since mining in the area is in decline, Kellogg has decided to try as hard as it can to make itself over into a popular ski resort and tourist destination. Mr. Clemets tells a joke to illustrate the spirit that underlies such an ambitious enterprise:

And you might have heard a story about a boy who was fishing. He was catching, oh, beautiful fish. He'd look at them and throw them back. If he got a smaller fish, why, he'd size it up and put it in his creel. A fellow went over to him and, "Hey, kid," he said, "you're an exceptionally good fisherman, but what do you keep throwing all those big ones back for?" "Well," the kid says, "it's like this: we only got a ten-inch frying pan at home." [. . .] That's one thing about the gondola down there in Kellogg. They didn't have a ten-inch frying pan on that one.

As long as such attitudes remain current, as long as the people of the district retain what Mr. Clemets calls "a wide open mind" instead of a "ten-inch frying pan mind," the dark and sobering aspects of the local sense of place will never overtake and overwhelm its bright and promising elements—and as long as narratives expressing those elements continue to enliven the district's landscapes, even those which are scarred and abandoned, the miner's traditional optimism will continue to live.

Landscape and Life—The Mining Camps

Images of forests, mines, and mountains bulk large in people's understanding of the valley. They are the most visually striking elements of the local landscape, and, through both the personal experience of individual residents and the historical experience of earlier generations in that landscape, they have accrued a cluster of related meanings which are bodied forth in memory and story. By no means, however, do people envision the mines and the wilderness in static isolation, their meanings separate from and uncluttered by the press and flow of life in the district. When valley residents think of the region, they understand its physical features to be inextricably bound to the social networks which those features witness, support, and embrace; they find it difficult to describe or envision their place without simultaneously evoking the friendships and families which bring to that place many of its most poignant and vivid associations. When asked if any particular image stood out in his mind when he thinks about the area, for instance, Bill Dunphy (who now lives in the city of Coeur d'Alene) replied, "Well, I'd just say people. [. . .] Yeah, we—oh, there were great people. I had real good friends in Kellogg, Mullan, Wallace, everywhere." As a popular grocer and a former Shoshone County commissioner, Bill Noyen has come to define his home ground primarily in terms of the boundaries of his wide circle of acquaintance rather than as the region where mining or logging is done, so that his personal sense of place pushes well beyond the South Fork valley: "My home area? Well, I think we're mostly known just here in Shoshone County. Well, we're well-known in Benewah County, too, and I know people in Kootenai and Bonner and Boundary County. [. . .] Yeah, the whole Silver Valley, and then up the river towards Prichard and Murray and everything like that; we know a lot of people; we're well-acquainted up the Coeur d'Alene River, and all around this area." Not all the meaning of this place derives from scrutinizing its surface and chasing its resources, then, no matter how large a part those activities play in local ways of life. After working in the mines and the woods, after hunting elk and picking berries, people always return to the towns strung through the valley. These towns collectively comprise the focus of social life in the district and lie along the geographical spine of the region as well; they are the gravitational center from which people go out and to which they return, from which ore-rich canyons and forested mountains physically and conceptually radiate—they are the "jar," to revert to Wallace Stevens's poem, which the slovenly wilderness surrounds (fig. 20). The themes which people draw from life as it has been lived in these towns form a lively and essential component of their sense of place, one which exists symbiotically with the lessons they have derived from the land.

Miners and their families think of their towns as physically and socially distinctive, as embodying qualities not found in other types of settlements. Even as a child growing up on the other side of the mountains in the Benewah County town of St. Maries, Bill Noyen was aware that there was something different about the mining communities along the Coeur d'Alene River in Shoshone County:

> Shoshone County is a loose county, in the sense that they're not—the miners have always been that way, from the time I remember, when I was just a kid and my brother worked here in the post office in Kellogg. We'd come over from St. Maries, and you could always—if you wanted a drink of whisky or something like that, you could get it in Kellogg. And it wouldn't make any difference what day of the week it was, it was always that way in Shoshone County. And Shoshone County's still that way today. Still that way today. It's a good place to live.

People who live in the towns strung along the South Fork continue to view them as exceptional, as encouraging and supporting a way of living and of viewing the world which is rarely found outside the valley. They encapsulate this feeling in the traditional term "mining camp," a phrase

Figure 20. A mining camp: Mullan, Idaho. 1989 photograph by the author.

which carries with it an allusive depth of meaning and association available only to people who live in such towns. It is a natural and reflexive part of the vocabulary of miners: in talking about the copper mining city of Butte, Montana, Bill Bondurant casually mentioned that "all mining camps have a certain feeling in common, that you know you're in a mining camp." Aware that the term would not mean much to a visiting interviewer, his wife, Helen, offered to translate: "You won't hear that very often. And when we were in Boise, you know, I'd always mention something about 'back to camp.' And he says, 'It isn't a camp, it's a town; it's your mobile home.' Well, we were used to living in a mining town, and mining towns are always called 'mining camp.' Wallace is a mining camp; Kellogg's a mining camp. And it's just been so instilled that you just do it automatically, and people correct me now because they don't know what I'm talking about." People *outside* the district correct her, that is. As Mrs. Bondurant makes clear, the phrase is an automatic and ingrained part of the language of the region; it is a richly meaningful item in the vocabulary of place. Outsiders—even in Boise— have no idea that "mining camp" is a synonym for "mining town," nor do they have any idea of the complex of memories and emotions which the term evokes in the people who use it. Much of the verbal folklore of miners serves to illuminate the meanings which cluster around the term "mining camp," to pin down in words the "certain feeling" which Bill Bondurant and others find in the towns in which they live.

Part of this feeling is a vague yet comforting sense of belonging, an instinctive understanding of local ways of life and a recognition of the distinctive landscape of a mining town that make a miner feel like he fits in no matter where he travels among the mining communities of the West. When asked how she would describe that feeling in a mining camp which Mr. Bondurant mentioned, Helen Bondurant replied, "You feel at home." Her husband laughed appreciatively and added a confirming anecdote: "Yes, she had to go back to South Dakota and for some reason or other missed bus connections and had to stay overnight in Butte. I asked her how she liked Butte. She says, 'I liked it! It was a mining camp! I felt at home there!' [laughs]." Mr. Bondurant had started as a "tramp miner," a worker who rarely settled in any one place for long but instead moved frequently in search of more lucrative work or simply a change of scenery: as Mrs. Bondurant explained it, "But we'd hear of another job where they were paying better, we'd pick up and go"—a practice which found the family at various times in South Dakota, Arizona, and California, as well as Idaho. The tramp miner has traditionally been a familiar type in the mining camps of the Western states, a type whose essence Maidell Clemets captures in a brief story:

> They always had what they called the tramp miner, you know, and a moving population. And they tell the story about, like, one fellow, he kept a pair of diggers in Butte and a pair in the Coeur d'Alenes. And he came down here to the Bunker Hill and he hit the foreman up for a job, and the foreman said to him, "Well, Eddie, as I remember, last time we hired you, you only worked ten days." "Well," he said, "that's right." He said, "As I remember, you only paid me for ten days, too" [chuckles]. And that's the way that was.

Perpetually on the move, more interested in collecting a good wage than in putting down any sort of roots or showing any sort of company loyalty, the tramp miner ensured that the population of any mining camp remained fluid, and he probably lived in dozens of camps in the course of his working life. Wherever he went, though, he felt at home; he knew how people thought and behaved, and he blended in quickly. While the mining camps of the Coeur d'Alenes are unique and distinctive towns, then, they bear a close family resemblance to each other and to many other settlements in the Western mountains. While rooted along the

South Fork, the sense of place of Coeur d'Alene miners sends out shoots to ore-laden patches of ground in many other states; these miners belong to a conceptual and generic "place," the mining camp, which is not finally anchored to any one spot on the earth's surface. What is true of one camp, they feel, is true of them all. Bill Bondurant never worked in Butte, but, like his wife, he instantly felt like he fit in there: "I always felt at home in Butte."

Part of this feeling of recognition seems to arise in response to the distinctive physical appearance of a mining camp. As Bill Bondurant commented after telling of his wife's feelings of being at home in Butte, "Butte was a dirty town, too, like Kellogg." Mining inevitably scars and pollutes the land, leaving behind an industrial residue which is instantly recognizable by people who have spent years living and working around it. Others note a certain impermanence in the cultural landscape of a mining camp, a jerry-built boom-town quality which arises in response to the fickleness of the mineral wealth on which the camps are founded and to the traditional transience of the population. As Maidell Clemets notes, "a mining camp is short-lived. Born to die, and no element's going to bring it back that I know of." Because the nature of mining encourages little regard for the future, and because miners have rarely been inclined to settle in a town for long, he says, "a mining camp is more crude and more rude, probably, in a lot of ways, and you don't see too many local improvements or civic pride." For these reasons, Mr. Clemets finds that towns like Kellogg and Smelterville are "ugly. If the people themselves don't have any interest in it, why, what can you expect? No incentive."

There is abundant evidence in the local landscape of the transient and temporary nature of mining camps. The abandoned Pine Creek district south of Pinehurst is littered with collapsing mill buildings, cabins, and other structures which miners and mining companies simply walked away from when metal prices plummeted after World War II (figs. 21, 22). In other parts of the district, too, silent remnants of once-active mines and mining camps dominate the landscape, as Don Long points out in conducting a mental tour of the district:

And if you go away from the Bunker Hill complex, which has the smelter, at least still the remnants of the old smelters—the lead smelter and the zinc plant—then you get into more of the mining, the old remnants of mines; that is, generally you'll see a head frame, like at the Sunshine, and the mill buildings. Of course, when they're gone, then there's the mine dumps that are left in a lot of places; they're kind of unique, I guess

Figure 21. Disused mine buildings on a hillside along Pine Creek. 1989 photograph by the author.

[chuckles]. [. . .] You can go around and show people where, for instance, the main mining operations were at Burke; for instance, the Hecla Mining Company's old Star-Morning complex is still sitting there: the Star mill. And you go a little further up and there's still remnants of the Hercules, or the Tiger-Poorman dumps, and not much of the buildings left. Ninemile Canyon, there was the Interstate mine, the Tamarack mine, and the Success, and the Dayrock. There is very little left but the mine dumps, except the Dayrock buildings are still there: the head frame and the mill buildings.

Still, despite dirt and disrepair, people feel comfortable with the cultural landscape of their place; they recognize its appropriateness, the way it grows out of the miner's habitual approach to life and work, and they appreciate the link with the region's past that it provides. Currently, as part of its effort to promote itself as a ski resort and attract tourists, the city of Kellogg is refurbishing some of its downtown buildings with mock-Bavarian façades. Maidell Clemets takes exception to this enterprise: "Sure, it's all right, but, you know, that's a mining town. [. . .] And you can't go out and get the spirit of a Bavarian town in a mining town. It isn't there. Just like me; I live here in north Idaho, I don't live

Figure 22. An abandoned wooden chute next to the road which leads up Pine Creek. 1989 photograph by the author.

in Bavaria. I live in a mining camp." People in the district retain a strong sense of what a mining town should look like, a sensitivity to the geographical surface which forms a large part of their feeling of belonging.

For the most part, though, mining camps stand out in the minds of the people who live in them not for their physical appearance but for their social ambience. Helen Bondurant describes a time when Bill had briefly left mining and taken up farming: "And when Bill left the farm, the last time he left the farm, he thought he wanted to farm—I didn't, but he did [chuckles]—and he said one night, 'You know, I'm lonesome for the fellowship of the mines.'" The next day he found work at the Homestake gold mine in Lead, South Dakota. That fellowship—the "camaraderie," as Helen Bondurant describes it, of both the mines and the mining camps—forms a large part of the attraction of living and working in such places. "We've had a lot of fun," said Helen Bondurant more than once in the course of an interview. "I just remember they were fun days. Fun times." Her husband agrees: "Oh, I enjoyed the camaraderie, and liked the people that I worked with. [. . .] I'm not sorry that I followed the game." The Bondurants find that, to a certain extent, the sobering pall that settled over the district after the Sunshine fire has never lifted, and that the spirit of mining-camp fellowship has never really recovered: "The Sunshine fire was the beginning of the end as far as I was concerned," says Mrs. Bondurant. "The camaraderie just seemed to—it just fell away." Nevertheless, the personal narratives that the Bondurants and others tell about their social experiences in the district keep the mining-camp atmosphere fresh—in memory, at least, if not in the mines, streets, and taverns that they live among today.

Part of that atmosphere derived from the spirit of rough play which enlivened the mines and spilled over into the surrounding camps. Pranks and practical jokes, for instance, are common in any industrial setting, and some miners in the Coeur d'Alenes became notorious for their talents and enthusiasm in this field. Helen Bondurant urged Bill to "tell about Tommy Barton and his jokes," and Bill cheerfully complied: "Oh, he'd nail your lunch bucket down. He would [laughs], he'd catch somebody at lunch time sleeping and he'd give him a hot-foot. Or he'd take fuse and tie them [. . .] when they was asleep at lunch time, tie them down; they'd jump up when it was time to go to work, they couldn't get up! [Chuckles.] He was always doing something like that." One day, though, Mr. Bondurant gave Tommy Barton his comeuppance:

He just carried one sandwich, wrapped in plastic paper, in his coat pocket; that's all the lunch he carried. And so he was always getting us, playing some joke on us, so I went to a drug store in Wallace, and I said, "I'll get even with that S.O.B." And so I asked the druggist if he had any capsules of quinine sulfate. If you know what quinine sulfate is, it's the bitterest tasting stuff that you can imagine, and it's pure white powder. So I opened up his sandwich and emptied a capsule—I told the druggist what I wanted it for, and he said, "Here, take three." He gave it to me!

And he opened up his sandwich, and took a big bite out of it; the funniest look got on his face. He knew he'd been had. And he carefully folded the sandwich up, and put it back in his pocket, and never said a word! [Laughs.]

Tricks like these are played in mines all over the West, not just in the Coeur d'Alenes; they make up an important part of that "certain feeling" which floats freely through all mining camps. After he told me about Tommy Barton, Mr. Bondurant's memory turned to another practical joke he saw played in a mine in the gold country of South Dakota: "These two hotshots in the Homestake were in a raise, and they never could get them to come down. And so this fella took the powder out of, the dynamite out of a stick of dynamite, filled it up with dirt and sawdust, and stuck a cap and fuse in it, and put it on his skip, and hoisted the skip up there while the fuse was burning! They come down in a hurry [laughs]; it wouldn't have hurt anybody." Jokes like these serve to lighten the burden of exhausting work and to both relieve the tension of a hazardous occupation and cut through the long stretches of tedium which that occupation often entails; they are a creative and raucous response to the particular conditions which men find in the mines. They also help bind miners together into a community, serving as an informal and ongoing initiation into the spirited and roughhewn world of underground workers.

This rambunctious fraternity rarely bothered to rein itself in once it left the mines for the day or the weekend. As Bill Noyen was able to discern even as a child, the mining camps of the Coeur d'Alenes were notorious for the drinking, whoring, and fighting with which the miners filled their leisure time. Wallace "was a wide-open town" when they arrived in the early 1950s, reports Mrs. Bondurant, full of taverns and "upstairs rooms." "They had five [brothels] when we came to Wallace, upstairs," adds her husband, "and every other building was a saloon [chuckles]." Miners—as well as loggers, their hard-working congeners of the woods—shattered the calm of the streets with predictable regularity, according to Mrs. Bondurant: "Like with Wallace when it was in its heyday, the week would be kind of quiet, but during the weekends, see, the miners would come in, the loggers would come in. And it would be a bo-o-oming town." Things got especially raucous on payday: many miners would think nothing of drinking and gambling their paychecks away in a single night and going back to work the next morning to start earning another one. Maidell Clemets tells the story of a particularly enthusiastic gambler whom he knew in a mining camp in Alaska—which, while far from the Coeur d'Alenes, is part of the same generic "place":

And like when I was in Alaska there, I worked for the Alaska Civic Mining Company; they contracted right out of Watertown over there, and paid once a month. Boy, those miners would really blow their money. Soon as they got paid, boy, the dice would come out, they'd have four, five, six games going, a poker game going. I had a friend one time by the name of John. I didn't live in camp; we lived in what they called Boomtown. He was a good miner, John was, but he had the spirit to gamble. And he could pick up the dice and roll for his paycheck, and if he lost it, fine; he was just as happy as could be. He come over and wanted to know if I had some change, and I told him, "Well, the only thing I got, John, is this check here." "Well," he said, "that'll do." I said, "You bring back some of that"; I said, "I want something out of that." Yeah, he'd bring some back. So I gave him the check. I went to work that evening at about six o'clock, and the guys told me the game was really going. Well, I looked, and there was John; he was drunker than hell, but he had a pile of checks in front of him about that high. Boy, he broke the game, too. Well, then he told me, "I won't be to work." He said, "I'm going to town." And he said, "I'm lucky." And I said, "Well, they got guys sitting around in Anchorage waiting for you to come, too. They'll clean you out pretty quick." Well, about ten days, why, I told some guys to go down and get John, and they went and got him and brought him back. He was sick, and way in debt in town; he had a bill about eight hundred bucks there. I'd got my check back, though, before he left [chuckles]. He was giving guys money back; I found out, hell, he'd borrowed from three or four different guys [laughs].

Such an enthusiastic eagerness to gamble seems entirely appropriate among miners. Mining itself is a gamble; at any moment the ore vein may vanish or the price of metals may plummet, throwing men out of work. The capriciousness which characterizes the mines in the local understanding carries over into attitudes which the men who work in those mines hold toward the profits they gain from their work: glorious wealth or bitter disappointment await at the gambling table as they do underground, and the miner rushes forth eagerly to meet whichever one is waiting for him. He is principled in his pursuit, though, seeking to enrich or harm only himself, scrupulously repaying all those from whom he borrows money in the same way that early-day prospectors reimbursed the people who had grubstaked them. This theme of miners' honesty and integrity recurs often in stories that people tell about the mining camps.

Not everyone in the camps, however, has always been upright and honest. The miners themselves may have been honorable men, but the people who followed them to the mining camps, especially during the boom years, often had nothing more in mind than enriching themselves at the miners' expense. "As far as the class of people that followed mining," says Maidell Clemets, "it was always a group of tinhorns and prostitutes and that type of people that always came to a mining camp; they were trying to mine the miners, you know." Con men found eager and willing victims in a region where everyone had dreams of instant, lavish wealth, as Mr. Clemets relates:

> There was a lot of stories told, you know, about a fellow come to town one time in Wardner. He had a confidential manner about him, and he walked up to a bar there, in Page's Hotel, and ordered a drink, and gave the guy a twenty-dollar gold piece; there was a lot of gold in circulation at that time. And after the bartender rang it up, he said to the bartender, "You notice anything wrong with that twenty-dollar gold piece?" "No," he said, "I didn't," and he took it back out and said, "Well, it looks good to me." "Well, I'll tell you," he said; "it's counterfeit." He said, "I've got a machine down in San Francisco to make them." He said, "I can make them for fifty cents apiece, but they got hot on me down there; I had to get out, and this looks like a good place to set up." If he had about five hundred dollars he could go back down to San Francisco and get the machine and come up and they'd be in partners. So the bartender, he thought it over, and he didn't have five hundred dollars, but he got a couple of his friends to go in with him, and they raised the capital, the fellow left, and he didn't come back in the prescribed time. They took the gold piece over to the bank, and they gave it every test they had. And they told them, well, that was sure a good piece of money. He was just out five hundred dollars, that was all. But those type of people are still in existence today.

The confidence man is the human embodiment of the sense of treachery and broken promises which the district's people often attach to the woods and mines of their place. Like a mining property which seems rich on the surface but which "hides" the ore body once the tunnel is dug, the con man offers what seems like certain wealth only to withdraw it cruelly and leave the would-be millionaires with nothing but a worthless claim. Still, he always found ready victims, because, as Mr. Clemets commented after finishing his story, "there's something about a mining town, though; there are a lot of optimistic people." As we have seen, the miners of the region continue to focus on and respond to the promise of the land no matter how often that promise is broken, and this lesson which the land teaches them carries over into other areas of their lives as well.

Independence Day was always the high point of the social year in the mining camps, providing an occasion for lively collective celebration. The annual festivities provided a means for integrating their participants into the local community. Shirley Horning, for instance, felt rather dubious about moving from Spokane to Wallace as a girl in 1914: "Well, being dropped down into this valley with high mountains all around us, we were a little [chuckles] sure that we had come to the wrong place, my brother and sister and I." Before long, however, "we found that with the Fourth of July celebration coming, Wallace was putting on a real show. They had baseball games, they had races of all kinds, and people climbing the greased pole, and of course that was all fun for us to watch." The most anticipated part of the festivities was the competition in mining skills, especially in rock drilling. These contests frequently transcended the local celebrations which spawned them and became popular exhibitions in their own right. As Maidell Clemets explains,

> The early days, the biggest-drawing event in the district was the rock-drilling contests. You could draw a bigger crowd to a rock-drilling contest than to a baseball game. And then the prize fights. [. . .] They did all the drilling, you know, by hand. And they'd have contests to drill by hand. And they'd have all the western mining camps, and they'd have maybe a national meet: mining camps would come in from Butte and Arizona and Nevada and Idaho, drill for the world championship, two men to a team. And they'd drill fifteen minutes in granite with a hand steel and a hammer. And those men were in extremely good physical condition, far better condition than probably any athlete of today. [. . .] At times they were hitting as high as seventy-seven blows a minute with that hammer, six- or eight-pound hammer. And when they'd strike with the hammer, they'd only bring the hammer up even with the top of the shoulder and down; if you brought it back over the shoulder you were lifting the hammer. [. . .] And then they had the hand drilling: the guy would hold the steel in one hand and hit it with the other hand.

Rock-drilling contests were more than a crowd-pleasing exhibition. They were a ritual demonstration and public proclamation of miners' skills, of their mastery over the rock in which the ore was encased and against which they struggled every day. In a region where people habitually eye their geography warily, where death lurks underground and the pursuit of any resource is attended with uncertainty and frustration, such contests publicly enacted the strength, indomitability, and determination with which miners faced their daily task, and provided them with an arena in which they could ritually defeat their adversary. Rock-drilling contests showcased the pride and confidence that miners had in their abilities, the confidence expressed in a tall brag which Bill Bondurant passed on to me: "Like I asked this old miner about it, where he'd mined. He said, 'From Alaska to the Witwatersrand.' He says, 'I can set up on the moon and collar a hole on the slick side of an egg!'"

Images of rowdy, lively play leavened by honesty and personal integrity dominate Bill Dunphy's impressions of the many years he spent in the mining town of Burke, at the head of Burke Canyon. Now largely a ghost town, the Burke of the late nineteenth and early twentieth centuries stands out in the minds and memories of many local residents as the epitome of all mining camps: "Boy," commented Wendell Brainard, "that was a lively town in the old days up there." Burke's physical appearance was striking, leaving abundant evidence of the haste with which people built the town so that they could get immediately to the important work of hauling ore out of the ground: "The town was really jammed in there," recalls Mr. Dunphy; "they were all just board houses; of course, like all mining camps, they just threw them up there for people to subsist in while they were working in the mines." Burke's ramshackle buildings were crammed tightly into a canyon so narrow that the railroad track ran by necessity down the middle of the town's only street, an arrangement so distinctive and bizarre that it remains lodged firmly in the local mind even today (fig. 23). As Leonard Heikkila reports, "the joke was the town was so narrow the dogs had to wag their tails up and down instead of sideways [laughs]." Bill Dunphy remembers similar exaggerations of Burke's narrowness; while he knows from experience that Burke was never as narrow as memory and story would have it, he appreciates these narratives for the way they capture the essence of Burke's unique appearance.

It was narrow; there was one track ran through town, with two railroads using it [chuckles]. [. . .] They always said that, when the train came through Burke, you had to hoist the awnings to get the train through, which wasn't right. But it's a good story. I remember one story they told: when the town of Burke burnt, in 1923, they had a lawsuit against the railroad for starting the fire. We had one real character in Burke; his

Figure 23. Burke, Idaho—looking East, 1912. No. 8-X37, Barnard-Stock-bridge Collection, University of Idaho Library, Moscow, Idaho.

name was Billy Monroe, and he was a dandy. And they got him for a witness, down in the courthouse, and this railroad lawyer—of course, he was one of their hotshots, you know—he said, "Now, Mr. Monroe, they tell me that, as you go through Burke, that you can reach out and you can touch the buildings with your hand." Billy says, "Well, maybe you could, but you'd have to have a pretty long arm!" [Laughs.] That was a good story; it lasted for a little while.

Mr. Dunphy appreciates this story for the way it allows a Burke insider to deflate a "hotshot" outsider who thinks he knows all about the town; Billy Monroe knows the truth about the dimensions of Burke's narrow main street and drily twits the railroad lawyer for his supercilious assumptions and the credence he lends to rumor and cliché. The story draws on a deep familiarity with Burke geography and is a statement of identity for old Burke residents insofar as that identity is rooted in an experiential knowledge of that geography—only Burke veterans can fully appreciate the point of the story. At the same time, it resonates with an amused fondness for the quirks of a town where, as Mr. Dunphy says, "when the train came up you had to move the cars off so it could get through. They'd have to go slow, and they'd go in the beer joints and drag the drunks out to get their cars off the track, which is a kind of an exaggeration."

"Yeah, Burke was quite a town"; Mr. Dunphy repeated this comment, or variations on it, several times during his interview. In his perception, the Burke of his youth was a frontier outpost, an enclave of the old West surrounded by the twentieth century. Isolated at the end of a long narrow canyon in a remote mountain range, it was a place where men routinely settled arguments with fistfights and rarely bothered to wait for a judge to rule on a point of law before they meted out punishment themselves. "She was the code of the West there," says Mr. Dunphy; "that's what made it such a fighting town." He tells the story of one memorable fight, an epic battle which summarizes Burke's fighting spirit for him:

> So it used to be quite a thing; there was a depot right at the foot of the stairs where you come down out of the Hecla mine, and it was like a pit. It had about a three-foot concrete wall around one side of it, and then the depot was on the other. And these miners would—"I'll meet you in the parking lot." And they'd fight there, and boy, oh, boy, would they fight. I saw one fight: there was a kid, he was from the University of Idaho; he was a basketball player, and he was working in the mine in the summertime. And he got into an argument with another guy, and they were going to fight, and they went out there in the street and started. And they fought the full length of Burke three times. And no sign of defense; just plunk, plunk! And one guy got one guy going backwards, and he'd just lace into him until they got down too far, and they'd get into a mix-up again and turn around and come back. Boy, I'll tell you, there was five hundred blows that were just plain smashes! [Chuckles.] I never saw anything like it. Neither one of them ever tried to duck or catch a blow on their arms; God, that was an awful fight.

Fighting was an important part of life in Burke, both as a violent expression of anger and as a form of recreation; the spirit of rough play which characterized life and work in the mines spilled out of the workplace and into the life of the town. Boxing was a favorite sport in Burke, both for participants and for spectators. Several regional boxing champions came out of Burke, and Mr. Dunphy himself fought in exhibition matches as a boy: members of the local fraternal organizations would regularly "have big feeds and stuff, and they'd get us kids to put on exhibition fights—boxing, up there; you'd pick a kid your size and go two or three rounds with him, and then they'd have what they called a silver shower. They didn't pay you, but they'd throw dimes and nickels and quarters—not too many quarters—into the ring there after you got through fighting, and you'd throw your gloves off and scratch, and sometimes you'd get a dollar or two. I did a lot of that." Violence was simply a normal and expected part of male life in Burke, the expression of a perceived frontier-like expectation that men would defend themselves with the strength of their bodies and refuse to be intimidated. "There were some pretty short-tempered guys working," explains Mr. Dunphy; "they'd say, 'Oh, God damn you, I'll meet you in the parking lot.' And nobody ever said no, because everybody would think they were chicken. [. . .] But they'd get out there, and we'd form a big ring around them and let them go until somebody won. That's why Burke had such a reputation as a fighting town."

For all its character as a fighting town, however, Burke's fights were always scrupulously fair. The "code of the West," as Mr. Dunphy put it, demanded not only violence and retribution but, as in other aspects of mining-camp life, integrity and self-reliance as well. "But nobody pulled a knife or hit a guy with a rock or something else," explains Mr. Dunphy; "it was fist-fighting. And anybody stepped in, somebody would plunk him one so fast it wouldn't even be funny. If your own brother was getting beat up there, you stayed back and let him get beat up; you didn't get mixed into it and try to rescue him. Then somebody would knock you cockeyed." The same qualities which guided the conduct of Burke fights also shaped the course of Burke justice. Mr. Dunphy talked about another exemplar of the frontier code—the local justice of the peace, who

was famous all over the West [for] the way he run the law in Burke. He said, "If you want law, go to Wallace. If you want justice, come to Burke!" [Laughs.] And somebody beat up on their wife, why, he'd really lower the boom on him. If you just got into a fight, and tried to say you got whacked, he'd laugh at you. He wasn't a hanging judge, like some of the famous ones in the Southwest, but he was famous in this part of the West as a judge. Burke had their own marshal, and a jail; a lockup, more like. There were maybe four or five cells in the jail when I first came there. And they took care of their own law. But it was just about like living in a big fraternity where they took care of their own troubles. You beat up on your wife, somebody was liable to tie a rope around your neck and drag you up that creek about a hundred yards and say, "Now, are you going to do it again?" [Chuckles.] That cured them better than throwing them six months in jail! [Laughs.]

Rather than rely on the legalistic hairsplittings of judges, people in Burke executed justice according to their own firmly held standards of right and wrong, standards which grew out of an elemental, common-sense grasp of basic concepts of fairness and decency. It was wrong to abuse the weak, and weak to call on the protection of the law if a self-reliant confrontation of fists and brawn could settle the matter. Miners were vigilant in making sure that no one took undue advantage of anyone else. Despite the brutal stance with which men in Burke faced the world and each other, then, their actions were ultimately motivated by a desire to look after each other as members of a close-knit community—or "fraternity," to use Mr. Dunphy's word. They may have been angry and violent when confronting one another, but a feeling of responsibility for the welfare of the group as a whole ultimately lay behind their behavior and social thought.

Instances of solidarity and mutual support occur repeatedly in people's memories and stories of life in the mining camps. Mining is a notoriously uncertain occupation economically: fluctuating metal prices bring periodic layoffs, and, while coming nowhere near the level of anger and violence of the labor wars of the 1890s, standoffs between miners and management continue to punctuate life in the valley. Wages were low in the early days of mining, and it was often difficult for men with families to support their wives and children comfortably. Through all these troubles, though, miners have faithfully stood by one another, rarely putting personal welfare before that of the community. Years of standing together in the face of economic pressures have instilled in them an unshakable sense of mutual responsibility and group cohesion. "If you want to say one thing about the miners," says Maidell Clemets, "they were good-hearted. I never saw a stingy miner; damn few of them." Helen Bondurant fondly recalls the spirit of solidarity which infused the community during an eight-month strike at the Lucky Friday mine in the late 1960s, an occasion which combined the wonted spirit of lively fellowship in a mining camp with an invigorating sense of mutual care and concern to the point where the strike seemed more like a picnic than a hardship:

It was fun times. You never saw the men that were so close. [. . .] Yeah, and the union, the international allowed so much per person. And I was working. I was selling Avon, and I took on Fuller Brush. And we managed; we just took groceries, that's all we took. And Bill and I managed, and we were paying the mortgage on the house until, just the last eighth month, I had to ask if I could get by with just the interest [chuckles]. And anyway, Bill had been negotiating—he was on the negotiating team—and he'd come home, and he'd be *so* tired. [. . .] He'd come home, and he says, "Let's go uptown and sneak in the back door at Albi's and have a beer so I can go to sleep." So we'd sneak in the back door at Albi's and sit in a booth and order a beer. Pretty soon there'd be more beer, and more beer. "Don't take any money from those people; they're on strike. Don't take any money from those people." Do you know, [whispering] I don't think I went to work any day half sober, any day; I had a headache all eight months! [Laughs.] [. . .] Then we had, up at Morning Club—it was kind of a social place up in Mullan; it used to be company; I think they've torn it down now. But we had a dance up there. And they had just like a . . . what is it when somebody just picks up something and—a jamboree or something? And we danced, and the union officials bought turkeys, and we brought whatever we happened to have, and we had the biggest pot luck! We had *more fun*!

Mrs. Bondurant's reminiscence encapsulates her understanding of the nature of a mining camp. She offers at least a tame glimpse—as extensive a glimpse as her participation allows—of Wallace's "wide-open" approach to life with her implication that taverns were the center of social life and that time spent there often centered on convivial drinking. The camaraderie that she and her husband felt among their friends and fellow citizens is clear, whether it be expressed at a bar or at a "jamboree." Most importantly, it is a camaraderie founded on a sincere concern for the welfare and happiness both of individuals and of the group as a whole. If a mining camp is a place where miners feel at home, it is because they feel that they belong and are nurtured there, that they have found a safe and supporting haven from the shelter of which they can face the hazards and uncertainties of life, work, and land. They gain a sense of identity from the mining camp; they define themselves as members of this select and cohesive group which calls this place home.

Bill Dunphy remembers similar episodes of care, concern, and cohesiveness among the miners in Burke. When money was short, miners took advantage of every opportunity they had to make sure that the more needy among them were comfortable. Single men in Burke lived and ate in "beaneries," company-run boarding houses which fed their occupants plentifully, although "a guy working in the mine, paying his board there, could just about barely pay his board and room." Married miners lived in nearby houses and found it much more difficult to buy enough food to feed their families.

And I can remember working in the stopes there with people, with men who maybe—one man would be staying at the beanery, a single man, and then there'd be a married man there with four or five kids, trying to get by on fifteen to seventeen dollars a week. So, at the beanery you made your own lunch; they had a great big table set up, and a guy'd just walk by, and they had the old pie can, which was a round can about twelve inches high, and the top of it had an insert that would hold coffee, and they'd put the coffee in that and then underneath it they'd fill it with sandwiches. Well, during the Depression I've seen those guys just fill the whole can with sandwiches and give them to the guys that they worked with who had families, to take home to feed the kids [chuckles].

This sort of concern for communal welfare was not limited only to miners; it permeated an entire mining camp to the point where merchants would do everything they could to aid miners who were finding it temporarily difficult to get by on their own. Maidell Clemets tells of an encounter he witnessed with a particularly helpful and trusting local merchant:

And I seen a fellow come into a store one time, said he had a job but didn't have any money, and he needed some diggers to go to work in the mine. Well, he asked him, the storekeeper, "Well, what do you need?" Well, he needed a pair of rubber shoes, and overalls, a jacket, a carbide lamp, a lunch bucket, and stuff. He laid them all out on the counter. Well, the fellow said, "I'll be in to pay you payday." He said, "Well, I hope so." Well, he said, "Don't you want my name?" "Hell, no," he said. "Your name don't mean nothing to me," he said. "If you ain't going to pay me, you won't be around" [chuckles].

Not only does the storekeeper feel a benevolent concern for the welfare and success of the miner, he assumes as a matter of course that the man is honest and that he will be paid back—an assumption that was quite safe, for a miner who welshed on his debts quickly became a local pariah. "If you didn't pay your bills, you were just out of luck," explained Mr. Clemets. "You couldn't buy nothing; you couldn't even buy yourself a meal if you had money." The same ethic held true in Burke, according to Mr. Dunphy: his aunt and uncle ran a boarding house and would often let men stay there while they looked for work, getting paid only when the men found jobs. "And the funny thing is that very few people in those days ever beat their bills on board and that stuff; they might have on other things, but it was a real disgrace to beat a board bill, because you might need that awful bad the next time." Miners' integrity was seen as a matter of character, though, more than of expediency: to be a miner was, by definition, to be generous and honest. Feelings of concern and obligation in mining camps were reciprocal, not merely extended from benefactor to beneficiary; they bound the camp together into a cohesive, mutually supportive community.

One indication of the extent to which miners identify themselves as members of a cohesive group united by place and occupation lies, as has been noted before, in the existence, use, and meaning of the term "mining camp." The phrase is much more than a simple synonym for "mining town" or a picturesque linguistic survival from the days when miners actually lived in tents or rough cabins clustered near the mine portal. As we have seen, it resonates with personal and social connotations which become clear only through exploring layers of memory and narrative. The camps of the Coeur d'Alenes were once rich with many other such words and phrases, bits of language which are meaningless to nonminers and which often grew directly out of miners' experiences in the workplace. Bill Bondurant explained some of them to me. "Rustling," for instance, meant looking for work: "Just hunting for a job. Go up to the personnel office, and when you go into the personnel office, you're rustling. You're looking for a job; rustling up a job." Another phrase peculiar to the "mining lingo," as Mrs. Bondurant put it, is "Tap 'er light," a leave-taking formula which, according to Mr. Bondurant, "means 'be careful.' What it come from was, don't hit the powder too hard. And another expression for being careful was 'Stay out from under the loose.' [. . .] That one come from Michigan. It meant, be sure and bar down before you went into a place"—that is, use a long pole to knock any remaining loose rock from the roof of a newly blasted passage before you enter it. "It meant take care. 'Short fuse and long run' [chuckles]. Meant you was in a hurry to get out of there." Bob Anderson notes that the now-familiar toast "Here's mud in your eye" could have "come from nowhere other than the mining industry." It alludes to the days of hand drilling, in which one man would hold and turn the drilling steel while another struck it with an eight-pound hammer. To keep the dust down and make the cuttings easier to remove, the men would pour water into the hole from time to time. Occasionally, a blow on the steel would send a jet of mud into the eye of the holder—"And so, the miner's toast."[16]

Phrases like these, drawn from miners' experiences in blasting and working with rock underground, provided those who used them with a private language of sorts, a code whose meanings outsiders did not know and the use of which signaled both membership in the local group of miners and an intimate familiarity with the workings of the mines themselves. Their use created and reinforced a sense of belonging, both to the group and to the place: they are "mining terms from the mining camp," says Mrs. Bondurant, and "they aren't in anything else."

Slang terms like these also provide a sense of the extent to which the miners of the district have projected the values of their place onto the rest of the world. They have used their mining experience as a rich source of metaphor, translating behavior in other contexts into terms peculiar to their place. Through the use of such phrases they turn everyone figuratively into a miner, everyone's behavior into the familiar activities in which miners engage daily. Rather than let the rest of the world exist on its own terms, they view it through the lenses that their place provides. As the milieu which suggests this language and encourages its use, then, a mining camp is much more than a place to live, a spot on the earth's surface: it provides both a standpoint for understanding the wide world surrounding the camp and a sense of identity so strong and confident that, through its distinctive slang, it playfully molds the rest of humanity to fit its own image.

Another way in which miners in the Coeur d'Alenes have used language to build and sustain a sense of community and belonging is through the liberal creation and bestowal of nicknames. "Up at the mine," explains Helen Bondurant, "everybody had a nickname," and a miner's nickname soon became the label by which he was identified in the community as a whole: "you'd *never* know what his real name was." These names often derived from some identifying characteristic of their holders, some distinguishing aspect of appearance or behavior which marked them off from their fellows. For instance, Mrs. Bondurant tells of "a fellow over there [at the Lucky Friday mine] that had a little farm on the side, and he sold milk to the little town of Mullan, and they called him Milk Bottle. I don't know how many knew his name." One miner, trying hard to think of the word for a male goose, called it a "rooster-goose"; the name immediately stuck to the man himself, and he was known only as Rooster-Goose from then on. Bill Bondurant mentioned other colorful names which make the listener wonder with amusement just what sort of people they were attached to: Screaming Gene, Biffo, Dum-Dum, Little Man. Mr. Bondurant himself, explains his wife, "was

Big Bill; I don't know how many Bills there were; maybe there was a Little Bill and a Medium-sized Bill up there [chuckles], but they called him Big Bill, and all you had to say was 'Big Bill' and that was him." Along with their mining-based slang, nicknames like these provide members of the community with a private language whose referents are known only to them, an unofficial home-grown nomenclature to parallel or supplant the official, legal names which are known to the world at large. To be able to pick Milk Bottle out of a crowd, to know who Big Bill is while finding no meaning in the name Bill Bondurant, is to prove that one belongs in the place, that one is a member of an exclusive society whose members have been given new identities which are valid and meaningful only in this particular location.

Nicknames like these call to mind the distinction which folklorist Mary Hufford draws between the various names attached to plants and animals in the New Jersey Pinelands—between "botanical names," which identify a species "in the format and language of an international classification system," and "local names," which "encapsulate human experience with the species on this landscape," which "spring from experience with a place." [17] The difference between the names *Sternotherus odoratus* and "stinkpots" for a smelly kind of Pinelands turtle is the same as the difference between the names "William Bondurant" and "Big Bill" for a north Idaho miner. One is official, suitable for a scientific paper or a driver's license; the other is vernacular, growing out of olfactory experience in a Jersey swamp or the daily round of work and relaxation in a mining camp. These unofficial names circulate only within the local group, serving to maintain and tighten its cohesion; they help cement a sense of identity, an identity rooted firmly in the speaker's and listener's intimate knowledge of the life of a place.

The extent to which a miner's local identity can be represented almost completely by his nickname, as well as the extent to which that nickname can become conceptually divorced in the local mind from his legal name, became clear in Bob Anderson's experience in the aftermath of the Sunshine mine fire. In discussing his impressions of the miners' memorial, Mr. Anderson noted that many of the names listed on the monument's plaque were literally meaningless to him: "And many of the men whose names are on the plaque I don't know, didn't know. Unfortunately, there are some whom I did know but knew only by a nickname, so when I see a name, a full name, it doesn't mean anything to me. [. . .] Somebody would say Little Joe or Red Fred or Mickey, something like that, I would know, but some of those names I didn't know. I knew the faces, of course." The memorial is a public proclamation of sorrow and regret, a means of immortalizing the memory of the fire's victims by announcing their names to passers-by. It is more an official gesture, however, than a home-grown expression of miner sentiment: it uses the victims' legal names rather than the nicknames by which they were known locally, names which they earned in the course of their work in the mine in which they ultimately died, and so does not mean as much to the local community as it might. The plaque is not written in their language; it does not take account of the identities that the dead men had crafted within the mining camps, the truest and most meaningful sense of identity that they had. The main function of the memorial is thus primarily the same as that of any public monument: it announces to those who see it that something important happened in the vicinity— here, something terrible and tragic—and, through its plaques and statuary, attempts to shape interpretation of that event. While the people of the district appreciate that the memorial was built, its physical form has little relevance to local ways of life and bonds of identity. Residents of the district bring their own interpretations to the memorial, their own memories and associations; the heroic statue and the plaque with its official names are ultimately superfluous, dissolving away and leaving their beholders with remembered images of Red Fred and Little Joe at work in the mines and strolling the streets of the mining camps.

Wendell Brainard habitually uses language both to identify outsiders and to cement his feeling of belonging in a mining camp. "I know the language," he says; "I get a kick out of some of these Spokane reporters or somebody; they don't know the mining language, like the shaft in there—you either go down in a cage, or the skip, as they call it, and they call it an elevator; well, the miners [chuckles] laugh at them." District residents in general are sensitive and interested observers of newcomers to their place; like Alida Sverdsten commenting on the ineptitude of the Missouri tourist, they tell stories that pass judgment, with amusement or condescension, on the frequent inappropriateness of visitors' behavior to the way that life in a mining camp is lived. Helen Bondurant remembers a recent display of environmental illiteracy on the part of a group of tourists:

The other day I was at the new restaurant in this end of Wallace. And WHOOM! A lot of tourists in there. Everybody said, "What was that? What was that? What was that? Somebody hit something with a truck!" So I says, "Oh, that's an air blast." I says, "Are you tourists?" "Yeah, we're tourists; what's that?" I says, "That's an underground earthquake. There's a lot of mining under here, and the earth moves, and it's called an underground earthquake." It was a big one; it shook. Boy, they were all— even the waitresses; I thought they were funny, because they were local people.

What the greenhorns thought was a horrible highway accident turns out to have a simple, mining-related explanation. Mrs. Bondurant is surprised that even the waitresses, "local people" all, could not properly identify the sound; she is amused and a little disappointed by this lapse in their knowledge of their place. They blur the line between canny Wallace residents and naive visitors in a way that Mrs. Bondurant finds slightly disconcerting: to be a local person, in her mind, is to know all about air blasts. No such blurring occurred when Maidell Clemets got off work one day to be confronted by Donald Callahan, a campaigning politician who had recently moved to the district "from back east":

> But he was a two-bit politician, a smart guy. I remember during the Depression, he was running on the Republican ticket; well, of course, there wasn't a Republican anywhere in the United States at that time. I worked at a mine, and he come up there on the mine dump, and of course we were going to work when the moon was shining and coming off work when the moon was shining. They run the cage up, and the miners were all standing there, and he climbed up on a wagon, and the first word he said was, "Unaccustomed as he was to rising this early in the morning" [chuckles]. That's the last thing he should ever have said, you see. [. . .] He got off to a poor start. When he got through talking, nobody applauded or anything. He had sort of a downhearted look on his face, and he left.

After his astonishing display of ignorance about the long hours of hard work that miners engage in daily, Callahan receives nothing but the scorn that he deserves. The pompous Easterner slinks off in humiliation, and the miners are left with their sense of identity and group solidarity strengthened and reaffirmed through their confrontation and contrast with this bumbling outsider—an affirmation which Mr. Clemets reenacts through telling his story.

Much of the mining camp spirit as embodied in nicknames, slang, and stories is by now lost in the past. The mining camps themselves have suffered decline and depression since the days when they were famous for their hard work and spirited play. Burke began losing population as long ago as the 1940s, according to Bill Dunphy: "it was when

Figure 24. The main street of Burke as it appears today. 1989 photograph by the author.

the automobile came in, when people could buy automobiles, and that was right after the Depression. Then people moved down to Wallace, and they drove to work, and people that had pickup trucks, they'd haul eight men to work, you see, so they could live in Wallace." Today only a handful of people live there, and its rickety architecture and narrow main street are preserved only in photographs, jokes, and memories (fig. 24). Even in the remaining towns, change has been constant and harsh. As the Bondurants sensed, the 1972 mine fire darkened the mood of the district, causing a depression from which they feel it has never fully recovered. The Bunker Hill mine and smelter shut down in 1981, throwing over two thousand people out of work; the mine has since started production again on a smaller scale, but the original shutdown sparked an exodus of unemployed miners from the district, emptying houses, threatening merchants, and eroding morale. Through hard times and tragedy, however, the pure idea of the mining camp remains vital in the minds of district veterans, who keep it alive in lore and memory. When they look about them, they still see and feel something of its valued sense of camaraderie and liveliness. After Bill Bondurant retired, he and his wife moved to Bremerton, Washington, to be closer to their son, a retired Navy officer. Soon, however, they moved back to the district and settled in Kellogg; as Mr. Bondurant explains, "I had a lot of friends in Bremerton, but it was just—even though my son was a Navy man—it's just a Navy town and I didn't fit. Oh, we were friends with a lot of retired Navy people there, raised beautiful gardens, and just some reason or another—it wasn't home." And to a miner, after all, only a mining camp feels like home, no matter how much it may have changed. Despite years of economic depression and social erosion, the towns along the South Fork of the Coeur d'Alene still claim a prominent place in the thoughts, memories, emotions, and folklore repertoires of the people who have lived, worked, and socialized in them.

The Individual, the Community, and the Sense of Place

Within the shared sense of place of any region there is, of course, a great deal of individual variation. Although all residents of a place participate in the same broad patterns of geographical and historical experience, each person's sense of place is altered to fit his or her personal experiences within those larger patterns: like jazz soloists, individuals create unique styles and interpretations of life while remaining within the rhythms and structures of a larger composition. Maidell Clemets, for example, was a devoted and energetic amateur historian and a keen and opinionated observer of life in the district. His knowledge of the district's past was encyclopedic, his fund of stories seemingly inexhaustible. Few people could have had as firm a grasp of the district's general sense of place as he did. When asked which landmarks in the area stood out most in his mind, though, his response slid gently from the communal to the personal:

Well, yes, there's always certain landmarks that stand out, you know. I wrote an article one time about the Pythian Hall, used to be in Wardner. It was a three-story building, and all the center of activity was in the Pythian Hall. And they had national figures come in there; matter of fact, Corbett fought there, and Jim Jeffries fought there, in Wardner. And the reception room was patterned after the Metropolitan Opera House reception room, all finished off in red. It was a three-story building; they used to have their balls there, and things like that, and all the women in town, if they had some money, they'd go to see who had the best gown, things like that. It was the center of activity. And I remember when I was a boy, we lived in Wardner, up on a side hill, and we were very poor. And we had a bulkhead in front of the house to hold the bank up that the house was built on, and the hillside was pressing against the house trying to push it down, and one wall looked like it was getting bowed. And when they tore down the old Pythian Hall, why, we got some of those boards out of the old Pythian Hall and put a false wall in there against that bow. When I was a kid and came home from school, why, I used to hang my coat and hat on that wall. So I hung them on part of the old Pythian Hall. And it was a landmark. It's gone.

The Pythian Hall had been an important landmark in the conventional sense: years ago, it had been the hub of social activity for the old mining community of Wardner. Mr. Clemets's discussion of this facet of the hall's significance, however, is that of a conscientious historian; identifying prominent past landmarks for a curious visitor, he feels obliged to share his derived knowledge, to mention the famous boxers who fought in the building and to talk of how the town's women used it as a showcase to display their finery. The hall's most vivid significance for him lies instead in the fact that its boards had been incorporated into the fabric of his childhood home and that he used to hang his hat and coat on those boards when he came home from school. That act, and the memory of that act, provide Mr. Clemets with a personal link to the local past which no one else shares. While he is well aware of the larger significance of the old Pythian Hall, he plays a solo on that theme to show how the vanished building also carries vital experiential meaning within the context of an individual life.

Moreover, people share in the communal interpretation of place to a greater or lesser extent depending on how deeply they have been involved in the valley's typical ways of life. Shirley Horning, for instance, is over ninety years old and has lived in the district since the day in 1914 when her father, a railroad mechanic, moved his family to Wallace. Despite her longevity in the region, however, her connection with the world of mining is tangential at best: she has read many of the published historical works about mining in the Coeur d'Alenes, and her late husband, an attorney, was once a part-owner of the Lucky Friday mine in Mullan, but the daily patterns of her life have rarely brought her in contact with the experiences and concerns of miners and loggers. When she contemplates Wallace and its environs, she sees them as the setting for the social life of a teenaged girl and, later, of the wife of one of Wallace's more prominent citizens. This is not to say that she has remained totally insulated from the often raucous life of the mining camp; she tells the story of one man who decided to dispense a little frontier justice, an important local politician named Herman Rossi:

He was the mayor. And one night he came home unexpectedly and found that his wife was entertaining [chuckles] a gentleman, or had been. The man was the cashier at the hotel downtown, on the corner there. Anyway, he went down and shot the man, and Mr. Rossi was tried for the murder, or for the killing—I guess they didn't call it murder. But the jury couldn't say he wasn't guilty, so he had to spend something like a year, I think, in the penitentiary. But it was no blot on his character. It was [chuckles] never held against him; he was a very prominent man. He came right back to Wallace as soon as he got out of the penitentiary, and ended his life here.

For the most part, though, Mrs. Horning devotes thought and memory to more personal matters. Local history never seemed very urgent in her youth: she supposes she must have heard about the early days of mining when she was growing up, "but didn't pay as much attention as we would have when we were older. You know, when you're sixteen and going to high school, and have a job after school at one of the dry-goods stores, and weekends you're going mountain climbing and that sort of thing, you're just kind of self-satisfied, I guess [chuckles]." When she looks now at the mountains which loom over Wallace, she thinks not of hunting and logging and mining but of gentler and more convivial forms of recreation: "And we did a lot of hiking, and had a friend who had a cabin up in the mountains—on the way to Mullan, not very far up the way there—and we'd take lunches and go up, spend the day. There was a shooting gallery up there, I remember, that the men used, and we'd play handball, and have a big bonfire outside." The changes which strike her most in the streets of Wallace are not the falling off in mining-camp camaraderie but the loss of the old Grand Theater and "the nice stores that we used to have." Mrs. Horning is deeply attached to Wallace and finds that memories adhere to almost every bit of the local landscape, to the point where no one image or landmark stands out in her mind when she thinks about her place: "Oh, just going to the grocery store, I'm surrounded by things that I've been looking at since 1914. That's a long time [chuckles]. [. . .] Well, it's just home, you see, because I was only fourteen years old when I came here, and this is where I met my husband, and had my children, raised them. My husband and I had a very, very happy life." Wallace is "home" to Shirley Horning just as much as it was in its mining-camp guise to Helen Bondurant, but for each of them that home takes on a very different form.

For the most part, though, local perceptions and ways of life are so dominated by the landscape, and by the economic and recreational pursuit of the resources harbored by that landscape, that the people of the region have been able to develop a common sense of place, a common set of geographical images and a shared set of themes and interpretations associated with and linking those images. As Maidell Clemets points out, "When you were raised in a mining camp, only the one thing for you to do: you graduated from high school and you went to work in the mine; maybe before you graduated, even. [. . .] That's all the work there was for you. Either you'd go to work in the mines or work in the smelters here; that's all there was. No choice." People like the Sverdstens who lived farther west in the valley, away from the mining camps, naturally went into logging. Even people who eventually went into different lines of work, like retired schoolteacher Leonard Heikkila, usually spent summers or a few years of their youth working for the mining companies. Retired newspaper editor Wendell Brainard worked in the mines for five years as a young man because, as his father told him, "I don't care if you want to be a miner, but you're living in a mining town; you might as well learn what goes on underground." And area residents who never worked in the mines or the woods, like grocer Bill Noyen, were still able to learn about the ways of life which characterize those environments simply by keeping their eyes and ears open. Moreover, people of all occupations swarm annually into the wilderness to go hunting, fishing, and huckleberrying. Few people in the area have been able to avoid participating in the distinctive ways of life which the geography of their place has suggested and supported, and few have not had occasion to sift through their own experiences and memories, and through the stories and comments they have heard from others, to find out what that place means.

Even when they do not concern the region's wonted topics of mining, logging, and hunting, people's stories about the piece of geography that they inhabit still tend to fall into locally familiar patterns. When asked what she considered to be some of the more important events that had happened in the region, Marylinn Heikkila mentioned the Sunshine fire first, "And floods. See, Pinehurst had a heavy flood in December of '64, and again in . . . When did that big flood hit up here on the river? '73, '74, somewhere in there. You judge things by floods [chuckles]." Floods sweep through various parts of the valley with great frequency. Leonard Heikkila tells of an epic flood that occurred during his childhood in Cataldo:

In 1933 we had a big flood in the area, and Highway 10 at that time went right through the little town of Cataldo, and the river used to overflow there, and it'd go over the road, and so for a while there it was cut off, you know, getting through on Highway 10. And Kellogg was once completely stranded from outside; they had to bring in the mail and food and stuff by plane. On the farm there, we were completely stranded; we were surrounded by water, actually, all around us; the only way out was by boat for about three weeks. See, the water ran right in between Sverdstens' and us there, and so we were isolated; we were on kind of an island.

These floods, it turns out, are caused by the same Chinook winds that once set off so many snow slides in Burke Canyon. Snow accumulates on frozen ground during the winter, and when warm southerly winds blow the melted snow, unable to soak into the ground, runs into the rivers and flows over their banks. Stories of floods provide corroborating evidence of the capricious, willful nature of the local geography, of the way in which it regularly seems to like to flex its muscles and remind the region's inhabitants of its power. These narratives contribute nicely to the sense of place as embodied in other forms of folklore, growing as they do out of the human encounter with a landscape that—no matter where or when—is consistent in the way it both rewards and frustrates its human occupants.

My most memorable experience in that landscape was an afternoon I spent with Bill Etherton exploring the abandoned Pine Creek district, the area where he spent his childhood and where he still lives. For Mr. Etherton, a drive up Pine Creek is a drive through time. He showed me a rutted dirt road leading up a narrow canyon to a mine where his father had once worked (and where he had once lived), the site of the one-room school he had once attended, the general store (now a tavern) where he had run errands, the abandoned mine where his brother had worked to earn money to go to college, the rock ledge that he had helped blast through so that a road could be built. He pointed out to me where the old mines and their mills and outbuildings and camps had been, and explained how they had functioned and when they had stopped running. The Pine Creek that he sees is both a world of personal association and a world of hard work, of miners blasting and hauling ore out of the mountains; in its blending of personal and communal experience, his understanding of Pine Creek epitomizes the nature of the sense of place. We ended the afternoon two miles up a rough dirt road at the abandoned

Figure 25. The Highland mine site: the disused portal. 1989 photograph by the author.

Highland mine, walking atop its towering dump, examining its collapsing mills.

I returned to the Highland site alone the next day so that I could explore it and think about it at my leisure. I began to realize that, for me, the abandoned mine crystallized both the image and the understanding of the district that I believed its inhabitants held. Tucked below the bald dome of Wardner Peak, surrounded by steep mountainsides and towering trees, the old wooden buildings and the enormous heap of rubble which lies behind them capture the juxtaposition of wilderness and industrial occupation which forms so large a part of the local visual image of the environment. At the same time, the mine site is manifestly decaying, its last shift having been worked over thirty-five years ago. The mine portal, blocked now by a metal gate, is overgrown with trees and bushes, a trickle of water flowing steadily from its roof and out onto the dump (fig. 25). The mill buildings are slowly falling to pieces, lucky

Figure 26. The Highland mine site: the abandoned mill building. 1989 photograph by the author.

Figure 27. The Highland mine site: an abandoned miner's cabin. 1989 photograph by the author.

so far to have escaped the fires and vandalism which have claimed so many decrepit mine structures in the area (fig. 26). Nearby, a miner's cabin sits on a hillside, its stove tipped over and covered with rust, sunlight streaming through gaps in its roof (fig. 27). The site mutely suggests, in terms as dramatic and eloquent as any narrative, the nature and qualities of the local land: the riches it offers, the way those riches can suddenly vanish, the uncertainty which always surrounds their pursuit. Behind and beneath the story that the abandoned mine suggested to me, though, lay the insistent presence of the region's striking beauty. To be sure, there is little aesthetic value in a heap of broken rock, just as it is difficult not to be at least momentarily appalled by the bald brows of the hills around Kellogg. In my eyes, however, the surrounding wilderness softens the jarring impact of industrial ugliness, and no matter where I traveled in the district I found myself agreeing with Don Long when he said that "this is a very beautiful area, actually."

The valley of the South Fork of the Coeur d'Alene River is, in a broad sense, neither famous nor remarkable. Its mines have always been among the richest in the country, but this fact has brought them little renown. When I told friends and colleagues where I had done my fieldwork, several of them asked half-jokingly if the people I interviewed had anything to do with the infamous band of white supremacists who have taken up residence in Hayden Lake, north of the city of Coeur d'Alene. (Emphatically not.) One person asked if that was where the red light on Interstate 90 was—a reference to the fact that the divided highway ended just east of Wallace, funneled its traffic through city streets, and began again just west of town, creating the circumstance that the traffic light in downtown Wallace was, as Wendell Brainard put it, "the only traffic light between Seattle and Boston." (Wallace has since lost this distinction, as the missing link was recently completed.) National significance, however, has nothing to do with the creation of memorable events. The people of the Coeur d'Alenes have been living, working, and playing in their distinctive landscape for generations, gathering experiences which have followed recurring patterns and blending those patterns into a cumulative sense of place. As I clambered over the Highland mine dump and took a few nervous steps into the abandoned portal, trying to absorb more of what I understood to be the essence of the place before I returned to Rhode Island the next day, I felt gratified that Bill Etherton and my other informants had, in Barry Lopez's words, been "glad to take the outlander in tow" as they mentally traversed their home terrain. Every local landscape has its geniuses, as Lopez recognizes, no matter how humble or obscure that landscape may be. Through their extensive repertoires of personal narratives, traditional historical narratives, and other forms of verbal lore, the geniuses of the Coeur d'Alenes vividly create a colorful portrait of a land, a people, and a way of life. Listening to their voices constitutes the study of geography in its most real human sense, that study being the earnest attempt to understand and appreciate the way that people live on and feel about the surface of the earth; listening to their voices reminds us that "geography . . . is finally knowledge that calls up something in the land we recognize and respond to. It gives us a sense of place and a sense of community."[18]

≈≈≈≈≈≈≈≈≈≈≈≈≈≈≈≈≈≈≈≈≈≈≈≈≈≈≈≈≈≈≈≈≈

4 A Walk in the Invisible Landscape: The Essay of Place

The test of imagination, ultimately, is not the terri-tory of art or the territory of the mind, but the territory underfoot. That is not to say that there is no territory of art or of the mind, only that it is not a separate terri-tory. It is not exempt either from the principles above it or from the country below it. It is a territory, then, that is subject to correction—by, among other things, pay-ing attention. To remove it from the possibility of correc-tion is finally to destroy art and thought, and the terri-tory underfoot as well.

Memory, for instance, must be a pattern upon the ac-tual country, not a cluster of relics in a museum or a written history. What Barry Lopez speaks of as a sort of invisible landscape of communal association and usage must serve the visible as a guide and as a protector; the visible landscape must verify and correct the invisible. Alone, the invisible landscape becomes false, sentimen-tal, and useless, just as the visible landscape, alone, be-comes a strange land, threatening to humans and vul-nerable to human abuse.

To assume that the context of literature is "the liter-ary world" is, I believe, simply wrong. That its real habitat is the household and the community—that it can and does affect, even in practical ways, the life of a place—may not be recognized by most theorists and critics for a while yet. But they will finally come to it, because finally they will have to. And when they do, they will renew the study of literature and restore it to importance.

—WENDELL BERRY, "Writer and Region"

Folk Narrative and Literary Narrative: The Essay of Place

In a 1978 article, geographer Edmunds V. Bunkśe called on scholars interested in accurately grasping the ways in which geography interacts and combines with real human lives to step beyond the confines of conventional academic geography and travel to places like the Coeur d'Alene mining district, talking to local residents, listening to their stories, seeing the land through their eyes. Contemporary approaches to geographical study, he feels, while cutting ever closer to the true nature of geographical experience, do not go far enough. "As part of their concern for a more concrete approach to the study of human interaction with the environment," notes Bunkśe, "a number of recent advocates of 'humanistic' geography have expressed concern about the representativeness of studied attitudes and inside views." Such geographers as Edward Relph and Yi-Fu Tuan, he observes, "call for viewing cultural and individual experiences in space and place from 'within'— through the eyes of a participant, and not an observer." While this is an important and laudable goal, Bunkśe objects that the work of such geographers is often maddeningly theoretical; while it may be "intended to bring research closer to the lives of people," he finds it "abstract in its language and devoid of life and its variegated flavors. . . . In order to get closer to life," Bunkśe proposes, "we must turn to the people themselves, to their expressions and evocations of life."[1] Folklore, he concludes, and as the people who live along the South Fork of the Coeur d'Alene River eloquently demonstrate, offers perhaps the clearest and most immediate and spontaneous view of a community's sense of place, of their particular fusion of landscape and imagination; it amply fleshes out the theoretical concepts broached by humanistic geographers.

The sense of place does not gain public expression, however, solely through the folkloric narratives of oral storytellers with deep roots in the life and landscape of a particular location. That sense is, after all, primarily a pattern of thought rather than the stories and musings which give body to that thought—it is a way of structuring and interpreting geographically related memory and experience which generates a distinctive style of verbal communication, one which is not necessarily limited to oral performance. There are other "expressions and evocations of life" which offer equally immediate access to the meanings that people read in their landscapes; the same impulse which gives narrative voice to the sense of place through folklore burgeons forth as well in more formal kinds of verbal expression. The essayist Scott Russell Sanders, for instance, has recently written an essay which takes as its very subject the confrontation of imagination with place.[2] Returning with his family to their Indiana home after having spent a year in Boston, Sanders finds himself noticing with new appreciation the fine details and unvoiced meanings of this familiar scene—"a freshening of awareness," as he calls it; exile yourself briefly from your wonted place, and "upon returning you will recognize with fresh acuity what you had known but forgotten." Sanders trains his essayist's eye and mind upon the surrounding scene; having previously taken it for granted, he now confronts his place self-consciously, seeking out its identifying, particularizing characteristics, writing down what is most noticeable, vital, and arresting to his newly sensitized imagination: "wishing to know the place where I have been set down," he writes, "I drive the back roads of Indiana, tramp across country, wade the streams, look about"—that is, he deliberately and thoughtfully reenacts in condensed and concentrated form the typical, repeated activities and movements of anyone who comes to know a place deeply and thoroughly. His essay takes shape as a careful analysis of his own sense of place and in the process becomes a reflection on the broader themes and subjects of any writer of place.

In part, Indiana is to Sanders a unique concatenation of physical details: he gets out of his car at a rest stop and smells the familiar odors of hay, dust from farmers' fields, and roadside weeds; he hears a Midwestern thunderstorm gathering strength on the horizon. "Only when I caught those smells, heard those sounds, did I realize how much I had missed them in the East, just as I had missed the sight of a level horizon broken by power lines, grain elevators, water towers, silos, and the shade trees around farmhouses"; such, for Sanders, are among the "hundred details that characterize this place." These characteristic, identifying physical qualities of Sanders's Indiana neighborhood are charged, made resonant, frequently heightened, and occasionally obscured by memories which the landscape evokes and reawakens: "It is never a simple matter actually to see what is before your eyes. You notice what memory and knowledge and imagination have prepared you to see." In Sanders's case, he takes special notice of silos and barns and hay bales and big climbable trees, all of which recall vividly to him his own rural boyhood: "My muscles know the ache and grace in such things. . . . What I see is stitched through and through with my own past." These personal associations are balanced and deepened by his awareness of how others see the scene: "What I see when I look at the land is also informed by the company I have kept," he comments, noting especially that "I learned what to notice and value in the landscape from both my parents, at first unconsciously and then deliberately." He realizes that his sense of the place is only one of many possible understandings; he learns the sense of place of others by quietly listening to them and watching what they do in the landscape. Finally, Sanders looks about him and expands the meaning of his place beyond the temporal bounds of his own life, examining the landscape for the sense of history that it suggests. "Like all landscapes," he notes, "that of Indiana is a palimpsest, written over by centuries of human scrawls and by millennia of natural ones. Every fence, highway, billboard, and clearing is an utterance, more or less eloquent, more or less durable." Through the evidence of square fields and right-angled roads, of the settlement pattern of rural homesteads, of the engineered structures of modern development, Sanders reconstructs and reviews the course and texture of human history in his neighborhood. Personal memory, community history, the physical face of geography, a sense of emotional attachment to it all: these are the essential qualities of place which stand out for Sanders, which comprise the meaning of Indiana for him. Closely mirroring the components of the folkloric sense of place, they form here as well the matter of the literary, essayistic contemplation of place.

As Sanders's example suggests, of all literary forms the familiar (or personal) essay that takes as its subject a particular piece of geography—what I will call the "essay of place"—may supply the closest parallel to place-based folk narratives as a verbal means of illuminating the sense of place, of making visible the contours of the invisible landscape; in either case, in the words of philosopher Stephen H. Daniel, "To speak or write the world is to make it accessible to a reading, that is, to make it into a place."[3] Both these forms of expression grow out of the same impulse—the urge, whether consciously held or subconsciously felt, to explain the meanings which a landscape holds—and they take on the same forms and themes as well. Narratives such as those which people tell about the Coeur d'Alene mining district are characterized by their distinctive manner, matter, method, and motive. Their manner is personal, anecdotal, and spontaneous, driven by the sound of the human voice and by the unique personality and experience of the teller. Their matter is the confrontation of an individual mind, of a curious and creative imagination, with the concrete facts of the landscape and of the ways of life that the landscape supports. Their method is episodic and peripatetic, marked by a sort of imaginative wandering over the local terrain: they do not reach for sweeping summaries and abstract, inclusive conclusions, but allow their meanings to accrete subtly through the piling up of telling examples as the storyteller's mind, working its way through its repertoire, alights in turn on a series of memorable personal landmarks. And their motive, finally, is the narrator's desire to make sense of and explain a piece of the world, to find pattern and meaning in the surrounding region—to explore, bring to conscious notice, reveal in words, and thus share the sense of place.

On reflection, however, these distinguishing qualities of place-based folk narratives seem perhaps to inhere not so much in their nature as folk narratives as in the particular demands of the drive to make sense of and accurately explain a place, no matter through which form of verbal expression that drive ultimately makes itself heard. Any portrait and explication of place must bring vividly to life both landscapes and the people who live in them if it is to bear any but the palest and most attenuated resemblance to local truth. It must attempt to recreate through words what it is like to experience the place, to follow its ways of life, hear its history, and sense its physical fabric; it must guide its audience through the place with as much immediacy as possible, giving a sense of the texture of local life through narrative and descriptive detail, making the members of that audience feel that they understand the place, that they grasp its rhythms and emotions and meanings, that they have looked deeply into the local sense of place even though they may not be of that place themselves. As a narrative genre, the essay is uniquely fitted by its nature to accomplish this difficult task, closely paralleling in its form and purpose those characteristic qualities which distinguish folk narratives. In literary critic Chris Anderson's summary, "the essay is reflective and exploratory and essentially personal. Its purpose is . . . to tell the story of the author's thinking and experience."[4] As a genre, that is, the essay blends perceptions of the world with thought about the significance of what is perceived; it complements a rambling, wandering intellectual sensibility with a persistent urge to puzzle out the meanings of what it has stumbled across on its ramblings and filters its blend of experience and rumination through the perspective and voice of a single inquisitive mind. Insofar as it takes as its subject a particular geographical location, then, the essay, perhaps more than any other kind of writing, is especially well suited to explore and explain the sense of place—to wander across an actual landscape, noting details, reflecting on the meaning of what it sees. Like the stories which enliven the Coeur d'Alenes, "essays . . . deal only in the concrete and particular," in Scott

Russell Sanders's words. "They are narratives; they speak about the world in stories, in terms of human actions and speech and the tangible world we inhabit."[5] They are blood relatives of place-based folklore, an expression in a different verbal arena of that same general sense of place which generates indigenous regional folk narratives.

In writing about the identifying generic characteristics of the essay, those qualities which critics and essayists repeatedly single out for discussion are qualities which the essay shares with place-based folk narratives. One of the most prominent of these is the essay's personal, anecdotal style. Often written in the first person, albeit lacking the face-to-face immediacy of an oral storyteller's performance, the essay nevertheless resembles such a performance in the way it sifts personal experience and idiosyncratic memory through the contemplative mind and distinctive voice of an individual narrator. As critic and editor George Core points out, an important hallmark of the essay as a genre is the extent to which it is written from an identifiable and idiosyncratic point of view: he notes that "the author will usually be standing foursquare in the middle of the essay or off to the side of the action (but still unmistakably there)—and, of greater importance, the essay will be in large part about him or her and about the author's reaction to the action as it is told and interpreted."[6] Essayists themselves recognize the centrality of this personal slant and personable style to their art: E. B. White, for instance, puckishly notes in the foreword to a collection of his essays that "the essayist is a self-liberated man, sustained by the childish belief that everything he thinks about, everything that happens to him, is of general interest. . . . Only a person who is congenitally self-centered has the effrontery and the stamina to write essays."[7] Sanders writes of his craft in the same self-deprecating, mock-critical fashion, comparing the essay to the noisy harangue of a soapbox orator he once encountered: "Nobody had asked him for his two cents' worth, but there he was, declaring it with all the eloquence he could muster. The essay, although enacted in private, is no less arrogant a performance. . . . It is an arrogant and foolhardy form, this one-man or one-woman circus, which relies on the tricks of anecdote, memory, conjecture, and wit to hold our attention."[8] As it addresses its audience, then, the essay creates its personal quality through the sense it projects of an individual mind casually divulging its thoughts and impressions through a distinctive and often memorable verbal style—it "is like the human voice talking," says essayist Edward Hoagland, "its order the mind's natural flow."[9]

Much of the essay's attraction lies in the perceived personality of the essayist—the nature and quality of the mind producing the words. The insistent presence of this mind is central to the essay, for writers as well as for readers: as Carl H. Klaus points out in his survey and analysis of essayists' commentaries on their craft, "Most essayists, in fact, give special attention to the role of the essayist in the essay . . . through their preoccupation with an author's implied personality" and "implicitly or explicitly make [personality] a defining feature of the essay."[10] Engaging or infuriating, earnest or lighthearted, it is the force of this personality which arrests the attention of the reader, which lends immediacy, power, and authority to the essay's words and makes the audience sit still to find out what the essay has to say; we react with warmth or irritation to the character of the person who seems to be delivering the words, just as we do when listening to an oral narrative. "Brassy or shy," says Sanders, "stage center or hanging back in the wings, the author's persona commands our attention. For the length of an essay, or a book of essays, we respond to that persona as we would to a friend caught up in a rapturous monologue."[11]

The essay, then, is in essence a form of personal narrative: it reveals an individual mind at work, telling us about some of the striking or significant things it has seen, done, or heard about, trying to find meaning in those objects and events in a way that would not occur to any other mind. Each essay springs from an idiosyncratic vision, the essayist's personal slant on the world derived from years of life and thought and experience—"once that writer finds the right post of observation or the right place on the stage," says Core, "he or she can see the world in a fresh and distinctive way and can find the right tone in which to write about that world."[12] Given the extent to which they are molded to the contours of one mind, then, "The essayist's truths are 'for me' and 'for now,' " in the words of critic Graham Good, "personal and provisional. The essay stays closer to the individual's self-experience than any other form except the diary." Because it grows out of personal experience, the essay rarely reaches definitive conclusions or feels comfortable making sweeping pronouncements but instead settles for humbler and more reflective statements; according to Good, "the kind of truth offered in the essay is . . . a mixture of anecdote (perhaps heightened and 'pointed' for effect), description (again selective), and opinion (perhaps changing)." The essay, Good concludes, "is an act of personal witness,"[13] a meditation on a particular facet of the world which only one mind could possibly produce. Like folk narrative, the essay grows directly and idiosyncratically out of experience with life and people and landscapes; like the performer of personal narratives, the essayist describes and tells stories about the world as he or she knows it, and tries in the process to convey a sense of the meaning of those stories.

In the course of this performance, the essayist's persona recounts anecdotes and delivers opinions in a style approximating that of oral exchange—in spirit, at least, if not necessarily carrying the tang and flavor of spoken words. Not seeking to be scholarly, definitive, or authoritative, the essay says what it has to say in a casual, conversational manner: "It is well known and much beloved for its egalitarian spirit," says critic William Zeiger—"the congeniality and deference of the writer toward both the topic and the reader."[14] And while the language which bodies forth this congenial spirit is carefully considered and finely shaded, literary rather than colloquial and immediate, the tone of voice of the essayist is as unique, gripping, and entertaining—and goes as far toward letting us gauge the character of the person producing the language—as that of any oral storyteller: as Edward Hoagland observes in commenting on the essay, "the style of a writer has a 'nap' to it, a combination of personality and originality and energetic loose ends that stand up like the nap on a piece of wool and can't be brushed flat."[15] The style of any essayist is as personal and distinctive as the voice of any storyteller: on his way to describing "the breathless, often giddy, always eloquent and spiritually hungry soul" who seems to speak Annie Dillard's essays, or the "stately, moralizing, cherishing voice" of Wendell Berry, Sanders notes approvingly that "the essay is a haven for the private, idiosyncratic voice in an era of anonymous babble."[16] Through this sort of distinctive, personally crafted language—the "right tone" of which Core speaks—as well as through the authorial persona which that language implies, the essay creates the impression of a thoughtful and approachable narrator, addressing individual readers as equals and under the assumption that they will be interested in listening, ruminating on where he has gone, what he has done, what he has seen, and what he happens to think about those travels, activities, and sights. As best it can through the poor substitute of the printed page, the essay attempts to capture something of the experiential roots, the comfortable style, the easy manner, and the face-to-face rhetorical context of the personal narrative.

It attempts to focus on the typical subject matter of the personal narrative as well. Broadly speaking, essays can be written on almost any topic that happens to swim into the essayist's ken. "In range of interest," essayist Joseph Epstein notes, the essay "is multivarious: there are literary essays, political essays, philosophical essays, and historical essays; there are formal essays and familiar essays."[17] Graham Good lists "the main essayistic activities: traveling, pondering, reading, and re-membering," and their concomitant objects, "books and places, mores, and memories,"[18] while E. B. White observes that "there are as many kinds of essays as there are human attitudes or poses, as many essay flavors as there are Howard Johnson ice creams."[19] Despite this bound-less range of subject matter, however, the impulse to write essays, as to tell stories, grows consistently out of a single source: the individual con-frontation with the hard facts and particularities of the world—of place, of any aspect of life—and the resulting effort of the imagination to seek meaning in what it confronts. As George Core points out, the work of good essayists "depends . . . upon their marshalling the facts that will always provide the bedrock that must underlie any familiar essay. The best essays in this vein have always been bound to what E. B. White called the eloquence of fact."[20]

Eloquent facts may be found anywhere, even in the most humble and unlikely of places, as long as they seem to the essayist to help illuminate a truth, to provide a field for the energetic play of thought and imagina-tion. As Scott Russell Sanders observes, "the essay remains stubbornly concrete and particular: it confronts you with an oil-smeared toilet at the Sunoco station, a red vinyl purse shaped like a valentine heart, a bow-legged dentist hunting deer with an elephant gun. . . . Clinging to this door, that child, this grief, following the zigzag motions of an inquisitive mind, the essay renews language and clears trash from the springs of thought."[21] The essayist does not describe facts merely for their own sake, but for the sake of the memories they spark, the insights they inspire, the meanings they make clear in the essayist's mind; as Graham Good writes, "Reflections in the essay rise from and return to particular experiences," with facts leading to thoughts which in turn lead the es-sayist's mind to new facts. "This is the essential uniqueness of essayistic discourse: neither the order of thoughts nor the order of things predomi-nates. Each constantly interrupts and interpenetrates with the other. . . . The essay's fabric is woven from these alternations."[22] The product of this distinctive style of thinking and writing, of this intermingling of experience, reflection, and words, is something very like the narratives which people tell about the places where they live, narratives in which they reveal the lived meanings which overlie their landscapes. William Zeiger notes the relationship between personal essay and personally re-vealing narrative: "The personal essayist, rather than arguing for a con-cept, endows it with presence—relates a story imbued with sensations and appetites, perceptions and visions, personal relationships and the experience of everyday life. We all have this knowledge, of course, but the personal essayist, like the poet and novelist, articulates this well— takes the time to notice casual objects and events and to cultivate the habit of noticing."[23] Zeiger could easily have added the place-based storyteller to his examples of the poet and the novelist. The essayist and the folk narrator both approach the world's particularities and filter them through language and imagination in the same basic way: both tell stories, filled with experiential detail, about what they have seen, what they have heard, what has happened to them, and what patterns they have found among the concrete facts amid which they live. They present the world's meanings not as they have researched them or reasoned them out but as they have lived them.

In the course of telling these stories, the personal essay rarely adheres to the strict formal demands of logical exposition. As opposed to a more structured and purposeful rhetorical means of making a point, such as the oration or the scholarly article, the essay proceeds by indirection and association, the order of its topics determined by the casual workings of the essayist's mind, its subjects suggested by the patterns of the essayist's life. As critic O. B. Hardison, Jr., writes, "the essay is the opposite of an oration. It is a literary trial balloon, an informal stringing together of ideas to see what happens. Let's be frank. From the standpoint of the oration, the essay is feckless. It does not seek to *do* anything, and it has no standard method for doing nothing."[24] Instead, each essay improvises its own method as it goes along; as Carl H. Klaus notes, the essay is "a form of writing whose distinguishing characteristic is its freedom from any governing aspect of form."[25] What form an essay does take on, then, is determined only by the thinking and experience of the essayist; it hews closely to the way that life and thought naturally intermingle, to the way that the mind finds pattern and meaning in memory and experience and turns its findings into words—descriptions, anecdotes, musings on the significance of what has been done, witnessed, and remembered. In this way, the essay parallels the process and matter of personal narrative: it molds itself to the patterns traced by the writer's movement, both physical and imaginative, over the surfaces—geographical, social, cultural—of the world, and, like folk narrative, brings to conscious notice the invisible layers of meaning which adhere to those surfaces.

This imaginative movement, this ruminative mental meandering among life's particularities, bears a close metaphorical resemblance to the process of taking a leisurely and contemplative walk. According to Graham Good, "the essay is *essentially* a peripatetic or ambulatory form. The mixture of self-preoccupation and observation, the role of chance in providing sights and encounters, the ease of changing pace, direction, and goal, make walking the perfect analog of 'essaying.' "[26] The walk by its very nature epitomizes essayistic thought and activity: it is a fusion of, or an incessant shuttling back and forth between, direct engagement with facts and dispassionate contemplation of those facts. "The walker observes things from a distance," in critic Jeffrey C. Robinson's words, looking at the world through which he or she moves in a spirit of "disinterested reflection" and critical detachment. At the same time, however, "the walker is in experience, feels and thinks in his movement through time and space, and is reaching out (or can) to the world in time. To deny either side of the walk is to deny half of experience."[27] Many writers have found walking an apposite metaphor for the craft of writing essays, to the point that the comparison has become something of a commonplace: G. Douglas Atkins feels, for instance, that through being "more interested, in fact, in the journey, in journeying, than in any destination finally reached, the essay *is* a walk (and at the same time a garden of delights made of its adventures),"[28] while critic R. Lane Kauffmann, in the course of commenting on "the essay's mission of disciplined digression," concludes that "essaying is an *extra*disciplinary mode of thought. Entering the road laid down by tradition, the essayist is not content to pursue faithfully the prescribed itinerary. Instinctively, he (or she) swerves to explore the surrounding terrain, to track a stray detail or anomaly, even at the risk of wrong turns, dead ends, and charges of trespassing."[29] Scott Russell Sanders concurs with these descriptions of the essayist's modus operandi, likening himself to a curious and enthusiastic dog scrambling through the woods, eager to be led far afield by whatever interesting scent or sound he happens to stumble across:

> For me the writing of a personal essay is like finding my way through a forest without being quite sure what game I am chasing, what landmark I am seeking. I sniff down one path until some heady smell tugs me in a new direction, and then off I go, dodging and circling, lured on by the calls of unfamiliar birds, puzzled by the tracks of strange beasts, leaping from stone to stone across rivers, barking up one tree after another. The pleasure in writing an essay—and, when the writing is any good, the

pleasure in reading it—comes from this dodging and leaping, this movement of the mind.[30]

Samuel F. Pickering uses the same metaphor to describe his practice as
a writer, but in human rather than canine terms, and in so doing clearly
suggests the basic unity of essayistic writing and the casual, hands-on,
everyday human experience of geography: after an afternoon spent avoiding his writing desk by taking a walk with his family, he notes that
"rarely does the familiar essay set out hiking boots afoot and compass in
hand; instead it meanders, picking cockleburs and cattails, hoping to
see an owl and eating ice cream," as he and his wife and children had
done that day. "Almost everything," Pickering concludes, "even a day's
dull walk, can be matter for a familiar essay."[31]

Or *especially* a day's dull walk. As Pickering suggests, it is a very
short step from noticing the similarities between writing essays and
walking to actually writing an essay *about* walking. To the essayist, the
act of walking and thinking gives way almost reflexively to the desire to
write about the terrain that has been traversed and the reflections that
the terrain has sparked. When the essayist's attention turns to places
and landscapes—landscapes experienced slowly and immediately, on
foot and with all senses wide open—metaphor and activity fuse; the
unplanned course of the essayist's footsteps over the terrain corresponds
perfectly to the wonted leisurely meandering of his or her mind, to the
point that the simple act of walking has itself become a perennially favored and natural subject for essayists. Jeffrey Robinson observes, regarding what he calls the "walking essay," that "the world of the last two
centuries has spawned many such pieces, that walkers, who are almost
always bona fide essayists, are urged from somewhere to ambulate on
paper about ambulation."[32] Given the close resemblance between sauntering and essaying, this urge, this quick succession of words on the
heels of a walk with the goal in mind of describing that walk, seems a
natural progression, two phases of a single seamless activity. The walking essay is a log of the physical and mental itinerary of the essayist's
walk, the permanent record of an ephemeral event; the essay's reader
walks in the essayist's footsteps, interpreting the passing scene through
the essayist's eyes and mind. In its mimetic reflection of the close un-
hurried interaction of mind and body with geography, then—in the way
that it easily and naturally applies its inherent concern with concrete
details, with human experience and reflection on the meaning of that

experience, to the world's landscapes—the personal essay, of all forms of writing, seems the one best suited to outlining and exploring the sense of place.

Essayist Tim Robinson provides perhaps the best summary of the fusion of walking, landscape, meaning, and words at which the essayist of place aims when he considers the incredible imaginative complexity involved in the simple process of taking a single step. Any step we take in the course of any walk, Robinson points out, takes us across some fragment of "our craggy, boggy, overgrown and overbuilt terrain, on which every step carries us across geologies, biologies, myths, histories, politics, etcetera, and trips us with the trailing *Rosa spinosissima* of personal associations. To forget these dimensions of the step is to forgo our honour as human beings, but an awareness of them equal to the involuted complexities underfoot at any given moment would be a crushing backload to have to carry." No one person, no matter how dedicated, can assimilate all the significance which lies within the space of a single stride; no one person, no matter how talented, can summarize and share all this information and knowledge—personal, cultural, social, scientific—in a single burst of expression. Nevertheless, the attempt is worth making and is uniquely available to the artist, the person who fuses senses and imagination and words to create something—an expression of place, a melding of individual insight and shared meaning which gives form, as adequately and completely as possible, to the bewildering tangle of human and natural significance which lies beneath his or her feet: as Robinson puts it, "the structure of condensation and ordering necessary to pass from such various types of knowledge to such an instant of insight would have the characteristics of a work of art, partaking of the individuality of the mind that bears it, yet with a density of content and richness of connectivity surpassing any state of that mind."[33] The essay of place is that work of art, that condensing and ordering structure which puts the unvoiced meanings of the terrain into words and makes them available to be shared. It is, says Robinson, "the guide-book to the adequate step," inviting the reader to re-create in imagination the physical and mental meanderings which the essayist has already traced. To conclude with the words of Wendell Berry which opened this chapter, the essay of place, while grounded in the visible landscape—the territory underfoot—provides signposts for those who would saunter through the invisible landscape which that ground supports, that territory of art and mind which cannot exist without the physical landscape but which ultimately makes that landscape meaningful.

The Essay of Place and Nature Writing:
Henry David Thoreau and Barry Lopez

This practice of walking through landscapes, examining them closely, thinking about them, and writing about them, impinges closely on the literary genre of nature writing or natural history writing—and, in fact, many of the best essayists of place are commonly categorized as nature writers. The works of these writers, however, are not contained within that type of natural history that focuses primarily on the natural as opposed to the human world, seeking to puzzle out and explain the lives of organisms, the nature and structure of ecological communities, our biological and moral relationship to nature, and the truths and responsibilities which nature can teach people. Writers who work in this tradition join essayists of place in discovering implicit words and narratives embedded in the landscape, but "what they hear in the earth," says Stephen Trimble, "are the voices of what Henry Beston called the 'other nations' of the planet." Their writings, Trimble concludes, are "translations of these voices." Like essayists who concentrate on place, natural history writers aim at "turning landscape and experience into carefully chosen words,"[34] but it is experience of a particular kind. Place is created when experience charges landscape with meaning; in the landscape of the natural history essay, however, experience is transparent, a conduit to discovery, a means by which the essayist comes to learn and write about the significant facts and connections which inhere in the natural world. The experience of the writer in studying and pondering the land, and the repeated, localized experience of the people who live on the land, are tangential matters in the natural history essay; such a piece of writing, while fueled by and suffused with the curiosity, emotion, perceptions, and personality of the essayist, teaches primarily about pattern and beauty and meaning in the natural landscape, not about the human presence and imaginative life which that landscape sustains.

Essayists of place, on the other hand, while often adopting much of the naturalist's perspective, take equal account of human history as well as natural history, assigning equal value and priority to each, writing both of the natural world and of the physical and mental structures of human life, experience, and imagining which people have built on top of it. Such writers, while deeply sensitive to the presence and value of nature, find it artificial to separate the life and history of nature from the life and history of humankind and tend to doubt that such an exercise is profitable or even possible. As an example, Robert Finch, who has written three books on the natural history of Cape Cod, recalls that he bought the land on which he built his house "primarily because it sat in the middle of what appeared to be unspoiled woodland, with a good chance of staying that way for some time." Over several years of living there, however, he has "gradually come to realize that, despite the landscape's wild aspect, there is hardly a square foot of ground in the immediate vicinity that does not bear, directly or indirectly, marks of the past hand of man"[35]—old roads and paths that have been all but reabsorbed by new-growth forests, orchards and decorative plants that have grown wild in the former yards and lots of long-vanished houses, derelict stone walls and crumbling foundations now concealed by trees, the memories of longtime residents which adhere to obscure and unremarkable landmarks. Seeking to surround himself exclusively with nature, Finch instead found himself enmeshed in a web of hidden human leavings and ghostly human history.

As Finch discovered to his surprise, few natural landscapes are unmarked in some way by human presence, and none, once it has become the subject of an essayist's experience and writing, is unmarked by human consciousness: the mere presence of a human observer—or, for that matter, the fact of its becoming the object of thought at second hand through reading or maps or photographs—imprints a landscape, however faintly, with the physical or imaginative marks of human history (be it only a single episode in one naturalist's life) and with the structures and frameworks of a creative, organizing, and interpreting imagination. To the essayist of place, natural and human life are inevitably and inextricably joined; concludes Finch about his Cape Cod landscapes, "in my mind the various overlapping layers of history, past and recently past, natural and human, blend and fuse together into one richly textured presence, as the accumulated leaffalls finally decay and merge to form new humus."[36] Penetrating and describing these visible and invisible layers of history, communicating the rich physical and imaginative textures of a landscape, is the work of the essayist of place. This work requires deep imaginative engagement with the landscape and with the lived significances it has accrued over time—it requires a sensitivity to and appreciation of its implicit narratives. Narrative is as inextricably fused to the natural landscape as is history, and to a writer sensitive to the presence of narrative the land's appearance and meaning are irrevocably altered, rebuilt; "stories create meaning," says Finch in a recent interview. "They create the way you see the land."[37] While walking in the neighborhood of her New England farm and listening to the landscape-anchored reminiscences of an elderly neighbor, the poet and essayist Maxine Kumin similarly finds that nature and the narrative annals of human memory inexorably converge and unite, and she decides that "the sense of place underwritten by private history is part of that natural order."[38] To be an essayist of place, then, requires that a writer listen carefully to these quiet human voices whispering in the landscape. It demands a close and sympathetic attention to geographical experience, that of the essayist and of the people who have lived in and interacted with the landscape for years prior to the essayist's arrival. It demands conscious and careful scrutiny both of the geographical surface and of the narratives and emotions anchored there—it is the explication of landscape as place.

Since the walking essay and the natural history essay both cut close to the heart of the essay of place, an examination of two nature writers who have written about their walks should help clarify and illustrate the nature of the thought and writings of the essayist of place. Henry David Thoreau is the best-known American essayist to take as his topic a walk through the landscape. For Thoreau, walking was not only a favorite subject and inspiration for writing, leading to such essays as "Walking," "A Walk to Wachusett," and "A Winter Walk," but was also an important activity in his daily life—indeed, it was the activity around which he often structured entire days. "I think that I cannot preserve my health and spirits," he notes in "Walking," "unless I spend four hours a day at least—and it is commonly more than that—sauntering through the woods and over the hills and fields, absolutely free from all worldly engagements."[39] He found these walks important not for the physical activity they provided—"the walking of which I speak has nothing in it akin to taking exercise" (97)—but for the opportunity they created for thought and reflection, for the interaction of mind with landscape and nature—"you must walk like a camel," he admonishes, "which is said to be the only beast which ruminates when walking" (98). Thoreau was an indefatigable exemplar of the essayist, the writer who strides across a physical or imaginative terrain, wonders and muses about the meanings of what he sees, and shares both the journey and the thoughts with his readers.

He was not, however, primarily an essayist of *place*, despite his extensive, intense personal and imaginative engagement with the natural landscapes of Concord (and, in book-length treatments, of Maine and Cape Cod). Thoreau's method and motive on his literary walks were not to seek out history in landscape, to describe and explain the conjunction of experience, narrative, and geography, but to look *through* the landscape over which he rambled and penetrate to the lessons and higher truths of nature, before which man's history appears ephemeral and shabby. "When we walk," he felt, "we naturally go to the fields and woods" (98); avoiding towns and roads, he believed that the only proper route for a walk was to the woods, the wilderness, the West: "Eastward I go only by force; but westward I go free" (105), he proclaimed, adding that "the West of which I speak is but another name for the Wild; and . . . in Wildness is the preservation of the world" (112). Accordingly, he had little interest in and use for human landscapes, for places overlaid thickly with local history and communal experience; he preferred being able to "walk off to some portion of the earth's surface where a man does not stand from one year's end to the next" and enjoyed hiking to hilltops from which, he said, "I can see civilization and the abodes of man afar. The farmers and their works are scarcely more obvious than woodchucks and their burrows. Man and his affairs, church and state and school, trade and commerce, and manufactures and agriculture, even politics, the most alarming of them all,—I am pleased to see how little space they occupy in the landscape" (100–101). This sort of physical distance from and personal disdain for the landscapes of human occupancy, the geography on which history inscribes itself, characterizes all of Thoreau's essays on walks and walking. For him geography matters not as place but as nature and the metaphysical truths which nature reveals. He is, as he admits in "A Winter Walk," "a worshiper of the unseen" (69), but the unseen component of his geography is not the invisible landscape of place but the immanent power and purity of the natural world.

Thoreau's dismissive attitude toward place becomes clear in "A Winter Walk," as he comes across a deserted woodsman's hut and reflects briefly on the experience which this spot has seen. The hut eloquently suggests the way that the woodsman lived his life on this bit of earth— the unremarkable things he did, the sensations he absorbed, the way "he has passed the long winter nights and the short and stormy days" (60)—and Thoreau attempts to puzzle out this history from the evidence at hand, achieving a remarkable subtlety and depth of observation, sympathy, and imagination; for as long as he pauses there in his mind, the abandoned hut comes alive as place.

These hemlock boughs, and the straw upon this raised platform, were his bed, and this broken dish held his drink. . . . I find some embers left as if he had but just gone out, where he baked his pot of beans; and while at evening he smoked his pipe, whose stemless bowl lies in the ashes, chatted with his only companion, if perchance he had any, about the depth of the snow on the morrow, already falling fast and thick without . . . ; and through his broad chimney-throat, in the late winter evening, ere he stretched himself upon the straw, he looked up to learn the progress of the storm, and, seeing the bright stars of Cassiopeia's Chair shining brightly down upon him, fell contentedly asleep. (60–61)

The hut and its artifacts are powerful place-creating elements, suggesting patterns of life and experience. They provide abundant evidence of human history in the landscape, implying narratives to which Thoreau responds and alludes. Even the ground surrounding the hut talks eloquently about the life of its former occupant, a story which Thoreau translates through sensitively reading the landscape: "From this stump we may guess the sharpness of his axe, and from the slope of the stroke, on which side he stood, and whether he cut down the tree without going round it or changing hands; and, from the flexure of the splinters, we may know which way it fell. This one chip contains inscribed on it the whole history of the woodchopper and of the world" (61).

Despite his sympathetic imaginative response to this landscape as place, to the history and narratives which it implies, however, Thoreau finds the scene's greatest value in the fact that it is abandoned, that it is being reclaimed by nature: "After two seasons, this rude dwelling does not deform the scene. Already the birds resort to it, and you may track to its door the feet of many quadrupeds. Thus, for a long time, nature overlooks the encroachment and profanity of man" (61). As with the view from the top of the hill, he prefers this imaginative distance from the evidence of man's life in the land, this sense of the proper proportion of things. Place is, after all, a human construction which requires human occupance of and activity in the landscape, and Thoreau has little use for such activity. He seems happiest when a piece of geography cannot be, or has not yet been, thought of as a place—when it has not supported lives and accumulated history. The layers of meaning which overlie a place may be temporarily beguiling, the stories they imply may be compelling, but for Thoreau they are ultimately distracting and their implications are disturbing. When he walks through a landscape and writes about his walk, he keeps his attention fixed elsewhere; in his essays, he interacts with geography not as a partner in experience but as a springboard to higher thoughts—or, alternatively, as a surface which he can observe and describe and then bounce off of into the well-stocked depths of his own mind.

"A Walk to Wachusett" is an account of a journey which Thoreau and an unnamed companion took over the course of four days from Concord to Wachusett Mountain and back—an account of the route he took, the things he saw and did, the thoughts and meditations which the journey inspired. Thoreau notes that, for years, "our eyes had rested on the dim outline of the mountains in our horizon, to which distance and indistinctness lent a grandeur not their own, so that they served equally to interpret all the allusions of poets and travelers" (31), until finally "we resolved to scale the blue wall which bounded the western horizon, though not without misgivings that thereafter no visible fairyland would exist for us" (33). The stated motive of the walk, then, is to transform the mountains from the stuff of literary allusion into experienced landscape, from a blank surface onto which fancies can be projected into place. Much of the essay, accordingly, is descriptive, a catalog of landscapes traversed and of the sights, sounds, and odors which those landscapes harbor: the "small, drooping, bell-like flowers and slender red stem of the dogsbane, and the coarser stem and berry of the poke, which are both common in remoter and wilder scenes" (38), for instance, or the "murmuring of water, and the slumberous breath of crickets" which they heard "throughout the night" (39). Moreover, Thoreau also makes occasional note of the particularizing, place-making elements of the villages and scenes through which he passes, the unique qualities of life and landscape which tell him that he is no longer in his familiar neighborhood. In the town of Bolton, he encounters the local dialect with delight, remarking that "we thought we had not traveled in vain, if it were only to hear a truer and wilder pronunciation of [the mountains'] names from the lips of the inhabitants; not *Way*-tatic, *Way*-chusett, but *Wor*-tatic, *Wor*-chusett. It made us ashamed of our tame and civil pronunciation, and we looked upon them as born and bred farther west than we" (35). Similarly, on reaching the nascent village of Stillwater, "We fancied that there was already a certain western look about this place, a smell of pines and roar of water" (38). Thoreau also writes from time to time of the residue of history on the land: "This, it will be remembered," he points out while writing of walking through the town of Lancaster, "was the scene of Mrs. Rowlandson's capture, and of other events in the Indian wars" (47). In the course of recreating his walk to and from Wachusett, Thoreau attempts to give a sense both of the landscape as he experienced it and of the local culture and memory which that landscape supports.

His attention to this sort of evocation of place, however, is sporadic at best, and secondary to his main purpose. Before launching into the narrative of his journey, Thoreau alerts his readers to his primary destination: "In the spaces of thought are the reaches of land and water, where men go and come. The landscape lies far and fair within, and the deepest thinker is the farthest traveled" (33). While Thoreau devotes much attention to the landscapes through which he travels, he is interested in them primarily for the associations, metaphors, and moral and metaphysical lessons that they provoke and reveal. His walk is an occasion for meditation more than for geographical experience, a journey through his inner landscape of learning and spiritual aspiration more than a simple stroll through the Massachusetts countryside. While he claims to want to strip away the haze of fancy and distance which shrouds Wachusett, the fact that he is walking through particular towns and climbing a particular mountain, that his route can easily be traced on a map according to his description, is secondary to the conclusions that he reaches; any mountain and any path to that mountain, finally, would serve his meditative and didactic purposes.

Thoreau frequently allows literary associations to get between himself and the landscape, so that he appreciates scenes not for their particular physical and cultural qualities but for the works of literature that they remind him of or for the literary patterns and paradigms into which they seem to fit. While walking through Acton and Stow, for instance, he observes the many hop fields which line his path, commenting on them not because they are a central element in the local culture and folkways, part of the indigenous pattern of living on the land, but because the hop "perhaps supplies the want of the vine in American scenery, and may remind the traveler of Italy and the South of France. . . . The culture of the hop, with the processes of picking, drying in the kiln, and packing for the market, as well as the uses to which it is applied, so analogous to the culture and uses of the grape, may afford a theme for future poets" (34–35). That which characterizes the life and landscape of Acton is assessed only in terms of its usefulness for literature. In viewing local agriculture through a literary lens, Thoreau seems to disparage and dismiss the very idea and possibility of place, deciding that "man's life is rounded with the same few facts, the same simple relations everywhere, and it is vain to travel to find it new. The flowers grow more various ways than he" (35). This universal similarity is what literature teaches us: "we read Virgil," he notes as an example, "mainly to be reminded of the identity of human nature in all ages" (37). Certain broad and inclusive patterns of significance, Thoreau feels, embrace all of life and all of history—and, as he discovers on his walk, all elements of all landscapes as well.

As Thoreau ascends Wachusett, he also climbs out of the realm of human history and experience. The mountain's summit, he notes, feels "infinitely removed from the plain, and when we reached it we felt a sense of remoteness, as if we had traveled into distant regions" (40). Upon awakening the next morning, he finds that this sense of distance and lofty detachment is intensified as the sun climbs higher in the sky, and he is confronted by "an immense landscape to ponder on a summer's day. We could see how ample and roomy is nature" (44). It is a landscape, however, oddly devoid of human presence—"As far as the eye could reach," he notes, "there was little life in the landscape" (44–45), that life being confined mainly to birds. As he noted in "Walking," Thoreau enjoyed the perspective which hilltops afforded, and his summary comment on his view from the mountaintop is telling: "There lay Massachusetts, spread out before us in its length and breadth, like a map" (45). He instinctively echoes the distant, dispassionate, abstract view of the cartographer, noting the names and locations of the mountains which he sees and evincing little concern for the layer of experience and narrative which is overlaid upon that "map" by the people who occupy it. Since he is not concerned with those elements which would turn the map into place and has climbed above their obscuring presence, his mind is freed to puzzle out the larger philosophical implications of what he sees, the meanings which are common to all places no matter what their details and histories. After contemplating the view from Wachusett of its neighboring peaks, Thoreau finally comes to

> realize the place mountains occupy on the land, and how they come into the general scheme of the universe. When first we climb their summits and observe their lesser irregularities, we do not give credit to the comprehensive intelligence which shaped them; but when afterward we behold their outlines in the horizon, we confess that the hand which moulded their opposite slopes, making one to balance the other, worked round a deep centre, and was privy to the plan of the universe. So is the least part of nature in its bearings referred to all space. (46)

This revelation is the goal of the essay, the point to which Thoreau's walk ultimately leads. The unity of the physical world which it reveals, the burgeoning creative force of nature of which it is the expression, is why the landscape matters here for Thoreau, not because of any layers of human meaning and feeling which it supports. Place is the invisible component of any landscape, and in Thoreau's hands it is irrelevant as well; as he turns his walks into essays, place remains invisible not because it leaves no physical trace on the landscape but because he chooses not to recognize it, instead delving beneath it for an unmediated encounter with the land and the lessons that the land imparts.

After having "returned to the desultory life of the plain" (49), Thoreau continues to train his attention to his inner landscape rather than to the terrain over which his feet pass; metaphor lodges itself firmly between his eyes and the landscape. The very act of walking suggests higher truths, as the path of any traveler is "perfectly symbolical of human life,—now climbing the hills, now descending into the vales. From the summits he beholds the heavens and the horizon, from the vales he looks up to the heights again" (48–49). Wachusett finally stands out in his mind not as a specific geographical fact, not as a spot of scenic beauty, not as the unforgettable stimulus and backdrop for a powerful metaphysical revelation, but as the source of a lesson and guide for life, a lesson which any mountain could have imparted: he resolves to "import a little of that mountain grandeur" into his life, noting that "there is elevation in every hour, as no part of the earth is so low that the heavens may not be seen from, and we have only to stand on the summit of our hour to command an uninterrupted horizon" (49). In "A Walk to Wachusett," as in his other essays about walking, Thoreau looks at the landscape without quite seeing its surface and the way that that surface interacts with human lives. His vision penetrates the physical face of the Massachusetts terrain in search of metaphysical truth; at the same time, it bounces off that surface as off a mirror, so that the landscape comes to reflect Thoreau's reading and philosophy and is reshaped accordingly in his writing. As William Howarth suggests, in his walking essays Thoreau took a sequence of experiences and perceptions, "linked by his movement through space and time, and expanded their facts into metaphors. In the essay, landscape becomes a map of his mind; each step of his journey is an increment of thought."[40] The "map of Massachusetts" which he saw from atop Wachusett and which his essays inscribe bear, at best, a tangential relationship to any actual map of the state, to the geography which that map would have reflected, and to the way that his fellow citizens would have interpreted both the map and the familiar landscapes on which it was based. Despite his stated intent at the beginning of his walk, it is doubtful that Wachusett, or any landscape, ceases "to interpret all the allusions of poets and travelers" once Thoreau finishes writing about it.

The Irish poet and critic Seamus Heaney, writing about how he has come to think about a particular tree which once stood by his childhood home, provides a useful parallel to the manner in which Thoreau thinks and writes about landscapes. By way of preface to an essay on the poetry of his countryman Patrick Kavanagh, Heaney reminisces about a chestnut seedling that an aunt had planted in front of his family's house the year he was born. As time passed, he tells us, "I came to identify my own life with the life of the chestnut tree"—its birth year was his own, he associated it with the nurturing affection of the aunt who had planted it, it was the only thing in the immediate landscape that also grew as he grew. The family moved away from that house while Heaney was in his teens, and the new owner eventually cut down the chestnut tree. Heaney admits that he forgot all about the old tree until recent years, when he suddenly remembered and began thinking about it again, but in a new and less intimate way. Now no longer "a living symbol of being rooted in the native ground," a crystallization of personal identity and communal associations, the tree as it stood in his mind came to be "all idea, if you like; it was generated out of my experience of the old place but it was not a topographical location. It was and remains an imagined realm, even if it can be located at an earthly spot, a placeless heaven rather than a heavenly place." So it is with Thoreau on the road to Wachusett, assiduously exploring and mapping the country of his mind: as Heaney has done in his childhood landscape, Thoreau experiences a location, but he converts it in his mind and writing into an atemporal, unanchored, inward place—a projection of a geographical location into his imagination where it can be purified of its layers of history and experiential meaning, where it can be thought about and written about not for its depth of association, not for the role it has played in a life and a community, but for its potential as idea, as a means for disclosing and symbolizing broader human and natural truths. As Thoreau walks, thinks, and writes, he presses place into service as the protean raw material of literature, passing it through the filters of philosophy and accumulated reading, transcending any significance inhering in the scene itself and achieving whatever literary end of effect or meaning that he, as a writer, desires. This, says Heaney, was also Kavanagh's practice in his later poetry; like Thoreau on his rambles through rural Massachusetts, Kavanagh in these poems is "not saying that the farmers and the

Monaghan region are important in themselves. They are made important only by the light of the mind which is now playing upon them."

Not all of Kavanagh's poetry, however, treats familiar landscapes as screens onto which the idiosyncratic literary and thematic concerns of the poet may be projected, just as Heaney's thought about his boyhood tree has not always maintained such a tenuous attachment to the landscapes and patterns of the past. While Heaney finds that, in much of Kavanagh's poetry, places "have been evacuated of their status as background, as documentary geography, and exist instead as transfigured images, sites where the mind projects its own force," elsewhere in his writings Kavanagh "gives the place credit for existing, assists at its real topographical presence, dwells upon it and accepts it as the definitive locus of the given world." He looks at the landscapes of these poems, that is, in the same way in which Heaney originally thought about his tree: each poem "is supplied with a strong physical presence and is full of the recognitions which existed between the poet and his place; it is symbolic of affections rooted in a community life and has behind it an imagination which is not yet weaned from its origin, an attached rather than a detached faculty."[41] Just as these two strains in Kavanagh's poetry contrast, there is an essayistic way of writing about locations and landscapes that is as anchored and "attached" as Thoreau's is visionary and "detached," that looks squarely at the geographical surface and attempts to comprehend and communicate the meanings worked into that surface by the lives of its occupants. While Thoreau may gently abstract a tree from its background, attempting to read universal patterns in its leaves and branches, other writers understand, with the young Heaney, that that tree loses much of its meaning unless we also know that it once stood in front of a particular family's house, that it was planted by a favorite aunt, and that a young boy used to gauge his own growth by watching it gradually tower and spread.

Contrast Thoreau's thoughts in "A Walk to Wachusett" and "A Winter Walk" with those of Barry Lopez on a wintry walk of his own, a walk which he took on Pingok Island—a flat barrier island of sand and tundra off Alaska's northern coast—and which he writes about in "The Country of the Mind," an essay-length chapter in his book-length contemplation of the North American Arctic, *Arctic Dreams*. In his preface, Lopez notes that he wrote the book in order to more fully explore the implications of two arresting moments in his life. One moment occurred one evening in the western Brooks Range of Alaska, when he went for a walk among the nests of the tundra birds and first became intensely aware of the admirable, harsh beauties of the Arctic: the tenacious vitality of the birds, the cold yet gentle clarity of the light. The other moment found Lopez at the grave in Michigan of Edward Israel, a young man who died on an Arctic expedition in 1884, lured to his death by dreams which only he could have articulated. Moments like these must be combined, Lopez realized, in order for any place to be fully understood and appreciated; surface perceptions must be supplemented and deepened by a grasp of the imaginative life and dreams which the landscape sparks and sustains:

> These two incidents came back to me often in the four or five years that I traveled in the Arctic. The one, timeless and full of light, reminded me of sublime innocence, of the innate beauty of undisturbed relationships. The other, a dream gone awry, reminded me of the long human struggle, mental and physical, to come to terms with the Far North. As I traveled, I came to believe that people's desires and aspirations were as much a part of the land as the wind, solitary animals, and the bright fields of stone and tundra. And, too, that the land itself existed quite apart from these.

"The mind," concludes Lopez, "full of curiosity and analysis, disassembles a landscape and then reassembles the pieces . . . trying to fathom its geography. At the same time the mind is trying to find its place within the land, to discover a way to dispel its own sense of estrangement."[42] Writing about a place simultaneously enacts these two impulses: the impulse to describe the landscape and, more important, the impulse to understand and explain how that landscape is felt and remembered both by the writer and by the people who live in it. It demands that the writer look not within, as Thoreau does, but outward, to the way that geography is experienced and shared, to the way that it works its way into lives. Such a writer follows the same path traveled by Scott Russell Sanders when he wrote about growing up on a military base: "I meant to preserve and record and help give voice to a reality that existed independently of me. I meant to pay my respects to a minor passage of history in an out-of-the-way place. I felt responsible to the truth as known by other people. I wanted to speak directly out of my own life into the lives of others."[43] This is Lopez's method in his book and is the method, consciously outlined or not, of any essayist of place. Such writing reenacts, demonstrates, and shares with others the fusion of mind—of a curious, constructive, observing imagination—with landscape. It seeks to discover what Lopez sought on his Arctic rambles: "the power of a long-term association with the land, not just with a specific spot but with the span of it in memory and imagination, how it fills, for example, one's dreams" (250).

"This is an old business," Lopez muses as he meanders across Pingok, "walking slowly over the land with an appreciation of its immediacy to the senses and in anticipation of what lies hidden in it" (227). It takes time, however, to develop this appreciation and anticipation, to get beyond the inscrutable, monochromatic surface of the Arctic landscape and discover its depth, details, and subtleties. Lopez tries to see and understand as much as possible about the landscape as he walks, but he confesses that "I know how much I miss—I have only to remember the faces of the Eskimos I've traveled with, the constant flicker of their eyes over the countryside" (233). He is fascinated by, and deeply respectful of, the Eskimo's navigational abilities and the profound geographical knowledge and expertise which these abilities reveal—the way in which "on shorefast ice in summer fog he travels between the voices of seabirds on landward cliffs and the sound of surf on the seaward edge of the ice" (261), or the way he keeps on course by checking the alignment of the fur on his parka hood with the wind. This expertise, however, comprises only a part of the Eskimos' interpretation of their landscapes. Memory makes up a large part of their navigational ability—the Eskimo relies heavily on remembered sights and sounds and directions of wind—and, as it achieves expression in narrative, memory is a vital, essential component as well of the Arctic landscape in the minds of its inhabitants: "over time," says Lopez, "small bits of knowledge about a region accumulate among local residents in the form of stories. These are remembered in the community; even what is unusual does not become lost and therefore irrelevant. These narratives comprise for a native an intricate, long-term view of a particular landscape. . . . The perceptions of any people wash over the land like a flood, leaving ideas hung up in the brush, like pieces of damp paper to be collected and deciphered" (244–245).

For Lopez, the "conservation of the stories that bind the people into the land" (266) is crucial, for they comprise the backbone of local culture, of local identity and ways of life—"it is the constant recapitulation . . . of all these stories that keeps the people alive and the land alive in the people" (267). Through memory, imagination, and narrative, people become "attached to the land as if by luminous fibers; and they live in a kind of time that is not of the moment but, in concert with memory, extensive, measured by a lifetime. To cut these fibers causes not only pain but a sense of dislocation" (250). Time and history and experience are basic to the definition and interpretation of geography for the people who live in it; stories—be they spoken or implicit, be they current in tradition, rehearsed quietly in memory, or left to be pieced together in imagination from clues left in the landscape—bring that geography to life, demonstrating how firmly it is woven into its inhabitants' lives. The writer, Lopez feels, is obliged to conserve these meanings and connections, out of respect and concern for the people whose place it is if for no other reason; while he captures the physical details of the landscape, he must also take the narrative landmarks of the country of the mind into account if he is to write at all truthfully of a place.

To attain this truthful vision requires sympathy, imagination, and sensory confrontation through sight and hearing and touch and movement; it requires walking slowly, with all senses wide open. Most non-natives think of the Arctic as monotonous, Lopez feels, because they learn about it "from staring at empty maps of the region and from traveling around in it by airplane"—a perspective which oversimplifies the land, turning it into flat blank space. In order "to learn anything of the land, to have any sense of the relevancy of the pertinent maps, you must walk away from the planes. You must get off into the country and sleep on the ground, or take an afternoon to take a tussock apart." Only then, after walking and sensing and thinking, will "you begin to sense the timeless, unsummarized dimensions of a deeper landscape" (255–256). Lopez's ramblings on Pingok make up just such a walk—they provide detail and human depth to the "empty maps," suffusing landscape with narrative—and the essay which results from this walk finally transcends the immediate terrain over which he strides and becomes a broad meditation on geographical perception and understanding, on the way in which landscapes work themselves into thought and memory and lives and dreams—and, by extension, on the task confronting the writer who would write truthfully about such landscapes. Lopez, like Thoreau, is a nature writer, a chronicler and philosopher of landscape. Whereas Thoreau tends to write of the landscape of his own mind, however, maintaining a disdainful distance from that empty map of Massachusetts that he sees from atop Wachusett, Lopez turns his attention firmly outward to the physical and imaginative terrain—to both the visible and the invisible landscape—and concentrates on what he calls "the country of the mind." He offers this phrase tentatively, as a provisional definition of this multivalent territory in which he walks and of which he chooses to write, this fusion of geography and imagination: "If one can take the phrase 'a country of the mind' to mean the landscape evident to the senses, as it is retained in human memory and arises in the oral tradition of a people, as a repository of both mythological and 'real-time' history, then perhaps this phrase will suffice" (265). If Thoreau's writings on walking ultimately trace a map of his own mind, Lopez seeks to create, as best he can through words, a map of place. The essayist of place is a cartographer of the country of the mind, and the essay which he writes is his map.

Lopez eloquently enacts the program of walking, thinking, feeling, and writing which he outlines in *Arctic Dreams* in a recent essay entitled "The Stone Horse."[44] In this essay, Lopez writes of his encounter with a 300-year-old intaglio of a horse in the California desert just north of the Mexican border, a larger-than-life outline created by Quechan Indians who carefully pried pieces out of the dark, hard-packed desert surface. Lopez begins his essay with a brief history of human occupancy and activity in this piece of desert, moving from the native cultures of pre-history as evinced by rock drawings, stone tools, and what may be ancient quarries—artifacts which "anchor the earliest threads of human history, the first record of human endeavor here"—to the modern world of railroads, irrigated fields, military installations, and four-wheel-drive recreational vehicles which heedlessly destroy such ancient sites. Having established this background of threatened obliteration and erasure, he next writes of his journey to the intaglio, an as yet undisturbed artifact whose existence is known to few and about whose location he is sworn to secrecy by a wary Bureau of Land Management archaeologist. He cannot drive all the way to the horse, for the rough trail is blocked by boulders; in order to successfully negotiate the broken terrain which surrounds the site, he must leave his vehicle and walk. Only by walking, he comes to realize, can his experience of the horse be at all true or accurate; only by walking can he see the horse as it was meant to be seen. He has been shown an aerial photograph of the intaglio and found it disappointing, for it does not provide a "fair and accurate description."

In the photograph the horse looks somewhat crudely constructed; from the ground it appears far more deftly rendered. The photograph is of a single moment, and in that split second the horse seems vaguely impotent. I watched light pool in the intaglio at dawn; I imagine you could watch it withdraw at dusk and sense the same animation I did. In those prolonged moments its shape and so, too, its general character changed—

noticeably. The living quality of the image, its immediacy to the eye, was brought out by the light-in-time, not, at least here, by the camera's frozen image.

"Intaglios," he concludes, "were never meant to be seen by gods in the sky above. They were meant to be seen by people on the ground, over a long period of shifting light." The stone horse, he realizes, is more than a mere picture on the ground, something which can be comprehended at a glance. It was a living element in its community; it demanded time, a duration of experience and phases of light, in order for its full complexity to emerge, in order to be fully understood and appreciated. In this regard, it resembles place, and in the course of the essay it emerges as a metaphor for place. Accordingly, Lopez approaches it and writes of it in the spirit which it demands.

He thus draws up to the horse on foot, slowly and respectfully, trying to experience it and think about it as its makers did, open to its beauty and eager to discover its meanings. Critic Sherman Paul describes Lopez's method in the essay: "He approaches the stone horse at dawn, observes it at sunrise, in process, animated as it were, not in the frozen moment of an aerial photograph. He is not above the object, recording it, mapping it; he is present with the horse, as its maker was, seeing it from various perspectives and in various lights, and summoning as a necessary part of the experience of wonder all that the essay tells of geography, cultural history, and personal recollection. The stone horse, to cite Kerouac, is the jewel-center of the associations awakened by the occasion."[45] Lopez opens his mind to the full range of sensations which the horse supplies, to the many associations which the intaglio suggests to his imagination and awakens in his memory. The meaning of the horse is complex and multivalent; it is a place, supporting a heavily textured layer of meaning, not amenable to summary by the cartographer's instruments or the photographer's narrow sliver of experience. To embody place requires time and narrative, not distance and snapshots, and Lopez seeks to accomplish this embodiment in his essay, to describe and explain the intaglio before it too succumbs to the pressures which have erased so many other artifacts in the desert. "The Stone Horse" is an eloquent account of Lopez's physical and imaginative encounter with a particular place; and, insofar as the horse stands symbolically for all places, the essay is as well a model and a metaphor for all such exercises in approaching, thinking about, understanding, appreciating, and writing about place in general.

Standing next to the horse in the burgeoning desert light, Lopez at first simply absorbs the sensory experience of the site, feeling "a growing concentration in all of my senses" to the point that "I was aware that I was straining for sound in the windless air and I felt the uneven pressure of the earth hard against my feet. The horse, outlined in a standing profile on the dark ground, was as vivid before me as a bed of tulips." In its majesty and silent mystery, however, the intaglio fires the imagination and inspires speculation and wonder, and soon his mind scrambles after meaning, trying to fit the horse into a context, an imaginative setting which will enable him to somehow understand its significance. His memory sifts through all that he has learned and experienced about horses as they have been seen and used in this part of the country, in the form of "a headlong rush of images": images of Pleistocene peoples hunting wild horses with spears, of Spanish explorers and Indian warriors riding horses through the Western landscape, of "a hoof exploding past my face one morning in a corral in Wyoming. These images had the weight and silence of stone." That is, they seem equal in presence and gravity to the stone horse which inspires them; the images, along with the meanings they suggest, are coextensive with the artifact, an inextricable part of its fabric. The thought which the artifact awakens is as much a part of the experience of beholding it as the feel of rough ground and the dazzling clarity of the growing dawn; it is as much a part of the horse as the stone of which it is built.

Lopez attempts to resist the insistence of learning, of an overly bookish, modern, or academic explication of the horse; he does not want "to feel again the sequence of quotidian events—to be drawn off into deliberation and analysis." Instead, standing alone in the desert with the horse, noting that "it looked as though no hand had ever disturbed the stones that gave it its form," he is struck by the similarity of his situation to that of the artifact's makers; history has stopped, time has gone backwards, he is alone with the horse as they were: "A human being, a four-footed animal, the open land. That was all that was present—and a 'thoughtless' understanding of the very old desires bearing on this particular animal: to hunt it, to render it, to fathom it, to subjugate it, to honor it, to take it as a companion." Much of the horse's meaning, he realizes, lies in these desires, these patterns of thought and feeling which he has been able to grasp, however tenuously, in this timeless landscape. To comprehend and explain the horse, he must first try to understand these old desires, the meaning of the horse for its makers. The horse is a mute story, an allusion to narratives, to the old patterns of use and imagination which structured the lives of the intaglio's makers; it summarizes years of experience with horses in this vanished Indian community. The Quechan Indians clearly knew horses well, and Lopez is impressed by the intaglio's anatomical accuracy. It is a picture drawn from life: "the angle at which the pastern carried the hoof away from the ankle was perfect. Also, stones had been placed within the image to suggest, at precisely the right spot, the left shoulder above the foreleg. The line that joined thigh and hock was similarly accurate." Still, the representation is not "perfect," an idealized representation of a horse, but contains physical quirks—"the suggestion of a bowed neck and an undershot jaw, and the tail . . . did not appear to be precisely to scale." Rather than indicating shoddy craftsmanship, however, Lopez decides that these imperfections mean that "I was looking at an individual horse, a unique combination of generic and specific detail." The artifact summarizes not only a community's extensive experience with horses but one artist's experience with his own horse; it speaks subtly but eloquently of the way in which a specific animal wove its way into an individual life. It is a site which tells both of communal experience and of a unique personal variation on and interpretation of that experience.

The interpretation of any place comprises both individual and shared meanings, and Lopez next reflects on his own experience with horses, from the days when "for parts of two years I worked as a horse wrangler and packer in Wyoming"; he remembers once again the hoof flashing by his face. Almost immediately, though, he feels that such memories are unworthy of the place and of the occasion, that they lack stature and gravity: "As I squatted there in the desert, however, these more personal memories seemed tenuous in comparison with the sweep of this animal in human time. My memories had no depth." A full account of the meaning of this or any artifact or place must move beyond personal experience and association, must move beyond even the history which this particular spot of ground has seen and the thought it has inspired; it must enfold as well the meanings to which the horse alludes in the broader culture of which Lopez is a product. The horse stands at the center of a system of concentric rings of meaning, sending out ripples from the past into the present, from the California desert to other landscapes where horses have run and been memorialized in the earth. Only when they are located within this historical matrix and connected to the experiences and imaginings of others, Lopez feels, do his personal memories add fruitfully to the meaning of the horse; they move beyond idiosyncrasy and contribute to resonance. He thinks about the old Spanish explorers, who must certainly have first brought horses to the Quechans: "The horse, like the stone animals of Egypt, urged these memories upon me. And as I drew them up from some forgotten corner of my mind—huge horses carved in the white chalk downs of southern England by an Iron Age people; Spanish horses rearing and wheeling in fear before alligators in Florida—the images seemed tethered before me. With this sense of proportion, a memory of my own—the morning I almost lost my face to a horse's hoof—now had somewhere to fit." The full meaning of this site, he understands at last, is complex and multivalent. It says much about the experience of the Quechan Indians in this harsh and desiccated landscape. It sends out threads to other times, other places, and other minds—to the White Horse of Uffington in Berkshire, to the first appearance of horses elsewhere in the New World. It reaches deep into Lopez's memory and imagination as well, connecting him to this landscape and to the mind of the anonymous artist. This obscure intaglio supports many layers of meaning—a wide-ranging congeries of personal, historical, and cultural factors—yet those layers are intimately connected; as Lopez contemplates one, the others push quickly and insistently into view. While not seamless, the complex of meaning which the horse suggests is tightly knit and immeasurably rich. Having experienced the intaglio through a long period of shifting light, satisfied that his mind has reached as deep into the horse as it can, Lopez takes his leave: "I came to a position of attention at the edge of the sphere of its influence. With a slight bow I paid my respects to the horse, its maker, and the history of us all, and departed."

This gesture of respect is central to the meaning and the purpose of the essay. After leaving the horse, Lopez reverts to the context within which he first placed his desert walk: the continuing and growing threat to such historic sites. Above all else, the stone horse strikes him as a crystallization of and perpetual reminder of history—and not simply the history of the Quechan Indians as it was played out on a particular patch of desert but the personal history whose memory it awakens and the shared cultural history to which it alludes. Its loss would mean the loss of things immeasurably greater: culture, continuity, a sense of interrelatedness with other times and other people, an awareness that thought and action have consequences beyond the present and beyond the line of sight. He thinks of the possible loss of the intaglio as a "horror, now that I had been those hours with the horse. The vandals, the few who crowbar rock art off the desert's walls, who dig up graves, who punish the ground that holds intaglios, are people who devour history." His fear, however, is soon replaced by a feeling of glad and profound respect for the value which the horse represents: "I thought about the horse sitting out there on the unprotected plain. I enumerated its qualities in my mind until a sense of its vulnerability receded and it became an anchor for something else. I remembered that history, a history like this one, which ran deeper than Mexico, deeper than the Spanish, was a kind of medicine. It permitted the great breadth of human expression to reverberate, and it did not urge you to locate its apotheosis in the present." Such intense, resonant loci of history—places, artifacts, any physical object or location which accrues and inspires memory—lie thick upon the landscape. "This great, imperfect stretch of human expression," concludes Lopez, "is the clarification and encouragement, the urging and the reminder, we call history. And it is inscribed everywhere in the face of the land, from the mountain passes of the Himalayas to a nameless bajada in the California desert." To write an essay like "The Stone Horse," finally, is to preserve in imagination and words both history and the places that anchor and embody that history, without which we are impoverished, diminished, and endangered both individually and collectively. Lopez's essay is at root a gesture of respect and an effort at conservation, both of a place and of the meanings and history which form its most vital component. Any essayist of place does no less.

The function of the essay of place is not only to make place visible, to outline its qualities and meanings and to preserve it in the face of threatened erosion and destruction (both of its physical being and, through the vagaries of memory, of the place it occupies in the mind), but, in an important sense, to *create* place as well, to bring it out of memory and imagination and give it being in the world. Writing an essay, by its nature, is a singularly creative process. The essayist thoughtfully scrutinizes the world, drawing out significances which until then may never have been clearly seen or fully understood, creating and explaining new artifacts of intelligence through the alchemy of mind and words. Essays wander, wonder, and make connections; they meander among and sift through the bewildering array of the world's physical, social, and cultural phenomena, creating meaning and structure in life which may never have been evident before. As Scott Russell Sanders puts it, in the essay "we relish the spectacle of a single consciousness making sense of a portion of the chaos."[46] To the essayist, even the self is ultimately a literary creation whose nature and characteristics are explored, worked out, elaborated, perfected, or despaired of on the page. Ralph Waldo Emerson was such a writer: "Speaking of the achievements of Plato, Shakespeare, and Milton," notes O. B. Hardison, "Emerson creates one of the great literary puns: 'I dare; I also will essay to be.' Writing an essay is an exercise in self-fashioning."[47] Writing an essay is an exercise as well in fashioning the world—and, notably, in fashioning the world's places. Unlike simple geographical locations, which exist objectively, places do not exist until they are verbalized, first in thought and memory and then through the spoken or written word. Only when they have coalesced in the mind, and then achieved narrative expression, can places have anything more than an idiosyncratic, private existence. Only when place has achieved verbal expression, in turn, can it have any sort of permanence and its meanings remain secure. It is the function of the essayist to write place into being.

5 *The Essay of Place: Themes in the Cartography of the Invisible Landscape*

When the anthropologist asked the Kwakiutl
for a map of their coast, they told him
stories: Here? Salmon gather. *Here?*
Sea otter camps. *Here* seal sleep.
Here we say body covered with mouths.

How can a place have a name? A man,
a woman may have a name, but they die.
We are a story until we die.
Then our names are dangerous.
A place is a story happening many times.
—KIM STAFFORD, "There Are No Names But Stories"

Map, Meaning, and Narrative

Kim Stafford, in his poem "There Are No Names But Stories"—a poem based on anthropologist Franz Boas's *Geographical Names of the Kwakiutl Indians*—demonstrates his awareness of the ultimate inextricability of history, landscape, and narrative. For the Kwakiutl of the poem, a map and a sequence of stories are one and the same; expecting to be presented a collection of lines on paper, the poem's anthropologist is instead given a richly textured tour of time and space, an anthology of narratives reaching back into the past and rooted sequentially on the ocean shore:

Over there? We say *blind women*
steaming clover roots become ducks.
We will tell that story for you at
place of meeting one another in winter.
But now is our time for travel. We will
name those stories as we pass them by:

and the poem ends with a long list of "names"—of allusions to stories—such as *loon on roof, hollow of stopping, place of hiding repeatedly cedarbark bedding of cradles*, and *insufficient canoe*.[1] A place-name, in the view of Stafford's Kwakiutl, is not an arbitrary label, a lifeless phoneme—it is not "something that is, but something that happens,"[2] as Stafford explains in an essay on Native American naming practices out of which his poem later grew. Similarly, a place, in this view, is not a named dot on a map; it is grounded history, experience fused to terrain, events constantly recurring and always present, their recurrence and presence guaranteed by the stories whose words renew and confirm them each time those words are spoken.

As oral narratives, such as those to which Stafford alludes in his poem and those told by the residents of the Coeur d'Alene mining district, keep experience and history perpetually alive and bind them to the land with words, so too do essays of place capture in verbal permanence the lived and learned meanings which the essayist reads in the landscape. Like oral narratives, such essays serve to annotate the flat objective map of that landscape, structuring themselves around those stories which, as Stafford's Kwakiutl affirm, comprise the identity of a place. As Stafford comments in his introduction to a collection of what he, too, calls "essays of place," writing such essays is a matter of "listening, remembering, telling, weaving a rooted companionship with home ground." It is a matter of bringing to notice and sharing with others the unselfconscious body of custom and practice common to the residents of a place, those bits of lore and learning necessary to both physical and spiritual navigation: "In coastal sailing guides, directions for crossing shoals to safe water often carry the refrain, 'local knowledge is advised.' Local knowledge is that story and place called 'Insufficient Canoe.'" It is a matter, finally, of fixing personal and collective history firmly to the terrain, of enabling landscapes and maps to speak: as Stafford explains in concluding his introduction, "This book travels for place, custom, and story. As water is pilgrim, I know the urge: to visit all the places I was healed. . . . By that pilgrim's urge, I listen to my family stories, one long generation from the primitive. By that urge, I seek out the speaking places of my own country: Montana battlefield, Oregon fallen barn, North California coastal midden, Idaho eccentric's hut. I listen for the way stories would name our country. This book is the listening."[3] While it is the listening, it is the transcription as well. Stafford's "Essays of Place" (the subtitle of his book) shares the goal of any essay of place: to replace a static, two-dimensional, cartographic view of geography with a living world of narrative—to map out, in Barry Lopez's words, a "country of the mind."

The work and career of artist-turned-cartographer-turned-writer Tim Robinson exemplify this melding of map and word—be that melding explicit or subconscious—in the essay of place. Robinson left the London art world in 1972 to live permanently on Ireland's Aran Islands; needing an income, he began drawing maps of the islands "for which endless summersful of visitors would thank and pay me." In the course of researching his maps, Robinson became immersed more and more deeply in the life of the place, seeking an understanding of Aran's cultural depth as well as its physical complexity, that sort of understanding which—as essayists by their very nature seem to understand—is best gained by walking: "I have walked the islands . . . with the custodians of local lore whom I sought out in every village, and have tried to see Aran through variously informed eyes—and then, alone again, I have gone hunting for those rare places and times, the nodes at which the layers of experience touch and may be fused together." This project of walking and listening, while intended to increase the accuracy of his maps, also awakened in Robinson an ironic understanding of the inability of his maps to be more than superficially accurate, to express the true significance of Aran; they are guides to the islands' tangible surface but tell nothing of the invisible structures of lived meaning which that surface supports. "But I find that in a map such points and the energy that accomplishes such fusions . . . can, at the most, be invisible guides, benevolent ghosts, through the tangles of the explicit; they cannot themselves be shown or named. So, chastened in my expectations of them, I now regard the Aran maps as preliminary storings and sortings of material for another art, the world-hungry art of words." This art of words, in Robinson's case, has taken the form of a collection of essays on the lore, landscape, and history of Aran. Robinson admits that "the maps underlie this book," entitled *Stones of Aran: Pilgrimage.* The "pilgrimage" of the title refers to the book's structuring device: "it explores and takes its form from a single island, Arainn itself; the present work makes a circuit of the coast, whose features present themselves as stations of a *Pilgrimage.*"[4] Robinson tours the Arainn shore on foot, in the best essayistic fashion, writing down what he has experienced and learned; like the Kwakiutl recalling tales as they travel down their coast, he believes that the only accurate map of that coast is a sequence of narratives—that there are no names but stories.

Essayist C. W. Gusewelle has written explicitly about the kind of connection between mapmaking and writing that Robinson discovered (and which any essayist of place must discover anew) and moves on as well to discuss the extent to which writing about a place, just as much as capturing its forms and structures on a map, can lend a sense of imaginative permanence to the fabric and meanings of a landscape which is quickly changing beyond recognition. In a recent piece entitled "Memories of a Country Neighborhood," Gusewelle takes as his subject exactly that intersection of geography, meaning, and expression—of paper map, mental image, and words—which oral storytellers illuminate with such bright, colorful light.[5] The catalyst of his essay, he tells us, is "the subject of change—in particular the change that in a bit less than three decades has overtaken a certain country neighborhood of my acquaintance." It is an intimate neighborhood, constructed on a folk scale through the unplanned vagaries of daily human activity, bounded by the range and pattern of local life and, again, by the limits of the essayist's physical and mental perambulations: "The dimensions of the neighborhood are arbitrary, established by the length of a comfortable walk. The greatest distance from any part of it to any other, even from its northmost tip all the way to the river on the south, must be approximately five straight-line miles. Certainly not more than six. No one can say authoritatively. No one has ever gone that straight-line way." Wary of romanticizing and distorting the vanished past of this comfortable place, respectfully wanting to write about the neighborhood as accurately and honestly as he can, Gusewelle seeks out a strategy to evoke and organize remembrance with clarity and detail: "So I have drawn on a sheet of paper a map of that neighborhood, taking care to make it as exact as memory will allow." This map becomes the organizing principle for his essay, giving rise to a sequence of geographically linked stories as Gusewelle lets anecdotal memory range freely over its features; the entire essay is an exercise in converting a congeries of locations into a vivid statement of place, of firmly grounded local history. Gusewelle's map emerges—like Robinson's, like the Kwakiutl's—as an inextricable fusion of location and narrative, of cartographic features and the stories he knows about the people who lived among them, as he allows his memory to ramble over each house and meadow and to patch together their collective human history. Such a map, of greater or lesser size and scale, lies implicitly or explicitly behind any essay of place.

As it turns out, the story of Gusewelle's neighborhood as revealed piecemeal through our tour of the map—far from being the stuff of nostalgic reverie—is a sobering saga of death and decay: the houses Gusewelle recalls have since collapsed or burned down, while their occupants have met sad ends. "The westernmost feature on this map is a house atop a cold hill"; its inhabitant, a lonely widower, will be crushed to death in a tractor accident. Both general stores on the map stand out in memory because of their common fate: both will burn down, and the keeper of one, in despair and "almost as if by mystic volition, will go to his bed and there cause himself not to waken." Other buildings vanish; other lives are visited by pain, death, and wasting change; farms are bought and enlarged by modern young farmers, electric lines appear, roads are paved and widened, so that finally "the neighborhood as I remember it, the one on the map we navigated by, was both more elaborate and richer in detail." Still, while the shape and structure of the physical location changes and becomes impoverished, for Gusewelle the sense of place remains constant; the map of the old neighborhood is drawn, in clear lines and fine detail, in his head as well as on paper. Gusewelle's map-borne evocation of place reinforces his sense of the inevitability of change, the sense he set out to explore at the beginning of the essay, but at the same time (and somewhat paradoxically) his map, his memory, his sense of place, and his essay allow these vanished landscapes and their colorful inhabitants to survive permanently.

Gusewelle's verbal map, then, is in a sense an archival document, telling as much about a certain location at a certain time as any dusty, yellowed map in a historical collection. It freezes place, arresting it in its headlong change, resisting its inherent ephemerality. In this way, it duplicates an important function of the ordinary printed map. Whatever their various strengths and weaknesses as media of communication, one thing that maps do is anchor their features firmly to the geodetic grid of latitude and longitude, pinning them down so that they can be found easily and reliably. They give a sense of permanence to the landscape—and, to those who read them with the mind's eye wide open, to the landscape's meanings as well. Those like Gusewelle and Robinson who draw maps with words accomplish the same function: they are metaphorical mapmakers, recognizing the abiding value and fascination of the world's landscapes and capturing them on paper. Their real field, though, is the invisible landscapes overlying the visible ones, the historical peaks and emotional valleys which personal and collective experience have carved there. In ruminating on his fieldwork in the Northern Irish community of Ballymenone, Henry Glassie clarifies this point by employing a topographical metaphor to describe the task of the folklorist—and, by extension, of the writer who also attends to the meanings of places: "Think of the past as space expanding infinitely beyond our vision. It is not a record of progress or regress, stasis or change; uncharted, it simply, smugly, vastly is. Then we choose a prospect. The higher it is, the wider and hazier our view. Now we map what we see, marking some features, ignoring others, altering an unknown territory, absurd in its unity, into a finite collection of landmarks made meaningful through their connections. History is not the past, but a map of the past drawn from a particular point of view to be useful to the modern traveler." Specifically, Glassie continues, "Ballymenone's is a relief map." Among its prominent metaphorical "features" is a "highway," representing the daily facts of local social and economic life which people use to navigate successfully through their lives—it is the "highway of workaday existence." Across the path of the highway rise several hills, "the artful, mythic compressions of great past events"—the lives of saints, important battles between Protestants and Catholics, the revered exploits of "individuals who endured or rebelled against socioeconomic conditions"—which comprise the substance of the local body of story.[6] The folklorist thinks and writes about the features of the map and the connections among them—about bits of local history and the narratives which encompass them, and the overarching themes which connect the stories and give them meaning. To extend Glassie's metaphor (and make it more literal), a folklorist is a relief mapper, a cartographer of the invisible landscape, exploring and recording the local memory and ways of life, preserving them from erasure and decay, demonstrating how individual features on the map coalesce and form a unified whole rooted to a particular geographical location.

So, too, is the essayist of place. The essayist is sensitive to subtleties in the terrain—both physical and imaginative—to which more casual observers remain blind and, like the cartographer, attempts to make those subtleties stand out clearly on paper. What writer Michael Martone says about "the flatness" which characterizes both the Midwest and his home town of Fort Wayne, Indiana, is true by extension of any place to which the essayist chooses to turn his or her eye and hand. Contrary to popular belief, Martone points out, Midwestern terrain is not in fact universally level. "But the people who know the place only by driving through it know the flatness. They skim along a grade of least resistance. The interstate defeats their best intentions. I see them starting out, bighearted and romantic, from the density and the variety of the East to see just how big this country is. . . . And, in the dawn around Sandusky, they have had enough, and they hunker down and drive, looking for the mountains that they know are ahead somewhere. They cannot see what is all around them now. A kind of blindness afflicts them, a pathology of the path. The flatness." Such drivers, encased in their automobiles on the carefully graded interstate, have no opportunity to alter or replace their outsiders' view of the Midwest. Nothing in their current experience challenges or alleviates their general impression of flatness and the boredom this impression engenders; they peer anxiously ahead in anticipation of something more dramatic while dismissing the present landscape out of hand. As a native, however, Martone knows better: the Midwest "is flat for the people who drive through, but those who live here begin to sense a slight unevenness." When Martone drives from Fort Wayne to Indianapolis on the interstate, he finds himself anticipating a gentle hill, a glacial moraine, which other drivers might very well miss. "I know it isn't much," he admits, "the highlight of a road trip a slight elevation that could be missed if you were fiddling with the radio dial. But to such a scale has my meter been calibrated. Living in a flat country, I began to read the flatness, to feel the slight disturbances in the field, to drive over it by the seat of my pants."[7] To convert Martone's topographical observation into metaphor, every place has its own kind of "flatness," its own subtleties—its unselfconscious ways of life, its unremarkable history—which, since they are quiet and undramatic, the outside observer will probably ignore but which the insider has internalized, responding sensitively to the textures and gentle peaks which they provide. Where the outsider may assume monotonous lives of unrelieved boredom, the native knows deep historical rhythms and bright flashes of drama. These subtleties, these bumps in Glassie's imaginative terrain, are the province of the essayist as much as the folklorist; rather than dismissing what appears to be a featureless surface, the writer, either by virtue of being a native or through exercising a carefully trained sensitivity and a sympathetic curiosity, is a mapper in words both of physical landscapes and the imaginative life which those landscapes support.

The essayist of place, then, necessarily combines and balances the perspectives of the insider and the outsider: the intimacy and closeness which enable exact and sympathetic depiction of a place on the one hand, the detachment and distance which bring larger patterns and connections into focus on the other. Such an essayist must adopt simultaneously the viewpoints of the loquacious native (or sensitive explorer) and the precise cartographer; he or she must be aware of, and capable of describing, both the invisible and the visible landscape. Glassie's folklorist must "choose a prospect," and so must the writer; it is difficult to discern the meanings of a place when one is totally immersed in its daily life, piecing together its sense haphazardly (if at all) through participating in the disorganized flow of its talk. The essayist of place is one step removed from the native storyteller, for, while bringing to light and sharing some of the narratives which inhere in a place, the essayist (like the folklorist) also labors to produce a work which links these narratives together in a larger structure of meaning, bringing out some unifying theme. Glassie's "prospect" is vital to this task; it is easier to absorb the lay of the land if one can contemplate it from a distance. Writing essays about a place creates such a distance, an imaginative distance: the detachment which writing demands, the contemplation and careful thought which it forces upon the writer, the unity and structure which shape careful writing—all enable the contours and patterns of life in a place to become clearer. The essayist of place achieves the state which geographer Edward Relph calls "empathetic insideness," the condition which is "essentially that of the outsider or stranger who seeks to experience places as openly as possible, to respond to their unique identities" in "an attempt to experience all the qualities and meanings of a place both as the people living there might experience them and also in terms of their functional, aesthetic, or other qualities that might not be apparent to existential insiders"—"existential insideness" being Relph's term for the state characteristic of the native storyteller, "in which a place is experienced without deliberate and selfconscious reflection yet is full with significances," in which the insider "is part of that place and it is part of him."[8] The essayist of place is both sensitive wanderer and conscientious cartographer, able to both feel the life and meaning of a place and to inscribe its patterns on paper.

This state of simultaneous intimacy and distance marks the essays of writers who contemplate their native places just as much as those of writers who arrive in new landscapes as complete outsiders. In an essay about thinking about places—in particular, his hometown of Columbus, Ohio—Michael J. Rosen tells about a semester he spent in medical school in Grenada and the personal experience narratives he told about his home to his new friends. This physical distance brought about a concomitant sense of objectivity, a newfound and somewhat unsettling ability to see Columbus as an outsider might, to seize on the significance of his own stories:

At a distance of thousands of miles, each image from the Midwest, as I held it up for my new friends to consider, looked precious as a souvenir with its locale wood-burned or glittered across it. Qualities sounded like quirks; opportunities, like crazes. I began to worry that anything—an object, a scene, a love—at a distance of memory or miles, must resemble a little photo at the end of a keychain viewer, reduced but enlarged again by the present eye. How could I keep anything I remembered about the Midwest from sounding like a tourist attraction, even an unattractive one? Do we live our lives once as ourselves, then repeatedly as everyone else?[9]

By thinking about Ohio, by self-consciously rehearsing his stories of the place to an audience of outsiders, Rosen simultaneously achieves a degree of insideness and outsideness; he is both himself and everyone else. Any essayist of place undergoes a symbolic reenactment of Rosen's trip to Grenada, using the process of writing to pluck out and organize meaningful patterns, connections, and insights from a welter of experiential knowledge and gathered impressions. (For Rosen, the pull of place was evidently quite strong: he left medical school after that semester to become a writer and is now the literary director of the Thurber House in Columbus and an editor of fellow native and memoirist James Thurber's writings.) To the essayist, a place—any place—becomes a coherent, structured object of thought to be picked up, turned over in the hands, and carefully scrutinized: it is a relief map, to return to Glassie's metaphor, geometrical and ordered yet full of fascinating detail, whose hills and roads, and the connections among them, are ever more sharply etched.

Landmarks: Worth and Preservation, Time and Identity

No two such maps are alike, of course; the patterns of life and experience which any two places harbor will necessarily be vastly different in both their outlines and their details. Nevertheless, writers about place have tended to identify certain common themes, certain patterns of significance which may structure any literary treatment of place and which connect and unify the details that they think and write about. Specifically, the essay of place is marked by two primary aims, both having their roots in different levels of the etymological history of the word "essay." As critic O. B. Hardison, Jr., points out, "The word 'essay' comes from Old French essai, defined . . . as 'a trial, an attempt.' From this meaning comes English 'to essay' in the sense of 'to make a trial or an attempt,' as in Emerson's statement, 'I also will essay to be.' The word also comes into English via the Norman French assaier, 'to assay,' meaning to try or test, as in testing the quality of a mineral ore."[10] The essay of place springs directly from the simultaneous impulses suggested by these dual sources. First, an essay of place is a trial, an attempt—an attempt to lay bare the meaning of a place. It is a trying out of narratives, of possible interpretations; it is an earnest stab at the difficult work of making maps speak, of turning names into stories. It is, finally, an *essaying* of place, of re-creating for the reader that complex of doing and hearing wherein lies the essence of place. The second root meaning of "essay" is to assay, to assess value, to tabulate worth. An *essay* of place is at the same time an *assay* of place, a statement—either explicit, through the author's heartfelt admonition, or implicit, through the lavishing of so much authorial intelligence and energy on a small patch of ground—of the worth and value of a place in at least one person's life.

To begin with this second meaning, the essay of place springs in part from a visceral awareness that places matter, that they are valuable presences in human life, that they provide a sense of stability and scale in an often alienating and confusing world. As writers like Barry Lopez and C. W. Gusewelle demonstrate, any essayist of place is at heart a preservationist, a self-appointed keeper of the world's places and the stories and meanings that they enclose. As a genre, the essay of place arises frequently as a response to the same sense of danger that drove Lopez to the California desert to see the stone horse: the threatened, or already achieved, destruction of a place. It often involves visiting a place whose future is in danger in order to record and preserve it before it vanishes, or visiting a place which has been altered by time in order to try to reclaim it from the lost past by recreating it in memory and words. (So too was Lopez driven to the Arctic by the threat of industrial development to Northern landscapes and ecosystems and by a concomitant countervailing urge to understand the Arctic as its natives saw it, as a "country of the mind"—a literary throwing of himself in front of the bulldozers.) The essayist of place is at once a cartographer, a landscape painter, a photographer, an archivist, and a folklorist, as well as a storyteller—a foe of mutability and ephemerality, a conscientious and dedicated chronicler both of landscapes and of the ways of life that those landscapes witness and support.

Such writers see their task as vital, and, like Lopez, are often driven by a sense of palpable urgency, because they understand the value of place and of the meanings anchored in place. As Edward Relph observes, "There is for virtually everyone a deep association with and consciousness of the places where we were born and grew up, where we live now, or where we have had particularly moving experiences. This association seems to constitute a vital source of both individual and cultural identity and security, a point of departure from which we orient ourselves in the world." Place is "home," he adds, "where your roots are, a center of safety and security, a field of care and concern."[11] It is, in short, a fixed center of meaning which, like Wallace Stevens's jar in Tennessee, enables us to order and structure the world; it is a vital component of our sense of identity as well, and its continued existence provides a reassuring sense of the world's continuity and stability. Places organize and integrate both the world and the individual; as literary critic Harold Simonson notes, "a sense of place restores one's relationship to the land and the community, and therefore to oneself."[12]

Identifying and capturing the local cultures which inhere in places is vital and essential work, then, because of this crucial role that they play in giving order and significance to both individual and communal lives. Accordingly, the potential loss of places and their cultures means something much graver than the necessity of altering the map: it means the impoverishment not only of the landscape but of the lives of the people who inhabit it. In pursuing this theme, essayist Wendell Berry writes of a battered old bucket which hangs on an abandoned fence on land which once formed part of his grandfather's farm, a bucket which has come to stand in his mind for the nature and meaning of all places.[13] Being a prolific essayist, Berry is also an inveterate walker, and the old bucket is a favorite milestone on his walks; he likes to look inside it to check on the formation in its depths of new layers of soil through the slow accretion and decay of organic matter. He also remembers the small role that the bucket once played in the life of the old farm, summoning from memory a brief story of "a bucket that must have been this one" and the way his grandfather's field hands used to boil eggs in it for their lunch. "However small a landmark the old bucket is," he muses, "it is not trivial. It is one of the signs by which I know my country and myself. And to me it is irresistibly suggestive in the way it collects leaves and other woodland sheddings as they fall through time. It collects stories, too, as they fall through time. It is irresistibly metaphorical. It is doing in a passive way what a human community must do actively and thoughtfully. A human community, too, must collect leaves and stories, and turn them to account. It must build soil, and build that memory of itself—in lore and story and song—that will be its culture." What is going on in that bucket calls to Berry's mind nothing less than the formation of place. (His bucket in Kentucky is a geographical and imaginative neighbor of Wallace Stevens's jar in Tennessee.) Each year a new layer of humus forms in the bucket, inextricably fused to a new layer of memory—of recent walks, of things and thoughts that occur on those walks. The bucket gathers layers of meaning to itself, the layers of meaning which form the topography of Berry's invisible landscape and which he sees everywhere in these woods—"my walks," he realizes, "after so long, are cultural events."

Berry finds the local cultures which the bucket metaphorically represents to be everywhere under attack—from centralized economies based in large cities, from electronic media which create and enforce a uniform national culture and discourage the exchange of talk and stories among neighbors, from modern patterns of schooling which educate children to leave their local communities and follow the dollar wherever it may lead them. Berry finds this erosion of local cultures, this washing away of patiently accumulated strata of local knowledge and experience and memory, to be disturbing and dangerous. The loss of a shared sense of locally rooted history fosters isolation and alienation: "when a community loses its memory, its members no longer know one another. How can they know one another if they have forgotten or have never learned one another's stories?" It has ecological implications as well, for a local culture brings with it a feeling of care for place, for both natural and cultural landscapes; without it, geography consists only of blank space which may be used and exploited heedlessly. The "pattern of reminding" which brings the meanings of place to mind, the armature of landmarks and stories which give conceptual structure to the local landscape, "implies affection for the place and respect for it, and so, finally, the local culture will carry the knowledge of how the place may be well and lovingly used, and also the implicit command to use it *only* well and lovingly." The preservation and maintenance of local cultures, and of a frame of mind which perceives and appreciates local cultures, is vital to the integrity of individual and social identities and to the integrity of the land as a whole. Places bind people to one another and to the landscapes which sustain and nurture them; ultimately, Berry feels, they play a profoundly ethical role in human life. The erosion of place degrades that life. Through its documentary and preservationist impulse, the essay of place stands as a brave and necessary attempt to stem this erosion, an effort to preserve much of what gives life value: "A human community, . . . if it is to last long, must exert a sort of centripetal force, holding local soil and local memory in place. Practically speaking, human society has no work more important than this."

Writers who capture and preserve places in words, then, tend to urgently recognize their importance to human life, their vital role in maintaining the world's coherence. What Harold Simonson says of the "real towns, rivers, mountains, and ranches" which feature in the works of

Western American writers is true as well of the unremarkable local land-scapes which spark the essay of place: in a postfrontier world of limita-tions and dislocations, these bits of landscape are "physical places that one can identify with and connect with inside his own soul. A certain place is thus seen as synonymous with *home*. Home is where tensions are lived out; home is the special place where connections and clarifi-cations occur. In the end home is what brings wholeness and axial cen-teredness to people, and is therefore perhaps the only resolution any of us can know."[14] Writing about place—fixing or reclaiming its geogra-phy, its history, its lived meanings in the face of inevitable physical and historical change—is important, for both writer and reader, to maintain-ing the integrity of the self and the world. It keeps alive the narratives which make the world meaningful, preventing the world from becoming flat, smooth, disorienting, alienating space, preserving the rough texture and the imaginative peaks which places provide. It examines the world, place by place, on an intimate, human, lived scale, maintaining it as a field for nourishing life and imagination. Essayists of place feel com-pelled to record and preserve visible and invisible landscapes because they see that place is valuable and necessary to human life—"as nec-essary and significant," argues Relph, "as a close relationship with other people."[15]

To place too much emphasis on the essayist's function as a sort of archivist of place, however, is perhaps misleading; such an emphasis smacks too much of the museum or library, of preserving place lifelessly behind velvet ropes or in an atlas, of thinking of place as something objectively "out there" that can be charted and signposted with dispas-sionate precision. Writings which concentrate only on pinning narratives to the map threaten to calcify places, reducing them to lifeless artifacts, siphoning off their energies and their importance to the people who live in them, reducing them to the status of curious antiquities which, as geographer David Lowenthal observes, are all too often "fenced off, sealed away, put under glass or kept in artificially cooled and dehumidi-fied premises. Like historical markers, these protective measures alter the conditions in which artifacts are experienced: they remove relics from the here and now, from continuity with the world around them, to an exclusive milieu."[16] Place is dynamic, equal parts geography and imagination; it is a complex intermingling and, ultimately, fusion of mind and landscape, so that neither is finally separable or meaningful without the other. The essayist of place finally moves beyond the *fact* of place to emphasize the *life* of place, exploring in depth its symbiotic relationship with his or her own life or with the lives of the residents of the place to which the essayist turns a keen eye and an empathetic imagination.

In the course of these explorations—of various literary essayings and assayings of place—certain basic themes consistently recur, highlighting those specific elements which make place valuable in the eyes and lives of the authors who produce these writings. We have noted that the essayist of place must approach his or her subject as both an outsider and an insider, and the simultaneous objectivity and subjectivity required by this stance manifest themselves in two primary ways: an intense awareness of time in the former case, an introspective exploration of identity in the latter. Time is an objective element beyond human control, its passage and effects to be gauged and assessed by the historian. Identity is the subjective structuring principle of a human life, its outline and components to be confronted and revealed by the autobiographer. A concern with time brings a sense of past narratives; a concern with identity brings a sense of the narratives which run through one's life. Both concerns are required to bring to light all the stories which comprise a place, and both make place valuable, keeping the past close at hand (thus resisting the often distressing changes which time inevitably brings) and keeping identity firmly grounded. Both concerns, then, firmly command the essayist's attention.

Time is a constant presence in the essay of place, either consciously or unconsciously evoked by the writer: the essayist either deliberately confronts the effects of time by comparing a present landscape with memories of earlier scenes or allows the inevitable presence of time to hover quietly behind his or her description of a place in the form of a shadowy awareness that any place is in part a concretion of history and that the future will bring both new layers of history and inevitable physical alteration. Time is obviously a central concern of those essayists for whom the preservation of place is a top priority, but it emerges as an essayistic theme in other ways as well. As geographer Yi-Fu Tuan observes, time and place are related in three ways: "time as motion or flow and place as a pause in the temporal current; attachment to place as a function of time, captured in the phrase, 'it takes time to know a place'; and place as time made visible, or place as memorial to times past."[17] Any place, that is, constitutes a stable center of gravity for a particular moment in one's life, marking an end point of a stage of movement through that life. The past stands behind a place, and place also implies the future: time will change it or will bring new places. Place is also an accumulation of experience over time in a location, involving the internalization of subtle patterns of landscape, history, and local culture, and its continued presence—in the landscape or in memory, verbal re-creation, or physical souvenir—is an aide-mémoire for earlier episodes of life. Any contemplation of place, then, is temporally complex, looking simultaneously at the formative past, the impending future, and the ephemeral present which separates the two; a meditation on place is necessarily a meditation on time.[18] Moreover, to understand any place is to look deeply into a period of the life of the person to whom it belongs.

To a writer like Thoreau, as we have seen, landscape ideally contains no component of time; he looks through the landscape to the eternal truths it clothes. To the true essayist of place, however, time is a palpable presence—sometimes a subject of interested contemplation, sometimes a force to be nervously resisted. Ivan Doig, for instance, is a writer for whom the accretions of time, of personal and collective history, are an integral, inseparable part of any landscape; as critic A. Carl Bredahl, Jr., argues, "the search for place" forms "the core of [Doig's] imaginative work." For Doig, that place for which he searches consists of far more than simply landscape, far more than a distinctive geographical surface; it encompasses as well the patterns which human activity, be it his own or others', has inscribed, visibly or invisibly, on its surface. He has made his understanding of the nature of place clear by giving his memoir of his Montana childhood the title *This House of Sky: Landscapes of a Western Mind*, a title in which, according to Bredahl's interpretation, " 'House,' 'sky,' 'landscapes,' 'western,' and 'mind' integrate to form an image of an imagination seeking its place within a world dominated by land and sky. The interrelating of physical and mental landscapes define the focus of the narrative."[19] And in Doig's writings, that mental landscape is created by memory and listening, by an awareness of time and of the depth of stories which time has deposited on the physical surface; he believes that landscape inevitably carries with it a body of narrative and that it is the writer's duty to interpret that narrative to others. As Doig reveals, he understands Montana primarily as a mosaic of stories, of individual grounded human histories; the people among whom he grew up sensed that landscapes were only comprehensible within a context of human experience and thus divided the land into a collection of what they intuitively called "places":

Anyone of Dad's generation always talked of a piece of land where some worn-out family eventually had lost to weather or market prices not as a farm or a ranch or even a homestead, but as a *place*. All those empty little clearings which ghosted that sage countryside—just the McLoughlin place there by that butte, the Vinton place over this ridge, the Kuhnes place, the Catlin place, the Winters place, the McReynolds place, all the tens of dozens of sites where families lit in the valley or its rimming foothills, couldn't hold on, and drifted off. All of them epitaphed with that barest of words, *place*.[20]

Each such name implies a story of arrival, hope, struggle, and defeat, a melding of life and landscape, generic in its failure, individual in its particulars. Being a memoir, Doig's book is of course primarily a work of individual memory, a map of one man's invisible landscape as constructed from a life spent on this harsh Montana soil. At the same time, though, it is the product of a mind that understands that his mental map is not the only one that the land supports, that his is merely one story among the many written there over time.

This sensitive awareness of the way in which time and place fuse forms the heart of Doig's *Winter Brothers*, an extended commentary and meditation on the voluminous diaries of James Gilchrist Swan, a nineteenth-century resident and explorer of the remoter reaches of Washington's Olympic Peninsula. Now a resident of Washington himself, Doig reveals that he decided to immerse himself in Swan's stories for the span of a winter in part as a result of his becoming "more aware that I dwell in a community of time as well as of people. That I should know more than I do about this other mysterious citizenship, how far it goes, where it touches."[21] His book is a form of time travel to familiar places in his life as they existed a century or more ago, as he passes Swan's daily jottings through his imagination and uses them to rebuild Indian villages and nascent port cities, to reconstruct vanished streets and settlements in his mind and populate them once more with colorful, long-dead frontier figures. In the course of his reading, Doig comes to think of Swan as the unseen paper equivalent of the sort of memorable storyteller who wanders into many people's lives—"the remembered neighbor or family member, full of years while you just had begun to grow into them, who had been in a war or to a far place and could confide to you how such vanished matters were. The tale-bringer sent to each of us by the past" (3). Like any inheritor of stories anchored in a landscape, Doig uses Swan's brief narratives to deepen his sense of his Western place, pushing its temporal boundaries back to the days of earliest settlement, tracing its routes and visiting its landmarks with eyes and imagination freshened and quickened by Swan's words. He then attempts to communicate this newly achieved fusion of time and place to his own readers as it has coalesced in his mind, alternating excerpts from Swan's diaries with accounts of the present-day wanderings and observations to which those writings inspired him. In the end, Doig takes as his primary subject what any essayist of place addresses at least obliquely: the nature and extent of his membership in the community of time. Any experience of reading, traveling, and writing "such as this of mine—or any season, of a half-hour's length or a year's, spent in hearing some venturer whose lifespan began long before our own—I think must be a kind of border crossing allowed us by time: special temporary passage permitted us if we seek out the right company for it, guides such as Swan willing to lead us back where we have never been" (11).

Swan's life and writings fascinate Doig for another reason as well: he hopes they will help him understand why he has come to "invest my life in one place rather than another, and why for me that place happens to be western" (4). Doig is an inveterate Westerner; as he reveals in the subtitle of *This House of Sky*, after all, the internal and external topographies of which he writes are "landscapes of a Western mind." Over the years, having lived first in Montana and later in Seattle, he has drawn closer and closer to the Pacific. Swan, he feels, is a personal avatar of sorts, an early trailblazer of Doig's own path, and in understanding Swan he hopes to come to a greater understanding of his own identity, an identity which he senses he cannot fully comprehend apart from its connection with certain longitudes of American earth. "Because, then, of this western pattern so stubbornly within my life I am interested in Swan as a westcomer, and stayer. Early, among the very earliest, in stepping the paths of impulse that pull across America's girth of plains and over its continental summit and at last reluctantly nip off at the surf from the Pacific, Swan has gone before me through this matter of siting oneself specifically *here: West*" (5). By the book's end, after a winter spent tracking Swan in his imagination through forty riveting years on America's damp and ragged Western edge, Doig feels his identity to be at once sharpened, its distinct and idiosyncratic edges given precision and clarity, and also absorbed into a larger regional identity, an identity shared by his community of time and place. Time has erased much of Swan's West, so that much of its current geography and meaning must necessarily be Doig's alone: "My West, or Wests, inevitably are going to be smaller and a bit more skewed than Swan's and the more intensely held, felt, worried over, for that reason." At the same time, however, "any separations between Swan's territory and mine mysteriously close at some moments. Scenes of this winter and of Swan's own western-edged seasons do flow together," so that a visit, or a recollected visit, to a place mentioned in Swan's diary resurrects Swan at Doig's side, Swan's world under Doig's feet. "Perhaps atoms merge out of the landscape into us," he muses. "However it happens, the places are freshly in me" (241). Through "listening" to Swan and traveling and thinking, through consciously confronting and deepening his relationship to place, Doig brings to conscious light the extent to which his sense of self has its foundation in Western soil, in the farthest margin of America's westernmost edge; he strengthens his imaginative grip on that country to which his inner nature instinctively responds, which draws him across the continent like a lodestone. Swan is Doig's template, he is Swan's doppelgänger: they are "bearded watchful men both, edge-walkers of the continent, more interested in one another's company than the rest of the world is interested in ours" (11). As he implies in his title, they are related by a lineage of place, enabling Doig to claim identity through family relationship; he and Swan are of different generations in a geographical community, brothers of a sort.

Any essayist of place shares Doig's fascination with this fusion of place, time, and self. A familiar landscape provides tangible reminders of the past, solid anchors for memory, and thus invites contemplation of the self who lived that past, whose acts provided those memories. Landscape comprises a field upon which writers locate memories and experiences fixed to the terrain, sifting them, replaying them, arranging them in patterns so that the identity to which those memories and experiences contribute is newly and revealingly displayed. "Landscape is a powerful catalyst upon the imagination," notes essayist Conger Beasley, Jr.; formative episodes in a life stand out in sharp relief, patterns and meanings resolve and clarify, and "the effect is salutary: landscape as a kind of cutting board upon which the identity is dissected and then fused back together into a new amalgam."[22] Contemplation of place brings an awareness not only of time but of self and of the evolution of that self, evoking the simultaneous presence of past and present versions of one's identity and thereby illuminating the full chronological depth of that identity with a new and poignant clarity.

Essayist Rockwell Gray amplifies on this realization, arguing that the entire point of thinking and writing about place is to discover and confirm the writer's feelings of identity as grounded in the past—and, by extension, to get the reader to think about the places, and the meaning of places, in his or her own life.[23] Says Gray, "One's sense of personal identity depends upon the recapture in memory of the key places in which one's life has taken place. The phrase itself—'taken place'—is a kind of pun: we live by occupying, by taking possession of, a succession of places. Human life is always concretely circumstantial. All experience is *placed* experience. . . . In short, we cannot know who we are without knowing where we have been; and recall of all those now absent places is necessary to a full sense of dwelling in the present." In part, this sense of identity derives from an imaginative reconstruction of our past attitudes and perceptions as we interacted with particular landscapes. "Through evocation of childhood roaming and of all my later residences and wanderings in the world, I recreate the angle of vision which rendered each place meaningful"—and thus recreate past versions of the self as well. In addition to reminding us of past angles of vision—reactions to and relationships with particular milieux—memories of places, and in particular of a sequence of places, also bring back to us vividly the chronology of our lives, the sequence of events that produced our present selves: "Such memories become our means of deciphering and constructing a sense of identity: I am the person who remembers this moment, view, encounter or place, and who binds them all together in a unique whole; no one else remembers exactly what I do of a certain city in a certain year." This accumulation of past episodes in the development of the self ultimately gives us a comforting, weighty sense of existence, of a deep and firmly anchored personal history in the world—which, in a world of rapid mobility and change where long-term intimacy with place is increasingly rare, serves well "to meet the threat of shallowness or excessive immediacy in the present. . . . [A]utobiographical memory serves as an antidote to such self-reduction, making present again layers of past life that have receded for lack of articulation or a mnemonic structure." Memories of places provide the structure for building a sense of identity and making it whole, for thinking about who we are—and, therefore, for writing about ourselves as well: in Gray's view, "The key symbolic places, precincts of charged meaning we will never forget, become the spinal column of our autobiographical structure." To Gray, finally, the essayist of place and the writer of autobiography are ultimately one and the same.

Essayist Douglas Bauer agrees, noting also that one's sense of identity is shaped not only by the memory of places from the past but by a continuing confrontation with those places in the present. Such renewed and periodic contact with familiar places not only provides us with a sense of continuity with the past but also makes time's passage unsettlingly palpable by reminding us baldly of the present: as our places have changed over time, so must we have changed; as our places' identities have altered, so must ours have. In an essay in which he examines the effect of recent hard times on the agricultural neighborhood in Iowa in which he grew up, Bauer reflects on the meaning that he finds in the face of his old home town:

> I've come to realize that what I'll lose if Prairie City dies is my most uncompromising mirror. . . . The myth of small places includes their timelessness, but only those who stay in them are privileged to live with that perception. For those who have left and periodically return, the sense of change—more exactly, of age—is dramatic. In the faces of people you last saw three years ago, and two years before that, but saw, just as memorably, when you were six, and ten, and seventeen. Or in now-shadeless streets, after Dutch elm disease, that had received huge blankets of shadow from the trees that used to line them. Or in noticing that there's now a wire mesh fence at the edge of an outfield that had been infinitely borderless when you played it. Seeing unmistakably how Prairie City ages, I've always seen, therefore, that I must have aged as well.

For Bauer, then, thinking about and writing about place is not only a means of confirming his sense of identity. It is as well a means of updating it, of fundamentally challenging it, and, unsettlingly, of reminding himself of its fragility: if Prairie City dies of economic strangulation, fears Bauer, "I'll have nothing more accurately reflecting than the dubious specter of memory, literally no way of life to have left."[24] Here too he echoes Gray, who feels that "the verifiable, continued existence, say, of one's birthplace and hometown . . . serves metonymously to confirm one's link to an earlier life. The life of one's youth is authenticated, we might say, by the mute witness of the things among which it took place." Writing about place, then—or, more accurately, commemorating place in writing—emerges not only as a means of maintaining control, at least in the imagination, over a world in which decay is sadly inevitable but as a way of keeping one's own sense of self from eroding as well: in both these ways, notes Gray, such a "cultivation of reveries upon the past counters the dominance of sheer change."

As we have noted, however, the idea of place implies the future as well as the past: as time passes, one's identity will become shaped in ways as yet unknown, in settings as yet unseen. As some writers have observed, place can take an integral role in this process; not only is an awareness of past places important to a continuing sense of identity and of the world's coherence, but accruing new places is central to a changing and developing sense of identity and to personal growth in general. As people change and mature, they form attachments to new places; conversely, becoming attached to new places enables and encourages them to grow. The lifelong construction of new invisible landscapes seems vital to a continued sense of well-being, to a feeling of belonging in the world. In an essay in which she seeks to explain the harsh, arid plains of Wyoming, Gretel Ehrlich realizes that the value of place for her is that it provides what she calls "solace," a feeling of certainty and security—that the simultaneous process of working yourself into a place and having a place work itself into you can make a person feel grounded, rooted, whole.[25] Ehrlich tells us that she moved to Wyoming after suffering an unnamed tragedy. After four years of living there, accumulating some seasons of her own and learning the Wyoming way of seeing, she feels reborn, healed; place has restored integrity to her life. "I suspect," she confesses, "that my original motive for coming here was to 'lose myself' in new and unpopulated territory. Instead of producing the numbness I thought I wanted, life on the sheep ranch woke me up. The vitality of the people I was working with flushed out what had become a hallucinatory rawness inside me. I threw away my clothes and bought new ones; I cut my hair. The arid country was a clean slate. Its absolute indifference steadied me." It did not remain indifferent for long, as Ehrlich's perceptive observations of life and landscape in the rest of the essay reveal; she has come to understand Wyoming deeply and thoroughly. Becoming part of a new place pushed Ehrlich through a crisis, awakening her to a new sense of possibility, providing her life with a fixed center from which to orient herself. Ehrlich's Wyoming can stand for any place: it is a blank "clean slate" at first but becomes over time both a firm foundation for building identity and a known environment which makes human sense, which invigorates the mind and sustains community no matter how inhuman it may appear on the surface.

Ehrlich develops her feelings of solace and belonging in spite of, not because of, Wyoming's forbidding appearance: it is not, at first encounter, a nurturing landscape. "Winter lasts six months here. Prevailing winds spill snowdrifts to the east, and new storms from the northwest replenish them. This white bulk is sometimes dizzying, even nauseating, to look at. At twenty, thirty, and forty degrees below zero, not only does your car not work, but neither do your mind and body. The landscape hardens into a dungeon of space. During the winter, while I was riding to find a new calf, my jeans froze to the saddle, and in the silence that such cold creates I felt like the first person on earth, or the last." Belonging to a place has little to do with the nature of that place's geography, however, but depends on shared perceptions, shared experiences, a local history that goes deep into the ground. People in Ehrlich's part of Wyoming belong because they can see and appreciate the cold bleak land in ways that others cannot, ways that define them as a community: says Ehrlich, "we seem to share one eye. Keenly observed, the world is transformed. The landscape is gorged with detail, every movement on it chillingly sharp. The air between people is charged. Days unfold, bathed in their own music. Nights become hallucinatory; dreams, prescient." The people belong because they are rooted in the landscape by generations of quiet history and the round of daily activity: in Wyoming, "a person's life is not a series of dramatic events for which he or she is applauded or exiled but a slow accumulation of days, seasons, years, fleshed out by the generational weight of one's family and anchored by a land-bound sense of place." Belonging to Wyoming, Ehrlich finds, consists of a deep appreciation of, and identification with, both of these factors—the unique landscape and history of the place: "People here still feel pride because they live in such a harsh place, part of the glamorous cowboy past." By working herself gradually and deeply into a unique local culture, a culture causally related to a particular landscape, Ehrlich finds restored to her a deep sense of the beauty and value of life.

Unlike Ehrlich, who chose to make a new life in a landscape bearing no evident culture, some writers deliberately seek out places which they know have great temporal depth and well-documented histories, searching in those places for a sense of belonging which they have been unable to find in other locations and landscapes, hoping they can acquire and strengthen a sense of identity by immersing themselves in and absorbing an easily available local culture, attempting to develop through will and imagination the feelings that Ehrlich earned in Wyoming through unreflective experience over time. Robert Finch, who has written extensively on his adopted home of Cape Cod, confesses that, after his nomadic early life, "part of what attracted me to [the Cape] was its storied quality, the local history, which went deep and was colorful, the fact that it had a literary tradition." This palpable sense of history met a previously unrecognized emotional need, making Finch feel "as though it were the place where I should have been born, as though it were the place where I would have had . . . rootedness." By transplanting himself to the Cape, by paying close attention to its human as well as its natural history and translating his observations into words, Finch has gained a comforting sense of home, security, and identity. The act of writing is indispensable to this process, for it crystallizes perceptions and reflections, giving them form and meaning, turning them into story; Finch's writing gives the same sort of narrative form to his newly developed feelings of belonging and his intimate local knowledge that natives of a place achieve orally through storytelling. He is not alone in his yearning to belong to a local culture:

> I think a lot of what I do is an attempt to imagine for myself that rooted-ness in the place where I have chosen to live. A lot of people do that, though not professionally. A lot of people come to Cape Cod not just because it's a pleasant place to live but because of its sense of history, which is ultimately a sense of story, and they can borrow a sense of history from the land. We're nearly all what they call "wash-ashores" on Cape Cod. And we all become instant natives, and outdo the real natives, and adopt all the trappings. It is a way of seeking identity for our age, which has trouble sensing identity. . . . I think a lot of what I do is making up stories about the place I live and how I live there—but make up by interacting with it.[26]

Essayists of place listen carefully to and translate the narratives implicit in the landscape—whether that landscape be their natal or adopted home or a place which they visit with keen eye and empathetic imagi-nation—presenting the places of which they write as fixed points of se-curity and stability in an uncertain world, as providing a firm anchor in a known and valued past. By sharing a place and its stories in an essay, the writer signals recognition of the value of place and makes available to readers, in at least a vicarious way, the feelings of order and personal wholeness which membership in a geographically rooted local culture provides. The reader in whom Finch's writings find a kindred imagina-tion travels to Cape Cod in mind and spirit just as Finch traveled there in life.

No matter how it is pursued, finally, there is great psychic sustenance in the sort of cultivation of place which these essayists celebrate; once a place is established on the land and in the mind, once it has been fash-ioned from the materials of landscape and time and experience and be-come lodged in memory, it remains as permanent and immutable as memory allows, a touchstone of value, a fixed center from which life can be contemplated and interpreted. Place stands in the mind as, in essayist Loren Eiseley's words, "an insubstantial structure . . . compounded of air and time," a structure which, despite its intangibility, provides a firm foundation upon which notions of self and patterns of living can be built—constructions of reassuring permanence in a world of disconcerting and threatening mutability. Eiseley writes of place in the context of the attachment which animals form to certain locations and landscapes and the way in which they seem to construct mental images of those places, images which guide all their further behavior.[27] A field mouse, fleeing a nearby construction project, invades Eiseley's living room and constructs a burrow in a flower pot, attempting in its disorientation "to build a remembered field"; a flock of pigeons continues to mill about hungrily in a newly abandoned elevated-railway station near his home, waiting for handouts from commuters who will never come again. "This feeling runs deep in life," muses Eiseley; "it brings stray cats running over endless miles, and birds homing from the ends of the earth. It is as though all living creatures, and particularly the more intelligent, can survive only by fixing or transforming a bit of time into space or by securing a bit of space with its objects immortalized and made permanent in time." To Eiseley, attachment to place is as natural and necessary a part of existence as eating or breathing, a force which motivates and sustains life. It gives the world structure and meaning; it makes it a comforting home.

Eiseley knows this attachment well, confessing that "I have spent a large portion of my life in the shade of a nonexistent tree." Like Seamus Heaney recalling a chestnut tree planted during the year of his birth in front of his childhood home, Eiseley writes of a cottonwood sapling that he and his father had planted together in their Nebraska yard one day during his boyhood. The family soon moved, the boy grew to maturity, "but the tree for some intangible reason had taken root in his mind. It was under its branches that he sheltered; it was from this tree that his memories, which are my memories, led away into the world." The tree came to stand for many things to Eiseley: childhood certainties, the reassuring continuity of life and self and memory, "my father and the love I bore him." It grew in his mind, an anchor for a life, a source of comfort and meaning which he depended on imaginatively and emotionally to the point that, as he reveals, "during a long inward struggle I thought it would do me good to go and look upon that actual tree." On his return to Nebraska, however, he finds that the tree is no longer standing, that in fact it had probably died soon after he left it. "It was obvious," he realizes, that "I was attached by a thread to a thing that had never been there, or certainly not for long. Something that had to be held in the air, or sustained in the mind, because it was part of my orientation in the universe and I could not survive without it. There was more than an animal's attachment to a place. There was something else, the attachment of the spirit to a grouping of events in time; it was part of our mortality." Place grows out of life and sustains life, as Eiseley comes to understand; it provides a stable imaginative refuge from change and flux. It pins down and organizes images and history, preventing memory from becoming random, identity from becoming episodic and fragmented. Time alters and transforms the world and the self; geography shifts and scrambles; landscapes scrape off old familiar surfaces and accrete new ones in a sort of fantastically accelerated, man-made process of erosion and sedimentation. Throughout these personal, physical, and temporal upheavals, however, place remains constant; invisible trees continue to grow and spread their restful shade. Place anchors the filament of continuity which runs through our lives, providing a richly evocative connection to the pasts which create us. It renews our memories, sustains our dreams. Like mice and pigeons, we revert as best we can in body or mind to valued places when we are feeling somehow displaced; it is an effort to build a world of known landmarks, a world in which moral and emotional compasses work dependably, a world in which we know we can survive. "We cling to a time and a place," concludes Eiseley, "because without them man is lost, not only man but life."

"Things Don't Change Much": The Example of E. B. White

As should be clear by now, essayists are very self-conscious and self-aware creatures who love not only to write about things but to write about writing about things. It is not particularly difficult to find abundant commentary by essayists about the role and meaning of places in their lives and writings, commentary which falls into certain thematic patterns. Given this common awareness of place, then, we may expect to find that the themes outlined in this chapter underlie the works of any essayist who has chosen to associate himself or herself with a particular patch of American ground, even a writer not ordinarily thought of as in any way "regional"—for example, E. B. White. White divided most of his life between New York City and the state of Maine, two locations which provide the settings and subjects for many of his writings. He was born in 1898 just north of New York City, in Mount Vernon, and lived there until he left to attend Cornell University. After spending a year crossing the country by Model T and working as a newspaperman in Seattle following his graduation from Cornell, White moved back to New York and, in 1925, began writing for the fledgling *New Yorker* magazine, a connection which he would maintain throughout his life and which would establish his reputation as one of America's finest and most respected essayists. While his personal and professional lives had deep roots in New York, White was drawn throughout his life with equal strength to the landscapes and ways of life of rural Maine. During his childhood, White's family rented a cabin every August at the Belgrade Lakes in Maine, a removal from the city which the young White always looked forward to eagerly. He continued to visit and vacation in Maine as an adult and in 1933 bought a farm on the edge of Allen Cove in the little coastal town of North Brooklin. In subsequent years, on the whole, White spent more time in Maine than he did in New York: he spent summers there from 1933 to 1938, lived on the farm year-round from 1938 to 1943, divided the year between Maine and New York from 1943 to 1957, and lived on the farm permanently from 1957 until his death in 1985. Maine and New York provided constant themes in White's life, then, and just as Maine came increasingly to serve as the setting of his life, so did it grow in value in his mind. In his essays, White establishes Maine as a source of value and sustenance, an imaginative counterbalance to what he sees as the sobering effects of the passage of time.

This is not to say that White did not like New York. He loved the city deeply; he found it an enthralling combination of excitement and comfort, of spectacle and intimacy, of history and memory, which exhilarated and refreshed him. Living there, he wrote in a 1948 essay entitled "Here Is New York," gave him "the sense of belonging to something unique, cosmopolitan, mighty, and unparalleled."[28] Part of the city's exuberant character derived from the sheer volume and variety of life which it contained: "New York provides not only a continuing excitation but also a spectacle that is continuing." The city contains millions of people and thousands of visitors, each pursuing his or her own purpose at breakneck speed, imparting to the city a dizzying pace and complexity. White does not find this complexity overwhelming, though, because as a resident he understands the city not as a huge tangled mass but as a mosaic of small, personalized places, self-contained realms in which the city's residents anchor themselves and which render the city comprehensible; it is, finally, a very human world. As he puts it, "the curious thing about New York is that each large geographical unit is composed of countless small neighborhoods. Each neighborhood is virtually self-sufficient. Usually it is no more than two or three blocks long and a couple of blocks wide. Each area is a city within a city within a city." These myriad neighborhoods may make New York's social geography seem impossibly complicated, but they also contribute to the city's fascination, its kaleidoscopic charm. Collectively, to White, they make New York a place of sorts, an intensely known and felt human world.

It is a place in a more personal sense as well; White sees New York through the unique filter of his own mind, as a combination of collective and personal history. New York, he feels, "carries on its lapel the unexpungeable odor of the long past, so that no matter where you sit in New York you feel the vibrations of great times and tall deeds, of queer people and events and undertakings." As he sits writing in a hotel room in central Manhattan, he points out that within a small compass lie locations where such well-known figures as Rudolph Valentino, Nathan Hale, Ernest Hemingway, Walt Whitman, and Willa Cather lived out parts of their lives—"and for that matter I am probably occupying the very room that any number of exalted and somewise memorable characters sat in, some of them on hot, breathless afternoons, lonely and private and full of their own sense of emanations from without." Anyone who spends even the briefest moment in New York occupies—whether he or she knows it or not—the center of a similar web of history, of past experience and accomplishment; each traverses a rugged invisible landscape of untold stories. At the same time, White blazes his own trail through this landscape by recalling his own movements and bringing to mind his own experiences as a budding writer in America's literary capital, "remembering what it felt like as a young man to live in the same town with giants"—the luminaries of that circle of columnists and critics which White burned to join, writers like Don Marquis, Christopher Morley, Franklin P. Adams, Ring Lardner, and Alexander Woollcott. White finds New York endlessly fascinating and invigorating; he knows its history, has lived in its confines, has its complex texture at his fingers' ends. It is to him a deeply known and felt place, one of the poles around which he has arranged his life.

At the same time, however, New York resists his embrace, refuses to return the affection with which he regards it; in the end, it does not fully provide the kind of psychic and emotional sustenance which people look for in place. In the end, it wears people down instead of supporting them. Writing in 1948, White notes that "New York has changed in tempo and in temper during the years I have known it. There is a greater tension, increased irritability. You encounter it in many places, in many faces. The normal frustrations of modern life are here multiplied and amplified. . . . The city has never been so uncomfortable, so crowded, so tense." There are too many people trying to move through not enough space; the physical fabric of the city changes constantly, continually rendering itself unrecognizable even to the longtime resident. White nevertheless chooses defiantly to embrace the city and affirm its worth, likening it to an old willow tree of which he knows in an urban park near his home, a tree which "symbolizes the city: life under difficulties, growth against odds, sap-rise in the midst of concrete, and the steady reaching for the sun." Still, time would bring more change, more tension, more frustration; writing in 1977, White notes that the New York of 1948 "has disappeared, and another city has emerged in its place— one that I'm not familiar with. . . . The last time I visited New York, it seemed to have suffered a personality change, as though it had a brain tumor as yet undetected."[29] Despite its many attractions, New York for White is finally too impermanent, too transient, too little capable of providing a reassuring anchor for a life, too much at the mercy of time and the decay which time brings. An unnerving inconstancy is built into the very nature of the city, it seems; in New York, as White notes in an essay which he wrote just prior to his permanent removal from the city in 1957, "a citizen is likely to keep on the move, shopping for the perfect arrangement of rooms and vistas, changing his habitation according to fortune, whim, and need. And in every place he abandons he leaves something vital, it seems to me, and starts his new life somewhat less encrusted, like a lobster that has shed its skin and is for a time soft and vulnerable."[30] Increasingly, White felt the need to belong to a place which would not leave him vulnerable, which would provide a solid and reliable foundation on which to build his life. As more time passed and New York continued to shift beneath his feet, White felt drawn more and more urgently to the life and landscapes of Maine.

Maine—be it the Maine of the Belgrade Lakes or of his North Brooklin farm—provided White with something that New York never could: a feeling of constancy, dependability, and security. He came increasingly to see Maine, not New York, as a comforting, nurturing, and sustaining home. In 1955, while he was still spending most of the year in New York, White wrote an essay about a drive to his Maine farm which he entitled "Home-Coming"—a title which, according to his biographer Scott Elledge, "made clear where [White] thought 'home' was."[31] And as the title clarifies the location of White's true home place, the essay itself clarifies the meaning and value of that home place for him. White begins the essay in rather sentimental fashion by musing on the emotional attachment that he has formed to the state over a lifetime of visits and off-and-on residence: "What happens to me when I cross the Piscataqua and plunge rapidly into Maine at a cost of seventy-five cents in tolls? I cannot describe it. I do not ordinarily spy a partridge in a pear tree, or three French hens, but I do have the sensation of having received a gift from a true love." He moves on to describe the basis of that love, the one quality which Maine possesses which warrants his investing so much of his inner and outer life within its bounds and which assures him that his feelings will be returned:

> Familiarity is the thing—the sense of belonging. It grants exemption from all evil, all shabbiness. A farmer pauses in the doorway of his barn and he is wearing the right boots. A sheep stands under an apple tree and it wears the right look, and the tree is hung with puckered frozen fruit of the right color. The spruce boughs that bank the foundations of the homes keep out the only true winter wind, and the light that leaves the sky at four o'clock automatically turns on the yellow lamps within, revealing to the soft-minded motorist interiors of perfect security, kitchens full of a just and lasting peace. (Or so it seems to the homing traveler.)[32]

Maine is to White a world of comforting predictability, of quiet steadiness. It takes on a certain timeless quality in his description: when he returns to Maine he knows that a familiar cluster of sights and sensations will be there to greet him, as though they had not moved since the last time he saw them, as though no time had passed in the interval. White eagerly embraces this changelessness and constancy; he understands and experiences Maine as an island of security and dependability in a world in which—as New York demonstrates in exaggerated fashion—change and the passage of time are inevitable. His home place gives value to life and to the world, a value which the chameleonic and enervating New York could never provide: it wards off the "evil" and "shabbiness" which lurk on the other side of the Piscataqua, providing a psychic counterbalance to much of what disturbs him in the world.

One of the most distressing elements which White finds in life is simply the passage of time itself and the progress and change which that passage brings. To White, time's flight is always faintly tragic: for the individual, it carries with it the inevitable spectres of aging and death, and for society at large he finds that "there is always a subtle danger in life's refinements, a dim degeneracy in progress."[33] White spells out his feelings about time most explicitly in a wistful essay entitled "The Ring of Time." In this piece, White writes of visiting the winter training ground of the Ringling Brothers circus and of watching a young, beautiful, graceful acrobat practicing her tricks on the back of a horse as it gallops around a ring. White finds this an exhilarating yet faintly sad and poignant scene, for as he watched the young girl he "became painfully conscious of the element of time." As the girl circles the ring again and again, White falls under the illusion that "time itself began running in circles," but at the same time he is unhappily aware that this is in fact only an illusion. "The girl wasn't so young," he continues,

> that she did not know the delicious satisfaction of having a perfectly behaved body and the fun of using it to do a trick most people can't do, but she was too young to know that time does not really move in a circle at all. I thought: "She will never be as beautiful as this again"—a thought which made me acutely unhappy. . . . Everything in her movements, her expression, told you that for her the ring of time was perfectly formed, changeless, predictable, without beginning or end, like the ring in which she was traveling at this moment with the horse that wallowed under her.[34]

For White, this is the central tragedy of human life: that time is linear and not cyclical, that it brings decay and death, that beauty fades, that experience cannot be recaptured. Against this realization, White holds fast to the familiarity of place, the feelings of timelessness and security which it provides, the memories which are woven permanently into its fabric; he embraces it in his life and explores it in his writings. His many essays about Maine emerge as dams in the stream of time whose headlong rush he deplores, providing imaginative resistance to the erosion which that stream inevitably causes.

The trepidation with which White views time's passage applies not only to individual human lives but to the course and direction of human history as well, and White's essays of place provide an imaginative counterbalance to the horrors of the twentieth century. In 1938, feeling increasingly dissatisfied with life in New York and restless in his role at the *New Yorker*, White moved to his Maine farm for five years to live the life of a New England poultryman and to write in a more personal vein than his usual forum, the *New Yorker*'s anonymous "Notes and Comment" section, allowed him. While living in Maine, he published a monthly essay in *Harper's* magazine under the heading "One Man's Meat," which also became the title of the book in which these essays were later collectively published. White has characterized these essays as "casual pieces depicting life on a saltwater farm in New England"[35] and *One Man's*

Meat as a whole as "a sustained report of about five years of country living,"[36] and on the whole the book concentrates closely on White's day-to-day life in North Brooklin. These are emphatically *personal* essays: we see White raising lambs and chickens, gathering eggs, chatting with his neighbors, hunting and fishing, ruminating on Maine's distinctive speech, fixing up the barn, and performing other such unremarkable tasks. The book provides a detailed and complete picture both of White's life and that of his rural community; it is a richly realized depiction and celebration of place. At the same time, however, events press in on White from the world beyond Maine and muscle their way inevitably into his essays. The "One Man's Meat" series ran from 1938 to 1943—that is, approximately from the appeasement of Hitler at Munich until the bleakest days of World War II. The war works its way insistently into White's thoughts, becoming a secondary theme of the book, sometimes forming the overt subject of an essay, more often lurking menacingly in the shadows just offstage. *One Man's Meat* does more than portray a place for its own sake, then; through portraying that place it provides White and his readers with a solid foundation of meaning and value from which to contemplate and imaginatively resist the nightmare of war.

White's favorite device for commenting on the war is to unobtrusively contrast a particularly sobering piece of war news with a scene of himself performing some unremarkable task on the farm, elaborating through that contrast a sense of the war's evil and horror as compared to the stability and reassurance provided by place. He tells us that, while Hitler was being appeased at Munich, he was reroofing his barn; he recalls with satisfaction "those clear days at the edge of frost, with a view of pasture, woods, sea, hills, and my pumpkin patch stretched out below in serene abundance. I stayed on the barn, steadily laying shingles, all during the days when Mr. Chamberlain, M. Daladier, the Duce, and the Führer were arranging their horse trade." White admits that this "seemed a queer place to be during a world crisis, an odd thing to be doing" but finally decides that "a barn is the best place anybody could pick for sitting out a dance with a prime minister and a demigod. There is a certain clarity on a high roof, a singleness of design in the orderly work of laying shingles: snapping the chalk line, laying the butts to the line, picking the proper width shingle to give an adequate lap. One's perspective, at that altitude, is unusually good. Who has the longer view of things, anyway, a prime minister in a closet or a man on a barn roof?"[37] Against what he sees as a cowardly caving in to Hitler's aggression and inhumanity, White opposes the steadying influence of work on his farm, the daily round of tasks and obligations which comprise part of the fabric of his place, and the larger perspective on life which this work provides; immersing himself in place reassures him that at least one thing in life is solid, nurturing, and dependable. Similarly, in a passage of Hemingwayesque detail and simplicity, White describes his activities on the morning when England and France declared war on Germany: "[W]ishing to put my affairs in order, I cleaned my comb and brush, pouring a few drops of household ammonia into the bowl of water, running the comb through the brush, then brushing the comb with a nail brush. . . . After breakfast I went to the garage and sorted some nails, putting the clapboard nails together in a bunch, the six-penny nails together, the boarding nails together, in cans. The blade of my jackknife being stiff, I eased it with a few drops of penetrating oil."[38] Like Nick Adams in Hemingway's "Big Two-Hearted River," healing the psychic wounds of war through his total immersion in the details of his fishing trip, White here seeks to fend off the ugly fact of war through a willed absorption in the physical facts and routine chores of his place, creating emotional order through putting his place in order. The farm emerges as a mirror of White's inner state, a seamless extension or reflection of his identity, a symbiotic partner in his life; its welfare and stability determine his own.

White discovers in the local landscape a welcome alternative to thoughts about the war, an island of meaning in the midst of a world which no longer seems to make sense. He contrasts a visit from Viennese friends, among whom "the only topic of conversation is genealogy" and for whom "the matter of blood is so vital, no one can think of anything else," with the healing and reassuring return of spring to his farm: "Under the spruce boughs that overlay the borders, the first green shoots of snowdrops appeared, the indestructible. When I walked to the mailbox, a song sparrow placed his incomparable seal on the outgoing letters."[39] He writes on occasion of his war work in the local community as a plane spotter and a blackout warden, but his attention is always drawn back to the reassuringly familiar fabric of his place: as he writes while describing a shift which he put in as a plane spotter, "I've observed in addition to this single plane (high, unknown) an unsurpassed example of an afternoon. . . . Flash—the distant sea, my secret post and secret joy, the distant and impending shower, cumulus, the fields beyond the little stream, the holy spire of the small white church, children playing (against the rules) around the post and trading glimpses through the old binoculars. Flash. A little portion of America, imperiled, smiling and beautiful as anything."[40] The war never enters an essay for long without being shouldered aside by a countervailing bit of farm work, a conversation with a steady old neighbor (like Mr. Dameron the lobsterman, who in pursuing his daily round of work is "as regular as a milk train" and whose "comings and goings give the day a positive quality that is steadying in a rattle-brained world"[41]), or an indelible image of the Maine coast and countryside. White's view of twentieth-century history struggles desperately to be optimistic; he seeks some means to combat the bugbears of war and, in later essays, of nuclear weapons. He finds that means by looking beneath his feet, at the place in which he has cast his lot, and in writing essays of place he erects a secure bulwark against history's blood tide.

When he chooses not to write directly about the war, then, but to focus only on his life as a Maine farmer, the contrast between his calm place and the European conflagration remains implicitly in his writings, a fact that is too big to be ignored even if it is not directly addressed. The omnipresence and reassurance of this contrast was true not only for White but for his readers as well, and, according to Elledge, it accounts for the great popularity of White's essays among his wartime audience: "White excelled as a commentator on the war because he reported the thoughts and feelings of a man who had to do his chores—of one who depended on the dailiness of daily life to keep himself sane and effective. . . . All White communicated was what his readers felt—a sense of helplessness in the face of forces too great for an individual to resist or influence, and a compensatory sense of the power to make decisions and do the work at hand."[42] White occasionally was troubled by feelings that he was not doing enough in the war effort, that his farm life was escapist and his writings too ephemeral to have any impact, but he always returned to a strong sense of the value of place and the importance of sharing a sense of place with his readers, an image of something that is valuable, steadying, and worth defending and fighting for. In the middle of an essay about the tasks which need to be done on his farm in spring and the trouble he is having with his brooder stove, White confesses that "I sometimes think I am crazy—everybody else fighting and dying or working for a cause or writing to his senator, and me looking after some Barred Rock chickens. But the land, and the creatures that go with it, are what is left that is good, and they are the authors of the book that I find worth reading; and anyway, a man has to live according to his lights even if his lights are the red coals in the base of a firepot."[43] Those lights shine steadily on the Maine that he knows intimately and to which he has become firmly and fervently attached, the Maine which he understands as a place—a place where time is cyclical and seasonal rather than linear and where evil can be vanquished by familiarity and order, a place which (in his essays at least) is forever immune to the depredations of history.

White is not concerned only with the direction of history and the evils which it necessarily seems to bring; the Maine of his mind enables him to sustain his sense of self and to imaginatively resist his *personal* vulnerability to the passage of time as well. To accomplish this resistance, White looks into the Maine of his past—the Maine of his childhood summers at the Belgrade Lakes—and attempts in his writings to make that past live once more in the present, throwing the inexorable flow of time back on itself and keeping his earlier self alive. In its function in his mind and writings, then, the old summertime camp is of a piece with the more recent coastal farm: in White's mind, while Belgrade and North Brooklin were separate *locations*, they were not separate *places* but were conflated into a single mental map—a map of a timeless Maine which provided him with a safe haven from the ravages of time. Even their landscapes looked somewhat alike to him, as though in some way they were part of the same neighborhood: in a letter which he wrote to his brother Stanley after he moved to North Brooklin, White describes the region as "Belgrade tempered with a certain bleak, hard-bitten character which the sea gives to the land."[44] White returned to Belgrade on occasion throughout his adult life, in times of doubt and trouble, and each time he did so the wealth of memory which had become lodged in that landscape proved an effective device for fending off, if only temporarily, the gloomy present and the threatening future.

White's parents died within nine months of each other, his father in August of 1935 and his mother in May of 1936. In 1937, temporarily dissatisfied with the direction that his career was taking, White took a leave of absence from the *New Yorker*, a leave which he would end in 1938 by moving to Maine year-round and beginning the "One Man's Meat" series. In the summer of 1937, uneasy in his life and with the double loss of his parents still fresh in his mind, White went alone to the Belgrade Lakes in search of a sense of stability and reassurance. In a long, eloquent letter to his brother Stanley which Elledge characterizes as being "full of a kind of Proustian ecstasy,"[45] White describes in delighted detail the unchanged appearance of this fondly remembered spot, concluding to his satisfaction that, as he tells Stanley in the letter's second sentence, "Things haven't changed much." This phrase recurs throughout the letter as a sort of refrain, a reiteration of his theme, a savoring on the tongue of his reassuring discovery. "Things don't change much," he repeats, as he paints a picture of the lake in calm, timeless, idyllic tones: "The lake hangs clear and still at dawn, and the sound of a cowbell comes softly from a faraway woodlot. In the shallows along the shore the pebbles and driftwood show clear and smooth on bottom, and black water bugs dart, spreading a wake and a shadow. A fish rises quickly in the lily pads with a little plop, and a broad ring widens to eternity." He continues with a loving catalogue of detail: the feel of the sun-warmed boards of the dock under his feet, the smell of a farmhouse kitchen, the sound of waves and wind, the look and smell of the camps, the sight of boats on the water, the comings and goings of the local fish and birds, and on and on. "Yes, sir," he concludes, "I returned to Belgrade, and things don't change much. I thought somebody ought to know."[46] Clearly, the person who benefited most from knowing this was White himself, and as a discovery and celebration of changelessness the letter was certainly of greater value to its writer than to its recipient. Nowhere in the letter does White mention his parents' deaths or his personal troubles, but his visit to Belgrade has evidently served to dispel the gloomy thoughts about life and the intimations of death with which he arrived; it has stopped the clock, replacing troubling visions of the future with images from an earlier, happier era when, like the young circus rider in Florida, he thought that time moved in a smooth unbroken circle and that change and trouble and death could never touch him. The past still lives tangibly in this place to which White feels such a firm attachment, and, as he discovers, he need only visit it to imaginatively halt the passage of time and suspend himself in an achronological moment of perfect peace.

One of White's best-known and most-anthologized essays, "Once More to the Lake," continues to explore the themes and techniques which he first outlined in this letter. Recounting a 1941 visit which White made to Belgrade with his young son, the essay is a meditation on time, place, the way in which place incorporates into its fabric a certain segment of the past and earlier versions of the self, and the use of place to resist and retard time's flow. Although he is now "a salt-water man," White admits that the lake still attracts him powerfully, and that it does so primarily because of its calm peacefulness, the sense it creates of offering immunity to life's vicissitudes: "sometimes in summer," he says, "there are days when the restlessness of the tides and the fearful cold of the sea water and the incessant wind that blows across the afternoon and into the evening make me wish for the placidity of a lake in the woods."[47] While he speaks here of meteorological turmoil, the buffeting tides and winds and cold which beset and disturb him seem clearly symbolic: he has revealed in his letter that the lake offers sanctuary from personal turmoil as well. Even as a child, White felt that the lake was somehow removed from the larger world and from the inexorable advance of time, that it belonged to the distant past or to no time at all: "although it wasn't wild, it was a fairly large and undisturbed lake and there were places in it that, to a child at least, seemed infinitely remote and primeval." Feeling the need for placidity and remoteness, White packs up his son and heads for Belgrade—and plunges deep into his own past.

As he approaches the lake, White reveals how large this piece of Maine looms in his memory and his past and frets about the probability that the lake has changed somehow, a circumstance which he finds threatening and disturbing. "I wondered how time would have marred this unique, this holy spot," he muses, choosing for artistic purposes not to reveal that he had in fact already made visits there since his childhood—"the coves and streams, the hills that the sun set behind, the camps and the paths behind the camps. I was sure that the tarred road would have found it out, and I wondered in what other ways it would be desolated." Happily, although he is right about the tarred road, the rest of Belgrade seems largely unaltered—as he told his brother, things don't change much—and this circumstance, coupled with his rediscovery of "how much you can remember about places like that once you allow your mind to return into the grooves that lead back," creates in White's mind the illusion that time has been reversed, that the past has been made present, that he is walking around in the world of his own childhood, and that his childhood self has been restored to life and granted immortality. As White lies abed in one of the old familiar camp cottages and hears his son sneak off the first morning to go canoeing, "I began to sustain the illusion that he was I, and therefore, by simple transposition, that I was my father." The changeless landscape and the old familiar activities of father and son combine to create the sense that the visit of 1941 coincides perfectly, in all its details, with the fondly remembered visits of White's childhood. Everything is exactly the same, and it is as if no time has passed; White's past lives forever in this place, and so does White, deathless and ageless and eternally ten years old.

The rest of the essay explores White's sense of the exact correspondence of past and present on this small patch of ground and water: he and his son perform some action, White realizes that it is the same action that he and his father once performed, and he is convinced more than ever that no time has passed. Father and son go fishing the first morning, for instance, and a dragonfly lands on the tip of White's fishing rod.

> It was the arrival of this fly that convinced me beyond any doubt that everything was as it always had been, that the years were a mirage and there had been no years. The small waves were the same, chucking the rowboat under the chin as we fished at anchor, and the boat was the same boat, the same color green and the ribs broken in the same places, and under the floor-boards the same fresh-water leavings and débris. . . . There had been no years between . . . this dragonfly and the other one—the one that was part of memory. I looked at the boy, who was silently watching his fly, and it was my hands that held his rod, my eyes watching. I felt dizzy and didn't know which rod I was at the end of.

They walk to a nearby farmhouse for dinner, and White notes that the weather and the house and the food and the serving girls all seem familiar and unchanged, "there having been no passage of time, only the illusion of it as in a dropped curtain." They go swimming, and, just as always occurred in his childhood, a neighboring swimmer has entered the water with a bar of soap. "Over the years there had been this person with the cake of soap, this cultist, and here he was. There had been no years." Everywhere he looks, White's memory is renewed and confirmed by the constancy of the scene: the local general store, the streams where frogs and turtles live, the drama of a midsummer thunderstorm and the delighted shouts of campers going out to swim in the rain once the lightning has passed—all are unchanged, all are the same as they were over thirty years earlier, reinforcing White's feeling that "everywhere we went I had trouble making out which was I, the one walking at my side, the one walking in my pants."

White is immensely heartened by Belgrade's constancy, by the presence of the past, for his childhood summers at the lake have great value for him as a world of peace and security and contentment, a world beyond the touch of trouble and evil; he is glad it is not gone forever, that he can seemingly inhabit that world again whenever he chooses. The summer world of Belgrade remains in White's memory as a timeless, changeless, privileged realm which he invokes in the language of song or prayer: "Summertime, oh summertime, pattern of life indelible, the fadeproof lake, the woods unshatterable, the pasture with the sweetfern and the juniper forever and ever, summer without end." He realizes with great force the value of this place in his life and holds on with renewed strength to the memories and the psychic and emotional benefits that it represents: as the past crowds in on him, he finds that "it seemed to me, as I kept remembering all this, that those times and those summers had been infinitely precious and worth saving. There had been jollity and peace and goodness." This sense of peace and happiness, along with the illusion of timelessness and immortality which it creates, are what the place represents in White's mind, are what he seizes on with wonder and joy. This is a place well worth embracing and preserving, and for this reason White reacts with distress when confronted by the possibility of change and the intrusion of the present. Where the dirt road once contained three ruts, two for the wagon's wheels and one for the horse pulling the wagon, now there are only two, and "for a moment I missed terribly the middle alternative." While reflecting on the lake's peacefulness, White notes that "the only thing that was wrong now, really, was the sound of the place, an unfamiliar nervous sound of the outboard motors. This was the note that jarred, the one thing that would sometimes break the illusion and set the years moving." These are the only threats which he can find, however, and they are greatly overshadowed by all the things that remain the same and by the power and comprehensiveness of White's memory. In inhabiting this place, he inhabits his past.

As White reluctantly recognizes, however, his sense of timelessness is only an illusion, an illusion which is baldly dispelled at the end of the essay despite the eagerness with which he clutches it; White is yanked back into the present, into his own body and his own aging forty-three-year-old self, and into a sobering awareness of the future as well. As the summer rainstorm winds down, "When the others went swimming my son said he was going in too. He pulled his dripping trunks from the line where they had hung all through the shower, and wrung them out. Languidly, and with no thought of going in, I watched him, his hard little body, skinny and bare, saw him wince slightly as he pulled up around his vitals the small, soggy, icy garment. As he buckled the swollen belt, suddenly my groin felt the chill of death." At first, the chill which he feels seems only to be a sympathetic response to his son's momentary discomfort: since White has spent the visit not feeling sure whose body he was inhabiting, it seems somehow natural that what one body feels, the other one will as well. At the same time, however, the chill brings him back to himself with a jolt, training his attention from the past to the future: it is a chill of death, putting time in motion as surely as the sound of an outboard motor engine, reminding him, in spite of his current sense of inhabiting a timeless world of changeless peace, of his own inevitable demise. He will age, he will someday die, he will step back into a world of war and violence as soon as he leaves Belgrade. This place—and the identity which it confirms and the memory which it evokes and contains—is only a temporary refuge from the inevitable passage of time and, in White's view, the equally inevitable decay, degradation, and annihilation of the self which that passage brings.

Nevertheless, it is a powerful and valuable refuge, and while the end of the essay reminds White and his readers that time and its effects are inescapable and tragic, the rest of the essay provides ample and eloquent evidence of the worth of place, the central role it can take in a person's life, the way in which it crystallizes time and makes it visible, and the close, inextricable, symbiotic relationship it creates with human memory and human identity. Belgrade clearly kept a powerful hold on White's mind throughout his life, and, despite the encroachments of the modern world and White's own advancing age (or, indeed, probably because of these factors), it retained its central place in his life and activities: for example, to celebrate his eighty-first birthday in 1980, he spent "a few days of swimming and canoeing at Great Pond, the same Belgrade lake where, seventy years before, he had received a green Old Town canoe from his father, a gift for his eleventh birthday."[48] This time, he used a borrowed canoe, but when the trip was over he drove to Old Town, Maine, and bought himself a new green canoe to use when he returned the following year—a man of eighty-two returning fondly and happily to the world of his youth, retracing the steps of his earlier self, visiting an island of the past in the midst of the present. While the modern world was already beginning to nibble at Belgrade's edges during White's 1941 visit, the place evidently remained changeless and placid in his mind even into the 1980s, and while death eventually found White as he knew it would, in the essay which captures his memories on paper and turns them into literary art that place and its meanings remain perpetually available to anyone who wishes to visit.

Following the Map: The Writer, the Reader, and the Essay of Place

This invitation to visit is a final, central component of the essay of place; to write such an essay is a gesture not only of explanation but of sharing as well. The poet William Stafford has alluded to the basis of this sharing. Stafford—the father of Kim Stafford, with whom this chapter began—shares his son's interest in listening to and passing on the meanings and stories of places and argues that in fact all producers of literary art are perforce interpreters of place simply by the circumstance of their living on earth. Resisting modern critical notions which claim that literary texts primarily derive from and refer back to earlier texts, Stafford firmly maintains that "you write from where you are," that all writing is on some basic level a response to life as it is lived in the writer's place, that "the way toward a fuller life in the arts must come by way of each person's daily experience. To deny that experience—even to veer from it in a minor way—is a false step." In Stafford's view, then, all writing is rooted in place and is in an important sense regional—not deriving from regions as they are defined by academics and planners, though, but from the folk regions of everyday life: "All events and experiences are local, somewhere. And all enhancements of events and experiences—all the arts—are regional in the sense that they derive from immediate relation to felt life. It is this immediacy that distinguishes art. And paradoxically the more local the feeling in art, the more all people can share it; for that vivid encounter with the stuff of the world is our common ground."[49] Literature, in this view, not only arises from the writer's experience of place but speaks to the reader's experience of place as well, even if the two places involved are thousands of miles and dozens of years apart. We respond to what we read because something about it rings true—something about it reminds us of something we have seen or heard or felt or done in our own homemade regions.

Understanding and writing about places is not a privilege available only to essayists; in fact, many of the writers whose essays have been considered above have written extensively in other genres as well and have tended to focus on subjects and settings and characters that are resolutely local. The Staffords *père et fils* are poets associated with the Pacific Northwest; Ivan Doig has recently completed a trilogy of novels about the fictional McCaskill family of his native northern Montana; Wendell Berry, rooted firmly in Kentucky soil, is a poet, critic, philosopher of agriculture, and author of novels and stories about "the Port William membership," a fictionalized version of the Kentucky community in which he has spent his life; and E. B. White transformed the world of his North Brooklin farm into the settings and characters of the children's classic *Charlotte's Web*. Nevertheless, the personal essay is the forum in which they choose to display and explain their feelings for place most openly and directly. These essayists address us in their own guises and in more or less their own voices, with the immediacy and honesty of an oral narrator telling us about something memorable that once happened in his neighborhood. Through the medium of the essay, these writers explain personably how places have mattered in their lives, those lives which lie behind all of their writings no matter what their genre may be. And at the same time, through the immediacy of their address and the accessibility of their thought, these essayists awaken a responsive chord in their readers, inviting them to contemplate how places matter in their lives as well.

In an essay entitled "The Long-Legged House," Wendell Berry testifies to the truth of Stafford's assertion that all writing is ultimately local, demonstrating with great insight and passion the manner in which a place is created and the influence which it can have on the life and mind and work of a writer, hinting as well at the way in which the notion of place forms a bond of sympathy and opens a direct channel of communication between writer and reader. Berry writes eloquently and at length about the most valued place in his own life: "the Camp," a small patch of ground alongside the Kentucky River upon which his great-uncle had built a two-room cabin in the 1920s and upon which Berry has since built a house of his own. The Camp is many things to Berry, its various qualities arriving in his mind not by turns but simultaneously: it is landscape, wildlife habitat, mirror, companion, home—it is Berry's "bucket," to refer to his essay mentioned earlier in this chapter, the geographical center which organizes his life and thought. The Camp has come through time and memory leaving behind it a trail of narrative, a history, and in recounting that history Berry seeks explicitly to explore as best he can the nature and significance of the bond between a particular piece of geography and an individual mind, explaining that "what has interested me in telling the history of the Camp is the possibility of showing how a place and a person can come to belong to each other."[50] His essay seeks to be at once a vivid evocation of a Kentucky River landscape and a cartographic expedition into the invisible landscape which life along the river has built up in his mind.

Berry's sense of mutual belonging, of knowing the Camp intimately and of feeling that his life is somehow tethered to its ground, is in large part a matter of familiarity, of the unplanned accretion of happy experiences; the Camp is an old friend in his life. From his earliest childhood, Berry's family would pay frequent visits to the Camp from their home in a nearby town. He locates many of his most vivid and pleasant memories at the Camp and writes of returning there again and again throughout his youth and early manhood; in the essay, he reveals the Camp to be the center of gravity of his life, the point from which he departs into different phases of life—jobs, travels—and to which he returns with the inevitability of a natural law. He would frequently spend weeks at a time at the Camp as a teenager, either alone or with a friend; he spent a summer there with his wife immediately after their marriage; while living elsewhere, he often returned to the Camp for the summer and spent weekends there while teaching at the University of Kentucky; finally, he built a house on the lot adjoining the Camp and moved his family there permanently, realizing that "the Camp, always symbolically the center of our lives, had fastened us here at last" (70). Each of these periods of his life has supplied him with valued memories, and their cumulative weight reveals the extent to which the Camp has become a guiding force in his life; as Berry notes while describing a period of boyhood residence at the Camp, he early on "began a conscious relation between me and the Camp, and it has been in my mind and figured in my plans ever since" (29).

Berry's knowledge of his place is deep and extensive, temporally complex and physically detailed. As he turns the Camp over in his mind, different facets of it become visible by turns, different aspects which give it value in his eyes. It is a constant reminder of the beloved great-uncle who built the cabin, Curran Mathews; it is an endlessly fascinating physical world, a rich habitat of plants and birds and animals. Finally, though, in Berry's life and thought the Camp is much more than a locus of memories, a catalyst for nostalgia, an enthralling landscape, or a concretion of local and family history; it is at base an integral component of his identity, a fundamental aspect of existence toward which he feels a deep emotional bond to the point that the life of man and of place are no longer distinguishable; his feelings of identity with his place have become elemental and profound.[51] The Camp is one of the most valued elements in Berry's life, a living presence to which he feels not only connected but wedded, in a bond of mutual support, nurture, and love—a state which implies not only union and intimacy but obligation as well:

By coming back to Kentucky and renewing my devotion to the Camp and the river valley, I had, in a sense, made a marriage with the place. I had established a trust, and within the assurance of the trust the place had begun to reveal its life to me in moments of deep intimacy and beauty. I had been a native; now I was beginning to belong. There is no word—certainly not *native* or *citizen*—to suggest the state I mean, that of belonging willingly and gladly and with some fullness of knowledge to a place. I had ceased to be native as men usually are, merely by chance and legality, and had begun to be native in the fashion of the birds and animals; I had begun to be born here in mind and spirit as well as in body. (69)

His life and the life of his place meld and fuse, so that he cannot contemplate the Camp without calling to mind the pattern of his days and the development of his thought; nor can he write of his life without writing of the Camp which has shaped it and directed its course. The Camp has become all the world he needs, encompassing all that sustains him and all that he values in life: he "believe[s] that everything I need is here. I do not strain after ambition or heaven. I feel no dependence on tomorrow. I do not long to travel to Italy or Japan, but only across the river or up the hill into the woods" (72).

As it has shaped his life, then—and in accordance with Stafford's implication—Berry's relationship with the Camp has decisively shaped his career as a writer. "I am a placed person," he tells us, and he finds that his goal as a writer of essays and poems and fiction has been to work out the meanings and implications of having sunk roots deep into this particular patch of Kentucky soil.

> For longer than they remember, both sides of my family have lived within five or six miles of this riverbank where the old Camp stood and where I sit writing now. And so my connection with this place comes not only from the intimate familiarity that began in babyhood, but also from the even more profound and mysterious knowledge that is inherited, handed down in memories and names and gestures and feelings, and in tones and inflections of voice. . . . I have loved this country from the beginning, and I believe I was grown before I ever really confronted the possibility that I could live in another place. As a writer, then, I have had this place as my fate. For me, it was never a question of *finding* a subject, but rather of learning what to do with the subject I had had from the beginning and could not escape.

"I was so intricately dependent on this place," he concludes, "that I did not begin in any meaningful sense to be a writer until I began to see the place clearly and for what it was. For me, the two have been the same" (42–43). For Berry, writing equals place, place equals subject; writing is place captured in words and transferred to paper. Behind his writings lie layers of memory and history, the kinds of personal and shared experience which give warmth and resonance to conversation, which subtly mold thought and speech, which work their way quietly yet insistently into perception and opinion, which tint the way that all of life is viewed and approached. Even when he is not writing specifically about the Camp, as in "The Long-Legged House," he feels that the "profound and mysterious knowledge" which his life there has transmitted to him has so fundamentally shaped his mind, imagination, and values that it inevitably expresses itself in his writings—the "inflections of voice" through which he came to know the life of the Camp are heard again in his literary voice. The stories he has heard about the Camp, the episodes of life he has passed in its precincts, the deep emotional bond which pulls him centripetally back to the river, the impulse toward care and preservation which that bond sparks, the identity he has formed with the Camp so that mind and landscape, voice and place, are one—all contribute to Berry's art; he reveals the complexity and profundity of the meanings which place can have for people, organizes them on paper, and shares them with his readers, hoping both to clarify his relationship to his own place and to guide others over the contours of the invisible landscape whose terrain he knows so well.

What is important for the writer, after all, is important for the reader as well; the passion and commitment which reverberate through Berry's essay echo far beyond his pages and the patch of Kentucky ground about which he writes. The physical and imaginative landscapes which any essay of place focuses on are equalled in importance by the very act of writing about those landscapes, of recognizing significance and value in the geographical surface and converting the mental artifact of place into the shared verbal artifact of the essay. The reader who joins Berry in the Camp—or who accompanies any essayist to any place—accomplishes more than an act of imaginary travel: to such a reader is made available (if he or she is willing to embrace it) a vision of the world as a mosaic of places, a patchwork of fragments of people's unwritten autobiographies, a universe of gravitational centers around which lives and memories and values revolve. Berry's essay alludes implicitly to the "Camps" in other people's lives, the countless centers of local culture symbolized by his backwoods bucket. The love and care he bears the Camp expand to embrace all places, all such centers of lives, all such locations—unremarkable in their humility—which nonetheless powerfully shape human values and the course of individual and collective histories. The Camp sets off sympathetic vibrations in the reader's mind, awakening thoughts of similar formative and deeply known places which have structured and illumined the reader's days, suggesting a world of places beyond the horizons of individual lives. "Uniqueness is what makes all regions alike," says critic Harold Simonson, "and the human response is what unites us as brethren."[52] In the feelings of care and responsibility and regard it expresses or implies toward each of the world's landscapes, and in the respect it accords the lives and histories rooted in that valued ground—lives and histories whose integrity may depend on the maintenance of those landscapes—the essay of place is a fundamentally ethical genre.

Any essayist of place shares Berry's motive in one way or another—the compelling impulse, central to his identity and purpose as a writer, to document, explain, and serve as tour guide for a single one of the world's countless places, and in so doing to advocate and celebrate the worth and importance to human life of all places. The essayist of place adheres to what Berry describes elsewhere (in terms similar to Stafford's) as a particular sort of "regionalism," one which "could be defined simply as *local life aware of itself*" and which bodies forth "a particular knowledge of the life of the *place* one lives in and intends to *continue* to live in. It pertains to living as much as to writing, and it pertains to living *before* it pertains to writing. The motive of such regionalism is the awareness that local life is intricately dependent, for its quality but also for its continuance, upon local knowledge."[53] What Harold Simonson says about Western regionalists applies as well to the many literary chroniclers of America's local cultures and landscapes: "By having a sense of real towns, ranches, mountains, and rivers—always in relationship to persons—the best regional writers create a sense of home, connectedness and clarification."[54] The essayist plies the same ground that the teller of folk narrative does, that same nebulous region staked out by the unplanned patterns of experience, by the body and imagination wearing paths and finding favorite resting places in the landscape. Each tries to translate those geographic regions, and the imaginative regions which are coextensive with them, into narrative, explanation, and interpretation—into story, believing with writer Terry Tempest Williams that "within this notion of people and place, story is the correspondence between the two. It informs our lives, it keeps things known. It's the umbilical cord between the past, present, and future. Story identifies the relationships, and I think that's what is essential in the heart of good storytelling . . . to be able to see those inherent relationships."[55]

The urge to pass on these stories is not necessarily an American phenomenon, of course, but one which appears whenever and wherever an essayist's mind is sympathetically engaged by life fused with landscape. Nor is it limited to those places where history and legend lie thick on the ground, easily available to the inquiring author. What Jan Morris says about the Wales of which she writes is finally true of any place which captures the attention and compels the curiosity of any writer: she summarizes the work of the essayist of place in her attempt to grasp and record the Welshman's vision of his land as "another country almost, somewhere beyond time or even geography, which has remained . . . a distillation of history and imagination, poetry and hard fact, landscape and aspiration, and which we may call, in the absence of any more exact definition, the Matter of Wales." This motive holds as true for the chronicler of the most humble and newly founded place—a camp in Kentucky, a lake in Maine—as it does for Morris as she explores, through misty reaches of space and time, cultural richness and historical depth of Wales, where Owain Glyndŵr still strides defiantly through the Welsh imagination, where legends, narratives, and associations line every fog-shrouded valley and cling with the tenacity of lichen to every rock; there is equal value in both kinds of place. Even the writer who gives voice to the most obscure byway, one whose stories are short and few, ultimately shares Morris's goal of trying to see and reveal "time, place, and people all conjoined: and by putting the whole of it between covers, mark the country more distinctly upon the map of our minds."[56] The Matter of Wales, in one form or another, is the matter of every place.

≈≈≈≈≈≈≈≈≈≈≈≈≈≈≈≈≈≈≈≈≈≈≈≈≈≈≈≈≈≈≈≈≈≈

Epilogue:

Feeling Every Bump in the Ground

When I was nine years old, my family moved from New Milford, Connecticut, to Neenah, Wisconsin. In the house that we moved into, the driveway was slightly lower than the floor of the garage, leaving a bump of about an inch and a half where the two concrete slabs met. That unremarkable bump insinuated itself into my daily life in several ways. During games of driveway basketball, any airball, errant pass, or baseline dribble would be drawn to the bump with a grim fatality, and the ball would go rocketing toward the street unless one of us hapless players could throw ourselves in its path. The sensation of passing over the bump became an expected, inextricable part of riding in the car as it entered the garage. When I learned to drive myself, I discovered that the bump had practical navigational uses as well: it slowed the car down as I drove it into the garage, and I unconsciously developed the reflex of pressing down on the brake a certain fraction of a second after the rear wheels cleared the bump.

A few years ago, my mother, who still lives in that house, decided to have the driveway mudjacked and brought up to the level of the garage floor. On my first visit back to Neenah after she did this, I learned just how deeply I had internalized this bump, how much a part of daily experience in that house it had become. The first time I drove my mother's car into the garage, I had to stab wildly at the brake at the last minute to keep from plowing into the back wall: not only was there no bump to slow the car down, but I also missed the expected signal to start applying the brake. I've readjusted my driving habits since then, but I still feel slightly strange whenever I drive a car into that garage, waiting for a little lift that never comes.

My close relationship to this small malocclusion between two chunks of cement reinforces for me an important truth, one which has driven this study from the beginning through a range of disciplinary perspectives and narrative texts: the nature and quality of a place can sink deep into you, influencing and conditioning the way you think, see, and feel, working far down into your very bones by simple virtue of residence and time. I occasionally suspect that my deep-seated awareness of the drive-way bump grows somehow out of my being a Midwesterner, of my having spent the last half of my growing-up years in a well-ironed, geographically subtle part of the country where any deviation from the horizontal gets itself noticed. Certainly Neenah is among the flatter places I've ever been, and even now I can close my eyes and remember every slope on its streets—they are that few and, therefore, that remarkable. I know, for instance, that if you are a kid on a bike and you pedal furiously north from Cecil Street on Congress Street and start coasting when you cross Laudan Boulevard, the slight downhill grade on Congress that starts there will carry you nearly all the way to Wisconsin Avenue (a considerable distance to a kid on a bike, believe me). I also know that living in flat country has shaped my landscape tastes: I now take a disproportionate delight in rugged terrain, experiencing a secret thrill whenever I'm in a place where the horizon is visible above the rooftops. Having grown up in a geologically restrained, topographically prudish part of the country, I find high mountains and deep valleys to be exotic, voluptuous, geologically shameless and exhibitionistic: when I am in the West, I ogle the Rockies like a schoolboy at a burlesque show. I can't look at them enough. My home landscape has conditioned how I experience the world.

Being a Midwesterner has shaped my perceptions in other often amusing ways as well. The Midwest is the land of compass directions, the place where the survey grid mandated by the Land Ordinance of 1785 achieved untrammeled expression. Roads go north and south, east and west, and lacking other obvious landmarks to use as navigational reference points, people learn to orient themselves by the compass. I never thought much about this until I moved back to the geologically rumpled New England, where roads follow some insane logic all their own, and began baffling my friends by asking them, upon receiving directions to their houses, if they lived on the north side or the south side of the street, or by referring to a room or a doorway as being in the northeast corner of a building. The blank stares I received in return brought home to me the fact that I didn't see the world in quite the same way that my friends did, that our experiences of place had put different standards in our heads for making sense of what we encountered.

I offer my experience as a metaphor. Just as I am sensitive to and appreciative of the bumps in Neenah's physical landscape, so does each of us develop a refined sensitivity to the bumps in the invisible landscapes of places in our lives; through the process of living and thinking and talking and listening, we create a sense of place out of the physical, imaginative, and verbal materials at hand. We know where the narrative hills are; we know when to expect that little imaginative jolt at the base of the spine; we feel every bump in the ground. Another part of my experience, however, suggests a more sobering metaphor: can the roughness in our invisible landscapes be mudjacked away, leaving a smooth blank surface where there used to be a memory and a story? Many academics and writers see this possibility as a great danger of modern life, one which carries with it grave consequences. Geographer Edward Relph warns of the rise of what he calls "a placeless geography, a labyrinth of endless similarities," one marked by increasingly standardized architecture, by the mushroom-like sprouting of identical commercial strips at the edges of America's cities and towns, by anonymous and interchangeable landscapes. Instead of being rooted in place, modern people, in Relph's view, are increasingly characterized by what he calls "placelessness," a word which "describes both an environment without significant places and the underlying attitude which does not acknowledge significance in places."[1] This attitude on the part of builders and planners can lead in turn to the destruction of significant landscapes and places in the lives of individuals, causing them physical disorientation and emotional distress—a "fading and discoloration of places," as Tony Hiss calls it in his recent *The Experience of Place*, which "has been going on around us for generations." Until recently, Hiss reports, "when people spoke about a vivid experience of place, it would usually be a wonderful memory, a magic moment at one of the sweet spots of the world." Today, however, people tell Hiss "that some of their most unforgettable experiences of places are disturbingly painful and have to do with unanticipated loss. . . . A curving road in front of an old suburban house, for instance, gets straightened and widened, and suddenly a favorite grove of oaks or pines that the winds whistled through is chopped down and paved over."[2] Other writers decry Americans' increasing geographical mobility, their propensity for moving every few years without allowing any feeling for a particular place or attachment to a particular landscape to develop. Scott Russell Sanders, in a recent essay arguing for the value of "staying put," warns of the costs of this mobility, of skating blithely on the earth's surface and never stopping to rest, and points out the benefits of taking root: "For even the barest existence, we depend on . . . the inherited goods of our given place. If our interior journeys are cut loose entirely from that place, then both we and the neighborhood will suffer. . . . When we cease to be migrants and become inhabitants, we might begin to pay enough heed and respect to where we are. By settling in, we have a chance of making a durable home for ourselves, our fellow creatures, and our descendants."[3]

We ignore critics like these at our personal, interpersonal, cultural, and ecological peril. When we allow ourselves to become estranged from physical landscapes and the invisible landscapes that they support, abuse and pain and loss are inevitable. The results of this estrangement are not difficult to find on the landscape and in human history and usually take the form of unconscionable irresponsibility. Estrangement from the land and its ecosystems leads to environmental abuse, to irresponsible waste and destruction. Estrangement from a sense of the shared past on the land leads to the bulldozing of historic landscapes, to the irreparable loss of the land's temporal depth. Economic development and building borne of placelessness lead to the erosion or obliteration of distinctive regional landscapes. Disregard of the invisible landscape— and impressing change upon the physical terrain that anchors that landscape—forces psychic pain and dislocation on others, pounding flat those imaginative bumps by which they orient themselves and which give meaning to their worlds. Nor is this sort of estrangement and its consequences confined strictly to the American present and the recent past: the history of European expansion on the North American continent, to name one prominent example, was accomplished at the continual expense of Native Americans, whose mythic interpretation of landscape was pushed aside and imaginatively paved over by whites who assumed that they were moving into blank geographical space and believed that, since they themselves could place no narratives on the territory they were settling, no such narratives existed. After all, we tend to think, if territory looks blank on the map, it must be blank in the mind as well.[4]

We need to know that, if we feel that we must disturb a visible or invisible landscape for some reason, we should consider very carefully what we are doing before we act: the consequences on many levels may be grave and, ultimately, not worth it; the many losses may well outweigh the gains. We need to look beyond our immediate concerns and perceptions and be sensitive to those of others, viewing the landscape through as many eyes as we can. I do not, however, share the utter fatalism of many modern critics. I don't believe that there is such a thing as a completely placeless piece of ground, no matter how rationally it has been constructed, no matter how many cookie-cutter houses it has on its surface; nor do I think there exists a person completely lacking any vestige of a sense of place—and as long as that vestige remains alive, there is hope. My fellow Midwesterner Michael Martone has written many essays about his home town of Fort Wayne, Indiana, a town situated squarely in the middle of the survey grid in that Midwest which he says "began as a highly abstract work of the imagination and lingers so today. The power of the grid that overlays it often prevents us from seeing the place itself. It has been characterized from its inception in two dimensions alone, flattened by fiat." Still, if we are alert, we will find ourselves enmeshed in place to a degree we may never have expected. Martone writes of a park—Hamilton Park, named after a prominent local family which included Edith Hamilton, the popularizer of ancient Greek myths—near his childhood home, in a neighborhood bordered by "streets that followed the original township grid," that was built on what used to be a trash dump. Occasionally, old pieces of garbage would work their way to the surface, a fact which Martone seizes upon as a metaphor. Even two-dimensional Fort Wayne, he realizes, has its own narrative depth; what looks like boring Midwestern space becomes richly defined place if we pay it close enough attention.

> I look back now and see how this little patch of ground surrendered up its history, how too it was a frame for the larger histories of the world. Somewhere along the way I realized that classical Athens was not much bigger than my own home town, and the stories I read of those golden ages, interpreted by someone from my town, were relentlessly local while they spoke to the larger human condition. I also realized that the stories of this place were just beginning to be told. Platting the landscape, subdividing the subdivisions of property would not be enough to kick-start the culture of myth. We who grew up in the Midwest would have to sit here awhile, within the borders of our own defined neighborhoods, . . . and watch as the junk of our too-recent past resurrected itself and appeared to us as treasure in the dust at our feet.[5]

Linguist Barbara Johnstone, a fellow Fort Wayner of Martone's, draws a similar broad conclusion from her study of the unremarkable personal experience narratives embedded in the daily conversations of the city's residents, positing that "our sense of place and community is rooted in narration. . . . There is a basic connection between stories and places: in human experience, places are narrative constructions, and stories are suggested by places."[6] With Martone and Johnstone, I recognize and argue that we all have a sense of place of some sort, on some patch of ground, even in the most unlikely places; if we sit and think and talk, we can all attach stories—even if they are brief and unremarkable, even if, comparing them to the narratives of other times and places, we think of them as "junk"—to the landscapes we inhabit. Our senses of place may be temporally shallow, but that does not negate their reality and power; every day, the newest suburb sees just as much human experience as the oldest and most tradition-rich village. Once we become aware of our own invisible landscapes, we can build on this knowledge: we can come to see and believe that other people live in invisible landscapes of their own, imaginative vistas built upon the actual physical landscape, and will then be less inclined to do either of those landscapes harm. The potential is there for us to learn responsibility. What we need to do first is pay attention to and cultivate our own senses of place. What we need to do is learn to feel every bump in the ground.

Certainly I find myself becoming something of a connoisseur of bumps. I have become increasingly aware both of the way they get ironed out on the land and of their resilience in the mind. When I finished writing the doctoral dissertation on which this book is based, for instance, curiosity (and beautiful March weather) drove me back along Route 101 to the Connecticut–Rhode Island border once more; I wanted to celebrate in a quiet and personal way, and to give my study a sense of closure both in my mind and on paper. I also wanted to confirm something that I already knew: that landscapes change. I expected that some alterations would have come to the border zone that I had first explored many months previously—everything I heard and saw and read in the course of my research drummed this inevitability into me—but I wanted to see just *how* it had changed.

Upon arriving, I see that the scene actually seems much the same as when I had last left it: the picnic grove still occupies its roadside hilltop, the big blue signs still try energetically to buttonhole passing drivers, the old faded border sign and the stone post still stand quietly and unobtrusively at the edge of things. I notice that the neighborhood crime watch sign is gone, although similar signs now stand several yards up each of the side roads that lead away from the highway on either side of the border; the neighbors are still wary, apparently, but have decided to be a little less aggressive about it. The sign warning Connecticut-bound motorists that they exceed the speed limit at their peril still shakes its finger sternly from the roadside, and its companion cheerily broadcasts its old welcoming message, although the name at the bottom of the sign is different: as of the last election, Governor Lowell P. Weicker, Jr., now extends his personal greeting. Rhode Island has a new governor as well, and I find evidence of his accession on the other side of the border. In fact, not only does Bruce Sundlun's name stamp its official sanction on the bottom of the sign, but the entire sign is new: "Welcome to Rhode Island, the Ocean State," it blares at me, filling the rest of its surface with a picture of a sailboat heeling over in the wind. Although at the moment the nearest water to me is a reservoir in Connecticut, and although I would probably seriously damage my health if I decided to splash around in the part of Narragansett Bay closest to where I live, I have evidently just strolled into a maritime paradise.

So far the changes which I see have arisen from political events, a fact which does not surprise me; politicians delight in shuffling and scrambling the physical, social, and economic surfaces of our lives, while the quotidian bedrock remains reassuringly steady. Despite the symbolic presence of the governors at the borders and the subtle evidences of their accession to power, things (as E. B. White once pointed out) haven't changed much. Even the marker stake that the surveying crew left behind them still sprouts from the ground, its orange ribbons badly faded and worn. I notice idly that the picnic ground's identifying sign is gone but attribute its absence to the effects of a winter windstorm or an inattentive snowplow driver. That is, I dismiss its absence until I stroll into the grove itself, when I realize that it has been closed permanently: its grills and picnic tables and outhouses are gone, and both ends of the gravel road which runs through it have been blocked off with boulders. Pine needles and cones blanket it thickly—the picnic-grove equivalent of the dust which coats the surfaces of an abandoned house. I pull from the depths of memory a briefly perused and all-but-forgotten newspaper story from several months earlier about state picnic groves being closed because of state budget cuts, and I realize that I am in the presence of one of the victims, a relic, a ruin. The cheerfully welcoming Rhode Island border landscape will be a little less welcoming from now on. This too is a political event, the result of a political decision, and while the actual alteration in the landscape amounts only to the removal of a sign and some picnic and sanitary facilities, that alteration hints at a larger, sobering, uncontrollable source of change: economic uncertainty, political whim, the simple unpredictability of the future, whatever combination of trends and events it is that makes budgets dry up and replaces DiPrete with Sundlun and O'Neill with Weicker. I suddenly feel that there is much less stability here than I first imagined, at least if I read the evidence of the most recent additions to (and subtractions from) the border zone: the big loud signs designed to be easily seen by manically speeding motorists, the defunct rest area for drivers worn down by travel, the concessions to the world of modernity.

Time plays easily with the top layers of a landscape: things are put down, picked up, edited, and erased. The oldest layers of a palimpsest, however, are the hardest to erase completely, and the old sign and the stone post remain unchanged and impervious: they have seen it all, and they will see a lot more. The sign looks even more rusty and faded than it did on my last visit and seems to be leaning a few more degrees into Connecticut. The letters on the stone post are obscured by dead grass and leaves at this time of year; I don't see any poison ivy guarding the post this time, but all the same I decide not to take any chances and refrain from brushing the leaves away. I merely stoop down to reassure myself that the carved letters are still there (as if there were any danger that they would not be), point myself back into Rhode Island, and leave.

One further thing about this border zone also has not changed: there is a story anchored here, a story which remains in my memory (indeed, it is what brought me out here today) and which I included in my prologue. This book has sent me out into the field as well as into the library, has let me experience as well as learn; the Rhode Island border and the Idaho mountains now stand out sharply in my invisible American landscape. In a way, I see this book not only as a scholarly study of place but as a personal mapping of place, an allusion to my own geographically rooted narratives, and those narratives will remain inextricably joined in my mind with the learning that I have accumulated in the course of my research—and I have to admit that the stories may well be more vivid and entertaining than the learning. If nothing else, I have at least been able to liven up the writing process: as mementos, I keep on my bookshelves a chunk of low-grade ore and a weathered grey piece of a wooden dynamite crate that I found on an abandoned Idaho mine dump—a mine dump on which I lost my footing and whose face I slid down baseball-style on the side of my left leg and hip, desperately holding my camera in the air out of harm's way and, as I was a good two miles from a paved road, fervently hoping that I wouldn't hurt myself—and, as much as I would like to forget it, I still vividly remember that Rhode Island poison ivy. Despite the bumps and bruises and itches, though, it has been worth it.

Notes

PROLOGUE: READING THE BORDER

1. Barry Lopez, "Borders," in *Crossing Open Ground*, 97.

2. Wilbur Zelinsky, "Where Every Town Is Above Average: Welcoming Signs along America's Highways," *Landscape* 30:1 (1988): 1.

3. Ibid., 10.

4. Karal Ann Marling, *The Colossus of Roads: Myth and Symbol along the American Highway*, 59–60.

5. John K. Wright, "*Terrae Incognitae*: The Place of the Imagination in Geography," *Annals of the Association of American Geographers* 37 (1947): 3.

6. John Noble Wilford, *The Mapmakers*, 302.

1. OF MAPS AND MINDS: THE INVISIBLE LANDSCAPE

1. See Wilford, *The Mapmakers*; see also Norman J. W. Thrower, *Maps and Man: An Examination of Cartography in Relation to Culture and Civilization*.

2. Elizabeth Bishop, "The Map," in *The Complete Poems, 1927–1979*, 3.

3. John McPhee, *Rising from the Plains*, 26, 103, 149, 23.

4. Joseph Conrad, *Heart of Darkness*, 12.

5. Wilford, *The Mapmakers*, 14.

6. John L. Allen, "Lands of Myth, Waters of Wonder: The Place of the Imagination in the History of Geographical Exploration," in *Geographies of the Mind: Essays in Historical Geosophy*, ed. David Lowenthal and Martyn J. Bowden, 58.

7. Wilford, *The Mapmakers*, 61.

8. William Least Heat Moon, *Blue Highways: A Journey into America*, xi, 5.

9. David Lowenthal, *The Past Is a Foreign Country*, 256–257.

10. Maurice Beresford, *History on the Ground: Six Studies in Maps and Landscapes*, 28–30, 50–51.

11. John R. Stilgoe, *Common Landscape of America, 1580 to 1845*, 52, 56.

12. Helen Hooven Santmyer, *Ohio Town*, 20.

13. E. V. Walter, *Placeways: A Theory of the Human Environment*, 118–119.

14. Wilford, *The Mapmakers*, 34, 45.

15. This is not necessarily to suggest that, in contrast to these earlier maps, modern maps are uniformly objective, purely scientific, and entirely value-free,

or that the only additional meanings that can be read into them are personal ones. As historians of cartography point out, all maps, not merely those of premodern times, reflect the cultures which produce them. J. B. Harley argues that any map can be seen as "a social construction of the world expressed through the medium of cartography," as much (and as accurate and revealing) a cultural text as any work of art or literature. According to Harley, "Far from holding up a simple mirror of nature that is true or false, maps redescribe the world—like any other document—in terms of relations of power and of cultural practices, preferences, and priorities. What we read in a map is as much related to an invisible social world and to ideology as it is to phenomena seen and measured in the landscape" (J. B. Harley, "Text and Contexts in the Interpretation of Early Maps," in *From Sea Charts to Satellite Images: Interpreting North American History through Maps*, ed. David Buisseret, 4). Thus, for example, maps of the British Empire with England at their centers stood as powerful statements of imperialistic ideology, modern American highway maps and road atlases speak to the nation's love of the automobile, and the United States Geological Survey's topographic maps argue subtly for the authority of the government to establish and proclaim geographical truth (a truth that may be more partial than many people realize: the USGS maps are meant at least in part to serve logistical military purposes—one reason that they emphasize such features as relief and woodland density—and they routinely omit sensitive sites such as military installations and nuclear waste dumps). While my emphasis here is on the role of personal experience and knowledge in the production and understanding of maps, we should keep in mind that this understanding is not achieved in a vacuum—that maps, and the interpretation of maps, are necessarily embedded in a matrix of social and political forces. See also J. B. Harley, "Maps, Knowledge, and Power," in *The Iconography of Landscape: Essays on the Symbolic Representation, Design and Use of Past Environments*, ed. Denis Cosgrove and Stephen Daniels, 278–299, and Mark Monmonier, *How to Lie with Maps*, 118–122.

16. Robert P. Emlen, *Shaker Village Views: Illustrated Maps and Landscape Drawings by Shaker Artists of the Nineteenth Century*, 15, 129.

17. Richard M. Candee, "Land Surveys of William and John Godsoe of Kittery, Maine: 1689–1769," in *New England Prospect: Maps, Place Names, and the Historical Landscape*, ed. Peter Benes, 9, 43.

18. Lowenthal, *The Past Is a Foreign Country*, 257.

19. Stilgoe, *Common Landscape of America*, 100.

20. James R. Shortridge, *The Middle West: Its Meaning in American Culture*, xiii.

21. Edward Relph, *Place and Placelessness*, 24.

22. Yi-Fu Tuan, *Space and Place: The Perspective of Experience*, 54.

23. Yi-Fu Tuan, "Place: An Experiential Perspective," *Geographical Review* 65 (1975): 152.

24. Walter, *Placeways*, 142–143.

25. Tuan, *Space and Place*, 6, 199.

26. Ibid., 183–184.

27. Relph, *Place and Placelessness*, 31.

28. Walter, *Placeways*, 117.

29. Tuan, "Place: An Experiential Perspective," 153.

30. Relph, *Place and Placelessness*, 33.

31. Tuan, *Space and Place*, 33, 198.

32. Yi-Fu Tuan, *Topophilia: A Study of Environmental Perceptions, Attitudes, and Values*, 99.

33. Relph, *Place and Placelessness*, 43.

34. Walter, *Placeways*, 213.

35. William James, "On a Certain Blindness in Human Beings," in *The Writings of William James*, ed. John J. McDermott, 630–631.

36. Barbara Johnstone, *Stories, Community, and Place: Narratives from Middle America*, 5.

37. Arthur H. Robinson and Barbara Bartz Petchenik, *The Nature of Maps: Essays toward Understanding Maps and Mapping*, 43.

38. Hugh Brody, *Maps and Dreams*, 147, 6–7.

39. Bruce Chatwin, *The Songlines*, 74.

40. Peter Sutton, "Dreamings," in *Dreamings: The Art of Aboriginal Australia*, ed. Peter Sutton, 19.

41. Barry Lopez, "The American Geographies," *Orion Nature Quarterly* 8:4 (Autumn 1989): 60–61.

42. Charles S. Aiken, "Faulkner's Yoknapatawpha County: Geographical Fact into Fiction," *Geographical Review* 67 (1977): 13.

43. Charles S. Aiken, "Faulkner's Yoknapatawpha County: A Place in the American South," *Geographical Review* 69 (1979): 331.

44. Jules Zanger, " 'Harbours Like Sonnets': Literary Maps and Cartographic Symbols," *Georgia Review* 36 (1982): 789.

45. Elizabeth Duvert, "Faulkner's Map of Time," *The Faulkner Journal* 2:1 (Fall 1986): 14.

46. Aiken, "Faulkner's Yoknapatawpha County: A Place in the American South," 348. The quote from Faulkner is on page 347 of Aiken's article.

47. D. W. Meinig, "Environmental Appreciation: Localities as a Humane Art," *Western Humanities Review* 25 (1971): 4–5.

48. Leonard Lutwack, *The Role of Place in Literature*, 31. For two recent collections of essays which deal specifically with the relationships between geography and the genres of fiction and poetry, see Douglas C. D. Pocock, ed., *Humanistic Geography and Literature: Essays on the Experience of Place*, and William E. Mallory and Paul Simpson-Housley, eds., *Geography and Literature: A Meeting of the Disciplines*.

49. Walter, *Placeways*, 116, 2.

50. Mark Twain, *Mark Twain's Notebooks & Journals, Volume II (1877–1883)*, ed. Frederick Anderson, Lin Salamo, and Bernard L. Stein, 455.

51. Horst H. Kruse, *Mark Twain and "Life on the Mississippi,"* 9, 11.

2. FOLKLORE AND THE SENSE OF PLACE

1. Kevin Lynch, *The Image of the City*, 4.

2. Roger M. Downs and David Stea, *Maps in Minds: Reflections on Cognitive Mapping*, 6–7.

3. Ibid., 83–84. The italics are theirs.

4. Peter Gould and Rodney White, *Mental Maps*, 31–81.

5. For a collection of essays discussing the relationships between media such as these and the images which people form of places in the world around them, see Jacquelin Burgess and John R. Gold, eds., *Geography, the Media, and Popular Culture*. For a fuller discussion than I include in this book of the ways in which people construct impressions of the geographical world from secondary sources of knowledge in the absence of immediate experience, see Kent C. Ryden, "Mapping the Invisible Landscape: Geography, Narrative, and the Sense of Place," chapter 3.

6. Downs and Stea, *Maps in Minds*, 27.

7. Richard M. Dorson, "Introduction: Concepts of Folklore and Folklife Studies," in *Folklore and Folklife: An Introduction*, ed. Richard M. Dorson, 8.

8. E. Estyn Evans, "The Cultural Geographer and Folklife Research," in Dorson, *Folklore and Folklife*, 518.

9. Henry Glassie, *Pattern in the Material Folk Culture of the Eastern United States*, 34.

10. W. F. H. Nicolaisen, "Folklore and Geography: Towards an Atlas of American Folk Culture," *New York Folklore Quarterly* 29 (1973): 10.

11. Fred B. Kniffen, "Folk Housing: Key to Diffusion," in *Common Places: Readings in American Vernacular Architecture*, ed. Dell Upton and John Michael Vlach, 7. See also Kniffen, "American Cultural Geography and Folklife," in *American Folklife*, ed. Don Yoder, 51–70.

12. Edmunds V. Bunkśe, "Commoner Attitudes toward Landscape and Nature," *Annals of the Association of American Geographers* 68 (1978): 556.

13. William E. Lightfoot, "Regional Folkloristics," in *Handbook of American Folklore*, ed. Richard M. Dorson, 189.

14. Ibid., 187.

15. Suzi Jones, "Regionalization: A Rhetorical Strategy," *Journal of the Folklore Institute* 13 (1976): 107.

16. Richard M. Dorson, *Bloodstoppers and Bearwalkers: Folk Traditions of the Upper Peninsula*, 2.

17. Richard M. Dorson, *Land of the Millrats*, 6.

18. Gary Comstock, "Grandma's Backbone, Dougie's Ankles," in *A Place of Sense: Essays in Search of the Midwest*, ed. Michael Martone, 112.

19. Ibid., 115.

20. Arthur Gribben, "*Táin Bó Cuailnge*: A Place on the Map, a Place in the Mind," *Western Folklore* 49 (1990): 277–291.

21. Henry Glassie, *Passing the Time in Ballymenone: Culture and History of an Ulster Community*, 664–665.

22. Alan Dundes, "Defining Identity through Folklore," in *Folklore Matters*, 2, 13.

23. Anthony P. Cohen, "Belonging: The Experience of Culture," in *Belonging: Identity and Social Organisation in British Rural Cultures*, ed. Anthony P. Cohen, 10.

24. Glassie, *Passing the Time*, 201.

25. Mary Hufford, *One Space, Many Places: Folklife and Land Use in New Jersey's Pinelands National Reserve*, 44.

26. Tuan, *Topophilia*, 4.

27. Rita Zorn Moonsammy, David Steven Cohen, and Lorraine E. Williams, "Introduction," in *Pinelands Folklife*, ed. Rita Zorn Moonsammy, David Steven Cohen, and Lorraine E. Williams, 1.

28. Robert Blair St. George, "Mind, Nature, and Art in the Pine Barrens: An Exhibition Review," *Winterthur Portfolio* 23 (1988): 265.

29. Hufford, *One Space, Many Places*, 49.

30. Jones, "Regionalization," 111.

31. John Brinckerhoff Jackson, *Discovering the Vernacular Landscape*, 15.

32. Lightfoot, "Regional Folkloristics," 186.

33. Barbara Allen, "The Genealogical Landscape and the Southern Sense of Place," in *Sense of Place: American Regional Cultures*, ed. Barbara Allen and Thomas J. Schlereth, 156, 160.

34. Richard A. Reuss, "Suburban Folklore," in Dorson, *Handbook*, 173.

35. Gerald Warshaver, "Urban Folklore," in Dorson, *Handbook*, 169.

36. Howard Wight Marshall, *Folk Architecture in Little Dixie: A Regional Culture in Missouri*, 1.

37. Glassie, *Passing the Time*, 351.

38. Robert D. Bethke, *Adirondack Voices: Woodsmen and Woods Lore*, 7–9.

39. David E. Sopher, "The Landscape of Home: Myth, Experience, Social Meaning," in *The Interpretation of Ordinary Landscapes: Geographical Essays*, ed. D. W. Meinig, 137.

40. Mary T. Hufford, "Telling the Landscape: Folklife Expressions and Sense of Place," in Moonsammy, Cohen, and Williams, *Pinelands Folklife*, 16, 23.

41. Moonsammy, Cohen, and Williams, "Introduction," 10.

42. Mary Hufford, " 'One Reason God Made Trees': The Form and Ecology of the Barnegat Bay Sneakbox," in Allen and Schlereth, *Sense of Place*, 50.

43. Hufford, "Telling the Landscape," 32.

44. Simon J. Bronner, *Chain Carvers: Old Men Crafting Meaning*, 81, 95.

45. Marshall, *Little Dixie*, viii.

46. Charles E. Martin, *Hollybush: Folk Building and Social Change in an Appalachian Community*.

47. Marshall, *Little Dixie*, 18–19.

48. Reuss, "Suburban Folklore," 173.

49. Bethke, *Adirondack Voices*, 38.

50. Johnstone, *Stories, Community, and Place*, 10.

51. Hufford, *One Space, Many Places*, 74.

52. Hufford, "Telling the Landscape," 19–20.

53. Hufford, *One Space, Many Places*, 42.

54. Hufford, "Telling the Landscape," 21–22.

55. Dorson, *Millrats*, 2–3.

56. Marshall, *Little Dixie*, 110, xiii.

57. William Lynwood Montell, *Don't Go Up Kettle Creek: Verbal Legacy of the Upper Cumberland*, 3.

58. Ibid., 7.

59. Martin, *Hollybush*, 9.

60. Marshall, *Little Dixie*, 3–4.

61. Montell, *Don't Go Up Kettle Creek*, 129.

62. Bethke, *Adirondack Voices*, 68.

63. Ibid., 72, 68.

64. For a text (collected in 1956 in Lowell, Maine) and a general discussion of "The Jam on Gerry's Rock," see Richard M. Dorson, *America in Legend: Folklore from the Colonial Period to the Present*, 158–162.

65. Bethke, *Adirondack Voices*, 66.

66. Reuss, "Suburban Folklore," 175.

67. Jan Harold Brunvand, *The Vanishing Hitchhiker: American Urban Legends and Their Meanings*, 2–4.

68. Ibid., 81–84.

69. Ibid., 160–171.

70. Jan Harold Brunvand, *The Choking Doberman and Other "New" Urban Legends*, 78–92.

71. Sandra K. D. Stahl, "The Personal Narrative as Folklore," *Journal of the Folklore Institute* 14 (1977): 20, 22.

72. Eleanor Wachs, *Crime-Victim Stories: New York City's Urban Folklore*, xi, 12, 2.

73. Ibid., 42–44, 64, 41.

74. Larry Danielson, "Tornado Stories in the Breadbasket: Weather and Regional Identity," in Allen and Schlereth, *Sense of Place*, 29–30.

75. Jones, "Regionalization," 115.

76. Barre Toelken, "Folklore and Reality in the American West," in Allen and Schlereth, *Sense of Place*, 25.

77. Jones, "Regionalization," 116.

78. Bethke, *Adirondack Voices*, 40, 51.

79. The story to which I allude is one of the most frequently reprinted and discussed of the Crockett almanac tales; it can be found, among other places, in Walter Blair, ed., *Native American Humor*, 285–286.

80. Edward D. Ives, *George Magoon and the Down East Game War: History, Folklore, and the Law*, 293.

81. Carolyn S. Brown, *The Tall Tale in American Folklore and Literature*, 34.

82. Jones, "Regionalization," 116.

83. Ken Mingis, "Doomed Tower a Ruin, but Memories Alive," *Providence Journal*, 22 May 1989.

84. Montell, *Don't Go Up Kettle Creek*, 185.

85. Comstock, "Grandma's Backbone," 123.

3. THE FOLKLORE OF PLACE: THE COEUR D'ALENE MINING DISTRICT, NORTH IDAHO

1. In transcribing the words of my informants, I have tried to give an accurate impression of the way that their comments and stories actually sounded. In the interest of readability, I have deleted false starts, "crutch" phrases, stammerings, and other such extraneous words when those deletions in no way change the meaning, clarity, or spirit of the texts, but otherwise offer my informants' narratives verbatim. In addition, I have indicated when they laughed, altered their tone of voice, or made other metanarrational additions to their texts. For the most part, I have followed the standard conventions for punctuating English prose in presenting my informants' narratives. I have also tried to use punctuation to indicate the length of pauses, and for this reason some of the oral texts may be punctuated in what appears to be a nonstandard way; such instances should be regarded not as errors but as attempts to impart to written text the flavor, however attenuated and imperfect, of oral performance. In these stories and comments, a semicolon indicates that the narrator ran two consecutive sentences together with no pause at all; a period stands for a clear pause between sentences; a comma means a clear pause within a sentence; a dash indicates that the narrator suddenly broke off a sentence midway and began a new thought. An ellipsis stands for a long pause for thought; I have put my editorial ellipses (usually indicating a tangential remark interpolated into the narrative by the speaker, or a brief exchange between informant and interviewer) within square brackets to avoid confusion.

2. Richard V. Francaviglia, *Hard Places: Reading the Landscape of America's Historic Mining Districts*, 4–5, 9.

3. I have drawn the following account of the early history of the Coeur d'Alene mining district from these sources: Russell A. Bankson and Lester S. Harrison, *Beneath These Mountains*; John Fahey, *The Days of the Hercules*; Fahey, *The Inland Empire: Unfolding Years, 1879–1929*, chapters 9 and 10; Patricia Hart and Ivar Nelson, *Mining Town: The Photographic Record of T. N. Barnard and Nellie Stockbridge from the Coeur d'Alenes*; Richard G. Magnuson, *Coeur d'Alene Diary: The First Ten Years of Hardrock Mining in North Idaho*; Carlos A. Schwantes, *In Mountain Shadows: A History of Idaho*, 92–96, 155–160; Schwantes, *The Pacific Northwest: An Interpretive History*, 237–249.

4. Montell, *Don't Go Up Kettle Creek*, 7–8.

5. Sandra Dolby Stahl, *Literary Folkloristics and the Personal Narrative*, 12, 19. The italics are Stahl's.

6. Timothy Cochrane, "Place, People, and Folklore: An Isle Royale Case Study," *Western Folklore* 46 (1987): 2–3.

7. Roger Mitchell, "Occupational Folklore: The Outdoor Industries," in Dorson, *Handbook*, 133. For other discussions and examples of loggers' folklore, see Bethke, *Adirondack Voices*; Dorson, *Bloodstoppers and Bearwalkers*, 186–210; Dorson, *America in Legend*, 153–184; Barre Toelken, *The Dynamics of Folklore*, 51–72.

8. Timothy Cochrane, "Commercial Fishermen and Isle Royale: A Folk Group's Unique Association with Place," in *Michigan Folklife Reader*, ed. C. Kurt Dewhurst and Yvonne R. Lockwood, 102.

9. Daniel J. Gelo, "The Bear," in *American Wildlife in Symbol and Story*, ed. Angus K. Gillespie and Jay Mechling, 133.

10. Jay Mechling and Angus K. Gillespie, "Introduction," in Gillespie and Mechling, *American Wildlife*, 6.

11. The story also incorporates a traditional motif in mining folklore: in discussing narratives about the birth, life, and death of Western mining boom towns, Bruce Rosenberg notes that "often through pure blind luck a rich strike is made," after which miners flock in and a boom town springs up almost overnight. Horses often play the central role in the lucky strike: for instance, one legend tells of a Pony Express horse which "unintentionally kicked a chip of silver from the Reese River field while fleeing from Indians. The chip turned out to be nearly pure silver." See Bruce A. Rosenberg, "The Folklore of the Gold Rush," *Huntington Library Quarterly* 44 (1981): 300.

12. This too is a traditional motif: as Rosenberg points out, "Lost-mine stories are among the most common staples of Western lore" (295).

13. Patrick B. Mullen, *I Heard the Old Fishermen Say: Folklore of the Texas Gulf Coast*, 7–8.

14. Hart and Nelson, *Mining Town*, 84.

15. Bill Dunphy, letter to author, 28 October 1992.

16. Bob Anderson, letter to author, 2 June 1992.

17. Hufford, "Telling the Landscape," 20.

18. Lopez, "The American Geographies," 60.

4. A WALK IN THE INVISIBLE LANDSCAPE: THE ESSAY OF PLACE

1. Bunkśe, "Commoner Attitudes toward Landscape and Nature," 554, 556.

2. Scott Russell Sanders, "Landscape and Imagination," *North American Review* 274:3 (September 1989): 63–66. This essay has also been included in a collection of other personal writings on the nature and meaning of life and landscape in the Hoosier State: *Where We Live: Essays about Indiana*, ed. David Hoppe, 1–8.

3. Stephen H. Daniel, "Reading Places: The Rhetorical Basis of Place," in *Commonplaces: Essays on the Nature of Place*, ed. David W. Black, Donald Kunze, and John Pickles, 18.

4. Chris Anderson, "Introduction," in *Literary Nonfiction: Theory, Criticism, Pedagogy*, ed. Chris Anderson, ix–x.

5. Scott Russell Sanders, "Introduction," in *The Paradise of Bombs*, xiv.

6. George Core, "Stretching the Limits of the Essay," in *Essays on the Essay: Redefining the Genre*, ed. Alexander J. Butrym, 215.

7. E. B. White, "Foreword," in *Essays of E. B. White*, vii.

8. Scott Russell Sanders, "The Singular First Person," in Butrym, *Essays on the Essay*, 31.

9. Edward Hoagland, "What I Think, What I Am," in *The Tugman's Passage*, 25.

10. Carl H. Klaus, "Essayists on the Essay," in Anderson, *Literary Nonfiction*, 170.

11. Sanders, "The Singular First Person," 35.

12. Core, "Stretching the Limits," 217.

13. Graham Good, *The Observing Self: Rediscovering the Essay*, 8, 13, 24.

14. William Zeiger, "The Personal Essay and Egalitarian Rhetoric," in Anderson, *Literary Nonfiction*, 236.

15. Hoagland, "What I Think, What I Am," 25–26.

16. Sanders, "The Singular First Person," 39, 33.

17. Joseph Epstein, "Piece Work: Writing the Essay," in *Plausible Prejudices: Essays on American Writing*, 400.

18. Good, *The Observing Self*, xii.

19. White, "Foreword," vii.

20. Core, "Stretching the Limits," 218.

21. Sanders, "The Singular First Person," 33.

22. Good, *The Observing Self*, 7–8.

23. Zeiger, "The Personal Essay and Egalitarian Rhetoric," 237–238.

24. O. B. Hardison, Jr., "Binding Proteus: An Essay on the Essay," in Butrym, *Essays on the Essay*, 14.

25. Klaus, "Essayists on the Essay," 160.

26. Good, *The Observing Self*, xii.

27. Jeffrey C. Robinson, *The Walk: Notes on a Romantic Image*, 4.

28. G. Douglas Atkins, "In Other Words: Gardening for Love—The Work of the Essayist," *Kenyon Review*, n.s., 13:1 (Winter 1991): 61.

29. R. Lane Kauffmann, "The Skewed Path: Essaying as Unmethodical Method," in Butrym, *Essays on the Essay*, 238.

30. Sanders, "Introduction," xiii.

31. Samuel F. Pickering, Jr., "Being Familiar," in *The Right Distance*, 7.

32. J. Robinson, *The Walk*, 29–30.

33. Tim Robinson, *Stones of Aran: Pilgrimage*, 12–13.

34. Stephen Trimble, "Introduction: The Naturalist's Trance," in *Words from the Land: Encounters with Natural History Writing*, ed. Stephen Trimble, 2, 10.

35. Robert Finch, *The Primal Place*, 78–79.

36. Ibid., 103.

37. Quoted in *Writing Natural History: Dialogues with Authors*, ed. Edward Lueders, 45.

38. Maxine Kumin, "A Sense of Place," in *In Deep: Country Essays*, 162.

39. Henry David Thoreau, *The Natural History Essays*, ed. Robert Sattelmeyer, 95. Further references to this volume will be made parenthetically in the text.

40. William Howarth, *The Book of Concord: Thoreau's Life as a Writer*, 29.

41. Seamus Heaney, "The Placeless Heaven: Another Look at Kavanagh," in *The Government of the Tongue: The 1986 T. S. Eliot Memorial Lectures and Other Critical Writings*, 3–6.

42. Barry Lopez, *Arctic Dreams: Imagination and Desire in a Northern Landscape*, xix, xxi. Further references to this book will be made parenthetically in the text.

43. Sanders, "The Singular First Person," 41.

44. Barry Lopez, "The Stone Horse," in *Crossing Open Ground*, 1–17.

45. Sherman Paul, *Hewing to Experience: Essays and Reviews on Recent American Poetry and Poetics, Nature and Culture*, 350.

46. Sanders, "The Singular First Person," 32.

47. Hardison, "Binding Proteus," 25.

5. THE ESSAY OF PLACE: THEMES IN THE CARTOGRAPHY OF THE INVISIBLE LANDSCAPE

1. Kim R. Stafford, "There Are No Names But Stories," in *Places & Stories*, 11.

2. Kim R. Stafford, "Introduction: Naming the Northwest," in *Having Everything Right: Essays of Place*, 3.

3. Ibid., 6, 4, 7–8.

4. T. Robinson, *Stones of Aran*, 11–13.

5. C. W. Gusewelle, "Memories of a Country Neighborhood," in *Far from Any Coast: Pieces of America's Heartland*, 53–63.

6. Glassie, *Passing the Time*, 621–622.

7. Michael Martone, "The Flatness," in Martone, *A Place of Sense*, 29–30.

8. Relph, *Place and Placelessness*, 66, 55.

9. Michael J. Rosen, "Under the Sign of Wonder Bread and Belmont Caskets," in Martone, *A Place of Sense*, 16–17.

10. Hardison, "Binding Proteus," 12.

11. Relph, *Place and Placelessness*, 43, 142.

12. Harold P. Simonson, *Beyond the Frontier: Writers, Western Regionalism, and a Sense of Place*, 14.

13. Wendell Berry, "The Work of Local Culture," in *What Are People For?* 153–169.

14. Simonson, *Beyond the Frontier*, 4.

15. Relph, *Place and Placelessness*, i.

16. David Lowenthal, "Age and Artifact: Dilemmas of Appreciation," in Meinig, *Interpretation*, 112.

17. Tuan, *Space and Place*, 179.

18. This sense of the simultaneous presence of many layers of time is similar to the Native American notion of "ceremonial time" which naturalist John Hanson Mitchell evokes when thinking and writing about the square mile of territory which surrounds his house in Massachusetts. Ceremonial time, says Mitchell, is a stance for viewing the world "in which past, present, and future can be perceived in a single moment" (Mitchell, *Ceremonial Time: Fifteen Thousand Years on One Square Mile*, 1–2). This sort of perception, which brings all strata of local meaning into simultaneous view, is an identifying mark of the essay of place.

19. A. Carl Bredahl, Jr., *New Ground: Western American Narrative and the Literary Canon*, 135, 138.

20. Ivan Doig, *This House of Sky: Landscapes of a Western Mind*, 22–23. The italics are Doig's.

21. Ivan Doig, *Winter Brothers: A Season at the Edge of America*, 4. Further references to this book will be made parenthetically in the text.

22. Conger Beasley, Jr., "Preface," in *Sundancers and River Demons: Essays on Landscape and Ritual*, xi.

23. Rockwell Gray, "Autobiographical Memory and Sense of Place," in Butrym, *Essays on the Essay*, 53–70.

24. Douglas Bauer, "The Way the Country Lies," in Martone, *A Place of Sense*, 61–62.

25. Gretel Ehrlich, "The Solace of Open Spaces," in *The Solace of Open Spaces*, 1–15.

26. Quoted in Lueders, *Writing Natural History*, 44–45.

27. Loren Eiseley, "The Brown Wasps," in *The Night Country*, 227–236.

28. E. B. White, "Here Is New York," in *Essays*, 118–133.

29. White, "Foreword," viii.

30. E. B. White, "Good-bye to Forty-Eighth Street," in *Essays*, 6.

31. Scott Elledge, *E. B. White: A Biography*, 317.

32. E. B. White, "Home-Coming," in *Essays*, 9–10.

33. E. B. White, "Progress and Change," in *One Man's Meat*, 29.

34. E. B. White, "The Ring of Time," in *Essays*, 144–145.

35. E. B. White, "Introduction," in *One Man's Meat*, xi.

36. White, "Foreword," ix.

37. E. B. White, "Clear Days," in *One Man's Meat*, 17.

38. E. B. White, "Second World War," in *One Man's Meat*, 84.

39. E. B. White, "A Week in April," in *One Man's Meat*, 49.

40. E. B. White, "Morningtime and Eveningtime," in *One Man's Meat*, 247–248.

41. White, "Second World War," 81.

42. Elledge, *E. B. White*, 222.

43. E. B. White, "Spring," in *One Man's Meat*, 190.

44. Quoted in Elledge, *E. B. White*, 214.

45. Ibid., 203.

46. E. B. White, *Letters of E. B. White*, 135–137.

47. E. B. White, "Once More to the Lake," in *One Man's Meat*, 198–203.

48. Elledge, *E. B. White*, 355–356.

49. William Stafford, "Having Become a Writer: Some Reflections," *Northwest Review* 13:3 (1973): 91–92.

50. Wendell Berry, "The Long-Legged House," in *Recollected Essays, 1965–1980*, 45. Further references to this long essay will be made parenthetically in the text.

51. James Campbell suggests that, in a less immediately personal sense, the notion of "geographical place and its importance to human self-understanding" is an important element in all of Berry's writings; see Campbell, "Place as Social and Geographical," in Black, Kunze, and Pickles, *Commonplaces*, 70.

52. Simonson, *Beyond the Frontier*, 140.

53. Wendell Berry, "The Regional Motive," in *A Continuous Harmony: Essays Cultural and Agricultural*, 67. The italics are Berry's.

54. Simonson, *Beyond the Frontier*, ix.

55. Quoted in Lueders, *Writing Natural History*, 46.

56. Jan Morris, *The Matter of Wales: Epic Views of a Small Country*, 4, 6.

1. Relph, *Place and Placelessness*, 141, 143.

2. Tony Hiss, *The Experience of Place*, xiii-xv.

3. Scott Russell Sanders, "Staying Put," *Orion* 11:1 (Winter 1992): 42–43.

4. This willful disregard of Native American uses and interpretations of the land continued when it came time to map newly settled territories: historian of cartography J. B. Harley notes that "as the frontier moved west, the traces of an Indian past were dropped from the [cartographic] image. Many eighteenth-century map makers preferred blank spaces to a relict Indian geography." See Harley, "Text and Contexts," 11.

5. Michael Martone, "Correctionville, Iowa," *North American Review* 276:4 (December 1991): 5–7.

6. Johnstone, *Stories, Community, and Place*, 5, 134.

Bibliography

Aiken, Charles S. "Faulkner's Yoknapatawpha County: A Place in the American South." *Geographical Review* 69 (1979): 331–348.

————. "Faulkner's Yoknapatawpha County: Geographical Fact into Fiction." *Geographical Review* 67 (1977): 1–21.

Allen, Barbara, and Thomas J. Schlereth, eds. *Sense of Place: American Regional Cultures*. Lexington: University Press of Kentucky, 1990.

Anderson, Chris, ed. *Literary Nonfiction: Theory, Criticism, Pedagogy*. Carbondale and Edwardsville: Southern Illinois University Press, 1989.

Atkins, G. Douglas. "In Other Words: Gardening for Love—The Work of the Essayist." *Kenyon Review*, n.s., 13:1 (Winter 1991): 56–69.

Bankson, Russell A., and Lester S. Harrison. *Beneath These Mountains*. New York: Vantage Press, 1966.

Beasley, Conger, Jr. *Sundancers and River Demons: Essays on Landscape and Ritual*. Fayetteville: University of Arkansas Press, 1990.

Benes, Peter, ed. *New England Prospect: Maps, Place Names, and the Historical Landscape*. Boston: Boston University for the Dublin Seminar for New England Folklife, 1980.

Beresford, Maurice. *History on the Ground: Six Studies in Maps and Landscapes*. London: Lutterworth Press, 1957.

Berry, Wendell. *A Continuous Harmony: Essays Cultural and Agricultural*. New York: Harcourt Brace Jovanovich, 1972.

————. *Recollected Essays, 1965–1980*. San Francisco: North Point Press, 1981.

————. *What Are People For?* San Francisco: North Point Press, 1990.

Bethke, Robert D. *Adirondack Voices: Woodsmen and Woods Lore*. Urbana: University of Illinois Press, 1981.

Bishop, Elizabeth. *The Complete Poems, 1927–1979*. New York: Farrar, Straus and Giroux, 1983.

Black, David W., Donald Kunze, and John Pickles, eds. *Commonplaces: Essays on the Nature of Place*. Lanham, Md.: University Press of America, 1989.

Blair, Walter, ed. *Native American Humor*. New York: Harper and Row, 1960.

Bredahl, A. Carl, Jr. *New Ground: Western American Narrative and the Literary Canon*. Chapel Hill: University of North Carolina Press, 1989.

Brody, Hugh. *Maps and Dreams*. New York: Pantheon, 1981.

Bronner, Simon J. *Chain Carvers: Old Men Crafting Meaning*. Lexington: University Press of Kentucky, 1985.

Brown, Carolyn S. *The Tall Tale in American Folklore and Literature*. Knoxville: University of Tennessee Press, 1987.

Brunvand, Jan Harold. *The Choking Doberman and Other "New" Urban Legends*. New York: Norton, 1984.

———. *The Vanishing Hitchhiker: American Urban Legends and Their Meanings*. New York: Norton, 1981.

Buisseret, David, ed. *From Sea Charts to Satellite Images: Interpreting North American History through Maps*. Chicago: University of Chicago Press, 1990.

Bunkśe, Edmunds V. "Commoner Attitudes toward Landscape and Nature." *Annals of the Association of American Geographers* 68 (1978): 551–566.

Burgess, Jacquelin, and John Gold, eds. *Geography, the Media, and Popular Culture*. Boston: St. Martin's, 1985.

Butrym, Alexander J., ed. *Essays on the Essay: Redefining the Genre*. Athens: University of Georgia Press, 1989.

Chatwin, Bruce. *The Songlines*. New York: Viking, 1987.

Cochrane, Timothy. "Place, People, and Folklore: An Isle Royale Case Study." *Western Folklore* 46 (1987): 1–20.

Cohen, Anthony P., ed. *Belonging: Identity and Social Organisation in British Rural Cultures*. Manchester: Manchester University Press, 1982.

Conrad, Joseph. *Heart of Darkness*. New York: Penguin, 1973.

Cosgrove, Denis, and Stephen Daniels, eds. *The Iconography of Landscape: Essays on the Symbolic Representation, Design and Use of Past Environments*. Cambridge: Cambridge University Press, 1988.

Dewhurst, C. Kurt, and Yvonne R. Lockwood, eds. *Michigan Folklife Reader*. East Lansing: Michigan State University Press, 1988.

Doig, Ivan. *This House of Sky: Landscapes of a Western Mind*. New York: Harcourt Brace Jovanovich, 1978.

———. *Winter Brothers: A Season at the Edge of America*. New York: Harcourt Brace Jovanovich, 1980.

Dorson, Richard M. *America in Legend: Folklore from the Colonial Period to the Present*. New York: Pantheon, 1973.

———. *Bloodstoppers and Bearwalkers: Folk Traditions of the Upper Peninsula*. Cambridge, Mass.: Harvard University Press, 1952.

———. *Land of the Millrats*. Cambridge, Mass.: Harvard University Press, 1981.

———, ed. *Folklore and Folklife: An Introduction*. Chicago: University of Chicago Press, 1972.

———, ed. *Handbook of American Folklore*. Bloomington: Indiana University Press, 1983.

Downs, Roger M., and David Stea. *Maps in Minds: Reflections on Cognitive Mapping*. New York: Harper and Row, 1977.

Dundes, Alan. *Folklore Matters*. Knoxville: University of Tennessee Press, 1989.

Duvert, Elizabeth. "Faulkner's Map of Time." *The Faulkner Journal* 2:1 (Fall 1986): 14–28.

Ehrlich, Gretel. *The Solace of Open Spaces*. New York: Viking, 1985.

Eiseley, Loren. *The Night Country*. New York: Scribner's, 1971.

Elledge, Scott. *E. B. White: A Biography*. New York: Norton, 1984.

Emlen, Robert P. *Shaker Village Views: Illustrated Maps and Landscape Drawings by Shaker Artists of the Nineteenth Century*. Hanover, N.H.: University Press of New England, 1987.

Epstein, Joseph. *Plausible Prejudices: Essays on American Writing*. New York: Norton, 1985.

Fahey, John. *The Days of the Hercules*. Moscow: University Press of Idaho, 1978.

———. *The Inland Empire: Unfolding Years, 1879–1929*. Seattle: University of Washington Press, 1986.

Faulkner, William. *Absalom, Absalom!* 1936; rpt. New York: Vintage, 1972.

Finch, Robert. *The Primal Place*. New York: Norton, 1983.

Francaviglia, Richard V. *Hard Places: Reading the Landscape of America's Historic Mining Districts*. Iowa City: University of Iowa Press, 1991.

Gillespie, Angus K., and Jay Mechling, eds. *American Wildlife in Symbol and Story*. Knoxville: University of Tennessee Press, 1987.

Glassie, Henry. *Passing the Time in Ballymenone: Culture and History of an Ulster Community*. Philadelphia: University of Pennsylvania Press, 1982.

———. *Pattern in the Material Folk Culture of the Eastern United States*. Philadelphia: University of Pennsylvania Press, 1968.

Good, Graham. *The Observing Self: Rediscovering the Essay*. London: Routledge, 1988.

Gould, Peter, and Rodney White. *Mental Maps*. 2d ed. Boston: Allen and Unwin, 1986.

Gribben, Arthur. "*Táin Bó Cuailnge*: A Place on the Map, a Place in the Mind." *Western Folklore* 49 (1990): 277–291.

Gusewelle, C. W. *Far from Any Coast: Pieces of America's Heartland*. Columbia: University of Missouri Press, 1989.

Hart, Patricia, and Ivar Nelson. *Mining Town: The Photographic Record of T. N. Barnard and Nellie Stockbridge from the Coeur d'Alenes*. Seattle: University of Washington Press, and Boise: Idaho State Historical Society, 1984.

Heaney, Seamus. *The Government of the Tongue: The 1986 T. S. Eliot Memorial Lectures and Other Critical Writings*. London: Faber and Faber, 1988.

Hiss, Tony. *The Experience of Place*. New York: Knopf, 1990.

Hoagland, Edward. *The Tugman's Passage*. New York: Random House, 1982.

Hoppe, David, ed. *Where We Live: Essays about Indiana*. Bloomington: Indiana University Press, 1989.

Howarth, William. *The Book of Concord: Thoreau's Life as a Writer*. New York: Viking, 1982.

Hufford, Mary. *One Space, Many Places: Folklife and Land Use in New Jersey's Pinelands National Reserve*. Washington, D.C.: American Folklife Center, Library of Congress, 1986.

Ives, Edward D. *George Magoon and the Down East Game War: History, Folklore, and the Law*. Urbana: University of Illinois Press, 1988.

Jackson, John Brinckerhoff. *Discovering the Vernacular Landscape*. New Haven: Yale University Press, 1984.

James, William. *The Writings of William James*, ed. John J. McDermott. New York: Random House, 1967.

Johnstone, Barbara. *Stories, Community, and Place: Narratives from Middle America*. Bloomington: Indiana University Press, 1990.

Jones, Suzi. "Regionalization: A Rhetorical Strategy." *Journal of the Folklore Institute* 13 (1976): 105–120.

Kruse, Horst H. *Mark Twain and "Life on the Mississippi."* Amherst: University of Massachusetts Press, 1981.

Kumin, Maxine. *In Deep: Country Essays*. New York: Viking, 1987.

Least Heat Moon, William. *Blue Highways: A Journey into America*. 1982; rpt. New York: Fawcett Crest, 1984.

Lopez, Barry. "The American Geographies." *Orion Nature Quarterly* 8:4 (Autumn 1989): 52–61.

———. *Arctic Dreams: Imagination and Desire in a Northern Landscape*. 1986; rpt. New York: Bantam, 1987.

———. *Crossing Open Ground*. New York: Vintage, 1989.

Lowenthal, David. *The Past Is a Foreign Country*. Cambridge: Cambridge University Press, 1985.

Lowenthal, David, and Martyn J. Bowden, eds. *Geographies of the Mind: Essays in Historical Geosophy*. New York: Oxford University Press, 1975.

Lueders, Edward, ed. *Writing Natural History: Dialogues with Authors*. Salt Lake City: University of Utah Press, 1989.

Lutwack, Leonard. *The Role of Place in Literature*. Syracuse: Syracuse University Press, 1984.

Lynch, Kevin. *The Image of the City*. Cambridge, Mass.: M.I.T. Press, 1960.

McPhee, John. *Rising from the Plains*. New York: Farrar, Straus and Giroux, 1986.

Magnuson, Richard G. *Coeur d'Alene Diary: The First Ten Years of Hardrock Mining in North Idaho*. Portland, Oreg.: Binford and Mort, 1968.

Mallory, William E., and Paul Simpson-Housley, eds. *Geography and Literature: A Meeting of the Disciplines*. Syracuse: Syracuse University Press, 1987.

Marling, Karal Ann. *The Colossus of Roads: Myth and Symbol along the American Highway*. Minneapolis: University of Minnesota Press, 1984.

Marshall, Howard Wight. *Folk Architecture in Little Dixie: A Regional Culture in Missouri*. Columbia: University of Missouri Press, 1981.

Martin, Charles E. *Hollybush: Folk Building and Social Change in an Appalachian Community.* Knoxville: University of Tennessee Press, 1984.

Martone, Michael. "Correctionville, Iowa." *North American Review* 276:4 (December 1991): 4–9.

———, ed. *A Place of Sense: Essays in Search of the Midwest.* Iowa City: University of Iowa Press, 1988.

Meinig, D. W. "Environmental Appreciation: Localities as a Humane Art." *Western Humanities Review* 25 (1971): 1–11.

———, ed. *The Interpretation of Ordinary Landscapes: Geographical Essays.* New York: Oxford University Press, 1979.

Mitchell, John Hanson. *Ceremonial Time: Fifteen Thousand Years on One Square Mile.* New York: Warner Books, 1984.

Monmonier, Mark. *How to Lie with Maps.* Chicago: University of Chicago Press, 1991.

Montell, William Lynwood. *Don't Go Up Kettle Creek: Verbal Legacy of the Upper Cumberland.* Knoxville: University of Tennessee Press, 1983.

Moonsammy, Rita Zorn, David Steven Cohen, and Lorraine E. Williams, eds. *Pinelands Folklife.* New Brunswick, N.J.: Rutgers University Press, 1987.

Morris, Jan. *The Matter of Wales: Epic Views of a Small Country.* New York: Oxford University Press, 1984.

Mullen, Patrick B. *I Heard the Old Fishermen Say: Folklore of the Texas Gulf Coast.* Austin: University of Texas Press, 1978.

Nicolaisen, W. F. H. "Folklore and Geography: Towards an Atlas of American Folk Culture." *New York Folklore Quarterly* 29 (1973): 3–20.

Paul, Sherman. *Hewing to Experience: Essays and Reviews on Recent American Poetry and Poetics, Nature and Culture.* Iowa City: University of Iowa Press, 1989.

Pickering, Samuel F., Jr. *The Right Distance.* Athens: University of Georgia Press, 1987.

Pocock, Douglas C. D., ed. *Humanistic Geography and Literature: Essays on the Experience of Place.* Totowa, N.J.: Barnes and Noble, 1981.

Relph, Edward. *Place and Placelessness.* London: Pion, 1976.

Robinson, Arthur H., and Barbara Bartz Petchenik. *The Nature of Maps: Essays toward Understanding Maps and Mapping.* Chicago: University of Chicago Press, 1976.

Robinson, Jeffrey C. *The Walk: Notes on a Romantic Image.* Norman: University of Oklahoma Press, 1989.

Robinson, Tim. *Stones of Aran: Pilgrimage.* New York: Viking, 1989.

Rosenberg, Bruce A. "The Folklore of the Gold Rush." *Huntington Library Quarterly* 44 (1981): 293–308.

Ryden, Kent C. "Mapping the Invisible Landscape: Geography, Narrative, and the Sense of Place." Ph.D. dissertation, Brown University, 1991.

St. George, Robert Blair. "Mind, Nature, and Art in the Pine Barrens: An Exhibition Review." *Winterthur Portfolio* 23 (1988): 265–272.

Sanders, Scott Russell. "Landscape and Imagination." *North American Review* 274:3 (September 1989): 63–66.

———. *The Paradise of Bombs.* Athens: University of Georgia Press, 1987.

———. "Staying Put." *Orion* 11:1 (Winter 1992): 40–48.

Santmyer, Helen Hooven. *Ohio Town.* 1962; rpt. New York: Harper and Row, 1984.

Schwantes, Carlos A. *In Mountain Shadows: A History of Idaho.* Lincoln: University of Nebraska Press, 1991.

———. *The Pacific Northwest: An Interpretive History.* Lincoln: University of Nebraska Press, 1989.

Shortridge, James R. *The Middle West: Its Meaning in American Culture.* Lawrence: University Press of Kansas, 1989.

Simonson, Harold P. *Beyond the Frontier: Writers, Western Regionalism, and a Sense of Place.* Fort Worth: Texas Christian University Press, 1989.

Stafford, Kim R. *Having Everything Right: Essays of Place.* New York: Penguin, 1987.

———. *Places & Stories.* Pittsburgh: Carnegie Mellon University Press, 1987.

Stafford, William. "Having Become a Writer: Some Reflections." *Northwest Review* 13:3 (1973): 90–92.

Stahl, Sandra Dolby. *Literary Folkloristics and the Personal Narrative.* Bloomington: Indiana University Press, 1989.

———. "The Personal Narrative as Folklore." *Journal of the Folklore Institute* 14 (1977): 9–30.

Stilgoe, John R. *Common Landscape of America, 1580 to 1845.* New Haven: Yale University Press, 1982.

Sutton, Peter, ed. *Dreamings: The Art of Aboriginal Australia.* New York: George Braziller in association with the Asia Society Galleries, 1988.

Thoreau, Henry David. *The Natural History Essays,* ed. Robert Sattelmeyer. Salt Lake City: Peregrine Smith, 1980.

Thrower, Norman J. W. *Maps and Man: An Examination of Cartography in Relation to Culture and Civilization.* Englewood Cliffs, N.J.: Prentice-Hall, 1972.

Toelken, Barre. *The Dynamics of Folklore.* Boston: Houghton Mifflin, 1979.

Trimble, Stephen, ed. *Words from the Land: Encounters with Natural History Writing.* Salt Lake City: Gibbs Smith, 1989.

Tuan, Yi-Fu. "Place: An Experiential Perspective." *Geographical Review* 65 (1975): 151–165.

———. *Space and Place: The Perspective of Experience.* Minneapolis: University of Minnesota Press, 1977.

———. *Topophilia: A Study of Environmental Perception, Attitudes, and Values.* Englewood Cliffs, N.J.: Prentice-Hall, 1974.

Twain, Mark. *Mark Twain's Notebooks & Journals, Volume II (1877–1883)*, ed. Frederick Anderson, Lin Salamo, and Bernard L. Stein. Berkeley: University of California Press, 1975.

Upton, Dell, and John Michael Vlach, eds. *Common Places: Readings in American Vernacular Architecture*. Athens: University of Georgia Press, 1986.

Wachs, Eleanor. *Crime-Victim Stories: New York City's Urban Folklore*. Bloomington: Indiana University Press, 1988.

Walter, E. V. *Placeways: A Theory of the Human Environment*. Chapel Hill: University of North Carolina Press, 1988.

White, E. B. *Essays of E. B. White*. New York: Harper and Row, 1977.

———. *Letters of E. B. White*. New York: Harper and Row, 1976.

———. *One Man's Meat*. 1944; rpt., with new introduction, New York: Harper and Row, 1982.

Wilford, John Noble. *The Mapmakers*. New York: Knopf, 1981.

Wright, John K. *"Terrae Incognitae:* The Place of the Imagination in Geography." *Annals of the Association of American Geographers* 37 (1947): 1–15.

Yoder, Don, ed. *American Folklife*. Austin: University of Texas Press, 1976.

Zanger, Jules. " 'Harbours Like Sonnets': Literary Maps and Cartographic Symbols." *Georgia Review* 36 (1982): 773–790.

Zelinsky, Wilbur. "Where Every Town Is Above Average: Welcoming Signs along America's Highways." *Landscape* 30:1 (1988): 1–10.

Index

Aborigines, Australian: traditional view of landscape held by, 44–45

Adamsville, Rhode Island, 5–7

Adirondack Mountains (New York): as folk region, 71, 76, 85; folksongs of and sense of place, 81–83; tall tales of and sense of place, 90

Aiken, Charles S., 46, 49

Alaska: mining camps of, 182

Allen, Barbara, 69

Allen, John L., 24, 30

Anderson, Bob, 109, 114, 115, 119, 124, 151, 156, 160, 162, 172, 192; on "mining wars," 107–108; on forest fires, 112–113; on mental image of region, 120–121; on Noah Kellogg legend, 149; on prospecting, 153–154; on miners' nicknames, 194

Anderson, Chris, 212

Aran Islands, Ireland, 244

Atkins, G. Douglas, 218

Barnard Studio, Wallace, Idaho, 165, 166

Barnegat Bay sneakbox, 73–74

Bauer, Douglas, 260–261

Bear: as regional symbol in Coeur d'Alene mining district, 127–128, 144–145

Beasley, Conger, Jr., 259

Beresford, Maurice, 26

Berry, Wendell, 52, 215, 220, 252–253, 281, 286; "The Long-Legged House," 282–285

Bethke, Robert D., 82, 83, 90

Big Creek (Idaho), 98

Bishop, Elizabeth, 21–23, 43

Black Bear, Idaho, 164

Black Bear mine, Coeur d'Alene mining district, 104

Boise, Idaho, 175

Bondurant, Bill, 131, 160, 167, 175, 176, 177, 180, 181, 185, 193, 197; on hazards of mining, 159; on Sunshine mine fire, 162; on mining superstitions, 163–164; on miners' practical jokes, 180–181; on miners' slang, 192

Bondurant, Helen, 176, 179, 180, 181, 192, 193, 200; on fishing, 131; on mining superstitions, 164; on the term "mining camp," 175; on mining camps, 180; on solidarity in mining camps, 189–190; on miners' nicknames, 193–194; on environmental illiteracy of outsiders, 195–196

Borders and boundaries: geographical, 1; as products of experience, 25–29; in medieval England, 26; in colonial America, 26–29; and survey grids, 36; as folk constructs, 68–72, 76; and local history, 69–70

Brainard, Wendell, 98, 147, 171, 185, 201, 206; on Noah Kellogg legend, 149–150; on gold mines, 151–152; on unpredictability of mining, 156–158; on mining-camp language, 195

319

Bredahl, A. Carl, Jr., 256
Brody, Hugh, 42–43
Bronner, Simon, 74
Brown, Carolyn S., 92
Brunetti, Perina, 94, 95
Brunvand, Jan Harold, 84
Built environment: and sense of place, 76
Bunker Hill mine, Coeur d'Alene mining district, 104, 105, 106, 107, 109, 116, 148, 150, 151, 152, 170, 197
Bunkse, Edmunds V., 57, 209
Burke, Idaho, 108, 112, 118, 190, 196; as mining camp, 185–189; narrowness of, 185–187; importance of fighting in, 187–188; spirit of fairness and community in, 188–189
Burke Canyon (Idaho), 98, 104, 105, 111, 151, 164, 166, 167, 168, 171, 202
Butte, Montana, 120, 175, 177

Calumet Region (Indiana), 79
Campbell, James, 308 n.51
Candee, Richard M., 34
Cape Cod, 222, 263–264
Cataldo, Idaho, 98, 122, 146
Chain carving, 74–75
Chatwin, Bruce, 44
Chorography, 50
Clemets, Maidell, 119, 169, 178, 189, 201; on "twilight houses," 118; on unpredictability of mining, 154–155; on hazards of mining, 158, 159; on miners' attitude of optimism, 172–173; on tramp miners, 176; on mining camps, 177; on miners' gambling, 181–182; on con men in mining camps, 183; on rock-drilling con-

tests, 184; on solidarity in mining camps, 191; on outsiders to district, 196; on personal landmarks, 198–199
Cochrane, Timothy, 119, 128
Coeur d'Alene, Idaho, 98, 99
Coeur d'Alene mining district (Idaho): folk names for, 99; as physiographical region, 99; historical significance of mining in, 103–107; early development of, 104; and "mining wars," 105–106; individual variation within sense of place of, 111–113, 114, 198–200; residents' mental image of, 119, 121, 168, 170–171; collective sense of identity within, 143–145; pollution of by mining, 168–171; role of social networks in residents' conception of, 173–174; economic decline of, 196–198; communal sharing of sense of place of, 201
Cognitive maps, 54–56; and narrative, 56
Cohen, Anthony, 65
Columbus, Christopher, 24–25
Compressed narrative, 115–116
Comstock, Gary, 61–62, 95, 96
Conrad, Joseph, 24, 52
Core, George, 213, 214, 215, 216
Crime-victim stories, 87–88
Crockett, Davy, 91, 141

Daniel, Stephen H., 211
Danielson, Larry, 89
Dillard, Annie, 215
Doig, Ivan, 256–259, 281; *Winter Brothers*, 257–259
Dorson, Richard M., 56, 79; and regional folklore studies, 59–61
Downs, Roger M., 54, 55

Dream Gulch (Idaho): legend of, 152–153

Dundes, Alan, 64–65

Dunphy, Bill, 113, 114, 115, 118, 168, 173, 196; on "mining wars," 110; on forest fires, 111–112; on snow slides, 164–165; environmental literacy of, 167–168; on unexpected successes in mining, 171–172; on narrowness of Burke, Idaho, 185–187; on fighting in Burke, 187–188; on justice in Burke, 188–189; on solidarity among miners, 190–191

Duvert, Elizabeth, 47

Eagle, Idaho, 103, 148

Ehrlich, Gretel, 262–263

Eiseley, Loren, 265–266

Elk: as regional symbol in Coeur d'Alene mining district, 127–128

Elledge, Scott, 269, 274, 275

Emlen, Robert, 31

Emotion: and sense of place, 39, 66–67

Environmental literacy, 72, 78, 150; of Idaho miners, 153–154

Epstein, Joseph, 215

Essay: characteristics of as genre, 212–219; and sense of place, 212, 219–220; and folk narrative, 213–217; and personal experience narrative, 214–215, 217; and walking, 218–220

Essay of place, xiv, 52, 220, 232, 235, 240–241, 243, 248–249, 250–251; parallels with folk narrative, 211–213, 286; and nature writing, 221–223; and value of place, 251–254, 264–266, 285–286; and time, 255–259; and identity, 255, 259–264; rela-

tionship between writer and reader created by, 280–282, 285

Etherton, Bill, 170, 202, 206

Evans, E. Estyn, 56

Faulkner, William, 46–49, 144

Ferry, Ham, 82, 83, 85, 90

Few, William, 27, 30

Fiction: treatment of sense of place in, 49

Finch, Robert, 221–222, 263–264

Finnish method (folklore methodology), 56

Floods: in Coeur d'Alene mining district, 201–202

Folk architecture: and sense of place, 75–76

Folk beliefs: as response to hazardous work environments, 162–163; of miners in Coeur d'Alene mining district, 163–164

Folk heroes: and sense of place, 91–92

Folklore: and sense of place, 45, 209; relationship with geography, 56–58; as revealing geographical meaning, 57–58. *See also* Regional folklore

Folklore genres: and sense of place, 61, 67–68, 93. *See also* Chain carving; Folk architecture; Folk heroes; Folk names; Folk narrative; Folksongs; Legends; Material folklore; Migratory legends; Oral historical narratives; Personal experience narratives; Tall tales; Urban legends

Folk names, 63; and sense of place, 78–80

Folk narrative, 243; and sense of place, 45–46; place-based, characteristics of, 211–212

Folksongs: and sense of place, 81–83
Forest fires: and history of Coeur d'Alene mining district, 106–107
Fort Wayne, Indiana, 293
Francaviglia, Richard, 99, 102
Frisco mine, Coeur d'Alene mining district, 104, 105, 106

Galena mine, Coeur d'Alene mining district, 121
Gem mine, Coeur d'Alene mining district, 104, 105
Geography: relationship with folklore, 56–58
Glassie, Henry, 56, 64, 65, 71, 246–247, 248, 249, 250
Godsoe, John, 31, 32, 34
Godsoe, William, 31
Good, Graham, 214, 216, 218
Gould, Peter, 55
Gray, Rockwell, 259–260, 261
Gusewelle, C. W., 244–246, 251

Hardison, O. B., Jr., 217, 241, 250
Harley, J. B., 298 n.15, 309 n.4
Hayden Lake, Idaho, 206
Heaney, Seamus, 230–231, 265
Hecla mine, Coeur d'Alene mining district, 104
Heikkila, Leonard, 146, 168, 185, 201; on hazards of mining, 158; on floods, 201–202
Heikkila, Marylinn, 107, 116, 170, 201; on pollution by mines, 169
Hercules mine, Coeur d'Alene mining district, 152, 171
Highland mine, Coeur d'Alene mining district, 203–206
Hiss, Tony, 291
History: and sense of place, 38, 63–64
"History park," 6–7

Hoagland, Edward, 213, 215
Hollybush, Kentucky, 75, 80–81
Horning, Shirley, 184; personal interpretation of Coeur d'Alene mining district, 199–200
Howarth, William, 229
Huckleberries: as regional symbol in Coeur d'Alene mining district, 127–129
Hufford, Mary, 67, 68, 72, 73, 78, 79, 194

Identity: and sense of place, 39–40, 64–66; and history, 65; and physical environment, 66, 76–77; and essay of place, 259–264
Independence Day: celebration of in mining camps, 184
Invisible landscape, xiv, 40–41, 45
Isle Royale (Michigan), 119, 128
Ives, Edward, 92

Jackson, J. B., 69
James, William, 40–41, 46, 62
"Jam on Gerry's Rock, The" (folksong), 83, 86, 126
Johnstone, Barbara, 42, 77, 293
Jones, Suzi, 59, 67, 68, 89, 90

Kauffmann, R. Lane, 218
Kavanagh, Patrick, 230–231
Kellogg, Idaho, 98, 106, 107, 116, 118, 149, 160, 172, 177, 197, 206; and pollution, 169–170
Kellogg, Noah, 104, 152, 171; legend of, 148–151, 153
Kingston, Idaho, 98, 116
Kittery, Maine, 31
Klaus, Carl H., 214, 217
Kniffen, Fred B., 57
Kruse, Horst H., 51
Kumin, Maxine, 223

Land Ordinance of 1785, 35–36; survey grid mandated by, 37, 290
Least Heat Moon, William, 25
Legends, 63, 68
Lightfoot, William E., 58, 69
Literature: treatment of sense of place in, 46–52. *See also* Essay; Essay of place; Fiction; Nonfiction
Little Dixie (Missouri), 70, 75, 76, 81; as folk name, 79
Logging: as basis of history of Coeur d'Alene mining district, 103, 104
Long, Don, 98, 111, 146, 152, 160, 161, 206; on "mining wars," 108–109; on mental image of region, 120; on Noah Kellogg legend, 148; on hazards of mining, 159; on abandoned mines, 177
Lonn, Ken, 161
Lopez, Barry, 1, 45, 50, 52, 97, 206, 231–240, 243, 251. Works: "The Country of the Mind," 231, 233–235; *Arctic Dreams*, 231, 235; "The Stone Horse," 235–240
Louth (county), Ireland, 63
Love, David, 23, 31, 36, 46
Lowenthal, David, 25, 35, 254
Lucky Friday mine, Coeur d'Alene mining district, 189, 199
Lutwack, Leonard, 49
Lynch, Kevin, 54

Mace, Idaho, 164, 166
McGowan, James, xiii
McPhee, John, 23, 46
Magoon, George, 91–92, 93, 141
Maps, 246; as communications media, 20; limitations of, 20–21; and imagination, 22–25; premodern, as reflections of experience, 29–31; and medieval worldview, 30; modern, and abstract view of land, 33–36; and narrative,

42–43; as cultural texts, 298 n.15
Marling, Karal Ann, 5
Marshall, Howard Wight, 70, 71, 75, 76, 80
Martin, Charles, 80–81
Martone, Michael, 247–248, 293
Material folklore, 56, 62, 67; and physical landscape, 73
Meinig, D. W., 49
Memorates, 114
Memory: and sense of place, 39, 75
Metes-and-bounds surveys, 27–29
Migratory legends, 83; and sense of place, 83–84, 85
Milo Gulch (Idaho), 98, 104
Miners: self-image of in Coeur d'Alene mining district, 109; traditional attitude of optimism held by, 171–173; as gamblers, 182; integrity of, 192
Mining: as basis of history of Coeur d'Alene mining district, 103–107; physical effects of on landscape, 116; similarities with logging
Mining (*continued*)
and hunting, 148
Mining camp: as basis of sense of place in Coeur d'Alene mining district, 121–122; as folk name, 174–176, 192; residents' feeling of belonging in, 176–177; physical appearance of, 177–179; social characteristics of, 179–185; spirit of solidarity and community in, 189–192
Mining districts, 99
Mining towns: as component of sense of place in Coeur d'Alene mining district, 174; residents' perception of, 174
"Mining wars," Coeur d'Alene mining district, 105–106; and oral tradition, 107–111

Mitchell, John Hanson, 307 n.18
Mitchell, Roger, 122
Montell, William Lynwood, 80, 94, 113–114, 115
Morning mine, Coeur d'Alene mining district, 104
Morris, Jan, 287
Mother Lode mine, Coeur d'Alene mining district, 151–152
Mullan, Idaho, 98
Mullen, Patrick, 162, 163
Murray, Idaho, 103, 148, 151, 171

National Geodetic Survey markers, 15–17
Nature writing, 221
Neenah, Wisconsin, 289, 290
New Milford, Connecticut, 20
New York City, 87–88
Nicknames: use of in Coeur d'Alene mining district, 193–195
Nicolaisen, W. F. H., 56
Ninemile Canyon (Idaho), 98
Nonfiction: treatment of sense of place in, 49–52
Noyen, Bill, 111, 114, 170, 173, 181, 201; on "mining wars," 109–110; on pollution by mines, 169–170; on mining towns, 174
Noyen, Hazel: on mental image of region, 120

Oral historical narratives, 113–114; and sense of place, 80; and physical landscape, 80–81; and individual experience, 111
Osburn, Idaho, 98, 118, 119

Paul, Sherman, 236
Personal experience narratives, 114; and sense of place, 80, 86–89; in Coeur d'Alene mining district, 114–115

Petchenik, Barbara Bartz, 42
Physical landscape: as defining element of place, 38, 72–73, 76; and oral folklore, 77
Pickering, Samuel F., 219
Picture postcards, 165–166
Pine Barrens (New Jersey), 66, 72, 73, 78, 194
Pine Creek mining district (Idaho), 98, 145, 170, 177, 202
Pinehurst, Idaho, 98, 116, 145, 177
Pinelands Folklife, 67
Place (geographical concept), 37–40; and words, 42–45; value of, 94–96, 264–266
Placelessness, 291
Poorman mine, Coeur d'Alene mining district, 104
Practical jokes: among miners, 180–181
Prichard Creek (Idaho): and 1884 gold rush, 103

Regional folklore, 58–61, 62, 63, 66, 67; and sense of place, 58–59; as field of study, 59–61
Relph, Edward, 37, 38, 40, 209, 249, 251, 254, 291
Reuss, Richard, 70, 84
"Roadside colossi," 5
Robinson, Arthur H., 42
Robinson, Jeffrey C., 218, 219
Robinson, Tim, 220, 244, 245, 246
Rock Bridge, Kentucky, 69–70
Rock-drilling contests: in Coeur d'Alene mining district, 184–185
Rosen, Michael J., 249–250
Rosenberg, Bruce, 304 nn.11, 12

St. George, Robert Blair, 67
Sanders, Scott Russell, 210–211, 212–213, 214, 215, 216, 218, 232, 240, 291

Santmyer, Helen Hooven, 28
Sense of place, xiv, 38, 40, 59, 61, 67, 99, 115, 209; as folk construct, 45; components of, 62–67; and physical landscape, 63, 72–73, 76; and history, 63–64; and identity, 64–66; and emotion, 66–67; as folklore genre, 68, 86; as underlying and generating folk expression, 68, 115; and memory, 75; as narrative construction, 77–78; value of, 95; and individual experience, 111
Shakers: cartography of, 30–31
Shortridge, James R., 36
Silver Valley: as name for Coeur d'Alene mining district, 98
Simonson, Harold, 252, 253, 285, 286
Slang: use of among miners, 192–193
Smelterville, Idaho, 98, 116, 119, 169, 177
Snow slides: in Coeur d'Alene mining district, 164–167, 202
Sopher, David, 72
Space (geographical concept), 37, 40
Spokane, Washington, 99
Stafford, Kim, 242–243, 280
Stafford, William, 280–281, 284, 286
Stahl, Sandra Dolby, 86, 114, 115, 172
Standard mine, Coeur d'Alene mining district, 171
Stea, David, 54, 55
Stevens, Wallace, 53, 57, 58, 96, 174, 252
Stilgoe, John, 27, 36
Striped Peak (Idaho), 121, 124
Sunshine mine, Coeur d'Alene mining district, 104, 152
Sunshine mine fire of 1972, 107,

159–162, 180, 197, 201; memorial statue for victims of, 160–162, 194–195
Surveying: and abstract view of land, 33–36. *See also* Metes-and-bounds surveys
Sverdsten, Alida, 98, 122–130, 132–144, 148, 153, 154, 195; on logging, 122–123, 124–127; on mental image of region, 123–124; and sense of identity, 124, 127, 132; and interpretation of place, 125–126; recreational narratives of, 127; and gender roles, 127, 134–135, 137–138; on huckleberrying, 128–130; on hunting, 132–139; on being lost in the woods, 139–143
Sverdsten, Ed, 122

Táin Bó Cuailnge (Irish saga), 63
Tall tales, 63, 68; and sense of place, 89–93
Thoreau, Henry David, 223–231, 234, 235, 256; attitude of toward place, 223–225. Works: "Walking," 223–224, 228; "A Winter Walk," 223, 224–225, 231; "A Walk to Wachusett," 223, 226–229, 231
Thorpe, T. B., 144
Tiger mine, Coeur d'Alene mining district, 104, 151
Time: and sense of place, 39; and essay of place, 255–259
Toelken, Barre, 89
Tornado stories, 89
Tramp miner, 176
Trimble, Stephen, 221
Tuan, Yi-Fu, 37, 38, 39, 66, 209, 255
Twain, Mark: *Life on the Mississippi*, 50–51, 52

United States Geological Survey: topographic maps of, 20, 25, 298 n.15
Upper Cumberland (Kentucky-Tennessee), 81, 94, 114; as folk name, 80
Urban legends, 84; and sense of place, 84–85

Wachs, Eleanor, 87, 88
Walking: as subject for essays, 219–220
Wallace, Idaho, 98, 106, 113, 116, 118, 119, 184, 190, 196, 199, 206; social characteristics of, 181
Walter, E. V., 30, 37, 38, 40, 50
Wardner, Idaho, 199
Wardner Peak (Idaho), 203
Warshaver, Gerald, 70
Welcoming signs, 2, 5
White, E. B., 52, 213, 216, 266–280, 281, 295; and New York, 267–269, 270; and Maine, 267, 269–280; attitude of toward passage of time, 270–271; essays of as imaginative resistance to World War II, 272–274; and Belgrade Lakes, Maine, 275–280. Works: "Here Is New York," 267–269; "Home-Coming," 269–270; "The Ring of Time," 270–271; *One Man's Meat*, 271–272; "Once More to the Lake," 276–280
White, Rodney, 55
Wilford, John Noble, 17, 24
Williams, Terry Tempest, 286
Woods: as basis of sense of place in Coeur d'Alene mining district, 121–122
Wright, John K., 17

Zanger, Jules, 47
Zeiger, William, 215, 216–217
Zelinsky, Wilbur, 2, 5

The American Land and Life Series